EPICS, SPECTACLES, AND BLOCKBUSTERS

A HOLLYWOOD HISTORY

EPICS
SPECTACLES
AND BLOCKBUSTERS

SHELDON HALL AND STEVE NEALE

Wayne State University Press
Detroit

14 13 12 11 10   5 4 3 2 1

Library of Congress Cataloging-in-Publication Data

Hall, Sheldon.
Epics, spectacles, and blockbusters : a Hollywood history / Sheldon Hall and Steve Neale.
p. cm. — (Contemporary approaches to film and television series)
Includes bibliographical references and index.
ISBN 978-0-8143-3008-1 (pbk. : alk. paper)
1. Motion pictures—United States—History.   2. Motion picture industry—
United States—History.   I. Neale, Stephen, 1950–   II. Title.

PN1993.5.U6H278 2010
791.430973—dc22

2009041796

Arts & Humanities
Research Council

Typeset by Alpha Design & Composition
Composed in Adobe Garamond, Myriad Pro and ITC Bodoni Seventy Two

CONTENTS

Acknowledgments

We would like to thank Barry Keith Grant, Annie Martin, and Wayne State University Press for their support and patience. We would also like to thank our publisher's readers for their comments and suggestions, Richard Chatten for his manuscript corrections, and the librarians and curators at the Margaret Herrick Library, Academy of Motion Picture Arts and Sciences in Los Angeles; the Bill Douglas Centre at Exeter University; the British Film Institute Library in London; the Library of Congress in Washington, DC; the Doheny Library and the Warner Bros. Archives at the University of Southern California; the Wisconsin State Historical Society at the University of Wisconsin–Madison; and the University Libraries at UCLA, Exeter, and Sheffield Hallam.

Sheldon Hall would also like to thank the Arts and Humanities Research Council and Sheffield Hallam University for funding a year's study leave, Paul Anderson and family for their hospitality on a research visit to Los Angeles, Tom and Maureen Hall for their loving support, and Cat Critchley for her love, understanding, and curiosity. His contributions to the book are dedicated to the memory of Perkins, the cat, who was present at most of the writing and who died shortly after its completion.

Steve Neale would also like to thank the British Academy for funding a research trip to the United States, Rudmer Canjels for providing a copy of his PhD dissertation, Frank Kessler for bringing it to his attention, the anonymous passengers at Paddington station who helped retrieve dozens of pages of photocopying blown away by the wind, and Karen Leigh Edwards for her love and her constant support.

Introduction

This is a book about the history, characteristics, and modes of distribution and exhibition of large-scale, high-cost films in the United States, and the industrial policies, practices, and conditions that governed their production or importation from the 1890s to the present day. It is also concerned, though to a lesser extent, with less expensive, smaller-scale films that have been major commercial successes, particularly where they have helped to inaugurate major cycles or have pioneered new and influential modes of distribution and exhibition, which have in turn affected bigger and bigger-budgeted pictures. It thus encompasses boxing films, biblical films, war films, westerns, dramas, action-adventure films, historical epics, costume adventure films and romances, science-fiction films, disaster films, horror films, animated features, comic-book adaptations, and fantasy adventure films. Some of these films were aimed at families and children, some at male or female adults, some at teenagers, some at the middle or upper middle classes, and some at proletarian audiences or the general mass of the population. Some were exceptionally costly to produce; others were less so. Some made a profit; others did not. However, they could all be called *blockbusters,* the current term both for major box-office hits and for unusually expensive productions designed to earn unusually large amounts of money.

As detailed in chapter 7, this term was first regularly applied to films in the 1950s. It would thus be anomalous to use it to label films made prior that. But its double meaning encompasses the films with which the book is concerned in a way that earlier or alternative terms such as *feature, special, superspecial, roadshow, epic,* and *spectacle* would be unable to do on their own. These terms have an important part to play as well, though. As the book's chapter titles and subheadings suggest, they are each indicative of key aspects of U.S. film history and the practices and films that have marked it since the earliest decades.

Features, Specials, and Superspecials

Chapter 1 deals with the 1890s and 1900s, chapter 2 with the early 1910s. Throughout this period, "feature" was an exhibition category, a film or a presentation of a film that was promoted as something out of the ordinary, as something worthy of special attention. At a time when films were rarely longer than a single reel (approximately ten to fifteen minutes), and at a time when most films in the United States were shown in programs, a feature was the equivalent of a headline act in a variety show and was thus dependent on factors other than its length, scale, or cost. Certain kinds of films were "exploitable" (promotable) as features because of their subject matter or because of their technological characteristics: biblical films, colored films, or films accompanied by prerecorded sound, for instance. (As detailed in chapter 1, Pathé's *Passion Play* [1907] was a colored biblical import. It clearly fulfilled the criteria for a feature and was judged to be one of the most commercially successful films of the period.) But a lecturer or live musical accompaniment could function as a feature, as could the scheduling of a program of films on Sunday, at Easter, or at other key points in the year. Only with the introduction of multireel films in the 1910s did the term *feature* come to mean a film that was longer than a single or double reel. However, by the end of the 1910s longer films had become the norm. Programs of feature-length films were produced and released throughout the year; in chapters 2 and 3 we look at some of the ways in which these programs were organized and at some of the ways in which films and programs of films were distributed, booked, and promoted. Feature-length films were no longer special in themselves. Special features were those that were built around popular film stars or that were longer or more expensive than routine productions.

As explained in chapter 3, *special* and *superspecial* were production categories. Along with more inclusive terms such as *big picture,* they were both in common use in the United States by the early 1920s. Although by no means always interchangeable, and although subject to hyperbolic use in the industry's publicity, both were used to indicate a particular type of production: a relatively lavish film, usually of longer than average duration, with higher-than-average production values and higher-than-average costs; a film that would bring prestige, profit, or both to those involved in its production and distribution. When distinguished one from the other, as happened increasingly in the 1920s, superspecials were generally characterized as even more lavish and expensive than specials. Both, though, were different from run-of-the-mill features and shorts, not only in terms of lavishness, cost, and length, but usually also in terms of promotion, distribution, exhibition, and presentation.

Roadshowing

As a practice, roadshowing—the touring of plays and shows—was rooted in the legitimate theater and other forms of live entertainment. The itinerant exhibition of films in the 1890s and 1900s was an extension of this practice, one that continued on a small scale for many decades. But roadshowing on a large scale, in a manner reminiscent of the major repertory companies in the legitimate commercial theater, came to be used in the late 1900s and the 1910s as a means of distributing and exhibiting early feature-length films and specials. At a time when the film industry in the United States was dominated by the production, distribution, and exhibition of programs of shorter films, when the seating capacity of most of the venues used for exhibiting films was limited, and when most programs lasted little more than an hour and were changed at least two or three times a week, the roadshowing of longer features in large theatrical venues for weeks and months rather than days was a means not only of showcasing expensive prestige productions but also of building individualized publicity campaigns and attracting audiences willing and able to pay higher-than-average seat prices in numbers large enough to cover costs and generate profits.

As detailed in chapter 2, many of the earliest films shown in this way in the United States were imported from Europe. Some were distributed on a "states rights" basis, in which case the rights to show or tour the films were franchised to distributors or exhibitors in specific states. The states rights system had previously been used to distribute boxing films in the United States. (These were often longer than the norm and were legal in some states but not in others.) It continued to be used for the release of imports such as *Robespierre* (1917) and U.S. productions such as *Civilization* (1916) and *Tarzan of the Apes* (1918). But other imports were roadshown in select major cities nationwide. Among the earliest were *Quo Vadis?* (1913) and *Cabiria* (1914), Italian productions that broke new ground in terms of length, lavishness, cost, prestige, and box-office earnings. In the United States, D. W. Griffith and Cecil B. DeMille sought to emulate films like these. Griffith produced and directed *The Birth of a Nation* (1915) and *Intolerance* (1916), DeMille, *Joan the Woman* (1916). All three were roadshown nationwide. As well as being the longest and most expensive U.S. film to date, *The Birth of a Nation* was a huge box-office success. It helped pave for the way for subsequent domestic roadshow productions of the kind listed above.

Although sometimes used to sell blocks of features to exhibitors, specials and superspecials generally received more individualized treatment than the norm, including roadshow distribution and exhibition. Following an extensive publicity campaign and premiere screenings in New York and/or Los Angeles, superspecials were often exhibited in major cities in the United States in large picture-palace cinemas or in even larger theatrical venues at "advanced" or higher-than-average seat prices. At a time when most films were presented in continuous performances, without breaks between showings, and a time when tickets were rarely sold or reserved in advance, seats for roadshows were bookable, the films themselves were shown at specified times (usually twice a day) with at least one intermission, and if "silent," as was of course nearly always the case until the late 1920s, accompanied by a specially composed score played by an orchestra. Roadshow runs of this kind continued for weeks, months, or sometimes years before versions of the films were released to regular movie theaters and shown in the usual manner at regular prices. Some of these films, such as *The Four Horsemen of the Apocalypse* (1921) and *Ben-Hur* (1925), earned record sums of money. Moreover, as noted in chapter 3, highly profitable productions such as *Salome* (1918) and *The Kid* (1921) were sometimes released in a less exclusive manner, with prints booked into a number of theaters at once in some major cities. *Salome* was roadshown as well. But the "concentrated booking plan" adopted for its release in New York City and Chicago was said to be extremely successful. Then as now, there was no necessary correlation between box-office success and any particular mode of distribution.

As we discuss in chapter 5, with the adoption of prerecorded, synchronized sound at the end of the 1920s, the meaning of roadshowing began to change. It was no longer necessary for a live company comprising managers, a stage crew, and orchestra to accompany each print of a film "on the road" as it traveled from one city to the next. But the term, though separated from its literal origins, remained in use to describe those elements of legitimate theater presentation retained in the exhibition of certain special and superspecial pictures, such as reserved seats, separate performances, in some instances an orchestral overture played before the start of the film, an intermission, and the availability of lavishly illustrated souvenir program booklets. Raised prices, higher than for regular first-run exhibition, were still charged for such films, and to encourage mass attendance party bookings were sought for the block sale of tickets. Extended engagements ran for as long as the box office would stand, or even longer in the case of bookings that had been made for a fixed period of time. Roadshowing a film in a large "pre-release" cinema, especially one on Broadway or in Los Angeles and other key cities, served to advertise it both to the general public and to other exhibitors prior to its general release at regular prices. Because of the greater investment in publicity and additional theater staff, roadshowing was inherently more risky than conventional presentation. The films exhibited on such a basis therefore had to be chosen carefully for their prestige value and their audience appeal in order to justify their special status.

With the cinema-going boom of the Second World War and following the precedents established by the exhibition of *Gone with the Wind* (1939), many of the theatrical trappings of roadshow presentation, such as reserved seats and separate performances, were largely dispensed with. But as we show in chapter 6, the pre-release showings of big pictures at higher than usual prices continued to be referred to as *roadshows,* a term that connoted prestige and importance as much as a specific mode of presentation. The legitimate-stage aura of roadshowing was revived in the 1950s and 1960s by the industry's response to declining cinema attendance. The introduction of wide-screen and stereo sound formats, and the raising of production budgets to display them, invited similarly spectacular theatrical exhibition. As discussed in chapter 8, increasing numbers of films were released on a roadshow basis, much as they had been in the silent era, in the hope that the combination of special projection and sound processes, a presold subject, and high-class, high-priced presentation would earn them the status of blockbusters. Only when roadshowing proved ineffective at attracting the majority youth audience, as explained in chapter 9, was it replaced by alternative distribution and exhibition methods, some of which had also been pioneered in earlier decades.

Epics, Spectacles, and Spectacle

Many special and superspecial productions were described as *epics* or *spectacles* (i.e., spectacular films). These terms were used rather loosely. The former was as indicative of size and expense as it was of particular kinds of historical setting, of protagonists who are caught up in large-scale events as it was of those who sway the course of history or the fate of nations. The latter tended simply—and tautologically—to indicate the presence of spectacular settings, actions, and scenes. Used in this way, epic and/or spectacle were as applicable to films such as *Way Down East* (1920) and *The Big Parade* (1925) as they were to *The Birth of a Nation, The Covered Wagon* (1923), and *Ben-Hur.* Spectacular historical romances such as *Gone with the Wind,* spectacular travelogues such as *Cinerama Holiday* (1955), epic comedies such as *The Great Race* (1965), epic disaster films such as *Earthquake* (1974), and spectacular science-fiction, comic-book, and action-adventure films such as *Star Wars* (1977), *Superman* (1978), and *Raiders of the Lost Ark* (1981) are thus as central to later chapters in this book as *Samson and Delilah* (1949), *Spartacus* (1960), *How the West Was Won* (1963), and *Gladiator* (2000).

As an aesthetic phenomenon, spectacle has proven easier to exemplify than to define. As Aylish Wood and Geoff King have both pointed out, it has been persistently associated in the cinema with space, with settings, and with narrative interruption rather than with narrative agents, actions, and events.[1] However, as they each go on to argue, spectacular elements in the settings of a film can and frequently do become agents of spectacular narrative action: the eruption of Mount Vesuvius at the end of the various versions of *The Last Days of Pompeii* would be an example; others include the tornados in *Twister* (1996), the stormy seas in *The Poseidon Adventure* (1972) and *The Perfect Storm* (2000), the asteroid in *Armageddon* (1998), and the ice and snow in *The Day after Tomorrow* (2004). And while narrative momentum can be slowed down by sequences of spectacle, key narrative actions—the chariot race in the 1920s and 1950s versions of *Ben-Hur;* the acts of alien destruction in *Independence Day* (1996) and *War of the Worlds* (2005); the battles in *The Birth of a Nation, The Big Parade, El Cid* (1961), and *Pearl Harbor* (2001); the hostile encounters between heroes and villains in *Superman, Batman* (1989), and *Spider-Man* (2002)—can be prolonged and their consequential status underlined by spectacular treatment. In these ways, spectacle can enhance what Vivian Sobchack has described as the "eventfulness" not only of large-scale or epic films, but also of the stories they tell.[2]

In chapter 11, drawing on work done by Higgins, Neale, and Brewster and Jacobs, we propose the term "Cinema of Spectacular Situations" to identify the characteristics of contemporary action, science fiction, epic, and comic-book blockbusters and, in particular, the extent to which the concept of the dramatic—or melodramatic—situation might be one way of conceiving the links between narrative, spectacle, and setting.[3] Brewster and Jacobs suggest that spectacular effects depend upon "the audience's perception of the disproportion between the reality represented and the means used to represent it—it is the very impossibility of having a train crash on stage that makes even a tacky simulation of it in the theatre impressive."[4] A train crash is a narrative event. But for Brewster and Jacobs the narrative status of spectacle is less of an issue than the effects produced by specific representational devices and technologies in specific representational contexts at specific times. In this respect, in the cinema, editing, framing, staging, and technological means and devices of all kinds (from special effects to wide-screen processes to computer-generated imagery) are particularly crucial. We discuss their presence and their role in the organization of films such as *Cabiria, The Three Musketeers* (1921), *The Big Parade, Old Ironsides* (1926), *The Broadway Melody* (1929), *A Midsummer Night's Dream* (1935), *Snow White and the Seven Dwarfs* (1937), *This Is Cinerama* (1952), *Ben-Hur* (1959), *55 Days at Peking* (1963), *Earthquake, Jaws* (1975), *Star Wars, Beauty and the Beast* (1991), and *The Matrix* (1999) at various points in this book. The choice of examples has been determined by the novel, influential, or unique and particular ways in which the means and devices they draw upon have been deployed.

The deployment of these technologies is one of the means by which large-scale productions exhibit what Ted Hovet has called "representational prowess."[5] Representational prowess can encompass the aural dimensions of a film or a film's presentation as well as its visual ones. Hence the many references to musicals, musical scores, musical accompaniment, and the uses made of sound and music throughout this book. The earliest uses and technologies of sound, along with those of color, large screen, large gauge, and wide screen, are discussed in chapter 4. It is here that we look at Kinemacolor, Prizmacolor, and Technicolor; Magnascope, Grandeur, and Realife; and the Kinetophone, Photophone, and Vitaphone. In chapters 7 and 10 we discuss later generations of visual and sound technology. However, in addition to these systems' technological characteristics and the effects they were used to produce, we also pay attention to the ways in which they figured as features in their own right or as hallmarks of special productions, the extent to which they involved or necessitated particular modes of distribution or exhibition, the costs involved in their production or exhibition, the extent to which they were commercially successful, and, in the case of sound, the extent to which they effected a permanent transformation of the industry and its films, both big and small.

Blockbusters and the Box Office

Details of revenues and production (or negative) costs cited throughout this book have been assembled from a wide range of sources that it would have been tedious to footnote individually. One of our most important sources is the show business trade paper *Variety.* Since 1946, *Variety* has published a regularly updated chart of "All-Time

Film Rental Champs," as well as annual lists of each calendar year's hits, ranked by their revenue performance. Since the late 1990s most published figures have been for box-office earnings (the exhibitor's gross, or the amount of money paid by customers for the purchase of tickets), but in earlier decades charts in *Variety* and other trade journals were based on distribution income (the distributor's gross, or rentals). Rentals were seen as a more reliable index of the ultimate profitability, or otherwise, of films for their producers and distributors. Although the distribution gross often worked out at around half the exhibition gross, for individual films, especially the more expensive ones sold at higher terms, rentals could rise to much higher proportions. They were also more verifiable: during the 1930s, 1940s, and 1950s, many films of lesser commercial importance, and almost all films in their later stages of release, were sold to exhibitors on a flat-fee basis, so ticket sales and takings for these engagements were not usually reported by theaters. Therefore, except where noted (such as in the discussion of individual theater engagements) we have generally followed *Variety's* example and quoted the distribution rather than the box-office gross.

For similar reasons of accountability, *Variety* has typically used figures for domestic (U.S. and Canadian) rather than worldwide revenue. This became its standard policy in 1940, when the advent of war in Europe persuaded the American film industry (temporarily, as it turned out) that it should be wholly reliant on the home market for profitability. Where specific rentals data are reported in *Variety* before this (which tended to be only sporadically) they were often for worldwide rather than for domestic performance. This was also the case with other trade sources, such as Quigley's annual *Motion Picture Almanac,* which published its own all-time hits lists from the early 1930s onward. The subsequent confusion of domestic and worldwide figures, and of rental and box-office figures, has plagued many published accounts of Hollywood history (sometimes including those in *Variety* itself), and we have attempted to be diligent in clarifying the differences between them.

There are other caveats to be borne in mind when citing published data for both revenue and expenditure. Figures released to the press by producers, distributors, and exhibitors were often either exaggerated to suggest greater success or largesse than was actually the case, or (in the case of planned budgets and actual negative costs) reduced to disguise undue extravagance, waste, or poor business management. Even revenues could be underreported to hide the actual scale of earnings from profit participants. In many instances, rentals performance was calculated by trade-press reporters on the basis of a sample of key-city earnings, rather than (or as well as) from "official" information declared by film companies themselves. As a result, figures in different publications, or in different issues of the same publication, are often widely at variance, and an element of hazard is involved in taking any one as definitive. It is hard to establish the degree of success or failure for post-1980s films in particular because of the nature and extent of ancillary and foreign earnings. The "annual grosses gloss" articles published in the March–April editions of *Film Comment* give some indication as to which films were or are perceived as box-office failures.

Where older titles are concerned, however, in recent years many collections of files, private or corporate correspondence, and other documents maintained by studios and individuals have been donated to libraries and archives, which have in turn made them available for inspection by scholars. Many of them contain financial data and other confidential material that, because they were not intended for publication or wide dissemination, are inherently more reliable than most press reports. Although these sources, too, are subject to variation (for example, ledgers pertaining to different companies may not be directly comparable due to different accounting practices and assessment dates) and always require careful interpretation, they provide an invaluable resource and a useful corrective to published accounts. Wherever possible we have drawn on such sources, either at first hand or as reproduced in other scholarly work.

Primary sources consulted include the George Kleine Papers at the Library of Congress, Washington, DC; the Kirk Douglas, Walter Wanger, and United Artists Collections at the Wisconsin State Historical Society, University of Wisconsin–Madison; the Sam Peckinpah, George Stevens, Howard Strickling, and Paramount Production Files Collections at the Margaret Herrick Library, Academy of Motion Picture Arts and Sciences, Los Angeles (AMPAS); the Twentieth Century-Fox Collection at the University of California at Los Angeles; and the Warner Bros. Archives at the University of Southern California, Los Angeles. Unless otherwise noted, cost and earnings figures for particular studios' films derive from the following sources:

MGM (1924–62): the Eddie Mannix Ledger, Howard Strickling Collection (AMPAS); excerpts reproduced in Glancy (1992).

Paramount: files for individual films in the Paramount Production Files Collection (AMPAS).

RKO (1928–50): the C. J. Tevlin Ledger, excerpts reproduced in Jewell (1994).

Twentieth Century-Fox: files for individual films in the Twentieth Century-Fox Collection (UCLA); excerpts reproduced in Solomon (1988).

United Artists: files for individual films in the United Artists Collection (Madison, Wisconsin).

Warner Bros. (1921–67): the William Schaefer Ledger in the Doheny Library and files for individual films in the Warner Bros. Archives (both USC); excerpts reproduced in Glancy (1995).

Unless noted otherwise, all dates in brackets following the first mention of a film title are for its first year of exhibition in the United States, regardless of its production or copyright date or earlier release in other countries.

Early Films and Early Features, 1894–1911

The earliest films in the United States were less than a minute long. Members of the public could view them on a peepshow machine in an arcade or a parlor or, a year or so later, as part of a program of films projected onto a screen in a vaudeville theater, an amusement park, or an opera house.[1] The peepshow films "were all simple recordings of some type of preexisting popular attraction: displays of boxing, wrestling, and physical culture; comic vignettes drawn from newspaper comic strips; specialty dances and other abbreviated vaudeville routines; Wild West exhibitions; historical reenactments; and highlights from theatrical comedy hits."[2] The projected films often also included "actualities," "scenics," and "travelogues"—outdoor views and scenes of everyday life, many of them made, initially, abroad.

The films were produced by organizations and individuals who manufactured cameras, peepshow machines, or projectors, who bought these machines or paid a fee for the right to use them, or who risked transgressing copyright laws by making versions or copies of their own. Some of the earliest producers of films and manufacturers of machines were based in Europe. They included Robert Paul, who was based in Britain, and the Lumière Company in France. The major U.S. producers and manufacturers were the Edison Manufacturing Company, the Vitagraph Company, Sigmund Lubin's Cineograph Company, William Selig's Polyscope Company, and the American Mutoscope and Biograph Company (AM&B).

Films were initially distributed to exhibitors in a number of different ways. Films for Edison's Kinetoscope, the first of the peepshow machines, were ordered by mail from a catalog. The films were sold rather than rented. Initial prices were high: in 1895 they ranged from fifteen to twenty dollars per film.[3] However, prices soon fell as sales of Kinetoscopes increased. Edison used a similar method to distribute its films for projection. Prices were based on the length of the films. According to Michael Quinn, the standard price for an Edison film in 1898 was fifteen cents per foot; according to

Tino Balio, the selling and pricing of films in this way became a standard means of distributing films for the remainder of the 1890s and the early 1900s.[4]

Through its agents, Raff & Gammon, Edison initially sold the rights to own and operate its Kinetoscopes and projectors on a territorial basis.[5] It thus became the first film company in the United States to use the states rights system, a method used to distribute and profit from goods and services by selling the rights to further sell or to subcontract them within specific regions and states. Edison later sold its machines and its films on the open interstate market. AM&B owned its peepshow machines and owned and operated its projectors, both of which it supplied with the films it made with its cameras. Along with Lumière and Vitagraph, AM&B was also one of the earliest companies to provide an integrated distribution and projection service to exhibitors.

As Michael Quinn points out, there were no standard exhibition sites for films in this period, so Lumière, Vitagraph, AM&B, and others "were effectively itinerant exhibitors, screening films at local vaudeville houses, town halls, churches or other such venues."[6] When vaudeville became established as a regular exhibition site for films in the early 1900s, this "self-contained-unit system" died out as most film companies now made their profits from selling films. Even then, though, companies such as Vitagraph and Kinodrome continued to provide an integrated distribution and exhibition service, supplying vaudeville houses with a new act comprising a projector, a projectionist, and a new set of films each week.[7] And even then, and for some time thereafter, rural communities continued to be served by itinerant exhibitors who bought their films from manufacturers and traveled from venue to venue equipped with a set of films, a projector, and a screen.[8]

Itinerant exhibition took two principal forms. One involved traveling to and from permanent venues, the other erecting temporary exhibition sites, usually under canvas, then moving on to another location. Traveling exhibitors were "the principal purveyors of films in towns and small cities where there were no vaudeville houses. Many films were shown in churches and opera houses (often for only one evening but, if the town was big enough, for two or three days)."[9] In addition to numerous "single-unit" companies, "multiple units" were toured by established showmen and even established film companies. Vitagraph toured a number of such units in 1904–5.

Itinerant exhibitors and companies like Lumière and Vitagraph were thus the first to roadshow films in the United States. In a large and predominantly rural country, the touring of shows and entertainments of all kinds—circuses and minstrel shows, variety shows and plays, tent shows, medicine shows, magic lantern shows and Chautauqua presentations—was a regular practice. The advent of a national railroad system, the growth in the size of the population and in the number of cities, towns and settlements, and the consequent growth in national and local markets for entertainments of all kinds helped spur the roadshowing practice. In some fields, in vaudeville, in burlesque, and in what was called the legitimate theater, these developments had already given rise to local, regional, and national exhibition circuits, to the centralized packaging, booking, and touring of companies, productions, and shows, to the establishment of highly capitalized agencies and businesses, and hence to the development of what Calvin Pryluck has called the "industrialization of entertainment" in the United States.[10] While companies like Lumière, Edison, and AM&B were highly capitalized, most of this capital was invested in the production and distribution of machines for making and showing films. Until the establishment of regular venues for film exhibition and of local and national distribution facilities, what might best be termed *rural* or *small-scale* roadshowing remained an essential means of showing and distributing films. In some rural areas it was to remain so until the 1950s and early 1960s.[11]

Boxing Films and Passion Plays

It would be anomalous to describe any of the films made in the 1890s as epics or spectacles. As Tom Gunning has pointed out, spectacle was a fundamental attraction in nearly all films made at this time.[12] While some may have contained more markedly spectacular moments than others, they do not appear to have been distinguished one from another on the basis of their quotient of spectacle alone. None was of a type or a scale sufficient to prompt the use of a term like *epic;* most of the films made in the 1890s were no more than a few minutes long. However, there were one or two films whose subject matter and length marked them out as special, novel, or unusual productions requiring special, novel, or unusual modes of distribution and exhibition.

One of the earliest peepshow productions was a boxing film. As Dan Streible points out, boxing films were relatively prominent in the 1890s and early 1990s. There were three major types: sparring films, recordings of prizefights, and fight reenactments.[13] The earliest recording of a prizefight was *The Leonard-Cushing Fight* (1894), which was specially arranged by its producers, Woodville Latham and Enoch J. Rector, and specially limited to six one-minute rounds for the purposes of filming. The length of the rounds was determined by the capacities of Edison's Kinetograph camera and Edison's Kinetoscope peepshow machine, the number of the rounds by the average number of peepshow machines in a parlor. Customers keen to see the whole fight could view each one-minute round in turn on a set of six different machines. In 1895, the Lambda Company made a continuous eight-minute film of a fight between Young Griffo (Albert Griffiths) and Charles Barnette for their newly invented projector. And in 1897, the Veriscope Company, an Edison subsidiary, filmed a fight between Robert Fitzsimmons and James Corbett that was first shown at the 2,100-seat Academy of Music in New York. The "program lasted for approximately a hundred minutes and was one of the first full-length performances devoted exclusively to motion pictures."[14] It was subsequently exhibited in Boston, Chicago, San Francisco, and other major cities, and it was one of the first films to be distributed by means of the states rights system when it was shown more widely later that year. When it played at the

Grand Opera House in Chicago, it was shown at matinees and in the evening at prices ranging from twenty-five cents for a gallery seat to a dollar per seat in the orchestra.[15]

In adopting the states rights system, the Veriscope Company established a precedent for longer-than-average films, multireel features, and other special or unusual productions and programs in subsequent decades. In adopting a price range and by booking venues used for legitimate theatrical productions in its premiere run, it established a precedent for the exhibition of large-scale roadshow productions. Such productions would generally be of a more culturally prestigious kind than boxing films. To that extent, more direct antecedents can be found in the realms of the passion play film.

Passion plays depicted the suffering and death of Christ at the hands of the Roman Empire. They had been performed in Europe for hundreds of years. Prior to the advent of films, illustrated lectures on passion plays, especially the one performed at Oberammergau in Austria, were common events. In 1896, Charles Smith Hurd obtained $20,000 from Mark Klaw and Abraham L. Erlanger to film the passion play performed each year at the Austrian village of Horitz. (At the time, $20,000 was a huge sum; production budgets for films rarely exceeded $1,000.)[16] Klaw & Erlinger were theatrical producers; their company was one of the biggest theatrical booking agencies in the United States. They were well used to organizing large-scale roadshow premieres, presentations, and tours. *The Horowitz Passion Play* was premiered on November 22, 1897 at the Philadelphia Academy of Music as "an hour-and-a-half exhibition that also included projected slides, a lecture, organ music and sacred hymns" before playing for a number of weeks in Boston, Baltimore, Rochester, and New York City.[17] Prices for seats at the Philadelphia Academy ranged from fifty cents to a dollar, the same as those charged for legitimate plays. The film itself was 5,000 feet long. It "consisted of 50 scenes and began with documentary footage of the town where the film was photographed, followed by tableaux that served to introduce and identify each of the principal actors."[18]

When it opened in New York in March 1898, *The Horowitz Passion Play* found itself competing with *The Passion Play of Oberammergau*. The latter was produced by Richard Holloman, president of the Eden Musée, the venue at which the film was first shown. It was made in New York and was in fact only loosely based on the passion play performed at Oberammagau. It consisted of "twenty-three scenes totaling approximately 2,000 feet. Shot at about thirty frames per second, they produced some nineteen minutes of screen time. The resulting scenes, with their sparse sets and simple, frontal compositions, evoked the long, powerful tradition of religious painting." Little is known about the film's presentation at the Musée itself, but it "was soon sending out traveling companies to present two-hour passion-play entertainments."[19] The success of *The Horowitz Passion Play* and *The Passion Play of Oberammagau* prompted the production of other passion play films and presentations. Along with boxing matches, passion plays, the life of Christ, and other biblical topics and stories were to act as the basis for unusually expensive, unusually lengthy, and unusually distributed and exhibited films for some years to come.[20]

Exchanges, Nickelodeons, and Multishot Films

The film industry in the United States experienced a number of problems in the early 1900s: problems with nonstandardized technology, patents and copyright, stereotypical subjects, and severe competition. Film production was in decline; a number of vaudeville theaters dropped films from their bills; many storefront theaters and other small-scale exhibition venues began to experience a shortage of films. According to Ben Singer and Charlie Keil, these problems began to abate in 1903:

[O]nce secure copyright practices had been affirmed by the courts, the main patent infringement disputes had been adjudicated, settled, or abandoned (at least for the time being), and the industry shifted toward longer, more engaging multi-shot fiction narratives. Chase films, like AM&B's ten-shot *The Escaped Lunatic* (1903), and sensational melodramas like Edison's big commercial hit, *The Great Train Robbery* (1903), displayed increasing facility with editing techniques conveying continuities of space, time, and action, while continuing to draw upon close intertextual antecedents in American popular culture.

By the end of 1905, fiction films running at least half of a 1,000-foot reel (or about eight minutes) had become the dominant product of all five major US production companies—Edison, AM&B, Lubin, Selig, and Vitagraph (as well as Pathé-Frères, which opened a New York distribution office in mid-1904 and quickly commanded a major share of the US market).[21]

Richard Abel has argued that some accounts exaggerate the nature and scale of the problems besetting the U.S. film industry in the early 1900s. For Abel, the films of Pathé, Méliès, and other French companies were central to a steadily expanding market in the U.S. in the period before as well as after 1903, especially if "cheap" or "family" vaudeville, itinerant exhibition services, and venues such as summer parks are taken into account.[22] Abel also notes that French companies were central to the emergence of a number of new genres and to the promotion of individual films as "headline acts" or "features" on vaudeville bills. These genres included "mystical," "mysterious," or "trick" films. They also included "spectaculars." Spectaculars were reproductions of pantomimes and other stage spectacles. When taken up by Vitagraph in 1903, they were "films of a full reel or more, running fifteen to twenty minutes in length, either based on 'fairy plays' like *Puss-in-Boots* and *Fairyland* or on historical subjects like *The Life of Napoleon*."[23] Like Méliès's *Cinderella* in 1900, Pathé's *Aladdin and His Lamp* in 1902, and Méliès's "Magnificent Spectacle," *A Trip to the Moon,* in 1903, these films were all promoted as features.[24] They helped to establish spectacle as a generic category, as a generic term, and as a differential ingredient in films of all kinds. They also helped to establish a relationship among spectacle, scale, and feature promotion that was to persist for decades to come.

The period between 1900 and 1903 was marked by several key developments in the field of distribution: the establishment of film exchanges, the practice of renting

Spectacle scenes in *Cinderella* (1900) and *A Trip to the Moon* (1903).

films, and the separation of distribution from exhibition. Prior to 1903, "distribution had been only one of several functions performed by exhibitors. Now, some established companies began to rent a reel of film to the theater for less money (about twenty-five dollars a week) and let its management be responsible for the actual projection." In this way, the theater "became the exhibitor, while the old exhibition service retained the more limited role of distributor."[25] The practice of renting old reels of films had been adopted by a number of dealers in films and in film equipment. These dealers became known as film "exchanges." Their numbers increased in the early 1900s. Among them were Percival Walters's Kinetograph Company, the New York Film Exchange, the Miles Brothers, William H. Swanson's company in Chicago, and the Kleine Optical Company, which by 1903 was the principal agent for distributing the films produced by Biograph and Edison.[26] Later that year, Lubin announced that "A Million Feet of Film of all the latest and Up-to-date Subjects will be rented."[27] During the course of the following year, Eugene Cline and Company, Alfred Harstin & Company, William Paley, and George Spoor all opened exchanges or began to rent copies of films.

As Michael Quinn points out, exchanges "allowed exhibitors to rent more films and change them more frequently, allowing for repeat customers and a better viewing experience. They further allowed manufacturers to deal with only a handful of exchanges rather than hundreds of small exhibitors."[28] These exhibitors included the owners of peepshow parlors, amusement arcades, vaudeville houses, and storefront theaters, all of which, fed by an increasing number of multishot fiction films and the hand- or stencil-colored features produced by Méliès and Pathé, experienced a boom in 1904 and 1905.[29] As the name implies, storefront theaters were shops or other kinds of small buildings converted into venues for showing programs of films. An early example was the Seattle storefront operated by the Miles brothers in 1901: "The capacity (seating and standing) was 160 people. Admission was ten cents and receipts were said to be as high as $160 a day."[30] Other examples included the Electric Theater in Los Angeles and the Searchlight Theater at the Donnelly Hotel in Tacoma. These were short-lived operations, but those that opened in 1904 and 1905, among them the Nickelodeon opened by Harry Davis in Pittsburgh in June 1905, were much more successful.

Nickelodeons, as they came to be known generically, rapidly became the dominant site of film exhibition in the United States:

By the spring of 1906, a dozen or more nickelodeons were operating profitably in each of several metropolitan areas—New York, Philadelphia, Pittsburgh, Cleveland, and Chicago. Within a year, their numbers increased exponentially to include hundreds in New York and Chicago, and *Moving Picture World* estimated that there were between 2,500 and 3,000 throughout the country. Within another year, the overall figure had more than doubled, and both the trade press and moral reform organizations agreed that New York City nickelodeons "entertained three to four hundred thousand people daily" or nearly three million a week.[31]

The layout and capacity of nickelodeons could vary, particularly as they accommodated standing as well as seated customers. In 1906, the number of seats could range from as low as fifty to as high as a thousand. Most, though, were housed in a narrow room with several hundred seats, "a raised projection booth at one end and nine-by-twelve foot screen hung in a small stage space or attached to the back wall at the other. A piano and drum set were placed at one side of and below the screen."[32] Exteriors could be more lavish, especially as the decade wore on, and it was "at this time that the box office, as a special architectural feature of the movie house, came into use."[33]

The length of programs of films in nickelodeons could vary as well. Generally speaking, the lower the seating capacity, the shorter the program and the higher the number of showings each day. In 1906, the number of showings ranged from fifteen to sixty in the smaller theaters and from fifteen to as low as three in the larger ones.[34] The length and the number of programs also depended on location and clientele: "some ran no more than fifteen or twenty minutes, with forty or more shows a day, if the theater was open from morning to midnight; others ran close to an hour, much like family vaudeville. . . . By 1907, many theaters were changing their programs daily, while the great majority changed theirs from one to three times a week."[35] Most programs were shown on a "continuous" basis, with audiences able to enter or leave whenever they wished, rather than scheduled to begin and end at specific times. This was one of the features of nickelodeon exhibition that linked it to vaudeville and other forms of variety entertainment rather than to the legitimate theater.

The advent and spread of nickelodeons helped create "a new kind of specialized spectator, the moviegoer, who did not view films within the variety format of vaudeville, as part of a visit to a summer amusement park, or as one of an opera house's diverse offerings over the course of a theatrical season."[36] They also helped consolidate the trend toward fiction films, which were easier to produce on a routine basis than actualities and topicals, and the trend toward renting films from exchanges, which helped to increase the number of films in circulation at any one time. Above all, "the lateral expansion of movie houses across the country and the vertical increase of program change caused a tremendous demand for films."[37] Moreover, demand was continuous rather than seasonal as most nickelodeons, unlike many other entertainment venues, were open to patrons throughout the year.

As Richard Abel has shown, this demand was initially met by Pathé and other foreign companies rather than by companies in the United States. Only Lubin and Vitagraph substantially increased the numbers of films they produced in 1906 and 1907. Vitagraph also built new studios and became the first U.S. company to open sales offices abroad. It was Pathé, however, that supplied the greatest number of films.[38] By September 1906, it was releasing six films a week; by April 1907, seven films a week. By 1908 it was releasing eight to twelve films a week "and selling, on average, two hundred copies of each title released in the United States." It had by then "achieved the remarkable feat not only of mass marketing the largest number and the greatest variety of film subjects for an ever-expanding exhibition market but also of producing one subject, the *Passion Play*, with the longest 'shelf life.'"[39]

The Passion Play was produced and released in 1907. It was an updated, stencil-colored remake of the version directed by Ferdinand Zecca for Pathé in 1902–3, a version that had also met with considerable success in the United States. Preceded in France by Lumière's *The Life and the Passion of Christ* (1898) and Gaumont's two versions of *La Vie du Christ* (1899 and 1906), all of which, like the U.S. passion play films, were longer in relative terms than average productions of the period, the 1907 version of *The Passion Play* was four reels long "and took a full hour to project."[40] In preparation for its U.S. release, Pathé issued a forty-four-page booklet for potential exhibitors and later produced a special poster with stills from the film. The film itself was extraordinarily popular. It was held over in nickelodeons throughout the country and was presented at special screenings to Christmas shoppers at Keith's Fifth Avenue Theatre in New York. During Easter week the following year, "the demand was so great that not a renter could secure enough prints."[41]

There were no equivalents to *The Passion Play* produced in the United States at this time. The nearest equivalent in terms of length was probably Edison's earlier *Parsifal* (1904), which was based on the New York Metropolitan Opera's 1903 production of Wagner's opera, and which at 1,975 feet ran for approximately half an hour. Partly funded by theatrical producer Harley Merry, "the film sold only a small number of copies, and Merry almost certainly lost a substantial portion of his $1,800 investment."[42]

The Motion Picture Patents Company

Pathé's dominance in a rapidly expanding and profitable market was one of the factors that prompted the formation of the Motion Picture Patents Company (MPPC) in 1908.[43] The MPPC, soon to be nicknamed the "Trust," was a holding company designed to control the U.S. film industry and to profit its members by pooling the patent rights to cameras and projectors held by a number of different companies and charging fees for their use, thus eliminating competition in the field of film production and, as far as possible, from the field of exhibition as well. The patent holders were Edison, Armat, Biograph, and Vitagraph. The other members were Essanay, Kalem, Lubin, Méliès, Pathé, and Kleine. In addition, in exchange for collecting royalties on each foot of film, Eastman Kodak was authorized early in 1909 to act as the sole supplier of film stock to producers licensed by the MPPC. Licenses were granted to the MPPC's producers in return for an annual fee. They were also granted to exchanges and to exhibitors, who had to pay an annual fee for the right to project licensed films on licensed projectors.

Kleine was an importer of foreign films. Méliès and Pathé were foreign producers. However, one of the aims of the other members of the MPPC was not just to profit from expansion of the film industry in the United States, but also to limit the dominance of Pathé and to open up the domestic market to its own licensed domestic producers. This they achieved, as Abel points out, by limiting the number of films that could be released each week by member companies, thereby cutting the number of films released by Pathé and ensuring a greater share for U.S. producers, by encouraging public campaigns in favor of U.S. films and against those made by the French, and by introducing a number of measures to improve the quality of its members' films as well as that of its overall service.[44]

The Trust was modeled on large-scale corporations in the tobacco, oil, and communications industries, and, in the neighboring field of entertainment, on the theatrical Syndicate and other similar organizations in vaudeville and burlesque. Its stated policies were to standardize, modernize, and reform the film business in the United States in line with these and other contemporary industries. In return for their fees, exhibitors were promised a regular supply of films from the Trust's producers. These films were to be released on specified days of the week. Prints were to be rented from distributors licensed initially on a states rights basis.[45] These distributors were to rent rather than buy copies of the films from the MPPC. After a specified period of time, prints were to be returned to the MPPC and thence to its licensed producers. This would help curtail the circulation of old films, worn-out prints, and illegally duplicated copies. All films were to be rented at a standard rate per foot. This would encourage competition among the MPPC's producers and raise the standard of their productions, since what would differentiate the films they each produced would be their quality rather than their price. In addition, the MPPC "initiated a systematic policy of theatre improvement, secured accident and fire insurance for licensed exhibitors and joined with the newly created National Board of Censorship in an effort to produce 'educational, moral (and) cleanly amusing' films."[46]

In the first instance, and indeed in the long run, many of these policies, along with the underlying aim of eliminating competition in the field of production, were to fail. Unaffiliated exhibitors and the distributors who supplied them with films continued to operate. Some of these films were imported, some were dupes, some were old prints of old films, some were copies of films that had not yet been released at the point at which the MPPC had been formed, and others were films produced by unaffiliated domestic producers. Initially, these were few and far between. Perceiving that the source of most of these problems lay in the field of distribution, a field in which a series of a oppositional or "Independent" organizations—the Independent Film Protective Rental Agency, the Film Import and Trading Company, Great Northern, the Independent Moving Picture Company (IMP), the New York Motion Picture Company (Bison), and the Motion Picture Distributing and Sales Company (Sales Company)—had already emerged, the Trust decided in May 1910 to buy out every licensed exchange in the country and to establish the General Film Company (GFC), the first national distribution organization in U.S. film history.

Failing only to acquire William Fox's General New York Film Exchange, an additional source of growing opposition to the Trust and its policies, the GFC established a number of significant and influential practices. Continuing the policy of renting rather than buying films from licensed producers, it rented films to exhibitors for a fee based on the amount of time that had passed since their initial release date or run. It ranked exhibitors according to location and offered them a service based on their ranking, an early form of what became known as "zoning." And it provided a "complete service" to exhibitors, meaning that it supplied them with enough films to constitute a complete program, an early form of what became later known as "block booking."[47] Block booking, along with the "run-zone-clearance" system, was a practice that came to be associated with the companies and organizations that came to supersede the MPPC and to dominate the U.S. film industry from the late 1910s and the 1920s to the late 1940s and beyond, as we shall see. They too offered programs of films. But the nature and length of the films that comprised the program and the nature and conception of the program itself were entirely different.

Programs, Features, and Reels

The notion of the program that governed the practices of the MPPC and the GFC was derived from vaudeville and other forms of variety entertainment. Variety programs consisted of a series of short, ten-to-twenty-minute acts, and this was one of the principal contexts within which films were exhibited in their earliest years. By the late 1900s, the principal exhibition sites for films were nickelodeons and "small-time" vaudeville houses, which mixed programs of films with vaudeville acts and song slides. These were the venues and this was the market to which the MPPC and its member companies principally catered. Most of these venues and the auditoria within them were relatively small. In rural and small-town locations, they catered to stable but small populations. In big city centers, they catered also to passers-by, to what Quinn calls "the transient audience."[48] Either way, and for all these reasons, nickelodeons and small-time vaudeville houses required a constant turnover of patrons and programs of films. In the early years of the MPPC, short, continuous programs of films, generally changed daily or every other day, were the norm. These programs were provided by the GFC, the films that comprised them by the MPPC's licensed producers.

As Quinn points out, a system of this kind allowed little time or space for the promotion of individual films. The films were different from one another, but they were distributed and advertised as well as shown in groups. Difference was important. But what mattered most were those aspects of difference that contributed to the variety of the program as a whole.[49] There was room in this system for "features," but only for features of a kind corresponding to headline acts in vaudeville: features of a sort that would allow them to be promoted in an individual or special way, usually at the point of exhibition, but which were compatible with the demands and parameters of the system as a whole.[50]

Features were not necessarily films. An accompanying lecture or vaudeville act could be a feature, as could an organ, an orchestra, and other live or recorded musical performances, sound effects, and speech. Prints of features could be distinguished by their use of color. And films themselves were often promoted as features on the basis of what was perceived to be their educational or cultural value or their pertinence at Christmas or Easter or at other key points in the calendar rather than on the basis of their length.[51] Only gradually did the idea of a feature as a longer film take hold. As Quinn explains,

The Trust experimented with feature production as early as 1909. Vitagraph, which had begun producing "quality films" prior to the formation of the Trust, continued to release features despite its affiliation with the MPPC. Their first MPPC features include *The Life of Napoleon* and *The Life of George Washington* (1909), both in two reels, the four-reel *Les Misérables* (1909), and the ambitious five-reel *The Life of Moses* (1909–10). These films, particularly *The Life of Napoleon,* received a number of screenings at Broadway houses and other prestigious locations. However, as William Uricchio and Roberta Pearson point out, "Vitagraph obviously did not make the quality films to drive away the current patrons of the nickelodeons, claiming on the contrary that biblicals, literaries, and historicals would perform well at the box office." These small theaters rarely screened all the reels of a multiple-reel film on the same day, showing instead a different reel each day—or even each week—along with a regular program of shorts. This mode of distribution and exhibition was hardly the way to differentiate the feature from the standard program: however expensive or spectacular Vitagraph's features were, such practices integrated them with the standard program.[52]

Thus, as Ben Brewster notes, the system as a whole was "was built around the constant module of the 1,000-foot reel. In 1909, most films were shorter than this, so producers supplied 'split reels,' two films making up the 1,000-foot unit. By 1912, most films were a single reel, within a few feet of the modular length."[53] The system by then could accommodate multireel films as single units in a distribution schedule and in an hour-long program of reels. Two-reel and even three-reel features were not uncommon in 1911 and 1912. Vitagraph released the two-reel *Auld Lang Syne* and the three-reel *Vanity Fair* on a single day in 1911, and other producers of quality films followed in its wake. By 1912, most theaters possessed more than one projector and could therefore screen multiple reels continuously. But "by no means all did so. In general they treated the multiple-reels films as they treated the multiple reels of the program of one-reel films they regularly showed, whether with or without a shorter or longer break between the reels."[54]

This was the system that governed the production, distribution, and exhibition of films by most independent companies as well as by the MPPC and the GFC. In 1912, though, it began to be challenged as feature films in the modern sense, films of four reels or more, began to be produced and imported in greater numbers; as larger cinemas began to be built to show them; as old ways were revived as a means to distribute them; and as a new generation of companies and a new set of cartels grew up around them.

MULTIREEL FEATURES, EPICS, AND ROADSHOWS, 1911–1916

During the course of 1911 and 1912, the term *feature* became ubiquitous. Coincident with a rise in the number of two- and three-reel films, its use was still largely compatible with the concept of the program feature. However, 1911 and 1912 witnessed the release of a number of longer films than these, films such as *The Crusaders; or Jerusalem Delivered* (1911), *The Miracle* (1912), *Richard III* (1912), and *Queen Elizabeth* (1912), each in four reels; *Dante's Inferno* (1911) and *From the Manger to the Cross* (1912), both in five reels; and *Cleopatra* (1912), in six reels.[1] As a result, although the term retained its traditional meaning, the concept of the feature began to change.[2] This change was reflected in the names of some of the companies that produced and distributed the films: the Jesse L. Lasky Feature Play Company, Warner's Features Inc., the Gene Gauntier Feature Players, Marion Leonard Features, and dozens of others. Some of these were production companies; some were distributors. According to *The Moving Picture World*, there were over 150 companies distributing feature films by the beginning of June 1912.[3] As Eileen Bowser points out, most of them were short-lived and some were established to distribute a single feature film. But "feature fever" was a sign of things to come. This was "the beginning of a limited number of major production companies that would end up with greater control of distribution and exhibition than the Trust companies had ever achieved."[4]

The features listed above could be described as either "biblicals," "literaries," or "historicals."[5] They were not just experiments in length. They also constituted a response to growing demands by legislative bodies, cultural organizations, and governmental agencies for uplift and reform in the U.S. film industry. Reflecting anxieties shared by the guardians of culture in other fields of contemporary commercial entertainment, these demands were aimed not just at films but also at audiences for films and at the nature of some of the venues in which the films were shown.[6] Hence the production of Vitagraph's quality films and of biblicals, historicals, and literaries by other companies inside and outside the MPPC: Kalem's *As You Like It* (1908), Biograph's *Resurrection* (1909), Edison's *Faust* (1910), Thanhouser's *The Winter's Tale* (1910), and many others.

Similar demands had spurred the production of similar films in Italy and France. In addition to its passion plays, Pathé's quality productions included *Samson* (1908), *The Kiss of Judas* (1909), *Cleopatra* (1910), and a two-reel version of *Drink* (*L'Assomoir*) (1909).[7] In 1908, Pathé contracted with Film D'Art and SCAGL (Société Cinémato-graphique des Auteurs et Gens de Lettres) with the express aim of distributing films that would raise the cultural status of film and disseminate classic works of literature to cinema audiences. They included *The Assassination of the Duke de Guise* and *The Return of Ulysses* (both 1909). Gaumont made films of this kind as well, among them *Christopher Columbus* (1910) and *A Priestess of Carthage* (1911). These films were all distributed in the United States. Most were single-reelers, but the number of multireel quality French films began to increase in 1911 and 1912. As well as a two-reel version of *Camille* (1912), *Queen Elizabeth,* a French-Anglo-American coproduction, helped pave the way for a twelve-reel version of *Les Misérables,* which was released as a serial in four three-reel parts in France in 1912, and as a reedited nine-reel-long single feature film in the United States in 1913.[8]

The move toward longer films in France was facilitated by Pathé's ownership of cinemas and national distribution facilities. As Ben Brewster has noted, the position enjoyed by Pathé in its domestic and foreign markets enabled it to sustain high production costs and hence to compete in quality with its rivals. Its control over the programs of films exhibited in its theaters also enabled Pathé to extend the length of the films it made. But the major impetus to produce much longer films in France "came from the import by firms outside the Pathé circle of films from abroad, particularly Italy."[9] These imports established the basis for a sustained period of production of longer films in France.

In 1909, Pathé established Film D'Arte Italiana, a branch of Film D'Art. Its films included *Othello* (1909), *Salome* (1910), and a three-reel version of *Romeo and Juliet* (1911). These films were made by Italian personnel and distributed by Pathé. Italy's own quality films were produced by Ambrosio, Cines, Itala, and Milano. Ambrosio produced *The Last Days of Pompeii* (1909) and *Nero, or the Burning of Rome* (1909); Itala, *Julius Caesar* (1909) and the two-reel *The Fall of Troy* (1911); Cines, *Macbeth* (1910) and the two-reel *Joseph in Egypt* (1911); Milano produced *Dante's Inferno,* one of the first five-reel features, as well as a three-reel version of *Homer's Odyssey* (1912).

These longer films were produced in the midst of a period of expansion and renewed investment in the Italian film industry. Central to this expansion, as Paolo Cherchi Usai has pointed out, was the involvement of "a new generation of entrepreneurs, with its roots in the aristocracy or in the world of high finance and big business."[10] These entrepreneurs sought to raise the status of Italian films. One way of doing so was to involve members of the Italian literary and artistic elite in film production. Another, in a distribution and exhibition market less constrained by single-reel programs, was to make longer films and to invest in larger cinemas. Yet another was to make use of Italy's light, and its historical, cultural, and architectural heritage. The result was a combination of prestige, spectacle, and scale that was to prove a major site for the emergence of "epic" as a generically descriptive term in the United States at this time.[11] By 1911, Ambrosio was being noted for its "spectacular productions"; Italian productions were being singled out for their "superior technique."[12] These ingredients were to prove a major factor in the promotion, distribution, and exhibition of these films in the United States and elsewhere abroad.

Distribution, Exhibition, and Promotion

Whether domestically produced or imported, whether distributed by independents, the GFC or, a little earlier, by licensees of the MPPC, the shorter as well as the longer quality features were all increasingly treated as "specials." This meant that they were often more expensive to produce than ordinary program pictures, especially if they were two or three reels in length. It also meant that they were increasingly given more publicity and longer-than-average exhibition runs, even in ordinary nickelodeon theaters, that theaters were increasingly charged more for these films by distributors, and consequently that theaters increasingly showed them at higher-than-average seat prices. In addition, as early as 1909, the Film Import and Trading Company issued a four-color poster and a sixteen-page souvenir booklet in order to publicize *Nero, or the Burning of Rome*.[13] Earlier that year, special posters were produced for each of the reels of Vitagraph's *The Life of Moses* (1909–10). One of the posters for a screening of the film at the Plumb Opera House boasted of a production budget of $50,000 at a time when the budgets for single-reel films averaged $500 to $600.[14] Vitagraph's *Bulletin* encouraged exhibitors to show all five reels at once: "Besides adding to your cash receipts you would thereby add immensely to your reputation and to the reputation of the motion picture business."[15]

Between 1909 and 1912, developments such as these were on the increase. To that extent, a process of differentiation coincident in its later stages with the advent and influx of feature-length films was already underway in the program system. However, as we have seen in the previous chapter, the scope for differentiation within the system was limited, particularly when it came to longer runs and longer films. As early as 1909, *The Moving Picture World* was asking why "a first-class Biograph, Pathé or Edison" should be denied the "chance of securing the suffrages of the public to the point of exhaustion."[16] Two years later, *The Fall of Troy* and *A Priestess of Carthage* were cited as examples of longer films that would benefit from longer runs. The booking of the former for a successful week-long run at the legitimate, 2,000-seat Lyric Theatre in Cincinnati subsequent to its initial run in local nickelodeon theaters was offered as proof.[17] The MPPC, the GFC and independent producers, distributors, and exhibitors were all well aware of the economic potential of features.[18] In 1912, the GFC introduced a special service for two-reel and three-reel program features. It also licensed the distribution of *Queen Elizabeth, Dante's Inferno,* and a number of subsequent feature-length imports. *From the Manger to the Cross* was produced and distributed by Kalem, a founding member of the MPPC. However, these and later feature imports, together with the feature-length films produced in the United States during the course of the next two years, were distributed outside the regular and the special program systems run by the independents and the GFC. Most were distributed instead on a states rights basis.

As we have seen, the states rights system had been used by Edison to distribute its peepshow machines. It had been used for the distribution of boxing films as well. It continued to be used for this purpose, not just because boxing films were often unusually long, but also because a number of states had declared the staging of boxing matches and the exhibition of boxing films illegal. The inherently selective states rights system was thus tailor-made for their distribution. It was also the only ready-made means for distributing feature-length films. The origins of the states rights system lay in the live entertainment industry: "exclusive rights to an act were granted to a regional franchise holder, who would then book it into theaters in his or her territory, guaranteeing the theater owner exclusive exhibition for a negotiable period, thus allowing for long runs and a run-up period for an advertising campaign."[19] According to *The Moving Picture World,* it was Pliny Craft, who had worked for a number of theatrical companies as well as for Buffalo Bill's Wild West Show, who helped pioneer its use for features other than boxing films: it was Craft who used it to distribute *The Fall of Troy* and *Dante's Inferno.*[20]

There were a number of variable aspects to the states rights system. The rights to distribute a film within any given territory were acquired by a regional distribution company, by a coalition of such companies, or by local or regional exhibitors. These companies and organizations could play a more or less active role in the film's exhibition. They could book the film into exhibition venues at the request of the venues themselves, leaving the latter to arrange for its presentation. Alternatively they could prebook the venues and tour or roadshow the film themselves. When Walter Rosenberg acquired the New York and New Jersey rights to the three-reel *Twenty Years in Sing Sing* (1912) on behalf of the New York Film Company, he played it "like a travelling troupe. Putting the picture on a percentage, he takes charge of the stage and billing matter, leaving the theatre to use its house staff. The percentages vary, according to the capacities, but average 50-50."[21] When exhibitor Marcus Loew paid $25,000 for the New York rights to *Queen Elizabeth,* the plan was to show it in his vaudeville houses "as a special feature on top of the regular bill, running the film by speeding it a trifle in an hour. . . . Outside the Loew houses, it will be given over the state in accessible theatres at one dollar top admission. A full evening's show will be given."[22]

Like many of the other aspects of the states rights system, the nature of a "full evening's show" could vary. Presentation was a key factor. As we have seen, elaborate modes of presentation had been a hallmark of features and specials since the 1890s. Indeed in some cases, the presentation *was* the feature. *The Moving Picture World* reported that one of the attractions of the Orpheum Theatre in Chicago was the quality of the orchestral accompaniment to the films it showed.[23] According to *Variety,* the presentation mounted for *The Miracle* was

remarkable. Before the rise of the curtain there are a few minutes of "atmospheric" orchestral music, followed by a parade down the aisle by the choir in church vestments and onto the stage. Incense is wafted into the auditorium. The rise of the curtain disclosed the screen onto which the films are to be projected. It is in the form of the exterior of a cathedral, stained glass window and heavy doors. As the "doors" are opened the white screen itself is "lighted" so as to give the illusion of gazing into the interior of a house of worship. At the close of each "act," these "doors" are utilized to shut out the picture.[24]

The presentations mounted by Samuel L. ("Roxy") Rothapfel at the various venues for which he worked were major attractions in their own right. When he exhibited Pathé's 1907 *Passion Play* at the Lyric in Minneapolis in December 1911, there was

a prelude of two silent films with no music and no sound effects: *Wild Birds in Their Haunts* and *The Holy Land,* both from Pathé. When the audience settled in, the doors closed, the house darkened, the stage curtain lowered. There was a distant pealing of chimes. "The Holy City" was played by the pipe organ. The curtain was raised and the perfume of lilies wafted over the house. Twenty choirboys in white vestments were onstage. The baritone sang "Holy City," the choirboys joined in, a pale blue light was gradually diffused, fountains played with pale blue lights beneath, and several dozen roses were carefully strewn on the steps and the stage.[25]

With 1,700 seats, the Lyric was one of the largest film theaters in the country. Film theaters of this size were by no means unknown.[26] But they were not as common—or as large—as legitimate theaters, opera houses, or concert halls. Prompted by the advent of feature-length films, which required auditoria large enough to accommodate audiences of a size sufficient to cover the costs involved in feature exhibition, larger film theaters and "picture palaces," some of them with thousands of seats, began to appear during the course of the next few years.[27] By 1913, exhibitor William Fox was able to identify a number of "large class" theaters devoted solely to the showing of films.[28] Prior to that, though, the longest and most prestigious of the new feature-length films were nearly always premiered or roadshown by states rights franchisees in legitimate theatrical venues: *Queen Elizabeth* was premiered at the Lyceum Theatre in New York, *The Miracle* at the Park Theatre in New York, and *Dante's Inferno* at the Auditorium, "one of the largest and best located theaters in the city of Baltimore."[29] *The Miracle* was accompanied by a score composed by Engelbert Humperdinck; *Queen Elizabeth,* at least in some venues, by a score composed by Joseph Carl Breil; and *Dante's Inferno* by a score arranged by W. Stephen Bush.[30] Ten different regional roadshow companies went on to play *Dante's Inferno* at the Grand Opera House in

Cincinnati, the Academy of Music in Richmond, the Garrick Theatre in St. Louis, and a number of other theatrical venues.

The Lyceum Theatre was owned and managed by Daniel Frohman, the Grand Opera House by Klaw & Erlanger, and the Auditorium Theatre by Lee and J. J. Shubert. J. J. Shubert was a *Dante's Inferno* franchisee. It was under his auspices that *Dante's Inferno* was premiered at the Auditorium. *The Miracle* was partly financed by A. H. Woods.[31] Klaw & Erlinger had been involved in feature distribution and exhibition in the 1890s, as we have seen. The Shuberts had been involved in exhibiting films in their theaters in 1908. They had also been partners with Marcus Loew in owning a chain of nickelodeons in New York.[32] Hitherto, though, their involvement in the film business had been largely piecemeal. With the advent of feature-length films, they and a number of other theatrical entrepreneurs, among them David Belasco, William A. Brady, Charles Frohman, and William and Cecil B. DeMille, began to engage themselves in the business in a much more concerted way

Theatrical Connections and Feature Film Programs

By 1911, the spread of nickelodeons and the increasing popularity of films had already had a major impact on audience numbers for popular plays. According to theater critic William Lyon Phelps, a decrease in the number of melodramas and farces began around 1907.[33] As "the cinema's drive for stability and respectability proved increasingly successful," it began to impact on audience numbers for comedies, dramas, classics, and spectacles, resulting in "the disastrous New York theatrical season of 1911–12, in which many of the legitimate houses remained closed for the entire season."[34] These developments coincided with the trend toward longer features and the need to use larger venues to show them. They also coincided with the emergence of film stars, a phenomenon modeled on and prompted by a similar well-established phenomenon in the theater as well as in other forms of contemporary entertainment.[35] Together, they prompted theater impresarios, directors, playwrights, and stars to turn to the cinema as an outlet for their talents and as a much-needed source of income.

One manifestation of this development was the production of films featuring well-known stage stars such as James K. Hackett, James O'Neill, Sir Herbert Beerbohm Tree, and Minnie Maddern Fiske.[36] Another was the formation of companies to make feature-length films based on plays, scripted by playwrights, produced by theatrical producers, or directed by theater directors.[37] Some of these companies, like The Protective Amusement Company formed by Klaw & Erlanger and A. H. Woods in 1913, were fairly short-lived. But others lasted much longer. They included the World Film Corporation, the Oliver Morosco Photoplay Company, the Famous Players Motion Picture Company, the Jesse L. Lasky Feature Play Company, Famous Players-Lasky, and Paramount Pictures.

These companies were devoted not just to the occasional or piecemeal production of feature-length films but also to the production of programs of films of this kind. Famous Players was the first to do so, initially planning to produce around a dozen films a year. The GFC had licensed the distribution of *Queen Elizabeth* and *The Prisoner of Zenda* (1913), Famous Players' first domestic production. However, when Famous Players approached the GFC to distribute its films nationwide on a regular basis, it refused. Along with most of the other national distribution cartels, the GFC was still geared to the supply of shorter films and shorter features and was unconvinced by the idea of an annual series of feature-length films. Famous Players therefore turned to the states rights system. But while this system facilitated longer runs, longer publicity campaigns, and higher admission charges, it also had a number of drawbacks. Each film had to be sold to potential distributors in specific regions and states. National distribution was by no means guaranteed, and in addition, the multiplication of buyers, agents, distributors, and exhibitors within and across different territories complicated the collection of fees and slowed the flow of income to producers. In order to rectify these problems,

Famous Players "induced" the formation of five states' rights distributors. These distributors signed long-term contracts with Famous Players, with rental prices agreed in advance, thus eliminating many of the producers' distribution problems with the stroke of a pen. This move was an undoubted success: Famous had released only two films in its first nineteen months of existence, but in the year following September 1913 it released twenty-one films.[38]

These distributors, among them William Hodkinson's Progressive Motion Picture Company, merged to form Paramount Pictures on May 8, 1914. In need of a regular supply of feature-length films, Hodkinson, as Paramount's president, offered five-year distribution contracts to Famous Players, the Lasky Feature Play Company, and Bosworth Inc. (which had been formed in January 1913 to produce feature-length films based on Jack London's novels). These companies had been unable to cash in on their most popular productions because states rights distributors paid production companies a fixed fee rather than a percentage of box-office income. In order to alleviate their concerns, Hodkinson combined a number of the practices pioneered by the GFC with a number of practices he himself helped to devise. Under his "percentage-distribution plan," "exhibitors paid a standard per-feature price based on the size of the town in which they were located and the number of days they wanted the film. From these rental fees, Paramount paid its producers 65 percent, while retaining 35 percent as the distribution fee."[39] In addition to reviving the GFC's policies of licensed theaters and program booking (i.e., booking an entire annual program of films from a single distribution source), Hodkinson extended its use of runs and zones and introduced a new policy that soon became known as "clearance."

Under this policy, after renting a film to an exhibitor, Paramount would refrain from renting the same film to a competing exhibitor for a pre-determined length of time. Clearance was a spatial as well as a temporal policy: no theatre a specified distance from a Paramount theatre could rent a film until after a specified period of time. The clearance plan addressed one of the major complaints exhibitors had against the GFC, which often rented the same program, or many of the same films, to houses on the same street. Clearance thus helped differentiate films at the level of exhibition, for exhibitors as well as audiences, allowing exhibitors to screen and advertise features without worrying that they were helping competitors who happened to have the same films.[40]

As Michael Quinn points out, most of these policies, like most of the films produced by Paramount's suppliers, were theatrical in origin.[41] As he highlights in doing so, the theatrical heritage and characteristics of these films, their stars, their production methods, and their production personnel, have either been ignored or dismissed as an immature phase in the history of films in general and of feature-length films in particular. They were even more evident, however, in the production, distribution, and exhibition of even longer, even more expensive features than these.

The Italian Epic and the Advent of the Nationwide Roadshow

On April 21, 1913, an eight-reel version of *Quo Vadis?* premiered at the Astor Theatre in New York City. It was the first time the Astor had been used as the venue for a film. The film's presentation was relatively simple. There was no lecturer and no conventional orchestral accompaniment. The film was shown in three acts with two intermissions and accompanied by a Wurlitzer Automatic Orchestra. Admission prices ranged from twenty-five cents to $1.50, and the screening lasted for over two hours.[42] The film was a huge success: "A *Quo Vadis?* craze resulted as booksellers encountered intense demand for the original novel by Henryk Sienkiewicz while leading theatrical companies produced play versions of *Quo Vadis?* on the stage. Numerous speakers toured the country giving lectures on the subject as two cheap motion-picture imitations . . . appeared on the market."[43] (One of these was a "Talkaphone" version.)[44]

By the end of the summer, advertised by the first thirty-two-sheet film posters, it was still playing at the Astor at admission prices of twenty-five to fifty cents.[45] According to *Variety*, it had earned an average of $5,000 a week for its first four weeks and an average $3,500 a week after that.[46] It was also playing twice a day at the Hippodrome in Cleveland, the McVickers Theatre in Chicago, the Garrick Theatre in Philadelphia, the Academy of Music in Baltimore, and other theatrical venues throughout the United States.[47] By October 4, 1913, total earnings from its roadshow engagements amounted to $268,792.38, total expenses to $173,466.45, and total profits to $85,325.93.[48]

The film's presentation in subsequent venues was sometimes more elaborate than its premiere presentation at the Astor. In January 1914, it played for a week at the Regent in New York. The Regent was managed by Samuel L. Rothapfel, who had moved on from the Lyric and who was shortly to manage the Strand, a 3,500-seat picture palace on Broadway. In order to introduce *Quo Vadis?*

Mr. Rothapfel had a competent dramatic speaker, William Calhoun, enter a box on the left side of the auditorium, and, with the answering of a question, as to the meaning of "Quo Vadis?", from a young man sitting in the same box the speaker started to give a succinct little talk on how the author of the book, Henry [*sic*] Sienkiewicz, obtained his idea for the story. After Mr. Calhoun had given a brief story of the film the heavy asbestos curtain was raised to singing and displayed the orchestra garlanded in flowers. The singers' romantic recesses on each side of the stage were also festooned in greenery. Three resounding blasts from trumpets accompanied by the rest of the orchestra started the entertainment proper on its way.[49]

By January 1914, the Regent had already screened a six-reel version of *The Last Days of Pompeii,* one of at least four different versions in circulation at this time.[50] The six-reel version had opened at the American Theatre in Washington in October 1913. Accompanied by a score prepared by Palmer Clark, it had also played at the Broadway Theatre in Denver, the American Theatre in Salt Lake City, and the Great DeLuxe and Ziegfeld Theatres in Chicago. An eight-reel version of *Antony and Cleopatra* opened on a similar basis in January 1914, with screenings at the Savoy in San Francisco, the American Music Hall in Chicago, the Vendome in Nashville, and the English Opera House in Indianapolis prior to its New York premiere at George Kleine's new Candler Theatre on May 16. And on June 1, a twelve-reel version of *Cabiria* opened at the Knickerbocker Theatre in New York City, accompanied by a forty-four-piece orchestra and a chorus of twenty-eight singers, at prices of a dollar per ticket, before going to play the Savoy in Long Beach, the Hippodrome in Cleveland, and a number of other theatrical venues.[51]

These films were all made in Italy. They were the first films to be roadshown in the United States on a national rather than a regional, states rights basis. *Quo Vadis?* had been produced by Cines and imported by George M. Kleine. Kleine made a point of advertising the fact that *Quo Vadis?* was not available for states rights distribution and could only be booked direct.[52] One of the reasons for this, in addition to the drawbacks to which the states rights system was prone, may have been the disrepute into which a number of states rights films were beginning to fall. Although the states rights system continued to be used to distribute large-scale prestigious imports such as *Les Misérables,* it was also increasingly used to distribute a series of crime, "vice," "red light," and "white slave trade" films.[53] Such films helped establish an association between sensation and states rights distribution that was to persist for decades to come, and that someone like Kleine would have been keen to avoid.[54] Either way, Kleine's success with *Quo Vadis?* seems to have prompted the World Special Films Corporation to distribute Pasquali's eight-reel version of *The Last Days of Pompeii* (1913) in a similar manner.[55]

It is possible that Sam Harris suggested to Kleine that he roadshow *Quo Vadis?* in this way. Harris ran a theatrical production company with George M. Cohan. Cohan & Harris were lessees and managers of the Astor Theater. Their business associates included Charles Frohman and Klaw & Erlanger. Like Frohman and Klaw & Erlanger, Cohan & Harris had been hit hard by the failures of the theatrical season in 1911 and 1912 and were considering a move into film production.[56] According to Benjamin Hampton, Harris attended a preview screening of *Quo Vadis?* in New York and offered to premiere the film at the Astor.[57] He and his company were subsequently hired to book the film into theaters and to assemble, train, and transport the twenty-two companies that played the film on its roadshow run. Cohan & Harris received 15 percent of the box-office income each week. The remainder was split between Kleine and the theaters that played the film in proportions that varied from 40 percent/60 percent at one end of the scale to 60 percent/40 percent at the other.[58]

George Kleine had been a long-standing importer of foreign productions and a long-standing advocate of quality in the field of film production, presentation, and promotion.[59] A founder member of the MPPC and vice president of the GCF from 1910 to 1913, he had signed a distribution deal with Cines in early 1912. Most of the films he distributed were one or two reels in length. However, prompted by the huge success of *Quo Vadis?*, in whose initial promotion and distribution he had invested over $200,000,[60] he set up the Photodrama Producing Company of Italy and commissioned Cines to produce *Antony and Cleopatra*, Ambrosio to produce *The Last Days of Pompeii* and a six-reel version of *Othello* (1914), and Pasquali to produce a six-reel version of *Spartacus; or the Revolt of the Gladiators* (1914). He also set up a company called George Kleine Attractions to distribute the films, and was in the process of building his own production studios at Grugliasco near Turin when the outbreak of World War I put an end to his plans.

These films were all lengthy, expensive epics in the mold of *Homer's Odyssey*, *Dante's Inferno*, and a number of other Italian films. Some scholars argue that they traded not just on Italy's cultural and archaeological heritage but also on the political appeal of its imperial past and the imperial dimensions of its current political aims and ambitions.[61] Arguments along these lines could certainly be made about *Cabiria*, which was produced and distributed by Itala and in which Kleine had no involvement. But given the extent to which *Quo Vadis?, The Last Days of Pompeii,* and *Spartacus* all highlight the limitations of Roman power, and given the extent to which Kleine provided Cines, Ambrosio, and Pasquali with advice as to what would appeal to audiences in the United States, these arguments are not always fully convincing.[62] More persuasive are arguments about the international appeal of the classical past, and the extent to which that appeal involved popular novels, plays, and entertainments as well as classical literature, painting, and other forms of high culture and art.[63] Either way, the ingredients that secured the films a roadshow run in the United

States were their length, their scale, and their production values, and the Italian film industry's growing reputation for epic grandeur, high-class spectacle, and high-class cinematography.

Quo Vadis?, The Last Days of Pompeii, *and* Cabiria

What impressed contemporary commentators on *Quo Vadis?* were its spectacular qualities. These qualities were particularly evident in the scale and three-dimensional character of its spaces and sets. As one reporter put it: "The scenes have depth, and the massive furnishings appear so genuine that the spectator feels as if he might walk down the orchestra aisle and enter Nero's banquet hall"; as another put it, in "none of the pictures is there the slightest suggestion of canvas and paint, all of them being taken with a natural background. It is said that a huge arena was specially built for the production, and the film gives visible proof of the statement."[64] The arena was used in one of several "spectacle scenes," as Eileen Bowser calls them,[65] scenes and sequences in which large casts are involved in large-scale events in large-scale settings: Nero's banquet, the burning of Rome, and so on. Such scenes stand out from others around them. As the *New York Telegraph*'s reviewer pointed out, they were used not just to punctuate the narrative, but to structure its division into acts and intermissions as well:

Scenes at a Roman banquet . . . are introduced in the first act, together with expository action which "gets over" the germinal idea to the audience that Vinitius, a nephew of Petronius, who is Nero's favorite, is deeply in love with Lygia, a Christian girl held by Rome as a hostage. In Act II, the burning of Rome is the main spectacle. Great columns crash to the ground. The streets are filled with rabble, hurrying hither and thither, taking their scanty luggage with them. Red flames and black smoke fill the air. Inserted scenes show Vinitius searching for Lygia and Nero, at last gratifying his desire to see Rome in flames that he might have inspiration for his Iliad. In the last act the mammoth arena is unrolled, crowded with people, with Nero in the royal box. The Christians are driven . . . into the arena. The lions come out by a trap door. As they get about ten feet from their prey the scene shifts to Nero gloating over the spectacle, then the action shows the great animals crunching the bones of the dead.[66]

As this description implies, a feature of nearly all these scenes is their use of editing and special effects as well as their use of large sets: miniatures and double exposures are used in the scenes of the burning of Rome; inserts and cutaways are used to show Vinitius (Amleto Novelli) searching for Lygia (Lea Giunchi) and to show Nero (Carlo Cattaneo) playing his lyre. Like the scene in the arena and the scene of Rome in flames, the banquet scene is highly edited, and the editing is used to mark Nero and Nero's gaze as a constant source of decadent power.[67] As is common in epics and spectacles, on-screen spectatorship, most evident in the arena scene, but evident, too, in the burning of Rome and banquet scenes, is one of the devices used to mark the spectacular nature of the scenes themselves.

In scenes like these, as Bowser points out, editing is also used to provide "through a variety of details an otherwise inexpressible sense of a larger whole."[68] Along with the extensive use of pans, particularly in the arena scene, it is one of the ways the film is able to exhibit what Ted Hovet calls "representational prowess."[69] This prowess is demonstrated by depicting events and settings on an unusually large scale and by showing details as well as panoramic views; it is also demonstrated by suggesting that the scale of these settings and events is so great that they cannot be encompassed by any one shot at any one moment.

The extensive use of editing in its spectacle scenes is one of the factors that mark them out from the rest of the film. As was common in European films at this time, most of the scenes in *Quo Vadis?* use long takes, deep staging, elaborate blocking, and gestural choreography rather than editing to articulate character interaction and narrative action.[70] Bowser suggests that when *The Fall of Troy* was released in the United States, it "successfully revived (for American audiences) some of the earlier forms of narrative construction. It used a variety of spaces within a single shot for laying out its actions without cutting, a practice not unknown in America but one that seemed fresh in 1911, which was a peak period for fast cutting of short shots, at least for those who worked at the forefront of modern American style."[71] The same may have been true of *Quo Vadis?*, which persistently uses entranceways and curtains at the back of its sets to stage exits and entrances, or, as in the first of the scenes in Lygia's villa, to reveal and to provide an internal frame for hitherto unseen figures, spaces, and views. The villa contains a large staircase that is used to stage a number of entrances and exits. In doing so it is used to emphasize the height as well as the width and depth of the set and its framings.

Similar stylistic ingredients can be found in *Cabiria* and in the Kleine-Ambrosio version of *The Last Days of Pompeii*.[72] Both are marked by the inventive use of long takes, fluid staging and the spatial parameters and recessive planes of their sets and exteriors; by the equally inventive use of entranceways and exits; and by the interior revelation and framing of figures, scenes, and views. *The Last Days of Pompeii* interweaves low-key and intimate sequences with an escalating series of spectacle scenes, all of which are as marked by editing as the spectacle scenes in *Quo Vadis?*. These include the scene that intercuts shots of a jealous Arbace (Antonio Grisanti) watching Jone (Eugenia Tettoni Florio) and Glaucus (Ubaldo Stefani) together on a barge at sea, the storm scene on the slopes of Mount Vesuvius, the scenes in the gladiatorial arena, and the scene at the end of the film in which Vesuvius erupts and destroys Pompeii.

The Last Days of Pompeii is relatively simple in structure and style. *Cabiria* is much more flamboyant. Indeed, although clearly affected by the extent to which the version released in the United States had been cut by the equivalent of at least a reel, it is notable that the reviews of *Cabiria* in *The Moving Picture World* and *Variety* exhibit an impatience with the proliferation of its characters and subplots and prefer to focus on its spectacle, sets, and style.[73] It could be argued, however, that proliferation is one of the film's major aesthetic devices. At a narrative level, the capture of Cabiria (Carolina Catena) by Carthaginian pirates gives rise to a series of overlapping story-lines that eventually encompass Fulvius (Umberto Mozzato), Maciste (Bartolomeo Pagano), Hannibal (Emilio Vardannes), Karthalo (Dante Testa), Sophonisba (Italia Almirante-Manzini), and a host of other real-life and fictional characters. It also gives rise to scenes such as those at the Temple of Moloch, at the siege of Syracuse, at the siege of Cirta, and a number of other battle, chase, and search-and-rescue scenes that eventually culminate in Sophonisba's self-sacrificial death, the final rescue of the adult Cabiria (Lidia Quarante), and the ultimate victory of Rome in the Punic Wars.

Proliferation is a hallmark of the film's style, sets, and spectacle scenes too. *Cabiria* uses an array of stylistic devices, among them cross-cutting, shot scales that vary in size from extreme long shots to extreme close-ups, superimpositions and composite shots (evident in the scenes showing Hannibal crossing the Alps, the burning of the Roman fleet at Syracuse, and the burning of the camp of Syphax), and occasional right-to-left and left-to-right pans as well as the diagonal tracking shots for which the film and its director, Giovanni Pastrone, have become famous. *Cabiria*'s sets are equally varied in size and function. Pastrone makes as much use of the inn, with its trap door as well as its exterior door and window, as he does of the multitiered interior and exterior sets of the Temple of Moloch. He also makes as much use of Sophonisba's chamber, which at one point he explores with a set of three separate diagonal tracks as she moves back and forth to the window, as he does of the walls of Syracuse, the walls of Cirta, or the other larger, more evidently spectacular palace sets.

A recurrent feature of all these sets, scenes, and spaces and the framings they involve is the emphasis placed on height as well as on width and depth, on vertical as well as horizontal or axial movement. This is evident as much in the use of the trap door or the window in the inn to stage vertical entrances and exits as it is in the use made of the testudo to enable Fulvius to scale the walls of Carthage; as much in the shot of Fulvius at the top of a wall before he dives into the sea to escape his pursuers at

The use of height as well as width and depth in *Cabiria* (1914).

Carthage as it is in the vertical compositions that mark the interior shots of the Temple of Moloch or the exterior shots of the various sieges that occur later on in the film. It is evident, too, in less action-filled form, in the scene of Batto's return to his villa in Catania prior to the eruption of Etna at the beginning of the film: along with the villa's vertical columns, female servants can be seen cleaning the balustrades and walking across the very top of the building on the right-hand side of the frame as Batto shows his wife the newborn lambs he and his servants have gathered below.

D. W. Griffith, Cecil B. DeMille, and the Advent of the Hollywood Roadshow

It would be hard to exaggerate the impact of *Quo Vadis?* and *Cabiria* on the U.S. film industry. Among those whose ambitions were fired by their scale and success were D. W. Griffith and Cecil B. DeMille. While DeMille had been producing and directing five-reel and six-reel features for the Lasky Feature Play Company's program, Griffith had been producing and directing one-reel and two-reel films at Biograph for the variety programs distributed by the GFC. Two months after the premiere of *Quo Vadis?* Griffith began work on a four-reel adaptation of *Judith of Bethulia,* eventually released by Biograph on March 8, 1914. By then, though, Griffith had already had talks with Adolph Zukor at Famous Players and Harry Aitken at the Mutual Film Corporation about producing and directing feature-length films for them. Tempted by a promise that he could produce and direct two special features of his own, Griffith signed a contract with Majestic, one of Mutual's production companies, in October 1913.[74]

It was at Majestic that Griffith began to plan what turned out to be *The Birth of a Nation,* a twelve-reel production that was to be both the longest and the most expensive U.S. film ever made to that time and the first U.S. film to be roadshown on a nationwide basis, a film that would, as one reviewer put it, make "*Cabiria* and *Quo Vadis?* seem tame."[75] The first public showing of what was at that time still called *The Clansman* took place at the Loring Opera House in Riverside, California on New Year's Day, 1915. Its official Los Angeles opening was at Clune's Auditorium on February 8, where it ran for a record-breaking twenty-two weeks, accompanied by a score compiled and arranged by Carli Elinor.[76] After two private screenings for President Woodrow Wilson, members of his cabinet, a number of Supreme Court judges, and members of Congress, the film opened as *The Birth of a Nation* for an unprecedented forty-four-week run at the 1,200-seat Liberty Theatre in New York City on March 3, 1915, accompanied by a score compiled and composed by Joseph Carl Breil and at prices that ranged as high as two dollars per seat.[77] Under the management of former Shubert employees Theodore Mitchell (who handled publicity) and J. J. McCarthy (who handled the bookings), it went on to open at the Tremont in Boston, the Illinois Theatre in Chicago, the Nixon Theatre in Atlantic City, the Colonial Theatre in Chicago, and the Savoy in Asbury Park, continuing its nationwide roadshow run into the summer and causing controversy and generating profits on a legendary scale before being franchised on a states rights basis in the fall.[78] It continued to play on a states rights basis until its first official re-release, in a newly edited version, in 1921.

The history of the production of *The Birth of a Nation* has been detailed at length in a number of publications, as has the nature and impact of the film's racist agenda.[79] Several points are worth stressing here. The first is that Aitken, like Zukor, wanted Griffith to supervise the production of routine feature-length films for feature-film programs.[80] The second is that although Mutual and its production companies were funded by a number of Wall Street investment banks, *The Birth of a Nation* was funded by Griffith, Aitken, and other investors in a purely private capacity.[81] (It was Mutual's refusal to fund the production of *The Birth of a Nation* that led Aitken and Griffith to form the Epoch Producing Company to produce and distribute the film.) The third is that *The Birth of a Nation* was one of a number of longer-than-average feature-length films in production in the United States in 1914, among them *The Wrath of the Gods* and *The Spoilers*. It drew directly as well as indirectly on a theatrical tradition of Civil War melodrama, and it capped a cycle of Civil War films that emerged during the course of the war's semicentennial.[82] It also added to the list of multireel films dealing with aspects of U.S. history, a list that included *Custer's Last Fight* and *The Coming of Columbus* (both 1912).

As Charlie Keil notes, *The Birth of a Nation* is often remembered as a series of set pieces, among them the assassination of Lincoln, the Battle of Petersburg, and the Ku Klux Klan's ride to rescue the Camerons. However, as he also points out, "style is not turned on and off like a faucet: the style of *The Birth of a Nation* ultimately resides in the systematic deployment of devices across the whole film."[83] Keil goes on to detail these devices, relating them to the stylistic ingredients that marked Griffith's later one- and two-reel productions at Biograph. One such device was the editing of "multi-pronged last-minute rescues":

Combining propulsive editing rhythms, predicated on diminishing shot lengths at key narrative moments, with the selection of increasingly more kinetic or even closer-scaled shots for the climaxes of such sequences, Griffith had learned to squeeze virtually every ounce of audience response out of the effective rescue scenario. *The Birth of a Nation* offers three variations on this formula: the attack on the Cameron home by guerilla soldiers, Gus's pursuit of Flora (and the subsequent tracking of both by Ben), and the tripartite rescue which serves as the film's narrative climax.[84]

Editing plays a part in the orchestration of recurrent framings, looks, and gestures as well.[85] But in a story about racial and national division, editing is just one of the ways in which division, segmentation, and alternation "penetrate not only Griffith's formal procedures, but structure his very conception of the diegetic material, including his view of the family, morality, sexual difference and history," as Thomas Elsaesser and Adam Barker have pointed out. As they go on to explain:

Griffith's narratives are always based on an act of splitting the narrative core or cell, and obtaining several narrative threads which could then be woven together again. By this act of separation, and his ability to subdivide even the smallest of episodes, Griffith was able to insert further plot-lines and complications opening up potentially infinite series, as in his epics, where the "expansive" tendency of the narrative stands in highly dramatic relation to its resolution and the bringing about of closure."[86]

These principles are most obviously apparent in *Intolerance,* to which we will turn in a moment. But they mark *The Birth of a Nation* as well. They are evident, for instance, in the sequence early on in the film that intercuts the farewell ball at Cameron Hall with the wider bonfire celebrations in the streets of Piedmont after the Confederate victory at Bull Run. Here, interior shots of the ball alternate with exterior shots of the celebrations. In addition, as the sequence proceeds, shots that focus on the public spectacle in the ballroom downstairs are intercut with and eventually displaced by more intimate shots of Dr. Cameron (Spottiswood Aitken) and Flora (Mae Marsh) discovered asleep upstairs by Ben (Henry B. Walthall). These too are displaced as the sequence moves forward in time and back downstairs, where the celebrations continue both in the ballroom and in the street. The effect is to highlight by contrast the scale, the spectacle, and the noise produced by public events and to demonstrate representational prowess by encompassing small-scale private events as well as large-scale public ones. The strategy is to divide and to alternate between different sources and segments of spectacle; it is also to prolong, elaborate, and modulate the sequence by cutting away from rather than into its constituent spaces, actions, and segments.

This is very different from the strategy employed by Cecil B. DeMille in the coronation scene in *Joan the Woman,* a scene that similarly articulates a transition from public spectacle to intimate privacy but that uses scene dissection and intrascene cutting to do so, as we shall see. DeMille had been a key figure in the Lasky Feature Play Company. A founding member of the company, he soon became its principal producer as well as its principal director. However, the company's policy had been to produce a program of five- to six-reel features for its affiliates rather than a series of roadshown epics or specials. By 1916, on the verge of the amalgamation between Lasky and Famous Players, DeMille had directed twenty-three films, none of them longer than six reels, and none of them more expensive than *The Warrens of Virginia* (1914), which had cost $28,359.95.[87] These figures paled in comparison with those associated with *Quo Vadis?, Cabiria,* or *The Birth of a Nation.* Aware of the status as well as the profits associated with films such as these, Lasky and DeMille set up the Cardinal Film Corporation to produce and distribute *Joan the Woman,* a ten-reel road-show production that would eventually cost $302,976.26, in June 1916.[88]

Joan the Woman was premiered at the 44th Street Theatre in New York on Christmas Day, 1916, with a score composed by William Furst and a number of stencil-colored sequences produced by using the Handschiegl process. It went on to play the Majestic in Los Angeles, the Colonial Theatre in Boston, the Colonial Theatre in Chicago, and a number of other theatrical venues during the course of its fifty-eight-week roadshow run, grossing double its negative cost, but barely breaking even once its distribution costs were taken into account.[89] The film tells the story of Joan of Arc. On the eve of battle in World War I, Eric Trent (Wallace Reid) is granted a vision of a time when his distant ancestor was part of an English force set on conquering France. The earlier Trent is wounded in battle and befriended by Joan (Geraldine Farrar), but when she defeats the English at Orleans, he betrays her to her enemies and she is burned at the stake. Trent's vision persuades him to atone for his ancestor by fighting for the liberation of France.

The coronation scene occurs after the victory at Orleans. A single public space is initially filled then eventually emptied of spectacular ingredients as the film articulates a series of transitions from the public spectacle of the coronation to the official and semipublic sequences in which Joan requests freedom from taxation for her village and freedom from imprisonment for Trent, to the private farewell conversation between Joan and Trent, Trent's departure along the petal-strewn aisle of the empty cathedral, and Joan's solitary approach to the altar. Framing and editing play a key role in the scene's modulation. Long shots and medium long shots are used initially to display the ceremony, and Joan's place within it, in the crowded cathedral. Once the ceremony is over, closer medium and medium long shots are used to articulate a series of conversations between Joan and others, and to include background figures, observers, interlocutors, and groups of participants in frame as well. Gradually, however, as these sequences proceed, the number of figures in frame tends to diminish. Medium shots and medium close-ups in the one-to-one conversations first between Joan and a villager, then between Joan and Trent, displace then dominate the handling, mood, and purpose of the scene. When Trent departs, and when Joan turns to the altar at the end of the scene, the use of long shots serves not only to emphasize the intimacy of the preceding conversation sequences but also to highlight the absence of the crowds,

The beginning and the end of the coronation scene in *Joan the Woman* (1916).

the pageantry, and the spectacle with which the long shots at the beginning of the scene had been filled.

Intolerance

While filming *Joan the Woman*, DeMille was well aware that Griffith was filming *Intolerance*. Robert Birchard notes that when *Intolerance* opened at the Liberty Theatre in New York on September 5, 1916, Jesse Lasky wired DeMille as follows:

Griffith picture Intolerance opened last night. It is being severely criticized on all sides and opinion everywhere is that it does not compare with Birth. The lack of consecutive story is the picture's worst fault in fact it proved a disappointment as far as the first night audience was concerned. However the part of the production which deals with the fall of Babylon is wonderful and in my opinion the picture will be a general success.[90]

Intolerance was not a "general success," but, as Russell Merritt points out, it was more successful, at least from a critical point of view, than has sometimes been thought.[91] Anything other than a full-scale discussion of the film is hampered by the fact that, even more than most other epics of the period, *Intolerance* exists in a number of versions, a reflection of its origins and evolution as a project, of the alterations made during the course of its roadshow and subsequent runs, and of the fact that Griffith decided to use the modern story and the Babylonian sequences from *Intolerance* as the basis for two new roadshow attractions, *The Fall of Babylon* and *The Mother and the Law,* in 1919.[92] What we can discuss here is the relationship among *Intolerance,* epic production, and roadshow distribution in the United States and the dominant aesthetic characteristics of *Intolerance* itself.

It was the commercial success of *The Birth of a Nation* and the prestige associated with its large-scale roadshow production that led Griffith to convert what was initially planned as a conventional program feature for Majestic into an epic of thirteen or fourteen reels that eventually involved the interweaving of four separate stories set in four different historical periods, each of them dealing with the theme of intolerance.[93] The structure and evolution of *Intolerance* (including the subsequent construction of *The Mother and the Law* and *The Fall of Babylon*) clearly exemplify Elsaesser and Barker's points about subdivision, segmentation, and alternation, and "potentially infinite series." They also exemplify Rudmer Canjels's arguments about seriality. As Canjels points out, seriality had been a hallmark of such Griffith two-reelers as *His Trust* and *His Trust Fulfilled* (both 1911) since the early 1910s. It was subsequently evident not just in the structure of *Intolerance,* nor just in the process of its construction, but also in Griffith's plan to show what he thought might turn out to be an eight-hour film "on two separate nights in two parts of four hours each, with a dinner intermission each night."[94]

AROUND THE WORLD TRIUMPH!

D. W. GRIFFITH'S

COLOSSAL
$2,000,000
SPECTACLE

"INTOLERANCE"

LOVE'S
STRUGGLE
THROUGHOUT
THE AGES

The "Birth of a Nation" Has Proved the Most Astounding Financial Success in the
History of Amusements in any part of the world. Read what "Intolerance" is doing

5 MONTHS at the LIBERTY THEATRE, NEW YORK	12 COMPANIES TOURING AMERICA

LOS ANGELES — Receipts for three months' run equalled those of "The Birth of a Nation" for the same length of time.

MILWAUKEE — Receipts $21,410.50 two weeks' engagement, a gain over "The Birth of a Nation's" first two weeks' gross of $3,900.00

CHICAGO — (Now Playing) 12 weeks' receipts exceeded by $11,320 those of "The Birth of a Nation" for same number of weeks.

RICHMOND — Monday, $788.00; Tuesday, $1,894.00; Wednesday, $2,268.00; just $243.00 less than what "The Birth of a Nation" played to.

ALL ATTENDANCE RECORDS — Broken at the Chestnut St. Opera House, Phila., where it is in its third month.

SAN FRANCISCO — Receipts $15,000 better than what "The Birth of a Nation" earned during its 8 weeks' engagement.

A SENSATIONAL HIT — At the Pitt Theatre, Pittsburgh, where it has reached its 8th week.

All the above figures and statements are authentic and can be verified
by application to the management of the various theatres mentioned.

Now being shown at Theatre Royal, Sydney, and Theatre Royal, Melbourne, Australia. London engagement commences at
Drury Lane Theatre, Saturday, April 7th. Arrangements completed for presentation in Buenos Aires, Argentine, in May.

NOTE: Mr. Griffith's "Intolerance" and "The Birth of a Nation" Are the Only Two Motion Picture Spectacles Continuously Presented in Regular Theatres at the $2.00 and $1.50 Scale of Prices.

Direction, The Wark Producing Corporation. General Offices, 807 Longacre Bldg., New York City

Trade press advertisement for *Intolerance* (1916) (*Variety*, February 23, 1917, 18).

Segmentation and alternation, exemplified above all by the use of parallel editing, form the cornerstone of Tom Gunning's discussion of *Intolerance*'s narrative structure. As Gunning notes, parallel editing is generally defined

as the intercutting of scenes that are distant in space but simultaneous in time, as in the canonical race-to-the-rescue scenes, cutting from those in peril to those coming to the rescue. However, cutting between events that are spatially separate but not clearly related in time (cutting between the rich and poor to emphasize semantic contrasts rather than causal or narrative interrelation) has also been closely associated with parallel editing, and usually been terminologically indistinguishable from it.[95]

Gunning points out that Griffith used both forms of parallel editing at Biograph, and that in *Intolerance,* alongside parallel editing of a traditional kind, "Griffith intercuts separate stories occurring not only in different spaces but also in entirely different centuries." In this way, he "transcends the primary signification of parallel editing—simultaneity—in favor of a timeless realm of semantic contrast and parallel."[96] This timeless pattern interacts with the time-bound patterns created by traditional dramatic structures and traditional uses of parallel editing to stage "an allegory of providential progress moving through historical catastrophe to religious redemption," an allegory, therefore, of truly epic proportions.[97]

During the course of this allegory, the established features of the 1910s epic (crowd scenes, battle scenes, and scenes of pageantry) find their place in specific segments (most notably those set in Paris, Judea, and Babylon). However, as Russell Merritt has noted, one of the film's peculiarities is the extent to which the staging and composition of these scenes leave the viewer "simply overwhelmed by the distractions of the mise-en-scène, surrendering to the spectacle laid out before us."[98] This is particularly apparent in the tracking shot that introduces the set for Belshazzar's feast in the Babylonian sequence. Here

the track exists as sheer ornament. It serves no narrative function, nor does it represent an affective point of view. More striking, the forward movement does not work to discover or pinpoint any particular detail. . . . The effect of the track is not to draw us centripetally toward a central focal point, but rather to propel the set outward, setting . . . architectural details in motion, and to pull us centrifugally to the margins of the screen as these drift out of view. The track draws us away from any single attraction, giving us too much to see to concentrate on details.[99]

This shot and this scene provide the most extreme examples. But Charlie Keil finds a number of others: the ballroom scene at the beginning of the modern story, the Jaffa gate scene at the beginning of the Judean story, and the scenes in the town square and the court at the beginning of the Paris story.[100] In all these scenes, staging, framing, and editing confound rather than aid our understanding of the settings and of the activities taking place within them. Insofar as this is the case, *Intolerance* was marked in more ways than one as a deviant film. As Lee Grieveson has pointed out, in addition to its formal eccentricities, its insistence on the cinema's capacity for message-making was increasingly seen as excessive in an era in which, partly because of the controversy generated by *The Birth of a Nation,* U.S. courts and U.S. censorship boards were busy defining the cinema as "a business pure and simple" and its social function as the provision of "harmless entertainment."[101] The participation of the United States in World War I was to modify these tenets, encouraging Griffith, among others, to message-make in a number of subsequent films. But what were perceived as the failures of a film like *Intolerance* were to play a major part, either directly or indirectly, in shaping the policies, the purposes, and the nature of feature-film, epic, and roadshow production and distribution in the late 1910s and the 1920s.

SUPERSPECIALS, SPECIALS, AND PROGRAMS, 1916–1927

A month after the premiere of *The Birth of a Nation* in New York the weekly release chart in *The Motion Picture News* marked the extent to which films were now available "in two distinct formats. The industry's oldest firms, and a few younger rivals, were marketing program releases of short films, one to three reels in length, which were issued like clockwork on a daily schedule," as Richard Koszarski has noted. Also listed were "the offerings of a half-dozen feature distributors, whose products were generally four to six reels in length and not necessarily tied to specific release dates." Charts such as these "plotted the end of a distribution system that was rapidly approaching irrelevance. Out of the dozens of producers listed, only a handful would survive three years hence, and most of these in significantly changed form. As for the daily change of program releases, its remaining tenure could be measured in months."[1]

Among the new longer features released in the mid-1910s were *Neptune's Daughter* (1914), *Civilization, A Daughter of the Gods,* and *20,000 Leagues under the Sea* (all 1916). *Neptune's Daughter* and *A Daughter of the Gods* were vehicles for Annette Kellermann, an Australian swimming star who had forged a career with a swimming and diving act in England and the United States. According to her biographers, Kellermann herself came up with the idea and the basic scenario for *Neptune's Daughter,* which was produced by IMP for Universal and directed by Herbert Brenon.[2] It was premiered at the Globe Theatre in New York in the roadshow manner, with reserved-seat, twice-daily performances at a top price of fifty cents per ticket. It played at the Globe for seven months prior to its release as a Universal Special Feature. *A Daughter of the Gods* was produced by Fox. It opened with simultaneous premiere runs at the Lyric in New York (at a top price of two dollars per seat), the Chestnut Street Opera House in Philadelphia, and the Pitt in Pittsburgh in October 1916. It was then roadshown more widely with a score composed by Robert Hood Bowers. Universal produced *20,000 Leagues under the Sea* and Thomas Ince produced *Civilization.* The former premiered at the Broadway in New York, the latter at the Majestic in Los Angeles under its initial title, *He Who Returned,* then at the Criterion in New York. Both were subsequently distributed on a states rights basis, the latter initially as a roadshow in New York State under the management of A. H. Woods.[3]

These films were all long and expensive. *A Daughter of the Gods* was ten reels long and was advertised as costing a million dollars. *Variety* estimated its true cost at $850,000, still well in excess of the average feature and more than the cost of *The Birth of a Nation* and *Intolerance* combined.[4] *Neptune's Daughter* (at seven reels), *20,000 Leagues under the Sea* (at eight reels), and *Civilization* (at ten reels) have been costed at $35,000, $500,000, and $100,000 respectively.[5] *A Daughter of the Gods* tells the story of Alicia (Kellermann), who falls in love with a prince and who enlists the help of the inhabitants of Gnomeland in order to aid him in his struggles against his enemies. *Neptune's Daughter* tells the story of a mermaid who seeks to avenge the death of her sister, but who falls in love with the king responsible for granting the fishing rights that led to her death. *20,000 Leagues under the Sea* was an adaptation of Jules Verne's novel with additional plot material from *The Mysterious Island* and additional flashback scenes set in India. *Civilization* was a pacifist allegory that culminated in a vision of the horrors of war shown by Christ to Wredpryd's king. All four films could be categorized as *fantasie,* one of the terms used to describe *A Daughter of the Gods.*[6] All four films use aquatic settings, underwater sequences, and special photographic effects. And all four films were box-office hits: according to *Variety, Neptune's Daughter* netted $480,000, *A Daughter of the Gods* $1,390,000, and *Civilization* $768,000; according to an advertisement in *The Moving Picture World, 20,000 Leagues under the Sea* broke every house record at the Broadway.[7] However, there were significant differences in their cultural status and ambitions and in the nature of their target audience.

Unlike the other three films, *Civilization* was seen as a prestigious pacifist allegory that would appeal to upper middle-class adults.[8] In this respect, it was more akin to *Intolerance, Joan the Woman,* and the earlier imported epics discussed in chapter 2 than it was to *Neptune's Daughter, A Daughter of the Gods,* and *20,000 Leagues under the Sea.* The latter were indicative of a widening of the generic and cultural scope of what were increasingly (and simply) called "big pictures."[9] Although its allegorical form was unusual, and although its pacifist preachings were topical, *Civilization* was more traditional in its overt artistry, in the wedding of its spectacle scenes to moral dilemmas and religious teachings, and in the respectably serious nature of its themes and cultural ambitions. Its success was probably due to its topical subject matter and to the popularity of its pacifist stance prior to U.S. involvement in World War I. But the relative failure of *Intolerance* and the success of *Neptune's Daughter, A Daughter of the Gods,* and *20,000 Leagues under the Sea* showed that big productions, nationwide roadshows, and states rights specials need no longer appeal exclusively to genteel values and the upper middle classes in order to make considerable sums of money.

Big Pictures and Cultural Values in the Late 1910s

Genteel values were on the wane in the late 1910s. Middle- and upper-middle-class culture was being reconfigured in ways that led on the one hand to an elite highbrow culture in which aesthetic and commercial values were increasingly seen as at odds, and on the other to a consumerist middlebrow culture that increasingly, if selectively, embraced the masses and aspects of their culture.[10] From the 1920s on, middlebrow culture was to provide the basis for the most expensive and prestigious film productions for the next forty years. In the meantime, in the late 1910s, Griffith and DeMille turned away from the Old World epic and either abandoned or modified the nature of large-scale roadshow and states rights productions. DeMille turned to program features with contemporary upper-middle-class settings such as *Old Wives for New* (1918), *Don't Change Your Husband* (1919), and *Why Change Your Wife?* (1920). According to Sumiko Higashi, films such as these "continued to address the genteel middle-class," but in ways that "constructed a showcase for conspicuous consumption that appealed to lower-middle-class and working-class female spectators."[11] They were thus central to the consumerist transformation of middle-class culture and to the construction of its cross-class appeal. Their release on a regular program to regular cinemas at regular prices was essential to the realization of that appeal.

Having left Triangle for Famous Players–Lasky (FPL) in 1917, Griffith went on to cofound United Artists with Mary Pickford, Charlie Chaplin, and Douglas Fairbanks in 1919. In addition to roadshow productions and states rights releases such as *Hearts of the World* (1918), *Broken Blossoms* (1919), and *Way Down East* (1920), he produced and directed program features such as *The Greatest Thing in Life* (1918), *True Heart Susie* (1919), and *A Romance of Happy Valley* (1919). Like DeMille's films, a hallmark of all these productions is their contemporary or near-contemporary settings. However, Griffith's films, unlike DeMille's, tend to focus on rural or small-town characters, locations, and values, to shun or satirize consumer culture, or, like *Broken Blossoms,* to draw attention to and disdain other aspects of city life. *Hearts of the World,* a roadshow production commissioned and supported by the British War Office, focuses on the destructive intrusion of World War I into the lives of the inhabitants of a small rural village in France.[12] The first half of the film, before its intermission, is set in the village prior to the outbreak of war, the second half after "the call to arms." However, as Richard Schickel points out, despite the scale of some of its battle scenes, it appears uninterested in conveying a sense of the scale of the war as a whole.[13] Indeed in many ways it uses the war largely as motivation for the separation of its lovers and as the direct or indirect source of threats to their lives. *Way Down East,* the biggest, most expensive, and most commercially successful of Griffith's roadshow productions at this time, was a revival of an 1890s stage melodrama.[14] Its rural setting and traditional melodramatic conventions provided the film not only with its cast of characters, its moral dilemmas, and its modes of dramatic conflict, but with its climactic spectacle scenes in a blizzard in the woods and on the melting ice floes on a frozen river as well.

Consonant with his artistic reputation and prestige among the upper middle classes, Griffith was by the far the most prolific producer of roadshow releases in the late 1910s. In keeping with his ambitions, *Broken Blossoms* was premiered at the George M. Cohan Theatre in New York at a top price of three dollars per seat as part of a Griffith repertory season that also included *The Mother and the Law, The Fall of Babylon,* and a new edition of *Hearts of the World.*[15] But even Griffith wondered whether "the money" lay "in the big picture . . . or the program," and even Griffith eschewed biblicals, literaries, and historicals in the late 1910s.[16] Marginal examples of literaries, such as the ten-to-fourteen-reel version of *Ramona* (1916), an adaptation of Helen Hunt Jackson's novel, were released on a states rights basis, for the most part by small-scale independents. But these, too, were few and far between: a twelve-reel adaptation of *The Garden of Allah* and an eight-reel adaptation of *The Whip* were released as states rights specials in 1917, and a ten-reel adaptation of *Tarzan of the Apes* received a roadshow premiere at the Broadway Theatre in New York the following year.

By this time, states rights specials, roadshow premieres, and roadshow premiere runs were increasingly common, the latter serving as a means of publicizing program productions prior to a conventional general release, of showcasing special features to potential states rights franchisees, or as a means of securing first-run exhibition.[17] The original meaning of "roadshow" as a film toured nationally or territorially, exhibited at set times in theatrical venues rather than in movie houses, and viewed at higher-than-average prices in pre-bookable seats, was beginning to change. It now began to encompass long runs in movie theaters and the showing of films at higher prices in premiere venues prior to a later conventional release. Its meanings became even more blurred in the 1920s, as the major companies began to provide premiere runs at higher prices on Broadway for nearly all their feature productions. In the meantime, first-run exhibition as a whole was becoming more important. As Benjamin Hampton has pointed out, "representative features" in 1915–17 "earned in the United States from $60,000 to $100,000 gross, or about $40,000 to $60,000 after deducting the distributor's charge." These earnings were sufficient to make a profit, but if "adequate first runs were lacking, the earnings in second and subsequent run houses would drop to $30,000 to $40,000, which was not enough to repay producers' costs."[18]

Most of the states rights and roadshow specials produced and released in the late 1910s were either war-related newsreels, features, or documentaries such as *Fighting for France* (1915), *The Italian Battle Front* (1917), *The Kaiser—The Beast of Berlin* (1918), and *My Four Years in Germany* (1918), or, like *The Honor System* (1917) and *The Fall of the Romanoffs* (1918), features on topical or newsworthy themes. *The Honor System,* a ten-reel film about prison reform, was produced by Fox. According to *The Moving Picture World,* it was designed to "inaugurate an annual motion picture event patterned on the lines of the Drury Lane production [*sic*] in London."[19] As well as *The Honor System,* Fox also produced large-scale literaries such as *A Tale of Two Cities* (1917) and *Les Misérables* (1917), and at least three films with conventionally historical epic settings, *Cleopatra* (1917), *DuBarry* (1917), and *Salome* (1918). Of the principal producer-distributors of features in the United States in the late 1910s, it appears to have been the only one to do so.

Les Misérables, Cleopatra, and *Salome* were all roadshown. Indeed, *Salome* was one of the first films to be roadshown nationwide prior as well as subsequent to its New York premiere run.[20] It was also one of the first films to be distributed according to what was called "the concentrated booking plan," a form of what might now be called local saturation releasing. As Louis Rosenblush, manager of Fox's New York Exchange, explained: "In Brooklyn seven houses in one neighborhood combined on a *Salome* campaign that broke all records of attendance at the individual houses and secured for each hundreds of new patrons. Next week three of the best houses in Harlem, all on 116th street, will show *Salome*—just released on an independent basis—at the same time."[21] A similar plan was adopted in Chicago. Partly for this reason, a record number of prints, nineteen in all, were used by Fox's Chicago exchange.[22]

Salome was not the first film to be released in this way, nor were nineteen prints a local record. In 1915, George Spoor at Essanay had persuaded the GFC to provide forty prints of Chaplin's *His New Job* for distribution in New York and a further thirty for distribution in the "southern centers."[23] Prints of Chaplin's two- and three-reel film had often been released in record numbers: 130 prints of *The Floorwalker* were released in Greater New York in 1916, and *A Dog's Life* was booked by "160 of the leading houses in Greater New York" and by 80 additional theaters in 1918.[24] In 1921, *The Kid,* Chaplin's first feature, was booked for local runs in seventy theaters in the Bronx and Manhattan, and in eighteen first-run and neighborhood theaters in Boston simultaneously, thus "violating . . . every booking tradition ever established."[25]

Salome, DuBarry, and *Cleopatra* were vehicles for the vamp persona of Theda Bara, and as such their status was mixed. Theda Bara was a movie star rather than a stage star, as those who had played Salome, DuBarry, and Cleopatra had been hitherto, a popular sensation rather than a purveyor of genteel prestige.[26] Her popularity helped mark a shift both in the nature and appeal of literaries, epics, and historicals, and in the social mix of those who went to see them. *The Moving Picture World* noted that "there was a great diversity of audiences" during *Cleopatra*'s initial run in Washington, New York City, and New York State: "In Washington the most fashionable people in the city attended and the business increased each day until toward the end of the week it was impossible to obtain seats. In Schenectady it played to the industrial workers and both days were sell-outs."[27] Theda Bara's films were among the first to be promoted as "superpictures."[28] As such they were at the center of a policy of product differentiation at Fox and in turn at the center of a series of debates in the industry about the merits and demerits of program production and distribution, "open booking," long runs, star series, and other means of organizing the production, distribution, and promotion of a range of features and other films.

Programs, Bookings, Runs, Series, and Stars

In August 1917, Fox announced that its exchanges had been divided into two departments: "Department No. 1 will handle the 52 one-a-week Fox special features as well as the comedy pictures. Department No. 2 will be known as [the] Standard Pictures Department, and will handle Theda Bara, William Farnum, *Jack and the Beanstalk* [1917], *The Honor System,* Fox Kiddies, as well as any other big productions released under the Standard emblem."[29] Standard Pictures were to be booked "in the open market as an individual attraction," a system known as "open booking."[30] The following year, Fox refined these categories, advertising its output for the coming season under six different headings: "Four Big Timely Pictures," "Standard Pictures," "Victory Pictures," "Excel Pictures," "Sunshine Comedies," and "Mutt and Jeff Animated Cartoons."[31] A year later, Fox advertised its output in yet another way. In addition to three "Extraordinary Specials," twenty-six Excel Pictures, twenty-six Victory Pictures, twenty-six Sunshine Comedies, fifty-two Mutt and Jeff Cartoons, Fox News Weekly, and a fifteen-episode serial, it announced the forthcoming release of three "Theda Bara Productions," eight "Pearl White Productions," eight "William Farnum Productions," and eight "Tom Mix Productions" too.[32]

Fox was by no means the only company to organize, identify, and promote its output in these kinds of ways. Nor was it the only company to distribute shorts, newsreels, and cartoons; to produce and to advertise its star vehicles in series; or to adopt a form of open booking. FPL experimented with a number of these and other means of servicing exhibitors and differentiating and distributing its programs of films as well. Indeed, some of its films were rented individually, in accordance with a policy known then as "selective booking." The formation of Paramount in 1914 had resulted in the resurrection of "program booking," in which exhibitors were forced to sign contracts for an entire season's output of films. However, the advent of longer specials and star-centered features in the mid-1910s had led to a conflict. W. W. Hodkinson at Paramount had "wanted to maintain his flat fee, program booking methods."[33] But Adolph Zukor at Famous Players devised ways of allowing exhibitors to rent films in smaller groups, and Hodkinson was ousted in 1916. With the formation of Famous Players–Lasky (FPL), Paramount ceased to exist as a separate organization and in essence became a trade name for the distribution wing of FPL and later on for the company as a whole.

Prior to 1916, Paramount's distribution contract with its producers limited the length of their films to six reels and the length of their runs in theaters to no more than three or four days. Consequently, when Famous Players wanted to release *The Eternal City* (1915), a $100,000, eight-reel production, it was forced to set up the Select Film Booking Company to distribute the film on the basis of minimum rather than maximum runs and at roadshow prices.[34] To have released *The Eternal City* on Paramount's program would have been a waste of its potential earning power. The same is true of *Tess of the Storm Country,* which was released on a states rights basis in 1914 and which grossed over $2 million.[35]

Tess of the Storm Country was neither unusually long nor unusually expensive. Its special status and its success were a product of the enormous popularity of its star, Mary Pickford. Mary Pickford had established her status as a star at Biograph, IMP, and Majestic. She had signed a contract with Famous Players in 1913 at a salary of $50,000 a year. During the course of the next two years, her salary rose to $200,000 a year plus 50 percent of the profits on her films, and Famous Players established the Famous Players–Mary Pickford Company for the purpose of producing her films.[36] A year later, in 1916, she went on strike when Hodkinson refused to meet her demands for a five-fold salary increase, the removal of her films from the Paramount program, and more control over her films. But when Hodkinson was ousted, Pickford was given "a two-year contract which would pay her fifty percent of her films' profits against a guarantee of $1,040,000, a bonus of $300,000 to be paid at the end of each year, and an additional bonus of $40,000 for continuing to consider scripts during her strike."[37] Zukor also formed a new company, Artcraft Pictures Corporation, to distribute Pickford's films outside the Paramount program, an early instance of what came to be called "star-series" distribution. Pickford was permitted in addition to nominate other stars for Artcraft. Among them were Douglas Fairbanks, George M. Cohan, Geraldine Farrar, and William S. Hart, though most of their films went into distribution after Artcraft had been absorbed by FPL in 1917.

Neither Zukor nor Pickford was the first to adopt the star series idea, or to use it to distribute films in smaller groupings. In April 1916, Lewis J. Selznick "founded a new distribution company to handle Clara Kimball Young's features, as well as films from any other star who was willing and able to sign on to his company. All of Selznick's films were to be sold in blocks, rather than programs."[38] A number of others followed suit. They included Goldwyn, and they included Fox, as we have seen. Goldwyn also advocated, and Fox also partially practiced, open booking. These practices, it was argued, would facilitate longer runs for popular films with popular stars and would thus allow the films to realize their earning potential without resorting to the roadshow and states rights systems. According to Howard T. Lewis, the vogue for star series as such was fairly short-lived.[39] Some companies turned to the adaptation of novels and plays as an alternative means of making films with commercial potential. Others turned to topical subjects. But stars remained a key ingredient in the industry's calculations and in the construction of its production and distribution programs, deals and groupings—and have done so ever since. In the meantime, as FPL, Fox, Universal, Goldwyn, and others experimented further with differentiated programs and pure or modified forms of open booking, and as FPL embarked on a new program of investment in the acquisition of the rights to film novels and plays,[40] the formation of United Artists in 1919, and the formation of First National by a coalition of exhibitors in 1917, exemplified the continuing importance of these and other issues. United Artists (UA) demonstrated the continuing power and importance of stars. First National played a key role in attracting investment from Wall Street and in restructuring the relationship between the industry's production, distribution, and exhibition sectors.

Along with an influx of income from overseas markets, these developments were to play a central part in the revival and spread of large-scale, high-cost production and roadshow distribution and exhibition during the course of the 1920s.

The U.S. Film Industry in the 1920s

The film industry in the United States underwent a period of recession in 1917 and 1918, then a period of sustained expansion, marred only by a brief (though severe) industry downturn in the winter of 1921/22. Domestic attendances rose from an estimated average of 34 million a week in 1920 to an estimated 65 million a week in 1928.[41] New and ever more lavish movie theaters were built. By 1926, there were 20,115 in all, of which 1,341 were first-run venues in cities with a population of 25,000 or more.[42] Some of these venues were picture palaces, newly built or converted movie theaters of a size, scale, and opulence rarely seen before or since. They included the Capitol, the Strand, and the Rivoli in New York; the Coliseum in Seattle; the California in San Francisco; Grauman's Chinese and Egyptian Theatres in Los Angeles; the Tivoli in Chicago; the Century in Baltimore; the Howard in Atlanta; and the Newman in Kansas City. Seating 6,214 people, the Roxy, the grandest of them all, opened in New York in 1927.[43]

Despite disadvantageous exchange rates, income from overseas markets rose as well. Although there were fluctuations, notably in 1921 and 1922, foreign sales amounted to $4,731,382 in 1918, nearly doubled to $8,066,723 in 1919, and had risen to $8,680,745 by 1925.[44] By then it was reckoned that "the gross income . . . from the foreign trade nearly equals the gross profits of the American producer's [sic] entire business."[45] By 1926, net annual income from motion picture theater ownership and motion picture production amounted to $33,050,729, nearly as much as the income earned by the legitimate theater and all "other amusements" combined.[46]

Many of these developments were fueled by outside investment. Noting its rapid recovery from the postwar depression, bankers and business leaders finally became convinced that the film industry offered opportunities for profitable investment and, as a result, "poured millions of dollars into the two or three dozen larger companies which seemed to be firmly established and reasonably well managed."[47] Although a lot of the money invested in the late 1910s and the early 1920s was wasted on speculative ventures, and although investment reached "zero point" in the winter of 1921/22, the industry soon recovered and its relationship with Wall Street was soon resumed.[48] Money was spent on more expensive features, on new production and distribution facilities, on the salaries of stars, and on overseas distribution. It was also spent on the acquisition of theaters and theater chains and hence on the infrastructure of what was becoming a vertically integrated industry.

Following the demise of the MPPC, the origins of this new wave of vertical integration lay in the competition between exhibitors and producer-distributors over the control of stars, features, and programs, and first-run distribution and exhibition in the mid- to late 1910s. The first vertically integrated company was Fox, which by 1915 was distributing the films it produced to its own and to other theaters. As a systematic practice, however, vertical integration was a consequence of the growing dominance of FPL in the late 1910s. Fearing the control FPL was now able to exercise over the terms and conditions of booking and contracts, a number of theater-owners banded together to form the First National Exhibitors Circuit in 1917. By April 1919, First National "controlled 190 first-run theaters and approximately 40 subsequent-run houses, not counting 366 theaters which were controlled under subfranchise agreements."[49] The key development, however, was First National's move into production in 1917. Making "the obvious countermove" in 1919, FPL moved into exhibition, acquiring over 303 theaters by the middle of 1921: the "battle for theaters" had begun in earnest.[50] By the mid-1920s, a handful of major corporations had become fully integrated, and were thus effectively able to dominate the industry.[51]

In addition to First National and FPL, these corporations included Fox, Universal, and Loew's. They later included UA, which set up the United Artists Theater Circuit in the summer of 1926. By then the Loew's chain was concentrated in New York State; the First National chain in New Jersey and Pennsylvania; the FPL chain in New England, Canada, and the South; and the Fox chain on the West Coast. Only in the major metropolitan centers did the companies who owned these theaters compete directly one with another:

In these key cities, the majors fought to acquire the largest theaters or vied for the best downtown locations to build their deluxe movie palaces. These theaters were the first-run houses and their importance was enormous. Their proximity to large concentrations of population meant they received the bulk of the business. No picture could earn a profit without a first-run showing in one of them. Typically, a producer received up to 50 percent of the total rental from these theaters, usually within six months after a picture's release. Further, a successful first-run showing became the greatest selling point for distributors in dealing with the thousands of small theater managers throughout the country. In short, control of these theaters meant control over access to the screen.[52]

To some, the formation of the United Artists Theater Circuit was a major surprise. UA had been established not just to produce its founders' films but also to sell them on an individual basis to individual exhibitors. UA was explicitly opposed not only to program production and distribution but to the growing trend toward block booking as well.[53] In various guises, block booking became the principal means by which most major producer-distributors were able to ensure booking fees or a percentage of box-office income for most of their films. According to Quinn, flat-rate fees were more common than percentage deals at this time: UA was the only major company "with the temerity to distribute all of its films under a percentage booking plan" until the late 1920s.[54] Percentage deals were otherwise only common with roadshows. However, roadshows were on the increase in the 1920s as the postwar boom, market expansion, and Wall Street's investments fueled the advent and spread of "superspecial" production.

Superspecials

On February 4, 1921, *Variety* reported, "The special feature of eight reels minimum, to be put down for runs of one and two weeks and longer in key theaters in the larger cities, is the newest planned step designed to solve the manufacturer-distributor problem." A consequence of the record-breaking success enjoyed by *Passion,* the "old cry of producers that big pictures are prematurely canned is behind the new resurrection of an old condition."[55] That "old condition" was the need for longer runs at higher prices in larger venues in order to realize the commercial potential of bigger-than-average features. *Passion* was a German import, a retitled and reedited version of *Madame DuBarry* (1919). Along with the release and re-release of a number of large-scale U.S. productions, *Passion* served to cement an emerging trend. Two weeks after its initial report, *Variety* noted that there would soon be "half a dozen 'big' pictures playing legitimate houses on Broadway," among them *The Four Horsemen of the Apocalypse, The Queen of Sheba, Orphans of the Storm,* and *The Three Musketeers* (all 1921).[56] Two months later, it was reporting "the success of the special feature offerings in legitimate houses at about legitimate admission scales," and "an emphatic big increase in the use of long film plays" by legitimate theaters throughout the country.[57]

The success predicted for some of these productions was by no means always forthcoming. *The Queen of Sheba* performed poorly during the course of its premiere run. Its roadshow tour was canceled, and Fox announced that it would be bookable by regular exhibitors during the course of the forthcoming season.[58] *Orphans of the Storm* performed poorly too. Following premieres and previews in Boston and New York in late December 1921, it opened to the public in New York in January 1922 and was toured as a roadshow. According to Joel W. Finler, it cost "just under $1 million to produce and failed to break even" (though according to *Variety* it cost $700,000 and eventually grossed between $2 million and $3 million worldwide).[59] However, other big productions, notably *The Four Horsemen of the Apocalypse* (which opened in April 1921) and *The Three Musketeers* (which opened in August), were major hits. Between them, these particular films helped establish all but one of the major generic paradigms that were to dominate superspecial production and roadshow distribution and exhibition during the course of the next six years.

The Three Musketeers was twelve reels long and cost $700,000 to produce.[60] It was premiered at the Lyric in New York at a top price of two dollars per ticket; it was accompanied by a score composed by Louis F. Gottschalk; and it was shown with an intermission.[61] It was also a major box-office hit. According to Tino Balio, it grossed $1,500,000.[62] *The Three Musketeers* was produced by Douglas Fairbanks and released by UA. Fairbanks had by now moved away from the comedies with which he had been associated in the 1910s and moved into the field of costume adventure. Earlier films such as *The Mark of Zorro* (1920) had already established the ingredients that characterize nearly all of his subsequent vehicles: a mix of humor, romance, and physical action in a series of period settings. These settings serve to facilitate as well as showcase "his usual acrobatics."[63] In this way, they become integral to the action rather than remaining as decorative backdrops. They are themselves a major source of spectacle. But the spectacle is ultimately centered on Fairbanks's body, on the athletic performances of which it is capable, and on the optimistic determination to overcome obstacles of all kinds that these performances serve to convey. For Gaylyn Studlar, these ingredients "give voice to masculine nostalgia for a world of childish play where heroic adventure and chivalrous innocence" provide an escape from the "adult prerogatives and impurities made synonymous with the Roaring Twenties."[64] The result in aesthetic terms is what Richard Koszarski has called a "harmony" of movement and environment.[65]

In *The Three Musketeers,* this harmony is complex and rhythmic. It is carefully modulated, and it is punctuated by stasis as well as by motion. As D'Artagnan, Fairbanks is first seen seated on the floor at the feet of his father (Walt Whitman). In the film's last shot, he is framed from above, kneeling at the feet of the King (Adolphe Menjou). In between, he is almost always moving: running, walking, riding, jumping, gesturing in an animated manner, fighting with a sword or with some other weapon. In this context, an inability to move becomes a sign of constraint, and constraint a sign of danger, of an obstacle or blockage that has to be surmounted by movement itself. The clearest instance of this occurs when he is waylaid on his way to meet the other musketeers and brought before Cardinal Richelieu (Nigel De Brulier). Richelieu has arranged for him to be shot by an assailant behind one of the curtains in Richelieu's room. D'Artagnan stands immobile as Richelieu questions him. However, as soon as he is able to turn, to move in any significant way, he spots the barrel of the pistol, draws his sword, lunges across the room, plunges his sword into his would-be assailant, rushes out of the room, slides down the banister on the staircase outside, runs into the street, swings through a shuttered window to evade his pursuers, grabs a nearby horse, and rides off to rendezvous with his fellow musketeers.

D'Artagnan (Douglas Fairbanks) stands immobile and in danger in *The Three Musketeers* (1921).

Along with *Orphans of the Storm* and *Passion, The Three Musketeers* helped inaugurate a cycle of costume films that came to include *Monte Cristo* (1922), *The Prisoner of Zenda* (1922), *Robin Hood* (1922), *When Knighthood Was in Flower* (1922), *Scaramouche* (1923), *Yolanda* (1924), and *Beau Geste* (1926). They were joined by *The Hunchback of Notre Dame* (1923) and *The Phantom of the Opera* (1925), two Universal "Super Jewels" designed not only to showcase the unique performance skills of Lon Chaney and the "aggrandizement of freak physicality" those performance skills served to convey, but also to mark a change of policy at Universal, which was at this point bent on upgrading its product and entering the upper echelons of the industry's hierarchy.[66] Universal also funded a number of expensive Erich von Stroheim productions, notably *Foolish Wives* (1922), which cost precisely $1,103,736.38.[67] Stroheim went on to produce *Greed* (1924) for MGM. *Greed* cost $585,250 and was initially forty-two reels long.[68] These and other Stroheim films can be seen not only as exposing the sordid underside of the values inherent in *Old Wives for New, Don't Change Your Husband, Why Change Your Wife?* and other Jazz Age dramas and comedies, but also as offering an expensive counterpoint to the equally expensive costume films that increasingly surrounded them.

Most of these costume films were specials rather than superspecials. *Superspecial* was a term in regular use by 1922. It came to indicate a particularly long or expensive production, a production worthy, perhaps, of roadshow distribution and exhibition. (In April 1921, *Wid's Daily* advised exhibitors not to bill Griffith's *Dream Street* as a "Super Special" because it "will be put out for regular release."[69]) However, the distinction was never absolute. As early as November 1921, Fox announced that two of twelve projected "super-specials" were ready for "launching on Broadway before going to exhibitors throughout the country."[70] The two films were *Footfalls* and *The Last Trail.* These were high-end features, but they were neither especially long nor especially expensive. Nor were they roadshown. "Super-special" here seems simply to indicate that they were worthy of more-than-average attention and promotion and, as specified, that they would be accorded a Broadway premiere run.

With the exception of *Orphans of the Storm,* the Chaney films, and some of Fairbanks's later productions, few of the costume pictures listed above were roadshown. *The Three Musketeers* was given roadshow premieres in a number of major cities, as we have seen. But it was released to regular cinemas fairly quickly thereafter, probably because UA was short of films to distribute in 1921 and needed income from exhibitors in order to sustain its cash flow and pay off some of its debts.[71] Along with *Way Down East,* it was *The Four Horsemen of the Apocalypse* that relaunched the traditional nationwide roadshow on a major scale.

Roadshows

The Four Horsemen of the Apocalypse was produced at Metro. Metro had been a small-scale company in the 1910s, but its acquisition by Loew's led to an injection of capital, a reorganization of the company's management, and an upgrading of its films.[72] An adaptation of the best-selling novel by Vicente Blasco Ibáñez, *The Four Horsemen of the Apocalypse* was to become Metro's most expensive production and one of the decade's biggest box-office hits. Its production costs have been estimated at "something between $600,000 and $800,000."[73] *Variety* estimated its worldwide gross at $4 million in 1925 and at $5 million in 1944; in 1991, it estimated its cumulative domestic rentals at $3,800,000.[74]

In its review, *Variety* noted that *The Four Horsemen* "will probably be put out in roadshows as Griffith has done with *Way Down East.* The only way for the company to get its money back is to adopt that method or to book it for long runs."[75] Metro and Loew's decided to take the former option. Preceded by a spoken foreword, a prologue, and an overture, and accompanied by a score composed by Louis F. Gottschalk and arranged and conducted by Hugo Riesenfeld, the film premiered at the Lyric in New York on March 6 and subsequently moved over to the Astor, where its takings in the first week of April broke the house record.[76] It went on to premiere with equal success at the Mission in Los Angeles and at the LaSalle in Chicago, at which point a company called the Four Horsemen Exhibition Corporation was set up by Loew's to plan the film's roadshow presentation, to train its roadshow companies, and to coordinate its nationwide roadshow run.[77] By October, *The Moving Picture World* reported, "More than 100 road companies, with special orchestras and in many instances with artists to enact the prologue, are engaged in showing *The Four Horsemen* to the people of America."[78]

According to Basinger, Leider, and Walker, it was June Mathis who not only scripted *The Four Horsemen,* but who also recommended Rudolph Valentino for the part of Julio and pushed for a bigger budget.[79] Whatever the case may be, Valentino was one of the principal reasons for the film's success, and Mathis built up his role in her script. Essentially a family saga built around a series of contrasts between the Old World and the New and between the values and behavior of the film's principal male

The proscenium effect, the contrast in light and shade, and distribution of figures in the tango scene in Argentina in *The Four Horsemen of the Apocalypse* (1921).

protagonists, the film begins on the cattle-strewn plains of Argentina as surveyed by Madariaga (Pomeroy Cannon), the family patriarch, and ends in a grave-strewn cemetery on a hillside in France at the end of World War I. Its spectacle scenes are marked by compositional permutations. These tend to consist of variations on the layout of the tango scene in Argentina, in which a pronounced proscenium effect is generated by contrasts in light and shade between midground, foreground, and background, by sets that include galleries, staircases, windows, and an archway (or archway effect), and by the distribution of characters (and character-movements) within all these spatial planes. Its crowd scenes are also distinctive, based as they are on rhythmic patterns and volumetric effects created by dominant directions of movement and subdominant variations of various kinds, a technique that was noted by the film's reviewer in the *New York Times*.[80]

In its analysis of the box-office potential of *The Four Horsemen, Wid's Daily* expressed concern as to whether a film "with such an extensive amount of war incident is desired at this day."[81] However, *The Four Horsemen* served not only to reinstate the war as a point of reference in U.S. films, it also put the production of war films as such back on the agenda. This agenda was to result in epic war films such as *The Big Parade* (1925) and *Wings* (1927). Along with westerns such as *The Covered Wagon* (1923) and *The Iron Horse* (1924), these productions augmented the general postwar trend toward epics evident in the re-release of *Quo Vadis?* and *Cabiria*, in the distribution of imports such as *Theodora* (1921) and the 1925 remake of *Quo Vadis?* and in the production of *The Queen of Sheba, The Ten Commandments* (1923), *Ben-Hur* (1925), and *The King of Kings* (1927). These were epics of a more traditional kind, films with biblical or ancient-world settings. They were all given full-scale roadshow releases, and *The Ten Commandments, Ben-Hur,* and *The King of Kings* in particular were major box-office hits.[82]

Ben-Hur and *The Ten Commandments* both used color and special-effects technologies to augment their spectacular qualities. The latter were especially evident in the chariot race in *Ben-Hur* and in the Exodus scenes in *The Ten Commandments. The Ten Commandments* marked DeMille's return to epic production for the first but by no means the last time in his career. *Ben-Hur* was eventually directed by Fred Niblo for MGM, but plans for a film version of Klaw & Erlanger's stage adaptation of Lew Wallace's novel had been in evidence since 1920. This was the year in which the rights to the stage adaptation had lapsed. Klaw & Erlanger's adaptation had been in continuous production since 1899. A film version was viewed as a commercial proposition and had been tried before, in 1907, when Kalem produced a one-reel version and was promptly sued for breach of copyright. Early contenders for the rights in 1920 included D. W. Griffith and FPL. These rights were eventually acquired by Goldwyn Pictures in 1922. However, partly because of production problems and a lack of competent supervision when filming began in Italy, *Ben-Hur* went over budget. It went further over budget when Goldwyn was absorbed by Loew's and it was decided to rebuild many of the sets and retake many of the scenes at the Goldwyn studios in

Trade press advertisement for the roadshow release of *The Ten Commandments* (1923)
(*Variety*, April 2, 1924, 13).

Hollywood.[83] As a result, although *Ben-Hur* grossed "more than $4.3 million domestically and $5 million internationally," its $3,960,000 production costs and $5 million promotion and distribution costs meant that it failed to break even until reissued in 1930.[84] Partly because they were less expensive, epic westerns such as *The Covered Wagon* and *The Iron Horse* and epic war films such as *The Big Parade* and *Wings* were much more profitable.

Epic Westerns

According to Heidi Kenaga, the rights to *The Covered Wagon*, a novel adapted by Emerson Hough from his *Saturday Evening Post* serial, were purchased by FPL in June 1922. At this point, FPL envisaged a routine program production, and a cast, a director, and a budget of $110,000 were assigned accordingly. However, Jesse Lasky read the novel and persuaded Adolph Zukor to produce the film on an epic scale. A bigger budget of $300,000 was provided and a new director, James Cruze, and cast were assigned. Filming began in October. Eight weeks later, a six- or seven-reel version was given a preview. Additional footage was shot in early 1923 and further revisions were made. Following an extensive publicity campaign and a series of pre-release screenings, an eleven-reel version was finally premiered at the Criterion Theatre in New York on March 16, 1923, at an eventual production cost of $782,000. The film was accompanied by a score and a prologue of folk tunes composed by Hugo Riesenfeld.[85]

Noting the film's appeal to "the classes" as well as the masses, Lasky wrote to Zukor and proposed that the film should be roadshown:

I am absolutely convinced that we have the greatest road show proposition of any of the big pictures we have ever produced. . . . I find that the picture appeals immensely to the very best classes, so much so that an endless number of distinguished people have not failed to express themselves, calling *The Covered Wagon* the epic American picture, and recommending it for school children and American patriots. At the same time, the picture has tremendous appeal to the masses. Starting with school boys, small town folk, and right up the line, *The Covered Wagon* seems to get to all of them.[86]

As Kenaga points out, this was not the first time that FPL and its constituent companies had been involved in making prestige westerns.[87] Nor was it the first time that westerns had been produced with epic ambitions. However, as Andrew Brodie Smith points out, "in an era in which the cinema was being promoted as a uniquely urban entertainment," the status of the genre suffered in the late 1910s and the early 1920s as the studios "increasingly associated such films with rural and small-town audiences."[88] The trick performed by *The Covered Wagon* was to use rural and small-town values as the basis for a national epic whose production values ensured its conversion into a form of up-to-date urban entertainment as well.

Following a further publicity campaign and a series of premieres at the Majestic in Boston, the Woods in Chicago, and the Egyptian Theatre in Los Angeles, *The Covered Wagon* was withheld from regular release while John C. Flinn at FPL and Theodore Mitchell and J. J. McCarthy organized its nationwide roadshow run. Ten traveling companies, each with a twenty- to twenty-five-piece orchestra, went on to exhibit the film in legitimate theaters in Asbury Park, New Jersey; Portland, Oregon; Columbus, Ohio; and a number of other cities. All the while, the film continued its runs at the Egyptian, the Woods, the Majestic, and at the Criterion in New York, where it played for fifty-nine weeks at a top seat price of $1.50.[89]

In addition to its cross-class appeal, Kenaga suggests that the film's success was underpinned by a number of contextual factors. Among them were a contemporary upsurge in nativist sentiment, a renewed interest in the regenerative aspects of the West and of pioneer life, a renewed interest in the country's landscape and hence in the authenticity of the film's locations, and a renewed commitment to the ideology of Manifest Destiny.[90] As far as *The Covered Wagon* is concerned, this commitment was evident not just in the nature of its story, about settlers crossing the country in a wagon train in order to settle in Oregon in the far West, but also in the film's expository titles, which lay emphasis on the fact that "the blood of America is the blood of pioneers," and on the extent to which "the men and women of the 'forties flung the boundaries of the nation westward." They are also evident in the nature, structure, and function of its spectacle scenes. Kenaga draws attention to the way in which the image that follows the shot of Westport Landing at the beginning of the film "shows hundreds of covered wagons blanketing the terrain: Westport Landing has disappeared from view. Any existing social organization or communal structure is replaced by the wagon train, which alone will bring 'civilization' to the wilderness."[91] Subsequent scenes, notably the arrival of the Liberty train, the crossing of the River Platte, and the Indian attack on the wagon train, are also founded on an opposition between stasis and blockage, on the one hand, and both literal and metaphorical progress on the other.

The commercial as well as the cultural success of *The Covered Wagon* led to a cycle of epic westerns that included *North of '36* (1924), *The Thundering Herd* (1925), and *The Vanishing American* (1925) at FPL; *The Iron Horse* at Fox; *Sundown* (1924) at First National; *Tumbleweeds* (1925) at UA; and *War Paint* (1926) at MGM. *North of '36* and *The Thundering Herd* were given experimental screenings in new large-screen processes, as we shall see. None of these films, though, was as commercially successful as *The Covered Wagon* or *The Iron Horse*.

Eventually costing $280,000, and eventually grossing $2 million, *The Iron Horse* was directed by John Ford. Shooting on location in the Sierra Nevada began in January 1924. Accompanied by a score composed by Erno Rapee, a twelve-reel version was finally premiered at the Lyric in New York on August 28, 1924 and at Grauman's Egyptian in Los Angeles on February 21, 1925, where it was preceded by a prologue titled "The Days of 1863–1869" featuring Shoshone and Arapaho Indians.[92] At a top ticket price of $1.65 per seat, *The Iron Horse* remained at the Lyric and Egyptian theaters for a number of months. An eleven-reel version went on to play at the Rivoli and Rialto in New York; the Rialto in Washington; the Fox in Philadelphia; the Liberty in Kansas City; the Majestic in Portland, Oregon; and a number of other venues at prices ranging from fifty to ninety-nine cents before going on general release on October 4. In other words, *The Iron Horse* received premiere roadshow runs in New York and Los Angeles and pre-release runs in a number of other cities, but it was "not . . . an out and out road show."[93]

Epic War Films

The epic western cycle overlapped with a cycle of epic films set in World War I. Aside from *The Four Horsemen of the Apocalypse,* the two biggest commercial successes were *Wings* and *The Big Parade. The Big Parade* was designed initially as a program production with a relatively modest budget of $200,000 and with John Gilbert as its only major star.[94] Despite the success of *The Four Horsemen* (which was reissued at the height of *The Big Parade*'s record-breaking run in 1926), there was still some uncertainty as to the market potential of war films. *The Big Parade* began life as one of a number of ideas proposed by director King Vidor. It took shape when producer Irving G. Thalberg hired Laurence Stallings to work with Vidor on a screenplay. It was Stallings who came up with a five-page outline he titled *The Big Parade.* The outline "focused on three young men, a millionaire's son, a riveter, and a bartender, who join the Army and become friends despite their divergent backgrounds. In France, the rich doughboy sees his two friends die in combat, falls in love with a French girl, and loses a leg in battle . . . it was precisely the kind of story Vidor was seeking, and the studio purchased it immediately."[95]

Filming began in Los Angeles, then, with equipment, troops, and planes provided by the War Department, at Fort Sam Houston in Texas. A studio preview screening was held at MGM in July 1924. According to *Variety,* it was J. J. McCarthy who helped convince Thalberg and Louis B. Mayer of *The Big Parade*'s potential as a roadshow and who subsequently handled its roadshow run.[96] Either way, the film's budget was extended in order to pay for retakes, for the shooting of additional scenes, and, according to the AFI Database, for sequences to be processed in the Handschiegl process and shot in two-color Technicolor. Even then, at a time when the budget for a feature averaged around $300,000, no more than $382,000 was spent on production.[97]

Preceded by a prologue titled "Memories of 1918" and accompanied by a score composed by William Axt and Daniel Mendoza, a thirteen-reel version of *The Big Parade* premiered at Grauman's Chinese Theater on November 5, 1925. A twelve-reel version premiered at the Astor in New York on November 19. Shorn of a further 800 feet to allow its screenings to begin later and end earlier in the evening, the film ran at the Astor for ninety-six weeks, breaking records for runs in a single theater previously established by *The Birth of a Nation, Ben-Hur, The Covered Wagon,* and *The Ten Commandments.*[98] It was also roadshown at the Aldine in Philadelphia, the Garrick in

Chicago, the Playhouse in Wilmington, and in numerous other cities prior to its general release at popular prices in August 1927.[99] According to the Eddie Mannix Ledger at MGM, it grossed $4,990,000 domestically and $1,141,000 abroad.

Vidor's own account underlines two key aspects of *The Big Parade*: the extent to which it was "the story of the average man in whose hands does not lie the power to *create* the situations in which he finds himself but who nevertheless feels them emotionally," and the importance of rhythmic cadences to its editing, staging, and impact.[100] As Vidor explains, both were central to the film's preintermission set piece, the sequence in which Jim is separated from Melisande (Renée Adorée) when the troops are called up to the front before they are briefly reunited and able to declare their love for each other as Jim and his company are driven away.[101] The sequence involves cutting to and from Jim and Melisande and interweaves both with the accumulating movement of troops, villagers, and various forms of mechanized transport. The cadences that mark it serve to articulate a series of relationships between stillness and movement, between the movement of human beings and the movement of machines, and between the movement of individuals and the movement of groups. They also serve to articulate a complex set of relationships among powerlessness, power, and the limits and possibilities of individual agency in a scenario in which, to modify Vidor's words, average people do not possess the capacity to create the situations in which they find themselves.

The sequence begins at a point at which Melisande is upset because she thinks Jim is still in love with the woman back home from whom he has received a letter. She walks hurriedly away from him and stands immobile beside a tree near the river that runs through the village. Jim remains slouched on a cart in silent contemplation. At this point a bugler summons the soldiers up to the front, the troops spring into action, and the movement of men and machines begins. As it does so, Jim and Melisande are alerted to the events and actions around them. They both become aware that they are about to be separated, and that they must see and declare their love for each other before Jim is transported away. As the scale of the actions around them expands and as the pace of these actions increases, Melisande searches more and more frantically for Jim, her movements increasingly in counterpoint to the movements around her. When they finally find and declare their love for each other, they are separated once again, literally pulled apart from each other, by the power, pace, and movement of the truck. Before sinking to the ground, before being still once again, Melisande struggles to halt the truck by pulling in the opposite direction and tugging at the rope that dangles from its tailgate. She is as inevitably overcome by its superior physical force as she is by the force inherent in the events that pull them apart. That force, however, is the force that has enabled them to meet and fall in love in the first place. While as dwarfed by the forces over which she has no control as she is by the space around her, Melisande has nevertheless been able to find and to declare her love for Jim. Jim, for his part, has been able to declare his love for her. He has also been able to throw her one of his boots as a token of his love. This is the boot she clutches as she sinks to her knees at the end of the scene. Significantly, it is his right boot. He later loses his left leg in battle, but he still has his right leg. He would thus still be able to wear the boot when he finds Melisande again at the end of the film.

The enormous success of *The Big Parade* helped prompt a cycle of World War I films that came to include *What Price Glory?* (1926), *Seventh Heaven* (1927), *Lilac Time* (1928), *Four Sons* (1928), *The Dawn Patrol* (1930), *Hell's Angels* (1930), *Journey's End* (1930), and *All Quiet on the Western Front* (1930), as well as *Wings*. These films were either fully or partially roadshown. Some were partially filmed in color, some fully or partially exhibited in one of a number large-screen or wide-screen formats, and some partially or fully filmed or exhibited using one of a number of new sound technologies. These technological developments are discussed in more detail in chapter 4. In the meantime, a new Standard Exhibition Contract permitted distributors to roadshow two productions per season provided admission prices for evening performances were "not less than $1" and to roadshow as many productions as they wished in New York and Los Angeles provided that no more than two per season were withheld from subsequent routine release.[102] As a result, war epics such as these were among a plethora of "two-dollar pictures" in receipt of nationwide roadshow and roadshow premiere runs in the late 1920s.[103]

Wings originated as an ordinary program picture at FPL called "The Air Mail," then as a special titled "The Menace." It eventually became a superspecial designed to "answer the resounding broadside that M.G.M. made with its *Big Parade*."[104] Produced at a cost of $1,927,087, a thirteen-reel version was previewed in San Antonio in the spring of 1927; a twelve-reel version was premiered at the Criterion in New York on August 12, 1927 prior to a roadshow run in Chicago and in the East, then at the Biltmore in Los Angeles on January 15, 1928 prior to a roadshow run in the West.[105] Drawing on the "'air-mindedness'" of the U.S. public in the late 1920s, *Wings* tells the story of Jack Powell (Charles Rogers) and David Armstrong (Richard Arlen), who enlist in the air force.[106] As directed by William Wellman, it demonstrates the representational prowess of late 1920s superspecial cinema in the United States. That prowess is evident in numerous ways. The film's storyline encompasses romance, comedy, pathos, irony and action, scenes of ground-based combat, aerial combat, and even a comic boxing scene. Uniforms, weapons, forms of transportation, and planes of all kinds, including the giant Golgotha, are put on display. Footage is shot from every conceivable position in the sky, on the ground, even below the ground as tanks, in particular, are filmed rolling toward the camera. Two of the film's most flamboyant camera movements are reserved not for its combat scenes, but for scenes of romance and comedy. Early on, the camera moves back and forth with Sylvia (Jobyna Ralston) on a swing in her garden; later on, at the beginning of the sequence in the Folies Bergère, the camera dollies forward on a boom over a tabletop in order to home in on Jack getting drunk on champagne.

The film's prowess was evident, too, in its roadshow presentation. As well as the horizontal split-screen effect used during the course of one of the battle scenes, Magnascope projection lenses were used in the aerial sequences to increase the size of the image on screen. Moreover, in addition to the orchestral score composed by J. S. Zamecnik, and in addition to the sound effects produced live by the orchestra's percussionists and by a team of hands backstage, "machines behind the screen recreated machine-gun fire and the take-off noises of aircraft, the latter with different sound effects to distinguish between the American and the German planes."[107] These effects were initially recorded and played back on a disc system devised by Roy Pomeroy at FPL; according to *The Motion Picture News,* they were later recorded and played back on strips of film on a machine parallel to the projector, a modification of a sound system known as the Pallophotophone.[108] In other words, along with a number of other contemporary productions, *Wings* had become a hybrid, a "sound" film as well as a "silent" one.

Color, Large Screen, Wide Screen, and Sound, 1894–1931

Whenever sequences in *Wings* were projected in Magnascope, whenever *Wings* was exhibited with a prerecorded soundtrack, whenever *The Big Parade* was shown in its colored versions, the latest technologies were as much on display as the films they were used to enhance. To that extent, these technologies were participants in a tradition, in the historically evolving set of practices associated with the production, distribution, and exhibition of special films of one kind or another with which this book is largely concerned. Color, sound, and large-screen and wide-screen technologies have all been central to that tradition at a number of points in its history. This chapter will focus on the 1920s, looking at each technology in turn. In doing so, earlier manifestations, the extent to which they played a part in special productions, and the extent to which they entailed exceptional distribution and exhibition practices will each be looked at as well.

Color

As Paolo Cherchi Usai has pointed out, most of the films produced between the 1890s and the beginning of World War I "were endowed with color"; as Tom Gunning has pointed out, color in this period was nearly always a "superadded feature" designed in particular to produce "emotional intensity."[1] The initial means used to color films were derived from traditions established in still photography; magic lantern displays; and popular postcards, engravings, and illustrations in the nineteenth century. Hand-applied color was one such means. It was routinely used in trick films, fairy-tale films, and biblicals.[2] However, it was labor-intensive and therefore expensive. Barry Salt has estimated that a hand-colored print would cost exhibitors three or four times more than a monochrome one.[3] As such it was one of the hallmarks of a feature attraction in the United States and elsewhere, not just in the late 1890s and early 1900s but in its occasional use thereafter. Thus when Gustav Brock offered a hand-coloring service in the United States in the mid- to late 1920s, its use was largely confined to specific sequences in specials and to a limited number of first-run prints.[4]

Because of its expense and labor-intensiveness, hand coloring tended to be replaced by tinting and toning, by stenciling, and by a number of "natural color" processes. Tinting involved the immersion of film stock into an aqueous solution containing a dye. The dye gave a uniform color to the lighter portions of the image and left the darker areas black. Toning involved coloring the darker areas of the image by using a dye that reacted with the silver compound in the emulsion, a process that left the lighter areas almost white. Tinting and toning could be combined, though because toning dyed the developed image, it could only be used to treat a processed release print.[5] Tinting was used in epics and specials such as *The Birth of a Nation, Intolerance,* and *Broken Blossoms.* According to A. R. Fulton, *Intolerance* used "blue for the Judean story, sepia for the French, gray-green for the Babylonian and amber for the modern. Night scenes were blue, sunny exteriors yellow, and night battle scenes red."[6] Tinting and toning were used together on *Way Down East:* "Tone stock was used, then the highlights would be tinted another color by a bath in chemicals. Particularly the scenes by the river: the sunset sky was pink and the rest of the picture blue."[7] However, tinting and toning were increasingly used on program productions too; according to the Society of Motion Picture Engineers, 80 to 90 percent of all films produced in the United States were tinted or toned by 1920.[8] They were thus not a hallmark of specials as such.

Stenciling was pioneered by Pathé. The system originally involved cutting stencils by hand. However, it was semimechanized in 1907, enabling copies to be made from a series of stenciled masters. Stenciling was a major ingredient in the success and high reputation enjoyed by Pathé and Pathé's films in the United States in the 1900s. According to Usai, its use established color "as a criterion of taste in the evolution of moving images":

The Pathé *Films d'Art* series and the adaptations from drama and literature produced by SCAGL and Film d'Arte Italiana between 1909 and 1912 displayed a refinement of color and precision of outline (impossible with manual hand-coloring) unequalled in the period; their palette and their audience mirrored an appreciation for academic painting then common among middle-class viewers (many films were made available in two versions— black and white and hand-tinted or stenciled—at varying prices for different audiences).[9]

Stenciling was thus associated not just with spectacle but also with cultural uplift and the tastes of the upper middle classes to which most epics, specials, and spectacles sought to appeal. Unsurprisingly, when Max Handschiegl devised a system for mechanizing the application of color dyes and increasing the accuracy of registration in 1916, it was used in a number of specials and roadshow productions, among them *Joan the Woman, The Big Parade, The Phantom of the Opera, Sally* (1925), and *Greed.*

In each case, color was used in select and specific sequences, a practice that *Variety* often called "spotting."[10]

Spotting often marked the use of natural color too. Natural color films are those in which the colors are selected from the spectrum by mechanical or optical means.[11] Using lenses, prisms, or dyes in the film stock to filter the light, natural color systems are dependent on the fact that every shade in the color spectrum can be reproduced by mixing the three primary colors—red, green, and blue—in different proportions. The earliest natural color processes were "additive"—that is, they involved adding one or more primary color to black. They were generally restricted to two primary colors, red (or red-orange) and green (or green-blue); they used filters in the camera and the projector rather than the film stock; and they involved the recording and reproduction of each primary color on separate frames or strips of film. The frames were alternated or the strips combined at the point of projection. Films colored in this way necessitated the use of nonstandard cameras, nonstandard projectors, and therefore nonstandard means of exhibition. Whenever and wherever additive films were shown, special arrangements had to be made.

Kinemacolor

One of the most successful additive processes was Kinemacolor. Kinemacolor was invented in the United Kingdom by Charles Urban and George Albert Smith. It was first demonstrated in London in 1908 and at Madison Square Garden in New York on December 11, 1909. The program consisted of several reels of actuality films and included shots of flowers and military parades.[12] *The Moving Picture World* declared these films "the finest bits of color work that we have ever seen on the screen in stationary or moving picture work."[13] The U.S. rights to the process were purchased by Gilbert H. Aymar and James K. Bowen, who founded American Kinemacolor in April 1910 "with the intent of exploiting the device in the big variety theaters rather than in motion-picture houses. Their Allentown plant was used for the manufacture of the special apparatus and they planned to sell territorial rights for exploiting the projection system and the films."[14]

Kinemacolor was first publicly shown in New York at the Eden Musée in January 1911, where it received an extended run.[15] By the summer, the Kinemacolor Company of America had been purchased by J. J. Murdock, who proposed "to exhibit only in the best and higher class theatres superior subjects."[16] Among these "superior subjects," the films of the king's coronation and a subsequent two-hour-long program of films of the Delhi Durbar in 1912 were particularly successful, so much so that Robert Grau was prompted to write an article titled "Is the Two-Dollar-a-Seat Picture Theater in Sight?"[17] According to Quinn: "The trade press was ecstatic about Kinemacolor; if there had been a term superior to that of 'feature,' undoubtedly it would have been bestowed upon these films. . . . *Variety* claimed in mid-1914 that Kinemacolor would remain a feature no matter what the future held in store for the standard single-reel program picture."[18] One of the reasons for this was that Kinemacolor played a key role in contributing to the cause of cultural uplift. Operating initially outside the regular distribution system, "it carried special prestige and offered serious competition to the shows of Lyman Howe and Burton Holmes. Like those traveling companies, it played in legitimate theaters, auditoriums, opera houses, and similar high-class venues."[19] As Kinemacolor's general manager, Arthur H Sawyer, explained, "Kinemacolor was not for the nickel houses."[20]

Sawyer's remarks were made in the context of U.S. government hearings against the MPPC, which had refused Kinemacolor a license. Almost certainly as a result of these hearings, a license was granted in 1913. At this point, Kinemacolor's films were integrated into the MPPC's program via its new exclusive service and its newly expanded but program-based concept of feature cinema:

Kinemacolor's importance lay in the fact that its films were marketable as features, in fact as quite remarkable features, though they usually were limited to one or two reels. Their length allowed distributors and exhibitors to fit them into a program, while they were clearly unusual enough to receive high-profile advertising, thus drawing new audiences to theaters. This, of course, perfectly fit the Trust's approach to the feature. . . . When the exclusive service began two months after the Kinemacolor licensing, Kinemacolor was included in this special feature program as well, becoming one of its highlights."[21]

At the same time, Kinemacolor modified its projector to allow it to project standard black-and-white as well as color films. It also began selling its projector, renting its films by the day and week, and producing fiction films. Its films acted not only "as a bridge between the expensive, one-of-a-kind feature, and the MPPC program short,"[22] but also as a bridge between different concepts and practices of feature cinema in the late 1900s and early 1910s.

Prizmacolor and Technicolor

For an array of reasons, including changes in management, the lapsing of its patent rights, and the fact that it failed to lease its facilities to other producers, Kinemacolor had more or less ceased operations by 1915.[23] The most commercially successful natural color processes thereafter were Prizmacolor and Technicolor's second, third, and fourth color systems. These were all "subtractive" processes; they worked by using filters to remove from white light, which contains all colors, those portions of red, green, and blue needed to produce each given shade. As such, they could be projected on standard equipment, and this was one of the main reasons for their success.

Initially, Prizmacolor subtractive release prints had one frame toned blue-green and the next red-orange, with the color image appearing "only when the projected film was viewed on-screen."[24] Later, however, its inventor, William Van Doren Kelley, "began using duplitized stock (that is, stock with an emulsion on each side), printing

A FEATURE ACT

As a feature act, few producers can offer vaudeville managers the variety and stability that

KINEMACOLOR

(NATURAL COLOR MOTION PICTURES)

does, and those who cannot show vaudeville on Sundays (tho' you pay rent for that day) can keep their houses open and do business—giving an *exclusive show*—something the little picture-stores haven't got and *cannot get*—

Worth while considering, isn't it?

Kinemacolor Company

1600 BROADWAY
NEW YORK CITY

Trade press advertisement for Kinemacolor (*Variety*, January 24, 1913, 29).

the red-orange record on one side and blue-green perfectly in register behind it. After toning each side the proper shade, he obtained a print in which every frame displayed 'natural color' when viewed through transmitted light."[25] Because Prizmacolor, like Kinemacolor, involved the sequential recording of separately color-filtered frames at the point of production, it, too, suffered from fringing.[26] It was used for color sequences in *Way Down East* and for filming *The Glorious Adventure* (1922). Soon after that, though, Technicolor became the dominant color process.

The Technicolor Corporation was founded by Herbert T. Kalmus and Daniel Comstock in 1915. The first Technicolor process was additive, and the first Technicolor film was *The Gulf Between* (1917). Kalmus and Comstock soon realized, however, that additive processes were unlikely to be commercially viable because they necessitated nonstandard projection equipment as well as nonstandard cameras: "exhibition was the sector of the industry where standardisation was most important. . . . This meant that whatever happened in the studio or laboratory . . . color film had to be showable via the hundreds of thousands of 35 mm projectors operating worldwide."[27] Technicolor turned to subtractive systems. The first two were two-color systems. Running at approximately thirty-two frames per second, a prism or "beam-splitter" in the camera recorded the two color records on the negative film stock simultaneously rather than sequentially, thus eliminating the possibility of fringing. In addition, "Skip-printing every other frame made it possible to separate the blue-green record onto one film-strip, the red-orange onto another. Prints from these strips were then toned the proper color and cemented back-to-back to form each release print."[28] This system was used for *The Toll of the Sea* (1922), which was produced by Technicolor and distributed by Metro, and which grossed over a quarter of a million dollars.[29] It was also used for color inserts and sequences in *The Ten Commandments* and *Cytherea* (1924), and for such subsequent all-color productions as *Wanderer of the Wasteland* (1924) and *The Black Pirate* (1926).

Of the five all-Technicolor features produced prior to 1928, *The Black Pirate* was the only one to be given limited roadshow exposure. As *Variety* stressed in its review, *The Black Pirate* ran for only eighty-eight minutes.[30] Its status as a special worthy of opening at the Selwyn in New York at a two-dollar top-seat price derived from its use of color, its consequent cost, and the presence of Douglas Fairbanks as its star. However, its length also enabled it to be paired with Mary Pickford's *Sparrows* (1926) as part of a unique roadshow double bill at Grauman's Egyptian Theater.[31] This fifteen-reel, husband-and-wife "Double Special" came about when Sid Grauman was unable to agree on terms for the booking of *Ben-Hur*. But despite a planned eight-month engagement it ran only fourteen weeks, vacating the theater to make room for *Don Juan* (1926).

Reviews of *The Black Pirate* praised the Technicolor process and the restrained and appropriate way it was put to use. Mordaunt Hall in *The New York Times* wrote,

Mr. Fairbanks realized that color must be subordinated to the action of the episodes, and therefore, although the telling prismatic effects occasionally reap their full reward, they are put forth with deliberation and restraint. In this photoplay . . . there is no sudden fringing or sparking colors, the outlines being always clearly defined without a single instance of the dreaded trembling "rainbow" impinging on the picture. For the most part modulated shades are employed, such as sepia, the dominating tone which is far more effective than a lavish scattering of reds and greens. In fact, decisive red is only depicted to show the blood on the hands of a man or on his sword.[32]

However, although it otherwise produced successful results on the screen, the cemented strips of film tended to buckle or "cup" during projection, causing the image to go out of focus and necessitating the constant repair and replacement of reels. As a result, Technicolor's next two-color process used a different system for making prints. Instead of producing a negative that was used to generate two dyed and cemented "matrix" prints, two gelatin relief images known as matrices were optically generated from the negative, dyed by means of a process known as "imbibition," then used to make positive prints. This "dye-transfer" process became the basis of Technicolor's subsequent three-color system, which was first introduced in Walt Disney's animated short *Flowers and Trees* in 1932. As Koszarski points out, the images produced by this process were "smooth" and "grainless," "with far greater uniformity of color than on any system based on chemical toning. *The King of Kings* and *The Wedding March* (1928) made use of this system, which remained in general use until 1933."[33]

The King of Kings and *The Wedding March* used Technicolor's system in spotted sequences. However, like Technicolor's previous two-color system, it was used in a number of all-color productions as well. These included *The Viking* (1928), MGM's first all-color production; *On with the Show* (1929), Warners' first all-color talkie; First National's *Sally* (1929); MGM's *The Rogue Song* (1930); and Samuel Goldwyn's *Whoopee!* (1930). Aside from *The Viking*, these were all major box-office hits: *On with the Show* grossed $2,415,000 worldwide; *Sally*, $2,198,000; *The Rogue Song*, $1,610,000; and *Whoopee!*, $2,655,000.[34] (*Whoopee!*, like Universal's *King of Jazz* and Paramount's *The Vagabond King* [both 1930 and both all-color], was reported as costing over $2 million to produce.)[35] However, as the exception of *The Viking* makes clear, color was probably not the principal reason for the success of these productions; although a synchronized soundtrack was added soon after its premiere in New York, *The Viking* was neither a talkie nor a musical, as the major two-color Technicolor hits of the late 1920s and early 1930s tended to be.

The vogue for color led the Technicolor company to launch a number of new services, among them training for cameramen and consultancy in matters of "color control." The capacity of Technicolor's plant was doubled, and by 1930 Technicolor had contracts for some thirty-six color productions.[36] However, natural color systems were rarely a box-office draw on their own, perhaps because films made in natural two-color processes in the mid- to late 1920s were insufficiently distinct from films that were tinted and toned. The increasing use of Technicolor may have been a consequence of the fact that established tinting and toning techniques could not initially be used with optical sound tracks. (The chemicals used to dye the prints interfered with the optical sound track.) Whatever the reason, there was a marked increase in demand for Technicolor in the 1929–30 season, and, following a price cut in Technicolor's services, in 1930–31 as well.[37] However, Technicolor experienced problems in meeting demand and in maintaining standards.[38] Thereafter, the use of Technicolor and other color processes was severely rationed as a result of the increasing impact of the Depression on the industry's policies, practices, and fortunes. As the 1931 edition of the *Film Daily Yearbook* put it: "Increased cost of production without sufficient increase in gross sales was . . . the greatest drawback. Indications point to the belief that only in prosperous times and under flourishing conditions will there be a recurrence of the 1929 boom in color films."[39] The impact of the Depression on the U.S. film industry will be discussed at greater length in chapter 5. The last two-color Technicolor feature, Warners' *Mystery of the Wax Museum,* was released just after its height, in 1933.

Large Screen and Wide Screen

By the mid-1920s, picture palace auditoria had grown in size and capacity, but the size of their screens and the images projected upon them had remained relatively constant. According to William Paul, writers on theater design in the nickelodeon era had "recommended that screen size be kept between twelve and fifteen feet wide in order to preserve the illusion of what were generally referred to as 'life-size pictures.'"[40] Noting the advent of closer framings and the showing of more and more films in larger auditoria in the late 1900s and the 1910s, Paul goes on to quote from a 1909 article in *The Moving Picture World*:

To our mind, a compromise between the ordinary and a moving picture stage is desirable. Let us imagine an ordinary stage opening. It may be forty or fifty feet across and proportionately deep. But you do not want a picture that size. It seems to us that the best plan in such a case is to set the moving picture screen well back on the stage and to connect the size of the house by suitably painted cloths or side pieces so that when the house is darkened and the picture is shown the audience have the impression that they are looking at the enactment of a scene set a little way back on the stage.[41]

With the advent of picture palaces, the stage was redesigned to accommodate an orchestra as well as a setting. The orchestra was usually located downstage, while the screen was located upstage. However, with the larger orchestras, larger stages, and larger auditoria in the picture palaces built in the 1920s, the proportional relationship between the screen and its surroundings began to change. As John Belton points out:

Most of the new movie palaces were built with fairly wide, 35-to-45-foot prosceniums complete with theater stages, which facilitated the presentation of live-action prologues, dramatic sketches, variety acts, and other theatrical spectacles. . . . The movie screen occupied only a small proportion of the total space of the stage. Indeed the routine shift during the standard theater program, from the live stage show which preceded the film presentation and which filled the proscenium to the dramatically smaller projected image on the screen, accentuated the disparity between the two events and drew attention to the diminished nature of the motion picture program.[42]

In this context, it is hardly surprising that a number of film companies began experimenting with the size of the projected image, with larger-than-standard-gauge film stock and film prints, and with wide-screen processes too. Among the former were Natural Vision, Magnascope, and Fantom Screen.

According to a report in *Variety* in 1924, George K. Spoor had been working on a "new-sized film" designed to "give theatres a full stage projection" for over eight years. In addition to manufacturing his own film stock and producing his own films, Spoor was "building his own projectors with a view to confining all his activities to roadshowing the productions, which will mean that with about a score of projection machines he will be able to tour the country and clean-up in the legitimate houses for one season at least on the strength of the novelty of a picture that fills the entire stage of a theatre, instead of a small screen space."[43] Spoor was working with John G. Berggren. Their plans appear to have been delayed. But Adolph Zukor paid a visit to Spoor's plant in Chicago in 1924, and Spoor's system, now called Natural Vision, was revived again as a roadshow prospect designed specifically for use in legitimate theaters in early 1926.[44]

In the meantime, whether influenced by Spoor or not, Zukor and FPL became involved in a number of large-screen and large-gauge projects in the mid- to late 1920s. In 1924, FPL acquired the rights to a three-and-one-half-inch wide-angle lens from its inventor, Lorenzo del Riccio. Experimental screenings using this lens to project *North of '36* and *The Thundering Herd* on a much larger than average screen were held at the Eastman Theatre in Rochester, New York in 1925.[45] In 1926, soon after Spoor and Berggren revived their Natural Vision project, FPL announced the production of *Old Ironsides,* a historically based naval adventure film, and went on to use Riccio's lens as the central component in the Magnascope large-screen projection system used for the film's premiere at the Rivoli in New York on December 6, 1926 and for its subsequent premiere run.

Scripted by Laurence Stallings, directed by James Cruze, and accompanied by a Vitaphone musical soundtrack composed by Hugo Riesenfeld, *Old Ironsides* was FPL's most expensive production to date and was planned as a roadshow from the outset.[46] Its sets were designed by Edward J. Smith, who had designed the sets for *The Ten Commandments.* They included a fort that was 750 feet wide, a sea wall that was 3,000 feet long, and full-size replicas of the *Constitution* ("Old Ironsides") and other early nineteenth-century ships.[47] Problems on location resulted in an increase in production costs way beyond its original million-dollar budget. But by the time the film was finished FPL had set up its own in-house roadshow department under the management of Albert Grey and Theodore Mitchell and remodeled the Rivoli as "a reserved seat theatre," one of eleven such theaters on Broadway designed for roadshow premiere runs, and one of three owned by FPL.[48]

For the film's premiere run, FPL replaced the Rivoli's fifteen-by-twenty-foot screen with a screen that was thirty by forty feet.[49] For the Magnascope sequences, a change of reel to a projector equipped with the Magnascope lens was timed to coincide with the gradual opening of the masking at the top, bottom, and sides of the screen, thus producing an effect of gradual enlargement. According to reviewers, the first use of Magnascope was in the preintermission sequence depicting the *Constitution* on its way to rescue a U.S. ship hijacked by Barbary pirates: "Just as Old Ironsides was shown approaching and had entirely filled the regulation screen, the screen itself was seen to enlarge until it filled the whole stage. The old ship kept growing bigger and bigger until it seemed life-size and to be actually coming right out of the screen. It literally brought the audience to its feet with tremendous applause."[50] The effect produced here, as Belton points out, recalled the effect produced by screenings of some of the Lumière films on Vitascope projectors in 1895; it also looked forward to the overwhelming sense of "emergence" produced by later large-screen processes such as Cinerama, 3-D, and IMAX.[51] Here, the *Constitution* sequence, which was apparently edited from outtakes by studio publicist Glendon Allvine, was clearly designed to accentuate the power and prowess of the ship and the technology used to present it.[52] Reviewers were impressed and *Variety* predicted that "no matter what investment the picture represents," FPL "are sure to get it back and a whole lot more."[53] In fact, although *Old Ironsides* ran at the Rivoli for twenty weeks, it grossed substantially less than its cost.

Despite the increase in grain and consequent lack of picture quality induced by the magnification process, especially in the larger theaters where it was most commonly used, Magnascope was subsequently employed in the screening of other FPL films. Aside from *Wings,* examples include the semidocumentary *Chang* (1927) and *The Four Feathers* (1929), both of which were coproduced by Merian C. Cooper, who was later involved in the innovation of Cinerama. The Paramount Theatre on Broadway used it for newsreels and for "novelty hook-ups with stage units," and Magnascope was employed intermittently by exhibitors for many years.[54]

Magnascope was succeeded in the 1920s by Fantom Screen, in which the image enlargement was achieved not by changing to an additional projector for the large-screen sequences, but either through the use of a variable focal length (zoom) projection lens or by moving the screen upstage on rollers to take it further from the projector, thereby increasing the "throw." *Variety* credited Joe Vogel of the Loew theater department with the original idea, "which was executed by A. S. Howard, Frank Norton, Peter Clark and Lester Isaacs of the Loew technical staff, under the supervision of J. J. McCarthy."[55] The process was introduced at the New York premiere at the Astor of MGM's epic western, *The Trail of '98* (1928), which McCarthy supervised.[56] As with Magnascope, the use of Fantom Screen was spotted, though unlike Magnascope, the image could be reduced as well as enlarged by moving the screen or adjusting the lens. For *Variety's* reviewer, this was an advantage: "Shrinking to normal size is done to take up the story and keep the characters from appearing out of proportion. To help mask the transition the screen comes forward and goes back on the titles."[57] *Variety* predicted that no future MGM spectacle would be without Fantom Screen; but although the Astor roadshow engagement ran for five months, no subsequent uses of the device have come to light.[58] (A possible exception is *42nd Street* [1933], which was apparently presented in some variation either of Magnascope or of Fantom Screen in its premiere run at the Strand in New York.[59])

In January 1930, *Variety* reported that a "movement is already underfoot for the installation of big screens to accommodate wide angle projections lenses of ordinary sequences on the present 35 m. (standard) releases."[60] Chicago neighborhood exhibitors were busy installing such screens in order to attract audiences away from downtown theaters. The downtown theater-owners themselves, however, preferred to wait for the next innovation: wide-gauge film with an aspect ratio (width to height proportions) greater than the standard 1.33:1 frame of silent 35 mm film.[61]

Wide Gauge and Wide Screen

Wide-gauge and wide-screen formats were seen by the industry as another novelty to attract audiences now that sound was becoming accepted. Films exhibited in the now-standard sound-on-film processes had their frame proportions shrunk to 1.15:1 in order to accommodate the soundtrack. An enlargement of the film gauge was a means of compensating for the reduced width of the picture while also improving the clarity and resolution of the projected image through the larger surface area of the negative, the positive print, or both, to the extent, indeed, that some observers reported a near three-dimensional effect.[62] Fox representative Courtland Smith was reported as explaining the significance of these developments in the following terms: "Mr. Smith pointed out that the present standard screen had been in use for something like twenty-five years and that keeping to the same dimensions would be tantamount to automobile manufacturers clinging to the cars that were made about twenty-five years ago."[63]

Smith also stressed the need for "increased dimensions of film and screen" now that sound-on-film systems such as Movietone "took up part of the picture space hitherto given over to the picture."[64] However, several factors militated against industry acceptance of wide film: "Cost of production. Facilities for distribution. Practicality for general exhibition."[65] The initial problem was lack of standardization. Following a period of multiple formats both for peepshow machines and for on-screen projection in the 1890s and early 1900s, a period in which different formats were adopted in order to avoid patent litigation, 35 mm film and an aspect ratio of 1.33:1 had been adopted as standard by 1909.[66] Now, demonstrations of several competing systems in the new sound era were expected to decide the standard wide-screen format, but no decision was forthcoming as companies sponsoring different formats failed to agree on the optimum width for a new standard gauge. Fox argued for 70 mm, FPL and RKO, a new company formed to exploit its own sound system, for 65 mm. Warner Bros. also opted for a 65 mm process and had twelve cameras built for the format, though reports suggest that it contemplated switching to Fox's 70 mm system, which MGM and Universal were also considering. Meanwhile, Technicolor held off from manufacturing color wide-film cameras until standardization was reached.[67]

There were questions, too, about the artistic suitability of wider aspect ratios. Cameramen and technical experts preferred the standard ratio for its greater height, and some directors were intimidated by the prospect of staging and composing shots for a new ratio.[68] Because of the increased costs of production and distribution entailed in wide-gauge filming, there was speculation that the industry might opt instead for enlargement of the standard 35 mm image by means of lenses, along the lines of

Magnascope and Fantom Screen. Most theater chains had or were having large screens installed in their bigger theaters.[69] The wider frame was designed to be fully visible even from the rear seats and even with a larger picture frame, but in many situations the top of the image would be cut off by the balcony or the proscenium.[70]

Fox, which had been examining the possibilities of wide film for longer than any of the other major companies, eventually went ahead with its plans to make films in 70 mm without waiting for industry standardization. It began tentatively with *Fox Movietone Follies of 1929* (1929), which was initially shown at the Roxy in regular 35 mm before its later debut in 70 mm Grandeur at the relatively small, 808-seat Gaiety Theatre on September 17, 1929. The delay had been caused by engineers experimenting with different types of projectors, and problems still remained in adjusting the new-sized soundtrack (a quarter-inch wide compared to the standard 35 mm width of one-tenth of an inch) to the acoustics of smaller theaters.[71] While already playing at cheaper prices in late-run neighborhood theaters, *Movietone Follies'* limited two-week, two-dollar run at the Gaiety was a commercial success, though it remained the film's only 70 mm engagement. Fox saw the new technology as offering a competitive advantage, partly through its ownership of patent rights that could profitably be licensed to other companies.[72] It was reported in October 1929 that William Fox had ordered all major new talkies to be filmed in Grandeur, and various titles were announced, but only three films—*Happy Days, Song o' My Heart,* and *The Big Trail* (all 1930)—were actually made.[73]

Reviewing *Happy Days* on its debut at the Roxy in February 1930, Mordaunt Hall pointed out that the world's largest movie theater now had the world's largest screen.[74] *Variety* remarked on the impressive scale of the musical production numbers (involving up to eighty-six performers on screen at once) and other "scenic and atmospheric shots," and suggested that "all class A and B houses will have to go to the big screen sooner or later. That's surefire when the boys turn loose color on the big film, which, incidentally, isn't so far away."[75] (Fox planned to use a new Eastman color process on future Grandeur titles and made laboratory facilities for striking prints, but only the standard 35 mm version of *Movietone Follies* was shown with color sequences; like all the other wide-format films, the 70 mm version was black and white throughout.[76]) Grandeur films in 70 mm were intended for roadshows, while reduction printers were constructed to allow the wide-gauge negatives to be reduced to 35 mm for general distribution.[77] A thousand Grandeur projectors were also ordered built and projection equipment was planned for installation in theaters in Philadelphia, St. Louis, Detroit, and San Francisco for showing *Happy Days* following its New York opening. Fox even began to install projectors in neighborhood theaters, including the Fox in Brooklyn, but the 70 mm version was ultimately shown only at the Carthay Circle in Los Angeles and, according to Richard Barrios, in Milan (if so, this may have been the only wide-gauge presentation abroad).[78]

Other companies also began shooting films in wide-gauge processes. Each used a different format: RKO produced a short subject, *Campus Sweethearts* (1929, apparently shown only in private test screenings), and the feature film *Danger Lights* (1930) in Spoor and Berggren's 63.5 mm Natural Vision. Warner Bros. made *A Soldier's Plaything, Kismet,* and *The Lash* (all 1930) in 65 mm Vitascope. MGM produced *Billy the Kid* (1930) and *The Great Meadow* (1931) in 70 mm Realife using Grandeur cameras borrowed from Fox but with the intention of printing down to 35 mm for exhibition, with thick racking bars separating hard-matted wide frames (frames with their tops and bottoms masked on the film print in order to produce an image with a wider ratio). Realife also used Warners' sound-on-disc system in order to allow the picture to extend into the area usually reserved for the soundtrack. Independent filmmaker Roland West shot *The Bat Whispers* (1930) in 65 mm Magnifilm, a process different from 56 mm Magnafilm, which was used for *You're in the Army Now* (1929), a Paramount Famous Lasky production (as FPL was now called).[79] Magnafilm had an aspect ratio of 2.18:1, Grandeur was 2.13:1, Vitascope and Magnifilm were both 2.05:1, Natural Vision was 1.85:1, and Realife release prints were 1.75:1.[80] In an effort to move toward standardization, RKO and Paramount reportedly altered the width of Natural Vision and Magnafilm stock to 65 mm. But while Fox refused to budge on 70 mm, Warner Bros. experimented with an adjustable projector capable of taking 35 mm, 65 mm, and 70 mm prints.[81]

After a meeting with leaders of the Motion Picture Producers and Distributors of America (MPPDA) in May 1930, it was decided to abandon further development of wide film until a standard gauge could be agreed and to refrain from releasing any more wide-screen pictures until the fall. While individuals were permitted to continue with technical experiments, theater installations of wide-gauge projection equipment and public exhibition of wide-gauge films would be limited to ten key cities.[82] As *Variety* put it:

The giant screen is to be tucked away as an emergency stimulus such as sound proved with its introduction. . . . Danger of wrecking the entire industry by placing, via wide film, a burden upon theatres which the majority could not be expected to survive and which would automatically reflect itself in circles, was conceded by filmdom's leaders.[83]

There still remained, of course, the question of what to do with the ten wide-gauge productions already completed and awaiting release. Paramount's *You're in the Army Now,* which ran for either two reels or four according to different sources, had been shown only once in 1929 at a New York press demonstration and was apparently never exhibited publicly at all.[84] Fox's Irish operetta, *Song o' My Heart,* and MGM's pioneer western, *The Great Meadow,* were never publicly shown in wide format, being exhibited only in standard 35 mm versions. MGM's other Realife production, *Billy the Kid,* was shown as a special attraction on large screens using Magnascope-type wide-angle lenses with 35 mm reduction prints in New York, Chicago, Detroit, Pittsburgh, Atlanta, Cleveland, Providence, Kansas City, Washington DC, and Los Angeles, the ten key cities permitted by the MPPDA. Dissatisfied with the results of *A Soldier's Plaything,* its first Vitascope film, Warners chose not to release it in 65 mm. It was also initially undecided as to whether *Kismet* would be shown in its entirety in the wide-screen version or only half, with the rest of the film shown in standard size, in the manner of Magnascope presentations; but *The Lash* (a Richard Barthelmess western) was planned for release in large format in the ten cities listed above.[85] In the event, both films played in the wide format in only one theater in each of New York and Los Angeles, as did *The Bat Whispers*. RKO, meanwhile, exhibited *Danger Lights* in single theaters in Chicago and New York, having played the rest of the country in 35 mm.

Billy the Kid earned a box-office gross of $76,000 in its sole week at the New York Capitol, though this was only "what a healthy programmer with no embellishments averages at this house."[86] At the Criterion in Los Angeles it grossed only $7,500 in its opening week. *Billy the Kid* fared better in Detroit and Kansas City, but, costing $605,000 to make, it went on to gross only $840,000 worldwide, leaving MGM with a loss of $119,000. Of the first four openings of *The Big Trail,* two were to be in 70 mm and two in 35 mm; the results would be compared to see whether wide screen made a difference at the box office.[87] At the Roxy, the film lasted only two weeks; at Grauman's Chinese, it stayed on for eight weeks, the longest engagement of any of the wide-gauge films, though the $1.50 roadshow run was still considered a disappointment.[88] Plans to roadshow *The Big Trail* nationally were canceled and retakes were ordered.[89] Of the first two 35 mm engagements, at the McVickers in Chicago and the Fox in Brooklyn, the former fared better than the New York or Los Angeles runs, but in most other big cities the film failed. Costing $1,900,000, it ultimately grossed only $900,000 in the domestic market. Following precedents such as these, other companies generally chose not to stress the wide formats in publicity for their subsequent films or to produce further titles in large format.[90]

The screen "revolution" was over by early 1931, even before the last wide-screen title (*The Great Meadow*) crept onto the market in standard 35 mm. In December 1930, the MPPDA issued a more emphatic statement than its earlier one in May, that wide film and other comparable innovations were henceforth to be abandoned for at least two years.[91] The reduced aspect ratio of the 35 mm sound-film frame was eventually "corrected" in 1932 by using a reduced portion of the film strip for the image, thickening the racking line between each frame, and printing the hard-matted image farther to the right of the soundtrack area, using a new standard of 1.37:1. (This, not 1.33:1, is the so-called Academy ratio, as it was introduced by the Academy of Motion Picture Arts and Sciences.[92]) As John Belton has argued, wide film at this juncture served no useful commercial purpose and only incurred unwarranted expense as the industry, and the country, entered a period of economic instability.[93] The MPPDA's ruling was explicitly motivated by a 4 percent drop in business for the just-ended fiscal year, the first sign that the industry was being affected by what the Hays Office called "the worst time in the financial history of the country."[94] The financial outlay necessary for further investment in new screens and new projection technology was beyond the means of exhibitors who had already invested considerable sums of money in equipping their theaters for sound.

Wagons roll in the wide-screen
version of *The Big Trail* (1930).

Sound

As Leo Enticknap points out: "It has become a recurrent cliché among cinema historians that 'there was no such thing as a silent film': rather there was a period during which the dominant cultural and economic mode of practice dictated that the film and the sound which went with it were produced and supplied separately."[95] Sonic accompaniment was usually arranged by exhibitors, "and tended to consist of one or a combination of four forms of live performance: a spoken lecture or commentary; a live musical performance, ranging from a single instrumentalist to a live ensemble or orchestra; sound effects corresponding to, and generated in approximate synchronisation with, the action in the film; and, more rarely (in the European and North American film industries, at least), a theatrical performance by actors" either in full view of the audience or else hidden behind the screen.[96] As we have seen, these arrangements could constitute a feature in their own right, and large-scale orchestras playing a specially composed or compiled musical score were a hallmark of roadshown specials.

It is a further cliché that Edison's Kinetograph and Kinetoscope were invented to do "for the Eye what phonograph does for the Ear," and that the "silent" era was peppered with numerous other devices used to record or to reproduce sound.[97] Among them were cylinders and discs. These were analog systems in which the patterns of vibration emitting from a sound source were recorded and reproduced on a continuous basis. Among the earliest was Edison's Kinetophone, a peepshow device that combined moving images with sounds played back on a cylinder. Discs were much more common. They provided the basis for Lubin's Cineophone and E. E. Norton's Cameraphone in the 1900s. However, these devices were expensive to hire. According to Douglas Gomery, the cost of a Cameraphone talkie to exhibitors was fifteen to twenty cents per foot at a time when the standard cost was around ten cents. The Cameraphone "required a specially trained operator at a higher salary. The necessary phonographs increased the outlay. In total, where the usual film expense was $30 to $60 per week, a talkie doubled that price. This precluded use by small 'store' theaters and caused larger theaters to demand exclusive rights."[98] As a result, the Cameraphone company was out of business by the 1909–10 season. In the meantime, Edison continued its experiments, and the cylinder format and Kinetophone label were both revived in 1913.

The Kinetophone

A number of limitations had marked the prerecorded sound systems used hitherto:

Firstly, acoustic recordings (both cylinders and discs) were what would now be termed a "write once" medium: after recording, the signal characteristics could not be altered in any way. Secondly, no editing of the recording's content was possible. . . . Thirdly, they were time-limited to (approximately) two minutes in the case of cylinders, and three for discs. Fourthly, there was the issue of synchronisation in playback. As all these systems relied on two separate carriers for the picture and the sound, a means was needed of regulating their playback speed. . . . And finally, the acoustic nature of the medium imposed severe limitations. Recording had to take place close to a large horn—so close, in fact, that it would be visible in frame if any attempt were made to actually record the picture and sound simultaneously. Therefore, almost all these "synchronised" films were produced by performers lip-synching in front of a camera while a copy of the record (which had been recorded earlier) was played.[99]

The new Kinetophone sought to overcome some of these limitations by using an oversize cylinder to increase recording and running times and amplification. It debuted in January 1913. As with nearly all the other early sound programs, the Kinetophone program consisted of prerecorded theatrical and musical performances. Like many early color programs, it was perfectly compatible with the program-based conception of feature cinema. However, Edison and the MPPC abandoned their daily-change exhibition policy and began to market Kinetoscope in a manner normally reserved for feature-length films. "Kinetophone films were rented for a minimum of three months per theater, at the highest prices yet seen for anything but the most prestigious features, as much as $500 per week."[100]

Like these features, the Kinetophone was usually roadshown. Despite its initial success, though, a fire at Edison's factory and problems with synchronization and amplification spelled the end of Kinetophone and with it all other acoustic systems. The successful revival of sound in the 1920s was based on systems that used electronic amplification, that permitted longer recording and playing times, and that eventually permitted the editing and mixing of sounds as well. The systems that became standard in the early 1930s were those that eliminated synchronization problems by recording sound on film and by incorporating the soundtrack on the same strip of film as the images. These technologies all "drew on research carried out by telephone, radio and consumer record industry engineers."[101] Feeding off and into a culture that was increasingly attuned to electronically mediated sound, the industrially successful ones were funded and developed by major corporations: American Telephone and Telegraph (AT&T) and General Electric and their respective subsidiaries, Western Electric and the Radio Corporation of America (RCA).[102] The first and least successful system from a commercial point of view, Lee de Forest's Phonophone, was the system that lacked substantial corporate backing.

Phonophone and Vitaphone

The Phonophone system was based on de Forest's own research. In 1906 he invented an early electronic device for amplifying sounds. The rights to this device were acquired by Western Electric in 1913, but de Forest retained the right to use it. Working with Earl Sponable and Theodore Case, he became seriously interested in the possibility of sound films in the early 1920s. An inaugural program of Phonophone films was held at the Rivoli in New York on April 15, 1924. The program consisted of musical and theatrical performances, albeit slightly longer ones than those recorded in the 1900s and 1910s. By 1924, live musical and theatrical performances, which had been a hallmark of special productions in the 1910s, were becoming a routine part of the show in many of the cinemas owned by the major companies. Known as "prologues" or "presentations," depending on whether they were thematically linked to the film being shown (in the case of the former) or not (in the case of the latter), they were often costly and necessarily dependent on the availability of live performers.[103] Star performers were even more costly and, by definition, even more scarce.

The significance of de Forest's program should be weighed in this context, as should its potential for recording full-scale orchestral scores. These, too, were becoming routine in the bigger theaters, but were still something that subsequent-run houses in suburban and rural areas could not afford. This was one of the reasons why Hugo Riesenfeld, musical director at the Rivoli, was one of Phonophone's most active proponents; for him it represented an opportunity for recorded orchestral scores to be heard throughout the country.[104] However, while Riesenfeld was able to secure showings of Photophone at the Capitol and the Rialto as well as at the Rivoli, de Forest was unable to secure the interest of Universal and Fox or the financial backing of major investors. He was thus forced to roadshow Phonophone in independent venues.[105] This made it a special attraction, albeit a minor one, but deprived it of the opportunity to become one of the industry's standard systems.

The fortunes of Vitaphone at Warners were very different. Vitaphone was a sound-on-disc system. The Vitaphone discs

were 16 inches in diameter, and rotated at a significantly slower speed—33 rpm compared to the 78 rpm which had been universally adopted by the recorded music industry as the standard speed for records for domestic sale in 1915. To compensate for the consequent loss of dynamic range, a thicker and softer shellac compound was used together with a larger groove pitch, which enabled wider and deeper modulations to be inscribed. This produced a comparable signal quality but a longer continuous playing time than the disc's domestic counterparts.[106]

Thanks to Douglas Gomery, it is now well known that Warner Bros. adopted Vitaphone as part of a strategy to increase its profits, its power, and its ranking in the U.S. film industry.[107] With the help of Waddill Catchings, head of the investment division at Goldman, Sachs, Warners "imposed a short-term debt on itself" in order to fund a well-planned program of expansion.[108] Still a relatively minor production company in 1924, Warners lacked a national distribution network and a theater chain. It raised the capital for its productions by trading a percentage of its potential earnings for loans from rich individuals or by selling territorial franchise rights to exhibitors. In the spring of 1925, these policies changed. Warners acquired majority control of Vitagraph, and with it a national and international network of film exchanges. It also acquired ten first-run theaters, leases on others, and a radio station in Los Angeles. Ownership of the radio station led to an encounter with Western Electric and in April 1926 to an agreement between Western Electric and Vitaphone, Warners' new subsidiary, to produce and distribute films using Western Electric's sound-on-disc system in exchange for annual royalty fees.

Vitaphone premiered as a "prelude" at the Warner Theatre in New York on August 6, 1926. There were seven "acts" in the prelude, followed by an intermission and a screening of *Don Juan*, a costume feature with occasional sound effects and a prerecorded score arranged and composed by Edward Bowes, William Axt, and David Mendoza. Initial reactions to Vitaphone "stressed the *musical* nature of the system,"[109] and tended to repeat Warner Bros.' own views on its potential and future use: "The Vitaphone is a step in a new direction and it should do much for the exhibition end of the business. Presensations [*sic*] through the use of Vitaphone, should become simplified."[110] According to an editorial in the *Film Daily:*

Dance and song numbers, vocal selections, violin solos, jazz bands in synchronized form sold on a weekly basis to offset the competition created for the little fellow by presentations at big theaters—that, too, is a potential Utopia for the average exhibitor. . . . It seems beyond human conception that the smallest theater in the smallest hamlet in this country can exhibit *Don Juan* with an orchestral accompaniment of 107 men in the New York Philharmonic Orchestra. It will not be to the de luxe theater that the Vitaphone will prove a boon. The relatively few houses of this type will look upon the process as a novelty. It is not to be expected that the Vitaphone will replace orchestras in theaters like the Capitol, New York or the Uptown, Chicago.[111]

However, it was in theaters like the Capitol and the Uptown that Vitaphone was initially exhibited. Although the wiring of theaters for sound began in earnest in 1928, it would be seven more years before "the smallest theater in the smallest hamlet in the country" was equipped to show sound films.[112] By then talkies rather than films with orchestral scores and musical performances alone had become the dominant form, and by then, sound-on-film rather than sound-on-disc had become the dominant process. In 1926 and 1927, roadshow premieres and long runs in exclusively equipped houses at premium prices were the norm, and were in accordance with Harry Warner's policies. According to Gomery, Warner

thought that Vitaphone should book its films in a selected number of the large cities in the United States. Each theatre need not be the largest, but should be big enough to attract attention, yet cheap enough so Vitaphone could *continuously* present a show before the public for at least one season. Then following that publicity, Vitaphone should gradually place shows in smaller, surrounding cities.[113]

In the interim, top ticket prices for the premiere of *Don Juan* and its prelude were $10 each, dropping to $3.30 for the first ten weeks, then to $2.20 thereafter. Warner Bros. initially planned to tour the program as a roadshow, but decided instead to pre-release it for extended runs at the Globe in Atlantic City, the McVickers in Chicago, and the Capitol in St. Louis. At this point, there were no theaters equipped to run sound in Los Angeles, so *Don Juan* opened as a silent at Grauman's Egyptian. The sound version finally premiered there at a top price of $5.50 in November 1926, the same month as it opened in Boston.[114]

Filmed at a cost of $546,000, an all-time high for Warners, *Don Juan* earned a box-office gross of $789,963 in its thirty-six-week New York run alone and went on to return $1,258,000 in domestic rentals and $1,693,000 in rentals worldwide, another Warners record.[115] Its immediate successors, *The Better 'Ole* (1926) and *When a Man Loves* (1927), also earned over $1 million apiece. *The Better 'Ole* opened at Moss's Colony Theatre in New York on October 7, *When a Man Loves* at the Selwyn in New York on February 4. Like *Don Juan*, *The Better 'Ole* and *When a Man Loves* included sound effects and musical scores. Only some of the short films in some of the preludes featured talking acts or presenters or included talking sequences. It was not until Warners produced *The Jazz Singer* (1927) that talking sequences were included in a feature-length film.

The Jazz Singer became Warners' biggest hit to date, grossing $1,974,000 domestically and $2,625,000 worldwide on a budget of $422,000 (slightly higher than the industry average at this time, but far from extravagant).[116] It broke house records at the Criterion in Los Angeles and ran

for five weeks each in Charlotte, Reading, Pennsylvania, Seattle, Washington, and Baltimore, Maryland. It also began to appear on return engagements. *The Jazz Singer* played the Fox Theatre in Philadelphia for two return weeks in mid-February, holding its own at Philadelphia's second largest theater. By mid-February, it was in its (record) eighth week in Columbus, Ohio, St. Louis and Detroit, and its (record) seventh week in Seattle, Portland, Oregon, and Los Angeles.[117]

WILL THRILL THE WORLD!

If you think the world has been thrilled before, wait until August 6th when—

WARNER BROS. will present the

VITAPHONE

AT THE WARNER THEATRE, NEW YORK, IN CONJUNCTION WITH THE

WORLD PREMIERE SHOWING OF
"DON JUAN"

STORY BY BESS MEREDYTH   **DIRECTED BY ALAN CROSLAND**

WITH THE WORLD'S GREATEST ACTOR

JOHN BARRYMORE

Featuring an Assemblage of World-Famous Artists
Unprecedented on Stage or Screen!

GIOVANNI MARTINELLI
the world-famous Metropolitan Opera tenor

EFREM ZIMBALIST
acclaimed the master violinist in both Europe and America

MISCHA ELMAN
known to every man, woman and child that loves music

HAROLD BAUER
the pianist numbered among the immortals of music

MARION TALLEY
the Metropolitan Operatic Sensation of the Year

ANNA CASE
the favorite of Europe's royalty and the American public

METROPOLITAN OPERA CHORUS
Singers heretofore appearing only with the Metropolitan Opera Company

HENRY HADLEY AND THE N. Y. PHILHARMONIC ORCHESTRA
Mr. Hadley, himself, conducting this unparalleled aggregation of 107 symphony artists

PRESENTED BY
WARNER BROS.
BY ARRANGEMENT WITH
THE WESTERN ELECTRIC COMPANY AND THE BELL TELEPHONE LABORATORIES

Opening Night ∿ **WARNER THEATRE** ∿ **$10 ADMISSION PLUS TAX** ∿ **August 6th**

Trade press advertisement for the premiere of *Don Juan* (1926) and Vitaphone shorts
(*Variety*, July 21, 1926, 13).

However, this was as nothing compared to the performance of *The Singing Fool* (1928), Al Jolson's next film for Warners. Although its advertising budget was set at $1 million and although it opened at the legitimate Winter Garden theater in New York, *The Singing Fool* was even cheaper to make at $388,000 than *The Jazz Singer*.[118] Nevertheless, it went on to gross a staggering $3,821,000 domestically and an even more staggering $5,916,000 worldwide, a box-office record for the early sound era that held until *Snow White and the Seven Dwarfs* (1937).[119] As Richard Barrios has pointed out, its domestic success was due at least in part to the fact that "a number of medium-sized American towns had just been wired for sound, and for many of them *The Singing Fool* was the premiere sound attraction, most likely the first talkie that many people saw."[120] Nevertheless, its thirty-one-week run on Broadway was not exceeded by another sound film until *Gone with the Wind* (1939).

As Douglas Gomery has emphasized, it was *The Singing Fool*, not *The Jazz Singer*, that convinced the two biggest companies in the film industry in the United States, Paramount Famous Lasky and Loew's/MGM, to convert to sound.[121] By then, though, there were other sound systems on the market aside from Vitaphone. Movietone and Photophone were available too. The choice made between them was to influence the structure of the industry for decades to come.

Movietone and Photophone

Movietone was a "variable density" sound-on-film system. It worked by converting patterns of vibration in the air into variations in electrical current that were recorded on film as variations in the density of silver salts in the film's emulsion. De Forest's Phonophone worked in a similar way. The essential difference between Phonophone and Movietone was the invention of a number of subsidiary sound recording and reproduction devices by Western Electric, and the involvement of Western Electric, AT&T, and Fox in its adoption, promotion, and use.

When Fox adopted Movietone it ranked higher than Warners but was still among the second tier of Hollywood companies. Like Warners, it was engaged in a program of expansion that encompassed the acquisition of theater chains and flagship Broadway theaters, and like Warners, it initially used its sound system to film and exhibit programs of shorts and to add recorded orchestral scores and sound effects to silent specials.[122] Among the latter were *What Price Glory?* and *Seventh Heaven*, both of which were accorded roadshow premiere runs at premium prices in New York when re-released with recorded scores and sound effects in 1927. *Sunrise*, the first Fox feature to premiere with a Movietone soundtrack, was given a roadshow run at the Times Square Theatre in New York later that year.

Fox was more cautious than Warners about producing all-sound or all-talking features. By the time it released *In Old Arizona*, its first all-talking feature, in January 1929, Loew's/MGM and Paramount had already chosen from a growing array of sound systems, started to produce their own all-talking features, and influenced the ways in which the industry and its representative bodies handled the final stages in the transition to sound. As early as 1926, Loew's and FPL were instrumental in setting up a committee with representatives from Universal, Producers Distributing Corporation, UA, and First National to consider the issue. The committee did not meet in earnest until February 1927, at which point it agreed to set up a subcommittee to investigate the available systems, to postpone making any decisions for a further year, and to insist on the importance of a single standard system. Among the systems available by then, aside from Vitaphone and Movietone, were an improved version of Movietone and a sound-on-film system called Photophone.

The improved version of Movietone was developed by Western Electric. It was a variable density system in which the light modulations produced by sound vibrations were recorded by means of a valve. Photophone was a "variable area" system. It worked by reflecting light onto a mirror, which vibrated in response to sounds and thus varied the patterns of light recorded on a strip of unexposed film. The Photophone system was devised by Charles Hoxie in 1921 and was further developed by RCA. It was an alternative to Vitaphone and Movietone. However, as a subsidiary of General Electric, RCA was a rival to Western Electric and AT&T. The subcommittee's recommendations would therefore have implications that were more than just technical. It eventually recommended the new Movietone system and on May 11, 1928, Loew's/MGM, UA, and Paramount Famous Lasky (as it had now become) signed an agreement with Western Electric's subsidiary, Electrical Research Products, Incorporated (ERPI), which would provide and install the technology. Most of the other major producers had signed by the end of the summer. But having been snubbed, RCA proceeded to establish RKO, its own vertically integrated film company. Combining the production and distribution facilities of the Film Booking Office with the nationwide Keith-Albee-Orpheum theater chain, RKO began to supply independent theater owners as well as its own theaters with Photophone equipment and to produce and release its own talking films under the trade name Radio Pictures. Its first films, *Syncopation* and *Street Girl,* were released in the spring of 1929. Subsequent releases included *Rio Rita* and *The Vagabond Lover* in 1929 and *The Cuckoos* in 1930, all three of which were box-office hits.[123]

RKO was now part of the new hierarchy that emerged with the coming of sound. Along with Paramount, Loew's/MGM, and Fox (later Twentieth Century-Fox), RKO and Warners were among the "Big Five" vertically integrated majors. Along with the "Little Three," Universal, UA, and Columbia, which largely confined themselves to production and distribution, they were to dominate the U.S. film industry and many of the markets for film around the world for the next twenty years. Among the practices that characterized this new industrial order were the renting of films to exhibitors at a percentage of the box-office gross and the weekly release of program productions on a run-zone-clearance basis. The roadshowing of sound films was initially restricted to movie theaters; theatrical venues were not at first equipped to exhibit sound films, and once the vertically integrated companies and affiliated and unaffiliated theaters alike had converted to sound, it made no sense to tour films to venues of this kind.[124] Legitimate theaters were used again once they had been fully equipped, but the number of theatrical roadshows declined.

Conditions in 1928 seemed propitious. Sound had not only proved a major attraction, it had also paved the way for new profit centers, synergies, and industrial and corporate alliances as well as new genres, new or modified aesthetic characteristics, and new talent, both on screen and off. The new talent included songwriters, musical performers, and musical directors such as Arthur Freed, Rodgers and Hart, Al Jolson, Jeanette MacDonald, Busby Berkeley, and Rouben Mamoulian. The new synergies and sources of profit included radio stations, record labels, music publishing houses, and the sale of songs on an unprecedented scale. The new genres included the musical.

Synergies and Musicals

Tie-ins and tie-ups with national newspapers, local stores, and other local businesses had been a feature of the industry since the 1910s, as had links with publishers like Grosset & Dunlap, who published novelizations and tie-in editions of source novels. As we have seen, synergies and links with the theater, with theater personnel, and with theatrical entrepreneurs had been a feature of the 1910s. They remained in force in the 1920s. Plays such as *What Price Glory?, Ben-Hur, Seventh Heaven,* and *The Bat* provided the basis for a number of big productions and box-office hits. Fox and FPL became involved in the financing of plays in order to secure adaptation rights, and there was a continual if fluctuating traffic of performers, actors, and writers to and from the theater.[125] With the coming of sound, this traffic increased. Most Vitaphone shorts were designed specifically to showcase performers and acts from vaudeville and the musical stage. The advent of part-talking and all-talking features placed a premium on theatrical source material, on plays such as *The Jazz Singer, The Singing Fool,* and *Abie's Irish Rose* (which was filmed in 1928) and on those with experience of delivering, writing, or directing dialogue for the stage.[126] It also placed a premium on musical numbers, performers, and writers and on those musical sources and forms in the theater susceptible to feature-length adaptation.

Synergies and adaptations already existed in these fields too. As Anthony Slide has pointed out: "Charles K. Harris's song 'The Virginian' was tied in to the 1914, and first, screen adaptation of the Owen Wister novel."[127] A song called "Mickey," which was commissioned for Mack Sennett's 1918 film of the same name, was the first "musical tie-up" to be recorded and sold on phonograph discs.[128] Soon, "music publishers began routinely linking their songs directly to a motion picture," and film companies continued to commission songs for special productions.[129] Among them were "Covered Wagon Days" for *The Covered Wagon,* "Your Love Is All" for *Old Ironsides,* "Charmaine" for *What Price Glory?* and "Diane" for *Seventh Heaven.* "Charmaine" and "Diane" sold over a million copies each in sheet-music form.[130]

With the coming of sound, the use of songs increased. Following an initial deal between Warners and ASCAP (the American Society of Composers, Authors, and Publishers) in 1926, ERPI negotiated an industry-wide royalty system on behalf of the MPPDA in 1928. In the meantime, Al Jolson's recording of "Sonny Boy" for *The Singing Fool* sold 370,000 copies on disc within the first three months of the film's release. Over a million discs and sheet-music copies were sold overall.[131] In need of a regular supply of music and the profits available from music sales, Loew's acquired a stake in the Robbins Music Corporation, Warners bought M. Witmark & Sons and went on to acquire the Max Dreyfus music holdings, and Paramount set up its own music division, commissioning songs from independent songwriters such as Irving Berlin.[132] All the while, the growing links between the film and radio industries were evident in the establishment of radio stations by Warners, by the substantial interests in radio held by RCA and AT&T, by the radio adaptations of MGM's films, and by the trade in stock between Paramount Famous Lasky and William Paley in 1929.[133] Paley owned the newly formed Columbia Broadcasting System (CBS). The stock trade gave Paramount a 50 percent stake in CBS, and CBS a "Hollywood connection."[134]

Earlier that year, *Variety* noted the imminent arrival of eighteen "musical talkers."[135] A major cycle of musical films was underway. By the end of the year, "it was the rare movie that was *not* a musical in some sense of the term."[136] Although the generic boundaries of musical talkers were "very fluid," the shapes and forms of musical comedy, musical drama, revue, and operetta were usually discernible nevertheless.[137] Drawing on European as well as U.S. traditions, these forms had been developed on the musical stage and above all on Broadway. Broadway, its culture, and, indeed, some of its musicals had already acted as a setting or as source material for a number of silent films in the late 1920s, among them *New York* (1927), *Broadway Nights* (1927), and *Show Boat* (1929) (which was initially shot silent and subsequently released in a silent version as well as in a version with two talking and singing sequences). A number of early sound films involved Broadway settings and were set in and around the world of musical theater too. Among them were *The Jazz Singer, The Singing Fool, Lights of New York* (1928), and *The Broadway Melody.*

The Broadway Melody premiered at Grauman's Chinese on February 1, 1929 and opened at the Astor in New York the following week. These and other premiere runs were roadshow engagements, with two or three showings a day at a top price of two dollars per seat. A novelization was written by Jack Lait and published by Grosset & Dunlap, and recorded and sheet-music copies of the songs were sold in lobbies by uniformed pages.[138] An advertisement in *Variety* called it "the most amazing and productive tie-up in show history."[139] Although it cost only $379,000 to make ($8,000 less than *The Singing Fool*), *The Broadway Melody* earned $2,808,000 in the United States (where it played for long runs in over sixty cities), and $1,558,000 overseas (where it was the first sound film to employ superimposed titles to explain the action and translate key lines).[140]

Richard Barrios has provided the most detailed account of the film's production.[141] MGM began planning the film in August 1928. Production head Irving G. Thalberg met with director Harry Beaumont and writers Edmund Goulding and Sarah Y. Mason to discuss the possibility of a part-talking musical. By September, they had an outline for a backstage musical about a vaudeville sister act, Hank and Queenie Mahoney, who go to New York hoping to land parts in Francis Zanfield's latest revue with the help of Hank's fiancé, songwriter-singer-dancer Eddie Kerns. Queenie becomes a star and Hank becomes disenchanted. When she discovers that Eddie and Queenie have fallen in love, Hank quits the show and sets up a new small-time double act with the help of Jed, her agent and uncle. At this point, Thalberg decided to make the film all-talking. Norman Houston and James Gleason were hired to provide the script with "greater urban wallop";[142] Arthur Freed and Nacio Herb Brown were hired to write songs tailored to the story. (Among them were "You Were Meant for Me," "The Wedding of the Painted Doll," and the film's theme song, "The Broadway Melody.") Bessie Love was cast as Hank, Anita Page as Queenie, and Charles King as Eddie. Shooting began in mid-October. A mobile camera booth was used in some of the scenes and "The Wedding of the Painted Doll" was filmed in two-color Technicolor. Most of the songs were filmed "live," with musicians playing off screen on set. But this particular number was retaken with the actors performing to the music recorded in a previous take, an early instance of what soon became known as "playback."

This was by no means the only innovative use made of music and sound. As Donald Crafton point outs, some of the numbers in *The Broadway Melody* are "overheard" by the spectator, "as when the arranger . . . spontaneously tries out some impromptu ideas on the piano" in the opening scene of the film, and Uncle Jed's stutter is an example of "vocal foregrounding."[143] There is more, though, to the use of sound in *The Broadway Melody* than that. The foregrounding of sound in the film is as much a product of the permutation of an array of acoustic effects, techniques, and possibilities as it is of local moments or individualized traits of speech. This is made apparent in the opening sequence, in which the spectator not only overhears the arranger but is also initially presented with a cacophony of sounds and snatches of music as the editing moves from one soundproof room to another in a Tin Pan Alley publishing house while an array of performers try out or pitch a series of songs.[144] A set of permutations in themselves, these snatches of musical performance lead into "The Broadway Melody," fragments of which are heard being played by the arranger as the camera cuts from room to room. Call for quiet having been made, "The Broadway Melody" is finally fully showcased when other musicians come into the room to accompany Eddie, who sings the song in a single take.

Further effects and permutations follow. In the next scene, Hank and Queenie are shown to their room by a hotel bellboy. The dishes and plates stowed in Hank's suitcase crash to the floor. Later on, Hank and Queenie are in the bathroom. Hank is washing clothes in the sink and Queenie is running a bath. Their conversation is initially barely audible over the sounds of running water. Uncle Jed arrives with his

Hank (Bessie Love) seen and heard sobbing in *The Broadway Melody* (1929).

stutter. Later still, Eddie arrives and sings "The Broadway Melody" again, this time to Queenie and Hank. They are all initially framed together, but as the singing proceeds Queenie and Hank are shown reacting in separate close-ups, a foreshadowing of the extent to which involvement with Eddie eventually splits up their act. This involvement culminates in the film's climactic scene, in which Hank pretends to Eddie that she has never loved him and tells him that he is free to rescue Queenie from her involvement with a millionaire playboy. Hank's motivation is laid out visually once Eddie has left. As she sits removing her makeup, she is shown looking at two photographs, one of Eddie, the other of Queenie, the two people she cares about most. However, the most extraordinary aspect of this scene is aural. Once she has seen Eddie leave and uttered a few almost indecipherable words through her howls of anguish, she cries and sobs for more than a minute. Her sobbing is intermittent as she struggles for self-control. It eventually abates as she decides to call Jed on the telephone. Until then, though, not another voice, not another sound, not another line of dialogue is heard. When she hangs up, the screen fades to black. As it does so one final sob can be heard. According to Barrios, there were "many reports of teary spectators bursting into applause at that same moment."[145] If so, it would not be surprising.

Tuners, Spectacles, and Prestige Pictures, 1929–1939

Following two decades of near-continuous growth for the American film industry, the 1930s marked a period of instability and a sharp downturn in profits. Economic and political problems, both within and outside the United States, left Hollywood continually needing to readjust its market strategies. Such problems made a particularly marked impact on the industry's premium products. Exceptionally expensive pictures were more than usually vulnerable to the various depressions, recessions, shocks, and crises experienced by Hollywood and by the nation at large. The two production categories most associated with large budgets were musicals and historical or costume pictures. Every major studio had its cycles of both types, waxing and waning with successive shifts in public taste over the decade and with fluctuating economic conditions.[1]

The 1929–30 season marked a peak in theater attendance and corporate revenues. For the next decade and more the film industry would look back on it as a benchmark in prosperity, with $720 million in box-office receipts earned in 1929 and $730 million in 1930, and an average 80 million movie tickets sold each week. However, the next few years would see most of the studios attempting to stave off heavy losses as the Depression took hold. Total U.S. box-office receipts fell to $482 million in 1933, and attendances to an average 50 million per week in both 1933 and 1934.[2] Business did not return to near-normal conditions until 1935, and by then several companies had suffered bankruptcy, receivership, and reorganization. Of the majors, only MGM-Loew's and Columbia survived the Depression without incurring a corporate loss or a change of management.

As early as the summer of 1930, the studios were already aware of the need to make sweeping cuts in production expenditure as the country entered a period of economic crisis.[3] Surveying the following year's production trends, *Variety* noted that with few exceptions "no efforts were made during the year toward the extra super type, but with every studio endeavoring to make pictures which at the outset wouldn't run above $300,000."[4] From 1931 to 1934, only around a dozen pictures from all companies combined cost more than $1 million. Although several of these films were also among the period's highest grossers, the contraction of the market meant that most of them still made a loss, or else scraped only a marginal profit through their success overseas. Among the highest spenders was Paramount. For the first half of 1932, Paramount's release schedule was expected to make an aggregate loss of $2,560,000; by the end of the year the company was reported to have lost a total of $21 million, much of it through the Publix theater chain.[5] The following year, Paramount-Publix filed for bankruptcy.

By the summer of 1935, as the national economy gradually emerged from the Great Depression, the industry was returning to near-normal conditions, with a significant increase in domestic revenues to support the many big pictures then in circulation. Around forty films in 1936–37 were predicted to earn a domestic gross of $1 million or more, the highest average return since 1929–30; a similar number had also cost the same amount or more to make, with several exceeding a $2 million budget. The costs of materials and labor rose dramatically in these years; a film that would have cost $1 million to produce in 1936 was estimated to cost $1,317,669 in 1937. Moreover, the box-office boom was temporary; it was due to increased admission prices rather than increased attendances, while competition from radio and sports increasingly cut into the movie business.[6] Few of the high-cost releases of the 1936–37 and 1937–38 seasons were major hits. Too many big pictures were pitted against one another, and fans could not see all of them. It was also thought that audiences had come to expect higher standards and were now "shopping" for their entertainment— a common complaint in times of recession.[7] A number of these films had also gone adrift by reviving the most costly and the most risky distribution method, which had largely fallen into disuse since its heyday in the 1920s: the roadshow.

Roadshowing in the 1930s

In their selling campaigns for the upcoming 1930–31 season, Warner Bros. and its recently acquired subsidiary First National each announced a release schedule of thirty-five films. Fifteen of each of their respective slates were classed as roadshows, the other twenty as specials. All would be in Vitaphone, some in two-color Technicolor, and they would feature stage as well as screen stars.[8] Yet, though several of these films played in Broadway theaters in twice-daily, reserved-seat runs at two-dollar-top admission prices, none was taken on the road by a specially mounted company. The meaning of "roadshow" had changed, and with it industry distribution practices.

In 1929 and 1930 combined, exactly one hundred pictures were given roadshow status in Broadway premiere engagements, more than at any other time before or since. As many as thirteen "two-dollar" films (actual ticket prices ranged from $1.65 to $2.20, including tax) could be found playing at one time around Times Square.[9] Most such runs lasted little more than a month, many only a week or two, but a few were spectacularly successful: MGM's *The Broadway Melody* ran at the Astor for twenty-six weeks, as did *The Hollywood Revue of 1929* for eighteen; Warner Bros.' *Disraeli* (1929) played for a total of twenty-six weeks in a premiere run split between the Warner and the Central. In 1930, comparably long runs were achieved by MGM's *The Big House* and *The Rogue Song,* and, in two adjacent theaters concurrently, by Howard Hughes's $3.2 million flying epic *Hell's Angels,* the most costly production since *Ben-Hur.*

Yet across the country, roadshowing as a *distribution* practice had virtually ceased. Barely a dozen of the hundred Broadway "roadshows" were exhibited in a similar fashion in more than one or two other key cities (usually Los Angeles). Even these were decidedly limited. Some were put rapidly into release following a handful of "hard-ticket" (reserved-seat) dates, with plans for subsequent roadshow engagements dropped. Tiffany's *Journey's End,* for example, had only five such runs before its sooner-than-planned general release. Other films intended for roadshowing, such as Paramount's *The Vagabond King,* played instead in grind (continuous-performance) runs with specially raised prices.[10]

The virtual abandonment of roadshow distribution by the industry from the early 1930s is often attributed to the effects of the Depression. As *Variety* remarked in its review of Samuel Goldwyn's *The Kid from Spain* (1932), "a $2 picture these days must also be considered in direct ratio to the proposition as to how many people have $2."[11] Yet though the Wall Street Crash occurred in October 1929, its full economic effects would not be felt by the industry for some time to come. Even in the worst years of the Depression, from 1931 to 1933, around a dozen two-dollar pictures annually were still exhibited on Broadway; their number actually decreased from 1934 onward, as the economy recovered. The reasons for the decline of roadshowing lie elsewhere.

The arrival of sound changed many aspects of the film business, distribution practices among them. In the silent era, collecting exhibitor rentals in the form of a percentage of the box-office take was relatively rare compared with the charging of flat hire fees. As we have previously noted, usually only roadshow engagements were booked on "sharing terms," with the proceeds from ticket sales split between the producer or distributor and the theater. The uncertainties of the fledgling sound market changed that, as distributors were willing to take a chance on the public responding favorably to the new medium, and many exhibitors gladly paid a cut of the gross in preference to a hefty rental charge up front. Although the "percentage system" was far from universal thereafter, it was regularly applied to the industry's more important pictures, thus removing one of the special advantages of roadshowing as a form of leverage against exhibitors.[12]

A second consequence of sound was the leveling out of movie presentation at all levels of exhibition. Among the distinguishing features of roadshow engagements had been a specially composed or compiled score played by a sizeable live orchestra. The larger the road company and the more lavish the theater, the better would be the musical accompaniment. But a prerecorded soundtrack sounded much the same in any class of house.[13] While audiences willingly paid $2 (and sometimes more) for early sound films when the medium was still a novelty and wired houses were in a minority, the more widely the technology spread—and it spread very quickly—the more it became taken for granted as a new norm. The coming of sound also made possible a new avenue of exploitation: radio. The ease of promoting a talking or musical picture through the leading mass-communication medium meant that film advertising could travel more widely, more rapidly, than ever before. In order to take full advantage of such an opportunity, speedier distribution was necessary. Roadshowing, being reliant on a small number of companies traveling a planned route one community at a time, was an inherently slow method of distribution.

Warner Bros., which particularly embraced the rapid-release strategy, trade-advertised its social problem drama, *I Am a Fugitive from a Chain Gang* (1932), as being released "in 200 road show runs at popular prices—day and date with Broadway!"[14] Warners had opened more two-dollar films on Broadway in 1929 and 1930 than any other company (forty-two), but *Chain Gang* was not a roadshow. Paramount's western remake of *The Spoilers* (1930) and Universal's *Back Street* (1932) were both advertised as roadshows, but they were not roadshown either. These advertisements are examples of the term *roadshow* being used to denote a mere special attraction, rather than a specific distribution strategy. The few 1930s films that *were* selected for a roadshow pre-release were often among the most expensive productions. To stand a chance of making a profit they needed the additional revenues possible with raised prices and extended runs. However, cost was not the only or even the most important factor in determining which films were roadshown. Roadshowing was essentially a promotional strategy, designed to advertise pictures to the public and to the trade, but it was also a mark of prestige. Prestige was provided on the one hand by production values and the sheen of "quality" that generally went with a large budget, but on the other hand by the cultural values of the subject matter, the source material, and in some cases the creative personnel involved.

Association with the legitimate stage remained (and in many ways remains) a mark of prestige. Among the "legit" stars who made a successful transition to the screen was the British-born actor George Arliss. Arliss made a number of screen adaptations of his Broadway hits in the silent period, including *Disraeli* (1921). In the early sound era he appeared in a series of films at Warner Bros., most notably a second version of *Disraeli*. Produced in 1929 for a modest $318,000, the remake enjoyed longer reserved-seat runs in New York and Los Angeles than any of the studio's films in the following decade and won Arliss an Academy Award as Best Actor. Other films given limited roadshow exhibition primarily because of their artistic qualities or upmarket appeal included Samuel Goldwyn's *Arrowsmith* (1931), Paramount's *An American Tragedy* (1931), and MGM's *Strange Interlude* (1932).

The most extensively roadshown film of the first half of the decade was MGM's *Grand Hotel* (1932), which offered no fewer than five stars in leading roles. Irving Thalberg explained the unorthodox casting: "Since it has been our experience as exhibitors, as well as producer-distributors, that only the unusual pictures are doing business, we want to help the exhibition end by fortifying each picture with star power."[15] *Grand Hotel* received as many as 721 twice-daily, reserved-seat runs at $1 top, playing even regular picture houses and small towns on this basis. Produced for $700,000, the film reportedly earned back its negative cost from the roadshow engagements alone.[16] MGM planned similar star casting and booking patterns for *Dinner at Eight* (1933), playing it first in legitimate theaters, then in picture houses on the same roadshow basis. Veteran roadshow manager J. J. McCarthy disapproved. He reasoned that while patrons would readily pay up to $2 at a legitimate house, where it represented a lower tariff than would normally be charged for a stage show, raised prices in regular movie theaters presented a psychological barrier: why should moviegoers pay more for some pictures than for others?[17]

On the heels of *Grand Hotel* and *Dinner at Eight,* several other big pictures were tried as roadshows in the 1932–33 season, including MGM's *Rasputin and the Empress,* Paramount's *The Sign of the Cross* and *A Farewell to Arms,* and Goldwyn's *The Kid from Spain.* All failed, and plans for further roadshow bookings outside of New York, Los Angeles, and a few other big cities were canceled in favor of regular release. On this basis, *The Sign of the Cross* and *The Kid from Spain* proved extremely successful, suggesting that it was the exhibition policy, rather than the product, that had kept patrons away.[18]

Despite having announced in 1930 that "it would never high-top on Broadway again," Fox set up a special exploitation department to roadshow up to five pictures in 1933–34.[19] Although *Berkeley Square, Pilgrimage, The Power and the Glory* (all 1933), and *The World Moves On* (1934) received limited hard-ticket exposure, only *Cavalcade* (1933) was widely roadshown, playing fifty-three such engagements, mostly in legitimate theaters at $1 top. *Cavalcade* was an exception to the usual pattern of failure with roadshows at this time. But even so it incurred the wrath of both exhibitors and the public when shown at normal prices in cities like Minneapolis and San Francisco only a month after its reserved-seat engagements. Such sharp practices soured the field for future roadshows, as many exhibitors, having been stung once, would refuse to book other films for twice-daily runs.[20]

Twentieth Century's adaptation of Victor Hugo's *Les Misérables* (1935, released by United Artists prior to the production company's merger with Fox the same year) was tested for advanced-price engagements in Pittsburgh, Indianapolis, and Columbus. It then played on a modified roadshow basis at the Geary, San Francisco, at $1.10 top, without reserved seats, and with three separate performances daily on weekdays and continuous performances on weekends. After five days under this policy it was switched to more traditional twice-daily shows with all seats reserved, but closed after only two weeks. The irregular exhibition pattern confused patrons, who simply waited for the film to arrive in cinemas on normal terms at lower prices.[21] When a further group of pictures was set to be roadshown in 1935–36, exhibitors resisted. Chicago-based theater chain Balaban and Katz (B&K) tried to persuade Paramount not to

RIGHT!
Typical
ad used in
New York

TODAY YOU'LL SEE STARS at

THE *Great* **ZIEGFELD**

M-G-M's Film Sensation starring
William Powell, Myrna Loy, Luise Rainer

BELOW ARE JUST A FEW OF MANY WHO HAVE ENJOYED IT:

★ BEATRICE LILLIE: "I'm mad about it."
★ LOU HOLTZ: "Greatest I've ever seen on stage or screen."
★ WALTER WINCHELL: "A cinemasterpiece."
★ ED WYNN: "Never saw anything to equal it."
★ RUTH ETTING: "Thrilled with its humanity, beauty, humor."
★ EDDIE CANTOR: "It has everything."
★ MILTON BERLE: "Ziegfeld would be proud."
★ GEORGE WHITE: "Fascinating tribute to the master showman."
★ ED SULLIVAN: "A new all-time high in production."
★ MARK HELLINGER: "Superb film entertainment!"

EVERY DAY IS CELEBRITY DAY
at the
ASTOR
Broadway at 45th St.

The Only New York showing this season!
Daily 2:40 — 8:40. Sunday 3:00—8:40. Matinees,
55c to $1.10. Evenings, 55c to $2.20. Saturday
Matinees & Saturday Midnite Show, 55c to $1.65.
MIDNIGHT SHOW EVERY SATURDAY

Metro-Goldwyn-Mayer
BRINGS BACK
THE ROAD-SHOW!

4th S.R.O. WEEK AT ASTOR, N. Y., AT $2 TOP AND BIG EVERYWHERE AT ROAD-SHOW PRICES, TWICE DAILY!

3rd Week Buffalo	1st Week Indianapolis
4th Week Detroit	1st Week Memphis
3rd Week St. Louis	Starts May 7th Cincinnati
3rd Week San Francisco	Starts May 9th Denver
4th Week Philadelphia	Starts May 17th Milwaukee
4th Week Boston	Starts May 8th Atlanta
4th Week Chicago	Starts May 8th Houston
3rd Week Los Angeles	Starts May 8th New Haven
2nd Week Washington	Starts May 8th Hartford
2nd Week Montreal	Starts May 8th Worcester
1st Week Cleveland	Starts May 15th Bridgeport
1st Week Pittsburgh	Starts May 7th Springfield
	Starts May 8th Albany

**Watch for
further dates
of "THE GREAT
ZIEGFELD"—
The Talk of
America!**

JUST CONCLUDED BRILLIANT ENGAGEMENTS:
Toronto, Miami, Miami Beach, Palm Beach, Jacksonville,
Daytona, Tampa, St. Petersburg, Orlando.

MGM's domination of the roadshow field in the 1930s is trumpeted by this trade press
advertisement for *The Great Ziegfeld* (1936) (*Variety*, April 29, 1936, 24).

roadshow Cecil B. DeMille's *The Crusades* (1935). When it was shown at $1 top in B&K's Roosevelt Theater in Chicago, the raised price kept patrons away and the film ran for only two weeks to "meager business." Following a few other roadshow engagements the picture was generally released to better results.[22]

MGM, which from 1930–39 presented thirty $2 films on Broadway (more than any other studio throughout the decade), pointedly decided against roadshowing its costly Clark Gable vehicles *Mutiny on the Bounty* (1935) and *San Francisco* (1936), in order to satisfy exhibitors who had bought them as part of blocks.[23] Both were among the decade's biggest hits, suggesting that roadshow exhibition was not necessary to produce outstanding results. However, with its three-hour musical *The Great Ziegfeld* (1936) the company was taking no chances. This was the first Hollywood production since 1930 to cost more than $2 million and the first film to be shown at what had been Los Angeles's premier roadshow house, the Carthay Circle, for four years; it ran there for fifteen weeks. Some 350 more roadshow bookings followed and, as with *Grand Hotel* before it, the film started a brief trend.[24] Twelve pictures opening on a reserved-seat basis in 1937, including a further three from MGM, constituted "the largest number of roadshow pictures since 1929–30,"[25] but they achieved very mixed results.

Of MGM's trio, *Captains Courageous* and *The Firefly* were profitable (the latter by a slim margin), but *The Good Earth,* costing $2,816,000 and earning $3,557,000 worldwide, made a loss of nearly $500,000. *The Life of Emile Zola* cost Warners $829,000 and returned $2,021,000 in rentals. It went on to win the Academy Award for the year's best picture, thus producing both profit and prestige. After the New York and Los Angeles runs of *Souls at Sea* lost money and *High, Wide and Handsome* achieved the "lowest grosses in the history" of the Carthay Circle, Paramount canceled all future roadshow plans.[26] Frank Capra's *Lost Horizon* was popular with audiences, but it had cost too much ($2,026,337) for a small company like Columbia to recover easily. It was more successful in general distribution than as a roadshow; five hundred prints were struck for this purpose, a large number by 1930s standards.[27]

A year later, MGM planned to roadshow *Marie Antoinette,* its longest picture after *The Great Ziegfeld* and its most expensive costume spectacle since *Ben-Hur.* Disappointing early engagements led the studio to change its mind. Although its $2,956,000 in worldwide rentals placed *Marie Antoinette* among MGM's top ten grossers of the decade, these receipts were almost exactly matched by production costs of $2,926,000, resulting in a net loss of $767,000. With this failure and that of *The Great Waltz* (1938), another expensive period piece, MGM decided against future roadshowing along with the rest of the industry.

Double Features and Day-and-Date Releases

Variety reviewers' most frequent pronouncement on roadshow pictures throughout the 1920s and 1930s was to suggest how much they would be improved after "trimming" or "pruning" for the "regular houses." Their length did have one advantage, however, in that they provided an alternative to double billing. The policy of offering two feature-length films on one program for the same price as a single feature had origi-nated in Boston in 1919 in a bid by independent theaters to fight competition from large chains. From New England the two-picture policy gradually spread to the rest of the country, becoming particularly common in the Midwest and on the West Coast, especially in Los Angeles. It was exacerbated when the major chains themselves began using double bills. In 1930, only 10 percent of theaters nationwide regularly played double features. By 1935, 75 percent of U.S. theaters were offering them for at least part of the week, and 40 percent were using them exclusively. The spread of double features lengthened the average theater program from a typical two hours in the silent period to three or even four hours by the end of the 1930s, as the average running time of films also gradually increased.[28]

The proliferation of "duals" was caused by various factors: the tendency of studios to make many pictures that were not big enough attractions to be played as single features; block booking, which obliged exhibitors to take weak as well as strong films; competition among rival exhibition chains or, in the case of "closed" towns (those in which one company controlled all the major theaters), from those in neighboring communities; and as a value-for-money incentive for patrons, especially during the Depression.[29] The problems caused by "dualing" affected the majors' production and distribution divisions, as well as exhibitors. The necessity of making more pictures to meet the demand for double-feature programs was a threat to quality, as less produc-tion money would be available for each one. Playing two features for the price of one also had the effect of undercutting rentals, threatening to reduce distribution returns for each film by half. This in turn would lead to the lowering of production values, as expensive features effectively playing at half-price admissions could not be profitable.[30]

In the early 1930s, any two films were liable to be arbitrarily coupled together, regardless of their production costs. Their status on the bill was determined only by the exhibitor's estimation of their relative appeal. One solution to this situation was for the studios themselves to designate films as having "A" or "B" status in advance of production, and to budget and sell them according to this predetermined box-office value. By 1935 distributors were making a clear distinction between "A-pictures" (those expected to head the bill), which had top-level budgets and would command a proportionately higher rental, and "B-pictures," anticipated as lesser attractions, which would be made more cheaply and be sold to exhibitors at lower rental rates. The most important A-films would invariably be sold on percentage terms: the more a film had cost to produce, or the more it was expected to earn, the higher the proportion of the box-office take demanded by the distributor. Percentages typically ranged between 25 percent and 40 percent. B-films, by contrast, were usually booked for flat fees.[31]

Of course, in practice exhibitors could still choose to advertise one picture over another; if a designated B-film seemed to hold particular appeal for their regular cus-tomers it could be elevated to A status. One way of insuring against the reduction of

A-features to B or "programmer" status was to stipulate in exhibition contracts that a film could be played in first run on single-feature programs only. RKO adopted this strategy with *Top Hat* (1935). The box-office value of a first-class single-feature attraction was demonstrated when it became the most successful of all the Fred Astaire and Ginger Rogers musicals and one of the year's biggest hits. Such films as *Broadway Melody of 1936* (released in 1935), *Anthony Adverse* (1936), and *In Old Chicago* (1937) were also set exclusively for single-feature exhibition.[32] However, only particularly strong commercial attractions ("super-A" pictures) could be sold in this way. There were too few of these for theaters to abandon duals completely. According to *Variety*, exhibitors wanted "AA pictures, and they backed up their position by pledging longer runs and higher rentals for class product, built from good stories, well directed, and played by personalities known to the theatregoing public."[33]

Extended runs were crucial to the profitability of costly productions. The rapid turnover of most theater programs, especially in "nabes" (neighborhood theaters), which relied on regular weekly, twice-weekly, or even thrice-weekly changes, left a large proportion of potential box-office revenue untapped. Runs were over so quickly that many prospective patrons did not have a chance to see a program before it was replaced. When the Fabian theater circuit pulled Twentieth Century-Fox's pioneer western *Drums along the Mohawk* (1939) from one of its first-run houses after only six days, despite its doing good business, studio production chief Darryl F. Zanuck wrote circuit head S. H. ("Si") Fabian an open letter of complaint. He pointed out the need to gain maximum revenue for big-budget productions and argued that curtailing a successful run was in no-one's best interests.[34] *Variety* spelled out the implications of Zanuck's letter:

Thus does Zanuck kick into the open the entire producer-exhibitor relationship which, in various terms, has kept the film industry in a dither lo, these many years. He builds up a strong case for the unusual, popular picture—the type of merchandise which merits special handling, not only in length of engagement, but in exploitation and advertising. . . . In all frankness, Zanuck's quarrel is not with any single exhibitor. His squawk is really against the prevailing system of film showmanship, which puts a premium on quantity production, block selling and routine double-billing of all pictures, good, bad and indifferent. Once tossed into the hopper of the distribution and exhibition machinery, the individual picture, with rare exceptions, leaves all hope behind. . . . Only occasionally does the system unbend itself for the unusual and outstanding film.[35]

The standardization of exhibition against which Zanuck was reacting was partly attributable to theaters' reliance on two-for-the-price-of-one to pull in regular, habitual patrons. But standardization was also an inevitable consequence of the system of mass production and block booking in which a studio's entire annual output (features, shorts, newsreels, and all) was sold by distributors in a single deal. This in itself seemed to discourage special efforts on the part of showmen, for whom each picture, with rare exceptions, was little more than a unit of the block package.[36]

Exhibitors, however, argued that extended playing time for one picture meant reduced playing time for others. The increased number of major studios (thanks to the rise of Monogram, Republic, and Grand National, the leading "Poverty Row" companies), the increased importance of Columbia, and the increased output of United Artists had all helped to overstock the market by the end of the 1930s.[37] Moreover, such practices as "holdovers" (retaining a film for longer than the original booking) and "moveovers" (continuing a film's run at another theater without any clearance or a reduction in prices) cut into the business of subsequent-run exhibitors, who complained that they delayed their own access to pictures and threatened to "milk" their box-office potential at the first-run stage. Fox's *Alexander's Ragtime Band* (1938), which had a record long run of five weeks at the Roxy on Broadway, performed much less well in the New York nabes than expected because it had been drained by the extended pre-release engagement.[38]

Some of the majors experimented with alternative patterns of distribution. This included the spread of regional and national "day-and-date" bookings: multiple simultaneous engagements covering a particular territory or community or in key cities nationwide. RKO released both *Check and Double Check* (1930), starring the blackface radio comedians Amos 'n' Andy, and the epic western *Cimarron* (1931) in some three hundred theaters, while Warner Bros.' *Captain Blood* (1935) opened in 483 first-run engagements over the Christmas holiday.[39] The danger of playing a film day-and-date in a large number of houses in one area was that the potential audience would be split among too many venues. Columbia's *Only Angels Have Wings* (1939) was booked into thirteen neighborhood theaters simultaneously in Minneapolis and none did well.[40]

Certain pictures particularly lent themselves to early release outside the sophisticated metropolitan centers. United Artists distributed David O. Selznick's *The Adventures of Tom Sawyer* (1938) in "secondary" areas such as small towns before the key cities, to exploit its grassroots appeal.[41] MGM released one of the Hardy Family series, *Out West with the Hardys* (1938), to nabes in the Greater New York area (which already had the shortest clearances in the country) without any clearance between first and second runs. The studio's declared goal was to determine in "just how short a time it can rake in top money from a speedy distribution of the film."[42]

Increased speed of distribution also, of course, increased the speed of rental returns to the studios, allowing them to amortize costs more quickly. The rise of day-and-date bookings increased the number of prints manufactured for each title—typically to between 180 and 300 for the domestic market in the mid-1930s, compared to between 125 and 175 in the silent period, but rising to 400 or more for the most popular attractions. This, along with double bills, helped raise print and distribution costs appreciably. Print shortages for a major hit put a severe strain on the busiest regional exchanges, such as New York and Chicago, which often resorted to borrowing prints from neighboring territories to keep day-and-date bookings fully supplied.[43]

In some instances, studios would "write down" the value of their own product in the face of disappointing results. One pointed example came in March 1940 with the coupling in New York of two big-budget A-films: RKO's *Abe Lincoln in Illinois* and Fox's *The Blue Bird* (both 1940). Both had played only two and three weeks, respectively, on their opening Broadway engagements in January. To improve their chances in general release, they were shown on the same bill in two RKO theaters (the Palace on Broadway and the Albee in Brooklyn) at a top admission price of only 50 cents. *Variety* estimated the investment in both films combined at around $3 million, thus posing "the mathematical problem of giving out dollars, taking in pennies, and then trying to wind up with a profit."[44]

Epics, Classics, and Foreign Adventures

After the last "silent" epic, *Noah's Ark* (1928)—which had in fact been released with a Vitaphone music and effects track and talking sequences—the technical difficulties of early sound recording and the costs of sets, costumes, and other production materials had generally kept large-scale historical films off the screen until 1932. Cecil B. DeMille's *The Sign of the Cross,* based on a stage play fashioned after *Quo Vadis?,* was "billed as the first talking picture spectacle." The director explained its appeal to *Variety:*

"You're always told," says Mr. De Mille, "that the people don't want ideas, that they shy away from period pictures, that they don't want costume stories, that they don't want films with a religious theme. Yet every smash picture, every picture that's grossed three millions has been made up of just those elements they tell you the people don't want."[45]

However, even DeMille—once described as "a super-salesman of entertainment," whose name was "a synonym for bigness"—had to submit to tight budgetary controls. Paramount reportedly insisted that the director pay all production costs over $600,000 himself.[46] Robert Birchard, citing DeMille's own records, states that the final negative cost was $694,065. This was achieved only through careful production planning and the use of special effects such as mattes, miniatures, and partially built sets.[47] The film climaxes with a lengthy arena sequence of unprecedented brutality, which was substantially reedited for later reissues. The variety of atrocities (massed gladiatorial combats, beheadings and impalings, women sacrificed to animals with strong suggestions of erotic bestiality) is, however, juxtaposed with an equal amount of footage showing the on-screen spectators, variously reacting to the slaughter with horror and excitement, boredom and amusement. Considerable time is spent showing the audience entering the circus and behaving in a manner typical of visitors to a theater (such as a couple complaining about their seats being too distant from the action). In emphasizing not only the Roman circus as a site of spectacular entertainment but also the act of communal spectatorship, the film contains, as Maria Wyke notes, "a self-conscious demonstration of cinema's virtuosity in the creation of spectacle,"[48] as well as an awareness of its own implication in the barbaric rituals.

Spectacle and spectators: the arena audience in *The Sign of the Cross* (1932).

DeMille's planned follow-up, *The End of the World*, due to be made for an unusually low $400,000, was canceled;[49] but with *Cleopatra* (1934) and *The Crusades* DeMille again revisited the epic. *Cleopatra* was made for under $900,000 and earned twice its production cost in rentals; but *The Crusades* went considerably over its original budget of $1,137,149 and lost $443,967 over two theatrical runs.[50] After these two films, DeMille turned to nineteenth-century American history with *The Plainsman* (1936), *The Buccaneer* (1938), *Union Pacific* (1939), *North West Mounted Police* (1940), and *Reap the Wild Wind* (1942), which proved more consistently profitable.

Following the disappointing commercial performance of both *The Crusades* and RKO's remake of *The Last Days of Pompeii* (1935), the ancient world epic was effectively put on hold until the 1950s. However, other generic cycles had already come to take its place. The producers of *Pompeii*, Merian C. Cooper and Ernest B. Schoedsack, also made the elaborate fantasies *King Kong*, *The Son of Kong* (both 1933), and *She* (1935) for RKO. These films showcased a number of innovations in the field of special photographic effects, such as stop-motion animation, process photography (back projection), and traveling mattes, as well as sound effects, which the industry continued to refine throughout the decade.

As Cynthia Erb has argued, *King Kong* was most likely seen by its original audiences less as a horror film than as an exotic adventure, in the vein of *The Lost World* (1925), *Trader Horn* (1931), and *Tarzan the Ape Man* (1932), and as a descendant of the popular ethnographic documentary tradition, which included Cooper and Schoedsack's own *Grass* (1925) and *Chang*.[51] *Kong's* initial commercial performance was more mixed than its celebrated status might lead one to expect; it was withdrawn from Grauman's Chinese in Los Angeles three weeks into its scheduled four-week run, thus setting a record for the shortest run in the history of the house.[52] But the film did reasonably well in New York, where it played in concurrent runs at two of the world's largest theaters, Radio City Music Hall and the RKO Roxy, and it was RKO's biggest hit of the 1932–33 season, with a world rental of $1,856,000.

The Last Days of Pompeii was the forerunner of a group of "disaster" films, which included MGM's *San Francisco* and *The Good Earth*, Samuel Goldwyn's *The Hurricane* (1937), and Fox's *In Old Chicago*, *Suez* (1938), and *The Rains Came* (1939). In all of these, a natural disaster—an earthquake, a fire, flood, storm, or plague—provides the climax and deus ex machina resolution to the personal conflicts of a diverse group of characters in a period setting. A cycle of sea adventures followed the success of *Captain Blood* and the Oscar-winning *Mutiny on the Bounty*, among them *Captains Courageous*, *Souls at Sea*, *Slave Ship* (1937), *Spawn of the North* (1938), *Rulers of the Sea* (1939), and *The Sea Hawk* (1940).[53] Both cycles allowed the studios continually to improve their mechanical equipment, such as rain and wind machines and hydraulic machinery, as well as the techniques of special photography.[54]

Other 1930s cycles depended less on spectacle than on the prestige appeal of their literary, theatrical, or biographical source material. Paramount filmed a version of Robert Louis Stevenson's *Dr. Jekyll and Mr. Hyde* (1931) on a budget of $535,000, for which Fredric March won an Academy Award as best actor. In the same year, Universal produced adaptations of Bram Stoker's *Dracula* and Mary Shelley's *Frankenstein*. Made for around $300,000 apiece, they earned approximate domestic rentals of $650,000 and $1 million, respectively.[55] As a result of their success, Universal continued to make Gothic horror pictures for the next two decades. Despite occasional big-budget productions such as the sequels *Bride of Frankenstein* (1935) and *Son of Frankenstein* (1939), horror became associated mostly with programmers and B-pictures. Later cycles of literary adaptations and costume dramas were designed for family audiences. RKO scored one of its biggest hits with an adaptation of Louisa May Alcott's *Little Women* (1933), the first film to play Radio City Music Hall for more than one week. It was followed by numerous versions of classic novels. They included MGM's *Treasure Island* (1934), *David Copperfield, Anna Karenina, A Tale of Two Cities* (all 1935), and *Camille* (1936); UA's *The Count of Monte Cristo* (1934), *Les Misérables,* and *The Last of the Mohicans* (1936); and RKO's *Becky Sharp* (1935)—the first three-color Technicolor feature, adapted from *Vanity Fair.*

The production of these films was often attributed to Hollywood's need to find respectable subjects that would not cause censorship problems and that would appease moral and religious lobby groups like the Catholic Legion of Decency. Such films were particularly encouraged by MPPDA president Will H. Hays as a way to improve the educational value of the cinema and thereby reach new audiences as well as raise the status of the industry.[56] Hays took a particular personal interest in Warner Bros.' *A Midsummer Night's Dream* (1935), which along with MGM's *Romeo and Juliet* (1936) and Twentieth Century-Fox's U.S. distribution of the British production *As You Like It* (1936), featuring the young Laurence Olivier, comprised a short-lived Shakespearean "cycle."

A Midsummer Night's Dream was based on a production of the play at the Holly-wood Bowl by the distinguished Viennese director Max Reinhardt, who had first staged it in Berlin in 1905. To make the film, Warners hired several of the show's creative personnel, including Reinhardt, and teamed them with contract talent from its Burbank studio as well as other leading theatrical figures, including ballet chore-ographers Bronislava Nijinska and Nini Theilade, costume designer Max Rée, and composer Erich Wolfgang Korngold, who arranged and adapted Felix Mendelssohn's classic score. Budgeted at $615,000, the film came in at a final cost of $981,000, though publicity subsequently inflated this to $1.3 million to emphasize Warners' lar-gesse. Production delays added to the total cost, preventing members of the "all-star" cast, including James Cagney, Olivia de Havilland, Dick Powell, and Joe E. Brown, from moving on to other pictures to which they had been assigned.

A Midsummer Night's Dream is as much a showcase of the studio's technical skill and resources as it is of the Warner brothers' cultural pretensions. (As a hallmark of prestige, the film's opening title billing reads, "Warner Brothers has the honor to present." On its regular releases the company billed itself simply as "Warner Bros. presents.") Filmed almost entirely on interior sets (bar a few location inserts and es-tablishing shots), including a forest covering two interlinked sound stages, it is replete with special optical effects (mattes, filters, superimpositions, misted camera lenses), sensuous visual textures (from the varied fabrics of the costumes to the use of real trees, leaves, and bushes, along with artificial materials like cellophane and glitter), and the elaborately patterned play of light. In the first sequence set in the forest, as Puck (Mickey Rooney) awakens amid a mound of leaves, he is joined by a chorus of fairies, elves, and goblins, which gradually emerge from the surrounding foliage, from ground mist, or from murky pools of water. Some of them fly, some play musical in-struments, while others dance on air and ascend heavenward "on a spiral path of light" circling a giant tree.[57]

The magical studio forest of *A Midsummer Night's Dream* (1935).

Tagged as "Three hours of entertainment that was three centuries in the making," *A Midsummer Night's Dream* premiered simultaneously in New York, London, Paris, Vienna, and Sydney on October 9, 1935. All the film's initial engagements, domestic and foreign, were on a roadshow basis, with twice-daily separate performances. Prices in the United States were set between $1.10 and $2.20 depending on the size of the community. Theaters playing it on these terms were given a guarantee of a year's "protection" (clearance) before it would be made available for general release. The film was booked for strictly limited runs of up to two weeks, with any extended or return engagements to be made subject to public response. By March 1936, 212 play dates had been completed, mostly of a few days each (in some cases only one), with plans for a total of around six hundred roadshow engagements prior to general release.[58]

A year after it had opened, *Dream* was put into grind release at "popular prices." It had been cut from 133 minutes (exclusive of overture and intermission) to 117 minutes to speed up the pace. Ad mats carrying the strapline "Now everyone can see it!" referred proudly to the high-priced roadshow runs in "the world's great theatres," thus stressing the established quality of the product and the value for money it now offered to ordinary motion-picture patrons. Exhibitors were instructed by the studio's press book not to stress "the 'highbrow' angle" but to "sell star value and all the romance, drama and thrill angles in this grand production." These later runs were largely a mopping-up exercise, the bulk of the film's rentals having come from the early roadshow engagements. Indeed, according to Robert Sklar's calculations, approximately 8 percent of all its domestic earnings came from the initial fourteen-week engagement at the Hollywood Theatre, New York, and a subsequent two-week grind run at the Strand: three times the normal proportion of receipts accruing from a Broadway run.[59] Yet despite all the energies that went into selling it, the film was ultimately a commercial disappointment. Warners had aimed for a $2 million gross, but its worldwide rentals amounted only to $1,229,000, of which $731,000 had come from the domestic market. This was taken to demonstrate that there was no automatic audience for Shakespeare on film, as "the public had to be led by the hand to the boxoffice."[60]

MGM's production of *Romeo and Juliet,* starring Leslie Howard and Norma Shearer in the title roles, opened in reserved-seat engagements in August 1936, while *Dream* was still taking roadshow bookings. *Variety's* reviewer suggested that *Romeo and Juliet* "will draw into theatres plenty of the casuals, and the star names will magnetize the regular fans. It will also attract a new crop of cinema patrons from the arty, cultural, literati and dramatic bunch."[61] But even allowing for its select commercial appeal, the film—which cost $2,066,000, grossed $2,075,000, and lost $922,000— was a major box-office disappointment. With a roadshow test engagement of *As You Like It* at the Geary Theatre, San Francisco, drawing little public interest, other studios' plans for Shakespeare adaptations were cancelled and *Variety* proclaimed "The Bard a B.O. Washout."[62]

After the success of Alexander Korda's British production *The Private Life of Henry VIII* (1933, released by United Artists), historical biographies appeared "in numbers so thick as to constitute the champion of cycles since sound came in."[63] They included Korda's own *Catherine the Great* (1934), Paramount's *The Scarlet Empress* (1934), Twentieth Century's *Clive of India* (1935), RKO's *Mary of Scotland* (1936), and a lengthy series at Warner Bros., mostly starring Paul Muni, who succeeded George Arliss as the studio's carriage-trade draw. Although several of these performed disappointingly at the box office, and exhibitors frequently expressed doubts about their popularity with audiences, both literary adaptations and biopics continued to be produced until the end of the decade and were frequently among the annual top grossers, especially in the crucial overseas territories.[64]

The studios had come to rely heavily on expected returns from the international market to make their profits, especially on the most expensive films, whose costs could not usually be recouped in the United States alone. Budgets were set with anticipated foreign revenues in mind, and these typically represented around one-third of all distribution income. In the case of major-budget A-pictures, however, the proportion could rise to more than half, especially for those with pronounced international appeal. Fox's *Cavalcade,* an adaptation of Noël Coward's play about several generations of an English family in love and war, cost $1.3 million. It was "expected to take in more than $3,500,000 by the time it ha[d] finished playing in the British Empire," with nearly three-quarters of its income "said to come from Great Britain and the Dominions."[65]

However, the expansion of foreign film industries following the introduction of sound, the rise of nationalism and fascism in Europe and Asia, and the erection of trade barriers of all kinds continually threatened to reduce overseas business. Germany, Italy, and Japan in particular became problematic markets. Soviet Russia was virtually a closed territory and other countries, including France, Britain, Australia,

103

and Czechoslovakia, had introduced import or exhibition quotas, increased taxation for foreign goods, and set currency export restrictions. Spain, Palestine, and China were also marked by political strife, while Holland had the toughest censorship regime in the world. Britain and Australia together accounted for 56.2 percent of all foreign revenues circa 1939, with the United Kingdom alone delivering nearly twice as much as the next-sized market and almost one-half of all foreign income.[66]

Two late-1930s film cycles were particularly aimed at Britain and the British Empire: a series of imperial adventures, which included Paramount's *The Lives of a Bengal Lancer* (1935), Fox's *Under Two Flags* (1936), Warners' *The Charge of the Light Brigade* (1936), and RKO's *Gunga Din* (1939); and a group of Warner Bros. productions that Nick Roddick has dubbed the "Merrie England" cycle, including *The Adventures of Robin Hood* (1938) and *The Private Lives of Elizabeth and Essex* (1939) as well as several titles already mentioned.[67] Most of these films, like other costume epics such as Fox's *Lloyds of London* (1936) and RKO's *The Hunchback of Notre Dame* (1939), earned around half or more than half of their revenues from the overseas markets.

With the outbreak of hostilities between Britain, France, Poland, and Germany in September 1939, the studios immediately announced drastic economy measures, reducing budgets and postponing or even canceling projects altogether in anticipation of lowered foreign revenue, and aiming more films exclusively at American tastes.[68] This included a renewed interest in the western. Although the decade is remembered more for its B-grade "oaters" than for frontier epics, the 1930s did produce a number of big-budget westerns. As well as the Oscar-winning *Cimarron*, they included MGM's *Viva Villa!* (1934), Paramount's *The Texas Rangers* (1936), *Wells Fargo* (1937), and *The Texans* (1938), and even a British-produced Canadian western, *The Great Barrier* (1937, released in the United States, initially on a roadshow basis, as *Silent Barriers*). An extensive new A-western cycle, lasting until 1941, was sparked by the release at the beginning of 1939 of Paramount's *Union Pacific* and Fox's *Jesse James*.[69] As both Tino Balio and Thomas Schatz have argued, the fact of these films' being produced and released as Europe entered into war is an indication of Hollywood's increasing commitment to more fully exploiting the U.S. market. When the imperial adventure and Merrie England films concluded their cycles at the end of the decade, their principal star, Errol Flynn, was cast by Warners in a run of westerns, including *Dodge City* (1939), *Santa Fe Trail, Virginia City* (both 1940), and *They Died with Their Boots On* (1941), thus marking a decisive reorientation toward the domestic audience.[70] (With the exception of the last named, a biopic of George Armstrong Custer, all performed significantly better in the United States than overseas.)

However, fears that the foreign markets would collapse altogether were never realized. Following a drop in the first few weeks of the war, overseas revenues quickly began to recover. British business in particular was gradually strengthened by its wartime economy, not weakened, and when currency export restrictions were lifted with America's eventual entry into the war, this helped Hollywood too. Some government economists even thought that the European war might actually benefit the U.S. film industry, as the belligerent nations would now be too preoccupied with fighting to be concerned with placing further restrictions on their film industries.[71]

Musicals and Animated Features

The backstage melodramas, variety revues, and operettas that characterized the musical in the early years of sound quickly wore out their welcome through overproduction. According to Clive Hirschhorn, 145 "tuners" were released from 1927 to 1930 inclusive.[72] The cost of mounting lavish production numbers would have militated against their continuance in the worst years of the Depression, even if the public had not made the studios' decision for them. Only twenty-eight musicals were released in 1931 and 1932 combined. But the genre's fortunes began to revive with the sensational success in 1933 of three Warner Bros. backstage comedy-dramas, all with production numbers choreographed by Busby Berkeley.[73] *42nd Street, Gold Diggers of 1933,* and *Footlight Parade* represented a new approach to the staging, filming, and editing of ensemble set pieces, as Berkeley himself explained in a *Variety* interview:

"Mere grandeur, static immensity, means nothing—except expense. Sets can never be more than the background for action. Motion, the building with motion from little to big, that's what makes production numbers for the screen." . . .

"Pictures are all ocular," Mr. Berkeley explains, "therefore the first thing to do is understand the camera." Now, when he starts out to conceive a production number, he visualizes its development shot by shot as the camera's going to see it. His imagination has learned to work in camera angles.

Unlike earlier musicals, which had typically used multiple cameras to capture a number, Berkeley used only one. With no excess "coverage" to choose from, the editor simply assembled the shots in the order specified by Berkeley according to his preconceived continuity. Commented *Variety:* "With his method there is expense, yes, but no waste."

As to the cost of his production numbers, Berkeley is convinced "you've got to spend to make." He convinced the producers, too, for the water number alone in *Footlight Parade* rang up a total of $97,000. "But then" he says, "get them to talk about something, get them to say, 'If only for that water number, you must see that picture!' That's the kind of comment that makes hits, that gives you your money back and a whole lot over."[74]

Berkeley's approach may have been extravagant, but it was also economical; none of his 1933 pictures cost more than a million dollars and the first two cost less than $500,000. All three were highly profitable, with *Gold Diggers of 1933* earning world rentals of $3,231,000, a remarkable sum during the Depression.

Most of Berkeley's films were set backstage, but several of the 1930s' most prestigious musicals looked to the live theater for source material, or traded on celebrated stage names, as in the cases of *George White's Scandals* (1934) and *George White's 1935 Scandals* (1935).[75] Universal remade its 1929 part-silent adaptation of Jerome Kern and Oscar Hammerstein II's "legituner"—to use *Variety's* term for a musical of stage origins—*Show Boat* with a lavish sound version in 1936. Paramount had its most disastrous failure of the decade with *High, Wide and Handsome*, another ambitious piece of Kern-Hammerstein Americana, albeit one written directly for the screen. Fox's immensely popular *Alexander's Ragtime Band* began a cycle of nostalgic "cavalcade" musicals based on the songbooks of popular composers (in this case, Irving Berlin). But with its fictionalized biography of Broadway impresario Florenz Ziegfeld, MGM created not just the highest-grossing musical of the 1930s and the year's Oscar-winner for best picture but also a new subgenre: the showbiz biopic.[76]

In its reliance on stage-based production numbers, *The Great Ziegfeld*, choreographed by Seymour Felix, harks back to the revue style of early sound musicals. Even the celebrated "A Pretty Girl Is Like a Melody," climaxing the first half of the picture and filmed virtually in a single take lasting some five minutes, depends partly upon theatrical frontality for its effect. This long take maintains a theatrical sense of spatial, as well as temporal, continuity. As the camera traverses an enormous platform set contained within a curtained proscenium (also enormous), the set itself revolves to meet the camera, rather than the camera entering the space of the set. Berkeley's numbers, by contrast, are typically staged for the camera's eye alone, fragmenting both space and performance and reconstructing them in montage.

MGM's attempt to follow *The Great Ziegfeld* with a $2,260,000 biopic of classical composer Johann Strauss II, *The Great Waltz*, was far less successful, though it did well overseas, where earnings nearly doubled domestic business. Despite its now-celebrated status, *The Wizard of Oz* (1939) created one of the studio's largest ever losses. With a negative cost of $2,777,000 (the highest of any musical to that date), the film grossed $3,017,000 worldwide on first release, two-thirds of which came from the domestic market, leaving a deficit of $1,145,000. According to *Variety*, in a comment that must have rankled, the trade consensus was that *The Wizard of Oz* "would have been more successful, both artistically and financially, if it had been made as a cartoon."[77] *Oz* had indeed been considered by MGM as a potential animated feature, as it had initially been undertaken in response to Walt Disney's phenomenal hit *Snow White and the Seven Dwarfs*.

Six months before it premiered, Disney combined five Oscar-winning short cartoons, including *Flowers and Trees* and *The Three Little Pigs* (1933), together with new linking material and released the forty-three-minute package on June 18, 1937 as *Walt Disney's Academy Award Revue*. Trade advertisements described the *Revue* as a "feature-length compilation," *Variety* referred to it as a "cartoon feature," and it was offered to exhibitors either for double- or single-bill programs on feature rental terms.[78] Of course it was not an original creation; nor did it tell a continuous story. But as far

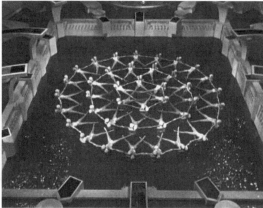

Theatrical and cinematic spectacle in *The Great Ziegfeld* (1936) and *Footlight Parade* (1933).

as the trade was concerned, it nonetheless constituted a feature attraction. However, when *Snow White and the Seven Dwarfs* made its public debut on December 21, 1937 (advertised as "Walt Disney's First Full-Length Feature in Technicolor"), the *Revue* was understandably forgotten. *Snow White* effectively created a new product for Hollywood. Its "specialness" as a feature resided, first of all, in the fact that it was perceived to be unique. In commercial as well as craft terms it set new standards, becoming the highest-grossing film of the sound era (though not for long). Although the phrase "Disney's folly" is repeatedly quoted by historians and Disney biographers (at least four accounts of the film's production take it as their title), Neil Gabler has pointed out that only one contemporary newspaper used that description and that the film was greeted on its world premiere at Los Angeles's Carthay Circle with eager anticipation by the industry.[79] Contrary to the mythology, it was not expected to be a disaster.

In addition to its use of Technicolor, the Disney studio's animation techniques seemed to have been brought to a new level of perfection, achieved by over a year's work of draftsmanship (the project had been in planning since 1933, was first announced to the press in 1934, and detailed preproduction began in 1935, but full animation did not begin until late 1936). For some of its scenes *Snow White* also made experimental use of the multiplane camera developed by Disney animator Ub Iwerks. By means of an elaborate structure in which several separate painted "cels" were placed at intermediate distances from the camera, each individually lighted and their positions relative to one another gradually adjusted from frame to frame, an appearance of three-dimensional depth and movement through space was created.

Snow White exploits the possibilities of the appearance of spatial depth in a number of ways. Its opening shot starts by moving into space past trees to the right and left in the foreground, toward the Queen's castle in the background. A dissolve moves us closer to the castle and in toward an exterior view of a window. Another dissolve takes us into the interior, showing the Queen, framed from behind, walking away from the camera toward the mirror on the wall. A shot of her reflection takes us into the space of the mirror itself. There are other sequences like this: the dwarfs' cottage is introduced in a shot similar to the opening one. But perhaps the most striking spatial effects in the film are created by the animation of the animals: the doves surrounding Snow White as she draws water from a well; the deer, squirrels, rabbits, birds, raccoons, and other creatures whom she meets in the woods, who guide her to the cottage, who accompany her inside and help her clean up, and who later flee with her as she herself flees from the Queen in the woods. In all these sequences, every animal is individually animated and moves in its own distinct way. Some hop, some fly, some run, some jump; some are fast, some are slow; some glide through the air, some run along the ground; some move in straight lines, some dart around, some move in arcs or expanding circles. In addition, each of the animals follows its own particular path even when as a group they are all heading in the same general direction. The result is a choreography of moving creatures whose changing configurations endow the space with an overwhelming sense of volume.

It was above all the telling of a full-length story in terms both credible and emotionally involving that drew the most contemporary praise. The film's triumph was to make its audiences, young and old alike, care about, identify with, and even cry for characters they were able to forget were merely drawings. Human characters, more difficult than animals to animate, were made to act and move convincingly partly through the "rotoscoping"—in effect, tracing—of live-action footage, a short-cut technique that the studio was understandably careful to keep out of the press.[80]

Originally budgeted at $250,000, Snow White's final negative cost was $1,488,423.[81] The expense was caused by the time and intensive labor necessary for the painstaking animation process, including the constant revision of ideas and materials and, inevitably, the creation of some footage ultimately unused in the completed film. In order to recover the investment, Disney and his distributor, RKO, sought to maximize revenues with a ruthless distribution strategy. The film was offered to first-run exhibitors on percentage terms only, running as high as 60 percent in some territories and no lower than 35 percent. Many independent theater chains in cities such as Philadelphia and Minneapolis declined to book it on such terms and held out for a better deal, but Disney-RKO refused to make concessions. Exhibitors were also asked to set higher than normal admission prices and even to charge the full adult price for children's tickets. They were permitted to show the film on single bills only; there were to be no supporting features, even in subsequent runs. Those theaters that were not put off by these conditions often booked return engagements even before their initial runs had opened, such was the word of mouth from the reception accorded the picture's first few situations.[82]

At the Carthay Circle, where it played on a twice-daily roadshow basis at $1.65 top, Snow White ran for eighteen weeks to a box-office gross of $178,880.[83] In New York, it played a record five weeks at Radio City Music Hall (no previous attraction

Exquisitely detailed figure animation in Walt Disney's *Snow White and the Seven Dwarfs* (1937).

having run longer than three), only being taken off because of other booking commitments and to prevent the film's being "milked" prior to subsequent runs in the nabes. Some 800,000 tickets were sold by the Hall, for a box-office gross of $530,000 and a rental to RKO of $148,000.[84] Partly because of the terms demanded, the film played a comparatively small number of theaters in its initial domestic release: 7,815, slightly more than half the expected number for a major hit.[85] This made it, according to *Variety,* "the highest money-getter per account in the history of the business."[86] Much of its earnings came from repeat visits or from out-of-town visitors, as many exhibitors reported admissions equaling or exceeding their local community population.[87] Up to 1952 *Snow White* had earned domestic rentals of $3,996,000 (which included reissues in 1940 and 1944) and almost equal foreign rentals of $3,850,000, for a total of $7,846,000.[88] RKO had been so keen to sign the film to a contract that Disney's company was allowed to keep 75 percent of the rentals rather than the standard 65 percent after deduction of distribution, print, and advertising expenses (which Disney shared: *Snow White*'s initial Technicolor print run alone cost $300,000).[89]

None of Disney's subsequent animated features was as successful as *Snow White,* though several were a good deal more expensive. The next two pictures put in work were *Pinocchio,* eventually released in February 1940 at a cost of $2.6 million, and *Bambi,* completion of which was delayed until 1942, by which time it had cost $1,741,000 (and this only after last-minute economies had resulted in several sequences being cut before their final animation). Although they were recognized by critics, as well as by the studio itself, as technically superior to *Snow White,* both failed to make back their costs on initial release.[90] Disney's most ambitious venture was *Fantasia* (1940), a two-hour animated feature without a continuous narrative, built around eight pieces of classical music (its working title was *The Concert Feature*) and costing $2,280,000 to produce. It employed an innovative stereophonic sound system developed by RCA, Fantasound, which limited the film's initial presentation to special roadshow engagements in legitimate theaters.[91]

The Disney company undertook the roadshow presentation of *Fantasia* itself, leaving RKO to handle the subsequent general release. Disney planned a premiere at Carnegie Hall, but opened the film instead at the Broadway Theatre in November 1940, where it ran for forty-nine consecutive weeks (a record long run for any sound-era film to that date). Twelve other roadshow engagements followed in 1941, including a thirty-nine-week run at the Carthay Circle in Los Angeles.[92] Up to eighty-eight roadshow engagements had been planned to take place over a five-year period, but U.S. Department of Defense demands on RCA for radio equipment prevented its manufacture of more than eleven sets, at a cost of $30,000 each.[93] By April 1941, the first eleven engagements had earned $1.3 million, but it is very likely that much of this was eaten up by the costs of installing and operating the sound system, consisting of "sound reproducers, amplifiers, and loud speakers so arranged as to reproduce sounds from a multiple sound-track film run in synchronism with the picture-film. . . . The weight of a complete Fantasound equipment was approximately 15,000 lbs.; it was packed in forty-five cases and required one-half of a standard freight-car space."[94]

At this point Disney turned the film's distribution over to RKO. It continued the roadshow booking policy using the regular monaural soundtrack, which had been recorded on the original prints for protection in the event of a breakdown in Fantasound's discrete four-channel stereo track. As many as 5,000 twice-daily engagements, with reserved seats at $1.50 top, were planned, beginning in May 1941. Exhibitors who had booked the Fantasound version protested that the playing of roadshows without special sound made the film seem "a sort of carnival gimmick, not in good taste and decidedly unfair to the public."[95] When the film was released at popular prices in 1942, it was cut from 125 minutes to 82 to allow its presentation in double bills.[96] Trade press advertisements addressed to exhibitors stressed the prestige and publicity that had accumulated from the initial roadshow engagements, from three special Academy Awards bestowed in 1941, extensive media coverage, and the direct mailing of "cultural groups" about the imminent national release:

Unlike most motion pictures *Fantasia* has a great *plus* audience waiting to see it . . . those hundreds and thousands of alert, educated and prosperous people in every community who are not regular theatregoers but whose patronage is so sorely needed by every theatre. These people are your *plus* audience for *Fantasia* . . .

Fantasia is a picture of Prestige and Profits—get both by going after both those vital audiences—the regulars by increased advertising in your newspapers, on the air, on billboards, and the *plus* audience by direct contact with the influential leaders of local groups whose membership can pack to overflowing the largest auditorium in any city, town or village.[97]

Variety reported that many exhibitors playing the film in general release continued to present it in single-feature bills with increased admission prices, and targeted their advertising at adults rather than children.[98]

In the event, RKO's distribution of the film made a small loss after grossing $2,120,000 worldwide, though the Disney Company sustained a much larger one.[99] Henceforward, Disney scaled down his plans for future animated features. Following *The Reluctant Dragon* (a documentary on the studio with animated sequences) and *Dumbo*, both made in 1941 for less than $1 million each, other features in preparation were postponed and did not finally emerge until the 1950s, including *Cinderella* (1950), *Alice in Wonderland* (1951), and *Peter Pan* (1953).[100] For the duration of World War II, the company devoted most of its energies to the production of government-sponsored films for instructional and propaganda purposes. The studio's remaining features of the 1940s were either purpose-made anthologies of short subjects or live-action films with animated segments, notably *Song of the South* (1946) and *So Dear to My Heart* (1948).

According to Gabler, "From working on *Fantasia*, Walt had become fascinated with the idea of presentation. It wasn't enough for a film to be great. It had to be mounted in such a way that the exhibition of the movie was also great. 'I wanted a special show' was how he put it."[101] Although these later films performed variably in the marketplace—*Song of the South* was Disney's biggest hit since *Snow White*—none was conceived, promoted, presented, or received as a "special show" in the way the company's earlier animated features had been. The full-length cartoon had become just another kind of picture.

Fewer but Bigger, 1939–1949

In the 1930s, MGM consistently had the highest production costs, and earned the highest rentals, in the industry. Between 1936 and 1940 it made eleven films costing $2 million and over, as many as all other studios combined. But even with the company's considerable distribution clout, only two of these—*The Great Ziegfeld* and *Maytime* (1937), the most successful of the Jeanette MacDonald–Nelson Eddy series of operettas—were profitable. With the number of feature films released by all companies in any one year averaging seven hundred, all competing for theater play dates and consumer dollars, it was virtually impossible for pictures above a certain budgetary level to make a good profit. Fox chairman Joseph M. Schenck suggested that the way for the industry to maximize business for each picture was to make fewer pictures. Currently, Schenck argued, exhibitors had too many films to choose from and too many to play, so each one was not earning its full potential gross. If the same overall costs were invested in a smaller number of pictures, each would have proportionately higher production values, hence greater audience appeal. With fewer films taking up playing time, each would be able to run longer and earn greater revenues.[1]

Production and release policies were slow to change. But from the 1942–43 season onward, all the studios gradually scaled down their operations to produce annual slates of fewer but more expensive films. Between 1939 and 1945, the total number of pictures released in the United States fell by slightly more than half. Although the impetus for reduced output and enhanced production values derived in part from the market conditions of the 1930s, the tendency was accelerated by two additional factors from the early 1940s: antitrust action against the film industry by the federal government and the involvement of America in the Second World War. Before we examine these, however, we must turn to the single most important picture for the film industry in the decade following its debut in 1939.

Streamlining the Roadshow: Gone with the Wind

David O. Selznick's production of *Gone with the Wind* (*GWTW*) is often taken to be the culmination of "classical" Hollywood, though in many respects it was an exception to all its norms and standards. With a running time of 222 minutes and a negative cost of some $4 million, it was the longest and most expensive American film yet made.[2] Adapted from the hottest literary property of the decade, Margaret Mitchell's best-selling 1936 novel of the Old South, it had the largest amount of pre-release publicity accorded any film to date, and was therefore quite reasonably described as the picture most eagerly awaited by the public. Once exhibited, it quickly broke all records for box-office performance, setting new benchmarks for admissions and grosses. *GWTW* had certainly been expected to be a success, but the scale of that success took everyone, including its producer, by surprise.

Nevertheless, both Selznick and MGM (which had invested $1,250,000 of the film's budget and loaned its contract star Clark Gable in exchange for the distribution rights and 50 percent of the profits) made every attempt to guarantee the film's profitability in advance and to make it an "event" (Selznick's term). The story of the production (and preproduction) of *GWTW* has been told many times.[3] Less often discussed are the distribution and exhibition methods used to bring it to audiences. They were not only significantly different from those of any preceding roadshow attraction, they also effectively changed both the practice and the very definition of roadshowing, setting a new pattern for big-picture releases from the early 1940s to the mid-1950s.

Although it had been widely expected in the trade that the film would be road-shown in the traditional manner, following its recent bad experiences with *The Great Waltz* and *Marie Antoinette* MGM instead wanted to put the film into immediate general release in order to get a quicker return on its investment. In a memo addressed (though not sent) to MGM vice president Al Lichtman, Selznick strongly objected to the company's plans, arguing that it would be "as wrong not to road show *Gone with the Wind* as it would have been not to road show *The Birth of a Nation*." Selznick pointed out that the length of *GWTW* precluded more than three shows a day "unless the first performance is held for night watchmen," and that the probable "speed of revenue" of three daily performances rather than two "might be a few months' difference at the most." He even had to argue for the necessity of an intermission in what would be a four-hour show.[4]

To arrive at the most appropriate release strategy for the film, MGM distributed questionnaires at public previews. Respondents were asked to suggest "the most convenient time of day to start the picture, both for matinee and evening performances," and the appropriate scale of admission prices; whether the picture should be played in continuous performances or in separate performances at specified times, "as is the case with a play"; whether it should have no intermission, one or two intermissions; whether patrons would be "prepared to pay a higher price if the producers went to the

Clark Gable as Rhett Butler and Vivien Leigh as Scarlett O'Hara in
Gone with the Wind (1939).

expense of having only two or three shows a day, with reserved seats"; and whether
they intended seeing the finished film more than once.[5]

Rather than commit to a definite, uniform nationwide exhibition policy from the
outset, MGM chose instead to treat the film's opening engagements as test runs, with
several different policies operating simultaneously across the country. Ten theaters in
seven cities were selected for this experiment following the world premiere in Atlanta,
Georgia, on December 15, 1939. The policies at these venues, all of which charged
increased admission prices, were as follows: two separate shows daily, all seats reserved
(Astor, New York; Carthay Circle, Los Angeles; Colonial, Reading, Pennsylvania); two
separate shows daily, matinee seats unreserved, evening seats reserved (State, Boston);
three continuous shows daily, no seats reserved (Loew's Grand, Atlanta; United Artists, Los Angeles; Orpheum, Boston; Capitol, Cincinnati; Loew's, Harrisburg, Pennsylvania); and three continuous shows daily, some loge seats reserved (Capitol, New
York). This approach was regarded by *Variety* columnist John C. Flinn as "more than
a violation of precedent: it is a theatre-man's nightmare. It is also the riskiest piece of
showmanship in memory, with little to win and much to lose." Flinn pointed out that

the film's length alone (the duration of an airplane flight from New York to Chicago) set a challenge for both exhibitors and audiences: "It will require more sitting through than the longest double bill program, with news, cartoon, travelog and screeno combined. From the posterior angle it is a six-day bike race."[6]

From these engagements a standard policy was evolved of two continuous matinee performances, without reserved seats, and a separate evening performance with a limited number of bookable seats. Ticket prices were set at a minimum of 75 cents for matinees and $1.10 for evenings, with up to $1.65 for "preferred" (best) seats or up to $2.20 for reserved seats (these were the top prices charged on Broadway at the Capitol and the Astor, respectively). Traditional roadshow arrangements were usually adopted only when the picture opened on concurrent runs at two theaters in a community, as with those in New York, Los Angeles, and Boston (and later in Detroit and Chicago), in which cases the two houses operated different policies, offering local patrons a choice. Theaters operating on a roadshow basis charged more than those on grind, for the additional convenience of guaranteed seats and advance booking (up to eight weeks ahead in the case of the Astor).

Selznick felt that too many concessions had been made and that the standard admission prices, higher than the norm for regular engagements but lower than those usually charged for roadshows, undersold the picture and reduced its prestige value. As he wrote in his undelivered memo to Lichtman:

You will recall that you laughed at the incident I reported to you of the woman who said she had been saving her money to pay $1.65 to see *Gone With The Wind,* and to pay $1.10 per seat for the members of her family for "second-best seats"; but who, upon hearing that she would be able to buy the best seats, unreserved, for $1.10, said that she certainly would not do this, and if that was to be the price of the best tickets, obviously the picture wasn't what it was cracked up to be, and would soon be playing at lesser prices, and she would wait until it got to the neighborhood houses at the regular price. Since then, I have had occasion to cross-examine a number of other people in the middle-class and lower-middle-class brackets. The reaction has in each case been identical, and has, in addition, been one of great disappointment that an event which they had looked forward to for so long was evaporating. . . . I believe there are countless thousands of people who will be enraged at being gouged for advanced prices to stand in line, to take their chances at seeing the picture partially, to see the picture in discomfort—but who would storm the box-offices to pay $1.65 to be sure of a seat, and to see it under the proper circumstances.[7]

If Selznick was unable to dictate distribution and exhibition policy, he was nevertheless determined to exercise some control over the standards of presentation in theaters. He prepared a nine-page booklet for house managers ("the link between the producers and the public"), containing detailed instructions on how to present the picture "in the perfect form in which the public demands to see it."[8] A signed memo from the producer began:

No time, effort, or money has been spared to make *Gone With The Wind* as perfect as possible. We have fully realized our obligation to the countless millions of readers of Miss Mitchell's beloved work, and have gone to elaborate pains with every detail of production. . . .

But all of the time, money and effort, and all of the new devices, will have been in vain if we do not have the complete cooperation of the exhibitor, without whose showmanship and presentation abilities a perfect show is impossible.

Among the recommendations in the booklet was that "*no light, especially colored light, is projected onto the screen, screen masking or stage proscenium* during the showing of the picture." All house lights should be fully extinguished during the screening so as not to "throw the color values of the picture off balance." Projectionists were instructed to check that projector sound and light levels were constant, to avoid shifts in volume or color temperature following reel changes, and to ensure that the machines themselves were kept spotlessly clean to avoid print damage. Ushers were to ensure that exit doors were properly closed before the picture started and not opened again until after the intermission and end titles had appeared, and to avoid anything that might distract the audience's attention from the screen. Souvenir programs were to be handed to patrons as they entered the auditorium, but not when they were seated. A staff rehearsal of the full show was suggested to ensure smooth running of the performance.

Perhaps most important were the instructions regarding the two-and-one-half-minute overture at the beginning of the first reel, the four-minute intermission music following the conclusion of the first part of the picture, the ninety-second entr'acte prior to the second part, and the four-minute exit music following the end title. All these pieces of atmospheric music—"designed to establish a mood for the enjoyment of the film," as well as to obviate any choice of inappropriate music by theater management—were to be played over closed curtains, with no light or other images projected on the screen.[9] The house lights were to be gradually dimmed during the play-in music before the curtains parted following a seven-second drum roll. Such exact timings allowed the operation of the screen curtains and house lights to be precisely synchronized.

For its first wave of release, the picture was exhibited "only in cities of 100,000 persons and up, and in theaters seating at least 850."[10] MGM charged a rental of 70 percent from the first dollar, but guaranteed exhibitors a profit of at least 10 percent of the gross on the run. A number of nonaffiliated theater chains refused to book the picture on these terms, leaving the way open for independent exhibitors to book it instead.[11] To speed up distribution, MGM again broke with precedent by permitting "nabes" to play the film concurrently with downtown situations. For example, *GWTW* opened in Brooklyn, Newark, and Jersey City in early 1940, while the twin Broadway engagements were still in progress. Normally they would have had to wait at least one week's clearance following the termination of the Astor and Capitol runs.[12]

MGM expected that wear and tear from long runs would require the entire inventory of 350 Technicolor prints (struck at a cost of $1,250 each for a total of $437,500) to be replaced.[13] *Variety* also reported wear and tear on theaters and their operators, with "nervous breakdowns, enforced vacations for managers and other members of house staffs, broken ribs among ushers, heavy toll upon rest-rooms, complaints from cleaners and no end of relief for cops who have had to handle unprecedented crowds."[14] The Capitol engagement was eventually cut short after twelve weeks (still a record long run for the theater) to free it up for new product, while the Astor run continued for a total of forty-four weeks, concurrent with neighborhood engagements around Greater New York. Following the advanced-price play-off, general release in January 1941 was preceded by a further set of eight test engagements to determine policy. MGM's plan to book the film into many of the same theaters that had already played it first time around, another break with tradition, was heralded by a duplicate premiere in Atlanta on the anniversary of its first public performance. Nationally, admission prices were around half those charged for the first release and exhibitors were now charged 50 percent rental, still higher than normal even for a premium release. Unusually for the general distribution of a very lengthy attraction, the film was not shortened but remained intact at its full original running time, a fact stressed in advertisements.[15]

In July 1940, Selznick reported a domestic rental to date of $12,402,463, already nearly three times the highest recorded previous gross.[16] His biographer Ronald Haver claims that earnings from the 1941 pop-price engagements reached an additional $9.7 million.[17] The rest of the available world market—where MGM had faced stiffer opposition to its booking terms, especially in Britain and Australia—contributed up to $10 million more.[18] *GWTW*'s success can be gauged not just by its epoch-making box-office figures but also by the extent to which later pictures took both the film and its marketing methods as their model. Having already sold the period costume drama *All This, and Heaven Too* (1940) as part of its 1939–40 program, Warner Bros. was not able to insist on special pricing arrangements, but it nevertheless encouraged exhibitors "to play the film . . . in the manner that 'Gone' was exhibited."[19] Charles Chaplin's political satire *The Great Dictator* (1940) was distributed by UA in a pattern that exactly duplicated that of *GWTW:* 70 percent rental terms with a 10 percent profit guarantee. Even its twin Broadway venues were the same as those for *GWTW,* the Astor and the Capitol.[20] RKO's release of Orson Welles's *Citizen Kane* (1941) was planned for the same policy but, because of the press campaign launched against it by newspaper tycoon William Randolph Hearst (on whom it was allegedly based), the film received only a limited number of bookings.[21]

Two aspects of what we might call the *Gone with the Wind* pattern were adopted on a longer-term basis. One was the opening of a major film in two theaters in a community simultaneously, one on a reserved-seat basis, the other on grind (with the former always charging higher prices). This policy was used for at least ten other films throughout the next decade, usually in only one or two key cities, normally

New York and Los Angeles. In almost every case the grind run outlasted the road-show engagement, though precedent suggested that the opposite should have been the case (round-the-clock performances using up patrons more rapidly than twice-daily shows). In several cases where the grind engagement closed first, the roadshow house subsequently switched policy to one of continuous shows at lower prices. Otherwise, the traditional practices of a single exclusive engagement per territory, advance booking of seats, and twice-daily separate performances were increasingly marginalized or eliminated altogether. Henceforth, throughout the trade "roadshowing" came to refer, more often than not, simply to pre-release runs at advanced prices with continuous performances.

A second practice established by *GWTW* was the selective raising of ticket prices for films exhibited on a grind basis. Although Selznick's picture was not the first to be presented in this way—it was anticipated on a limited scale by, for example, the 1935 version of *Les Misérables, Anthony Adverse, The Gorgeous Hussy* (1936), *Snow White and the Seven Dwarfs,* and *The Goldwyn Follies* (1938)—it was followed by such a large number of films adopting the advanced-price policy that its influence can scarcely be in doubt. In 1940 alone there were at least a dozen such releases. There was considerable debate in the industry over the wisdom or otherwise of raising ticket prices for particular pictures. On the one hand, it was believed that the public might accept it if the films were seen to merit the additional expense. Some were "justified" by their high production costs, or by the high demand for them, or their prestige status. On the other hand, if advanced prices were seen as arbitrary and undeserved, audiences might very well turn away at the box office, or express their resentment with fewer subsequent theater visits. They might even become skeptical about "ordinary" pictures whose prices were *not* raised, and that might therefore be bypassed as inferior attractions. Some also feared that if theaters were appealing primarily to the relatively wealthy they might find it difficult to claim tax relief as providers of "the poor man's form of entertainment."[22] The studios countered by arguing that the public was in fact getting big films cheaper than it would have done under the old pattern: the usual top price for grind "roadshows" was $1.10 rather than the $2 or $1.50 for two-a-day engagements.[23]

Warners' military biopic *Sergeant York* (1941), starring Gary Cooper as World War I hero Alvin York, opened on Broadway on a reserved-seat basis. But after six weeks at the Astor at $2 top it was moved over to Warners' Hollywood Theatre with a top price of $1.10 on grind. This latter engagement established the national distribution strategy. Warners offered the film for grind runs at slightly raised prices (a minimum of 55 cents for evening performances or 40 cents for matinees), with a rental of 50 percent. It was not made available for popular-price engagements until July 1942, a year after it had opened. Under this deal, *Sergeant York* earned higher domestic rentals than any previous film except *GWTW*: $5,671,000 from over 17,500 bookings in eighteen months of exhibition, more than half of which had raised prices.[24] Warners successfully applied a similar policy to another prestige biopic, *Yankee Doodle Dandy*

Extended runs and raised prices marked U.S. exhibition in the early 1940s: trade press advertisements for *All This, and Heaven Too* (1940) and *Yankee Doodle Dandy* (1942) (*Variety*, July 24, 1940, 19, and September 23, 1942, 12).

(1942), starring James Cagney as showman George M. Cohan. These were the only two films of the decade the studio opened on a reserved-seat basis. But its highest prices of all were charged in the name of charity rather than commerce. All the profits from Warners' film of Irving Berlin's service benefit show *This Is the Army* (1943) were donated to the Army Emergency Relief Fund. Some 4,450 advanced-price "premieres" had been held by December 1943 (tickets for the New York world premiere were sold at a minimum price of $55) and total world rentals eventually amounted to $10,445,000, four-fifths of which came from the domestic market. Thus, *This Is the Army* earned the highest U.S. gross of the wartime cinema boom.[25]

Bottlenecks, Logjams, and Backlogs

Fox suffered badly in 1940. For the first three quarters of the year it declared a net operating loss of $1,075,611.[26] This was largely due to heavy losses overseas and disappointing earnings for a number of expensive productions, including *The Blue Bird,*

Lillian Russell, Brigham Young, Chad Hanna, and *Hudson's Bay.* Joseph Schenck told *Variety* that the "'Epic' type of film is 'finished at Fox. . . . In 1941–42 there's going to be complete concentration on the U.S. market. We're going to have only pictures that will appeal to 100 percent of America's potential audiences.'"[27] A mere eighteen months later the company had changed tack completely. Its president, Spyros P. Skouras, announced that no budgetary limits would be set on top productions; whatever needed to be spent to ensure quality and box-office value would be spent.[28] What had occurred in the interim was, of course, a substantial improvement in market conditions due largely to the switch to a wartime economy.

The first signs of prosperity were felt even before the Japanese attack on Pearl Harbor brought the United States into World War II in December 1941. The government's investment of $16 million in a national defense program began to have an effect on public spending in late 1940. It ensured reduced unemployment, higher wages, more disposable income, and increased currency circulation. The relocation of defense workers meant an expanded urban population with plenty of money to spend on entertainment. Downtown first-run theaters in particular experienced a surge in business matched only by the early years of sound. Each successive year from 1943 to 1946 saw the industry surpassing its previous records for both revenues and admissions. The boom was such that even mediocre pictures could earn a healthy profit. For the most successful films, business went through the roof.[29]

As admissions steadily increased, the extended runs distributors had long been demanding became almost universal, as movies continued to draw patronage for longer periods than ever before. Whereas Broadway runs of two or three weeks were the norm in the 1930s, in wartime runs of two or three months were not uncommon. With first-run and pre-release theaters enjoying the greatest surge in attendance, this created a "bottleneck" that increased the waiting period for subsequent-run exhibitors. In some instances, limits had to be placed on the length of early runs, and successful engagements were deliberately curtailed by the distributors. MGM pulled *Mrs. Miniver* (1942) from Radio City Music Hall after ten weeks—a record long run for the house, soon to be exceeded by MGM's own *Random Harvest* (1942)—in order to benefit the New York nabes. But fears that product would be excessively "milked" in early runs often proved unfounded; the word-of-mouth and prestige built up by the downtown engagements meant that even subsequent runs could be profitably held over. To relieve the bottlenecks, many sub-run cinemas were upgraded in run status. Not only did this allow them to receive pictures sooner, they were also able to raise their customary ticket prices and thereby increase both their own and distributors' revenues.[30]

The very popularity of moviegoing created its own set of problems. It led to frequent "logjams" as films filtered through the exhibition system more slowly than hitherto, and others were forced to wait longer on the shelf. As a consequence, the studios built up considerable backlogs of unreleased product. Films with immediate contemporary relevance or potentially transitory appeal (war combat movies, say, or musicals with new hit songs) were given priority, while less topical titles were often withheld for one, two, or even—in the cases of Paramount's period sea adventure *Two Years before the Mast* and Warners' Brontë sisters biopic *Devotion* (both filmed in 1943 but not released until 1946)—three years after completion.

In such conditions, the virtually complete abandonment of traditional roadshowing made good sense. Twice-daily performances were simply inefficient at handling the large volume of patronage. Pictures were already taking long enough to work through the release system without artificially limiting the number of shows. Indeed, the government specifically requested the studios not to delay the release of films potentially useful to the war effort.[31] *Mrs. Miniver* (set on the British home front) was given a quick general release at normal prices, with MGM taking out trade advertisements to explain that the company wanted to bring the film "to the greatest number of people in the shortest possible space of time."[32]

Contributing to the first-run bottlenecks were the inflated running times of many major films. The 1943–44 season saw the release of a large number of big-budget productions of unusual length.[33] Darryl Zanuck, whose company produced *The Song of Bernadette* (158 minutes), *The Keys of the Kingdom* (137 minutes), and *Wilson* (158 minutes), stated:

There is no such thing as a trend toward longer pictures. There definitely is a trend toward bigger productions. . . . We plan in the future to make the major part of our schedule on an elaborate and epic scale. To give such pictures their needed scope and production value it is necessary naturally to give them adequate footage. The exceptional picture could not be exceptional unless it was given the required length for telling the story.[34]

But exhibitors protested that such length limited turnover. Although Selznick's American home-front drama *Since You Went Away* (1944) earned $4,918,412 in domestic rentals despite playing only at normal prices, it was claimed that the film's 172-minute running time prevented it from earning millions more. UA, its distributor, had even asked theaters to extend their opening hours to accommodate it.[35] Excessive length also used up extra film stock (rationed for the duration) and added to theater staff overtime. *Variety* speculated that some films might have been artificially padded to justify higher rentals or higher admission prices, or perhaps simply reflected their makers' sense of self-importance.[36]

One of the longest pictures of this period, and one of the most successful, was Paramount's *For Whom the Bell Tolls* (1943). Like *Gone with the Wind* it was adapted from a recent best-selling novel, in this case Ernest Hemingway's story of the Spanish Civil War. The studio had paid a record price for the screen rights: $100,000 plus an additional ten cents for every copy of the book sold up to a maximum of $150,000. This "sliding-scale" rights deal helped drive up the cost to other producers of buying literary works for the screen. Despite their common elements of love-against-a-background-of-war, *GWTW* and *The Bell* (as it was usually abbreviated) were hardly comparable in other terms. The overt left-wing dimension of Hemingway's work invited problems with censorship, and the film had to be approved by the State Department, which consulted with a representative of General Franco's government (this when the United States was engaged in an antifascist war). But the studio's hopes of another *GWTW* were clearly manifested in its attempts to stir up publicity over casting choices (Gary Cooper, at whose instigation the studio had acquired the book rights, had already been fixed as the hero, while Ingrid Bergman eventually played his lover) and with a release policy directly modeled on MGM's.[37]

The Bell opened in July 1943 with advertisements proclaiming that it would "not be shown at popular prices before 1945."[38] For the first half of its twenty-eight-week Broadway run at the Rivoli the film was a $2-top traditional roadshow; reserved-seat engagements were also played in Los Angeles, Chicago, Detroit, and San Francisco. It played in up to 1,000 grind engagements at $1.10 top before being temporarily withdrawn in August 1944. Regular-price general release followed in February 1945. *The Bell,* which had cost $2,986,231 (Paramount's highest budget to date),[39] returned total domestic rentals of around $6.3 million. The film's original running time was variously reported as being from 166 to 172 minutes (the difference may be attributable to overture and entr'acte music). Seventeen days after the world premiere, director Sam Wood reduced it to 156 minutes, and for general release it was cut again to 130 minutes. Such postrelease editing of long films, while rarely so drastic, was extremely common. Warners' *Mr. Skeffington* (1944) was cut from 146 to 127 minutes, MGM's *An American Romance* (1944) from 151 to 123 minutes, and Paramount's *Frenchman's Creek* (1944) from around three hours to 113 minutes prior to release.[40]

Although budgets were now being recouped in record time, not all films shared in the general riches. *Wilson, The Keys of the Kingdom, An American Romance,* and MGM's *Dragon Seed* (1944) all cost from $2.5 million to $4 million, and none earned a profit. *Wilson,* a biopic of the late U.S. president, which was the personal project of Darryl Zanuck, alone made a loss of $2.2 million.[41] Raising prices for such films was a tacit acknowledgment that they needed an additional boost at the box office. Budgets rose as dramatically as earnings during the war. This was partly due to the scarcity of materials for sets such as lumber and metal, but also because of the wage rises demanded by an increasingly militant and unionized work force, the inefficiencies caused by using inexperienced labor to replace contract staff absent on war service, and the extended shooting schedules that had come to be standard. The studios' reduction in output itself increased film costs, as overhead charges had to be spread across a smaller number of releases than before. Budgets of at least $1 million became the norm for A-pictures and the number of multi-million-dollar productions increased markedly.[42]

Postwar Hollywood

As the war drew to a close and the film industry reached its zenith of profits and admissions in the first full year of peace (partly thanks to returning servicemen flooding into city centers), Hollywood remained hopeful that the good times would continue.[43] In September 1946, in the first edition of what became an annually updated chart of the "All-Time Box-Office Champs," *Variety* noted that "virtually as many films hit the magical $4,000,000 domestic rental figure during the past year as in the entire history of the film industry up to that time."[44] In its subsequent year-end survey, the journal listed nineteen films entering what it called the "Golden Circle" of hits, compared to "only 25 films having reached that category in the entire history of picturedom preceding 1946."[45] The following year, another fifteen titles were listed as having grossed $4 million or more. But far from giving rise to unreserved optimism, this was instead taken to prove that "only the big pictures are paying off with the grosses now and the mediocre and smaller films are dying."[46]

By 1948 it had become clear that an industry recession was fast approaching. Social conditions were changing, as Paramount president Barney Balaban observed:

The cost of living kept on rising and there was less money left for pleasure. Some of the easy war cash vanished and a portion of the population gathered in the big centres for war-work purposes dispersed. The increasing numbers and uses of new automobiles, the booming of outdoor sports and other forms of recreation made stronger competition for pictures.[47]

According to a Gallup survey, the U.S. industry's all-time peak month for cinema attendance was November 1946, with an estimated 87,800,000 weekly admissions.[48] Thereafter, there was a pattern of continuing decline, at first gradual, then increasingly precipitous; by 1955, the figure for weekly ticket sales had sunk to around 50 million, and by 1960, 30 million.[49] The reasons for this mass desertion of the hitherto loyal movie audience are too familiar to require more than brief summary here: population shifts from urban areas to the newly built suburbs; the domestic sequestration of younger married patrons because of the postwar "baby boom"; increased disposable income (and concomitantly higher standards of living), partly absorbed by the greater availability of automobiles and home-based consumer durables; and the diversification of leisure pursuits, many of them centered on the home, including most famously the rise of commercial network television as an alternative form of motion-picture entertainment. All these combined to divert the potential audience into recreational patterns in which cinema occupied a diminished, if still important, role.[50]

As a consequence of this situation, by the late 1940s theater engagements were becoming shorter (Broadway first runs now typically lasted four weeks rather than the six to eight of the recent past) and average films were beginning to do average box-office. Overseas income was seriously hit by trade wars, as countries including Britain, Italy, and France imposed restrictions on imports and limits on currency remittance overseas in order to protect their own fragile economies. Around one-third of all the majors' releases were now losing money, overall profit margins were appreciably slimmer, and the studios began making serious efforts to economize.

Overheads had reached record levels during and immediately after the war because of the reduction in output as well as the increased expense of maintaining studio lots. These costs were passed on to picture budgets. For example, in July 1946 Paramount's *The Emperor Waltz* was budgeted at $2,855,000, of which $2,122,677 represented the direct production cost, and the remaining $732,323 studio overhead, calculated at a rate of 34.5 percent of the direct cost. But the film, a Viennese musical comedy in Technicolor starring Bing Crosby, was not released until May 1948 and was therefore subject to additional overhead figured at 44.5 percent in 1947 and 32.8 percent in 1948. Its final cost was $4,071,948.53, of which more than one-quarter, $1,053,649.90, was overhead. Although *The Emperor Waltz* was one of the top hits of its year, estimated domestic rentals amounted to only $4 million.[51]

According to Paramount, production costs overall had risen 50 percent since prewar days.[52] Jack Warner put the increase at 150 percent, "because the studios must pay more for stories, talent, labor, materials, and the average shooting time has more than doubled as a result of more big-scale productions."[53] Spyros Skouras advocated passing the costs on to exhibitors, but admitted that to justify higher rentals, "the product must be 'super-A,' or else."[54] "Super-A" budgets were certainly common enough. In the 1947–48 season, RKO's average negative cost was $1,222,000, Warners' was $1,943,000, and MGM's a staggering $2,249,000. These studios' average picture earnings for the same period were $1,250,000 (RKO), $2,426,000 (Warner Bros.), and $3,156,000 (MGM), each scarcely sufficient to cover distribution costs and return a profit.[55] But the number of exceptionally high-cost pictures also reached a peak in the early postwar period. From 1946 to 1948, Hollywood produced at least twenty films costing over $3 million, plus three costing over $5 million: Selznick's *Duel in the Sun* (1946), Fox's *Forever Amber* (1947), and UA's *Arch of Triumph* (1948).[56]

As the majority of overheads came in the form of staff wages and salaries, one solution was to reduce the size of the workforce. But budget cuts were more problematic, as their effects would take longer to show up on the ledger when amortization was a year or two down the line. Even more serious was the legacy of the backlogs the studios had been amassing for several years; pictures completed when costs were at a peak were now being released when the market had slipped into a trough. As these pictures were rushed into distribution so that they could be amortized as quickly as possible, too many films competed for a limited number of play dates and therefore often played shorter runs than they needed to break even.[57] Distributors had to devise ways of generating a larger than usual box-office gross, and extracting a larger than usual proportion of that gross from exhibitors. Paramount set up special publicity "task forces," each dedicated to one big-budget film for which they were solely responsible, such as *The Emperor Waltz* and Cecil B. DeMille's *Unconquered* (1947). The releases of such pictures were carefully spaced out to avoid cutting into one another's business.[58] However, the usual methods of contractually imposing minimum ticket prices on theaters were rendered problematic by the results of antitrust legal action that had been pending for the last decade.

Selling Singly, Auction Selling, and Antitrust

In 1940, the "Big Five" theater-owning corporations had signed a Consent Decree agreeing to desist from some of the common practices claimed by many independent exhibitors to be iniquitous and in restraint of trade.[59] In particular, block booking was now limited to a maximum of five features in any one block, and blind selling was outlawed.[60] National arbitration boards were also established to deal with exhibitors' complaints of unfair competition or excessive clearances between runs. In return, the Department of Justice agreed to waive its demand for the complete divorcement of exhibition from production and distribution. The principal effect of the 1940 decree was to make production and distribution more competitive; each film now had to stand largely on its own merit. Blocks of five typically included one or two high-budget pictures along with several medium- and low-budget pictures, titles in each category being charged at varying rental rates. But an increased number of films were now booked on percentage terms and at generally higher percentages than before.[61]

Another new tendency was to sell pictures singly in one-off deals. In the 1930s, only UA, which had the smallest output of any major distributor, regularly sold all its films individually (at the insistence of producers like Selznick and Goldwyn), and usually only roadshows were offered separately from the other majors' annual blocks. However, with the new limitations on block booking, an increased number of films were designated as being of special value and sold separately to maximize their rental revenues.[62] The larger number of percentage bookings, the higher percentages, and the practice of selling films singly all increased the rentals paid by exhibitors, as did the studios' stipulation of increased admission prices for top product. By 1944 the term of the decree had lapsed, the arbitration boards were deemed lacking in sufficient force, and the Justice Department resumed its campaign for divorcement.[63]

The District Court of New York issued its ruling on the case on June 11, 1946. It again stopped short of calling for full divorcement, but stipulated that the theater-owning majors be prevented from acquiring further theaters (including those temporarily hired for roadshow purposes) unless specifically approved by the courts. It also placed a total ban on block booking (all films now had to be sold singly), on the setting of unreasonable clearances, and on the fixing of admission prices. The implications of these decisions for big-budget pictures were crucial. Although the judgment contained no specific prohibition against or even mention of roadshows as such, *Gone with the Wind*, *For Whom the Bell Tolls*, *Wilson*, and *The Song of Bernadette* were specifically cited as instances of price fixing and unreasonable clearance. When their distributors "were not satisfied with current prices [charged by exhibitors], they would refuse to grant licenses unless the prices were raised."[64] The setting of minimum prices and protection periods for expensive pictures was of course central to roadshowing in any of its forms. Only by controlling them could distributors hope to guarantee a certain return on their investments. (In the same period, the government was putting pressure on all businesses to reduce prices in order to bring inflation under control.)

Selznick's Vanguard Films approached the court with a proposal to exempt big-budget, "extra-length" features from the price-fixing ban in order to permit exhibition at advanced prices. The company argued that

"a producer was willing to invest his time and energy and to venture his capital beyond the ordinary in motion pictures of that type because, traditionally, he could protect his larger capital investment and justify the expenditures of his time and energy by having such pictures roadshown at increased admission prices and thereafter released generally." Many of the landmarks in the advance of the motion picture art were only possible because of the road-showing practice, Vanguard said.[65]

The majors in turn submitted a plan for "blanket roadshow exemption," along with other proposed alternatives to the decree rulings, to the New York federal court on November 6, 1946. The court informally agreed to make an exception for roadshow-type pictures made by independent producers and "non-theatre owning companies,"[66] and eventually agreed that all companies should be permitted up to one roadshow release a year, so long as its production costs were over $3 million. However, the distributors were still forbidden from fixing admission prices except in four-wall-hire situations (which themselves, as we have noted, had specifically to be approved by the courts). There also remained the problem of definition: what actually constituted a roadshow under current conditions? Although historical precedent suggested that reserved seats and twice-daily separate performances were integral to roadshowing, the more liberal recent use of the term to designate only raised admission prices and an extended clearance before general release swayed the court to accept this as the basis of the agreement.[67]

As many as a dozen raised-price "roadshows" were announced for 1947–48, and studio executives privately admitted that the market could not "possibly absorb [them all] without serious permanent injury to the industry."[68] Allied Theatre Owners asked all exhibitors to resist them as "harmful and shortsighted," creating ill will among patrons.[69] Nevertheless, the six highest domestic grossers of 1947 included five such films: *The Best Years of Our Lives* (1946), *Duel in the Sun, Unconquered, Forever Amber,* and *Life with Father* (1947). (Only Columbia's *The Jolson Story* [1946] was not shown at increased prices.) Yet their chart positions suggested a more successful performance than had actually been the case. All five films ultimately grossed less than early predictions had anticipated, allegedly due to public resistance to the high prices asked.[70]

"Roadshow" releases planned for a number of other high-cost productions, including Fox's *Captain from Castile* (1947), MGM's *Green Dolphin Street* (1947), Universal's *All My Sons* (1948), and RKO's *I Remember Mama* (1948), were subsequently canceled and they were offered instead at normal admission prices but with rental terms set at 50 percent or more. Some circuits accused the majors of colluding to fix high rentals.[71] RKO's release of Walter Wanger's *Joan of Arc* (1948), which cost $4,650,506 to produce and needed at least twice that amount in rentals to break even,

NO BOOK EVER PRINTED CAN MATCH THE PUBLISHING RECORD OF

FOREVER AMBER

3 Years on ALL best-seller lists!

32 gigantic Printings!

668,000 1st Printing!

360,250 2nd Printing!

275,000 3rd Printing!

125,000 4th Printing!

115,000 5th Printing!

141,000 Overseas Edition!

50,000 1st Printing England!

Condensation in Pageant!

Condensation in Coronet!

Translated into 9 foreign languages!

More than 2,000,000 copies in print!

300,000 copies new movie edition to be printed in October, 1947!

NO PICTURE EVER PRODUCED CAN MATCH THE BOOKING RECORD OF

FOREVER AMBER

COLOR BY TECHNICOLOR

4 WEEKS BEFORE RELEASE DATE IT HAS BEEN BOOKED IN MORE THAN 1300 OF AMERICA'S AND CANADA'S TOP THEATRES!

THE PICTURE   THE PLAYDATE   YOU'LL REMEMBER FOREVER   20 CENTURY-FOX

Literary tie-ups and saturation bookings are highlighted by this trade press advertisement for *Forever Amber* (1947) (*Variety*, September 24, 1947, 12).

played around 2,500 raised-price engagements (compared to 4,500 for *The Best Years of Our Lives* and 5,300 for *Duel in the Sun*), but was ultimately left with a net loss almost equal to its domestic gross of just over $2.5 million. Forbidden from fixing its own prices in theaters, RKO had at one stage planned to release the film through Samuel Goldwyn's company, a nonparticipant in the antitrust proceedings.[72] Although Columbia was judged to have acted illegally by insisting on a "per-ticket minimum rental" for *Jolson Sings Again* (1949)—which after playing "a few more than 100 dates" at advanced prices was moved swiftly into regular release[73]—the courts generally declined to intervene in rentals disputes unless a conspiracy to fix prices could be proven.

The 1946 court ruling had also recommended the "auction selling" of films on an individual basis through competitive bidding. This was an effort to break the established system whereby theaters had been placed in advance in a particular run, and in which they were required to charge the admission prices approved by the distributors.[74] But it was greeted with dismay by many exhibitors, who correctly realized that it would entail increased rentals. Exhibitors in a given area would each submit a proposed rental, without being told what their rivals had bid (hence "blind bidding"). Distributors would then give the picture to those who offered the best deal. MGM was the first major to try auction selling, beginning with the musical *Holiday in Mexico* (1946). Despite its slowness as a method of selling, the generally satisfactory results meant that other companies took up the bidding system and continued using it even after the Justice Department and the Supreme Court later reversed position and specifically recommended against it.[75]

In order to stimulate bidding, product had to be especially attractive, and that usually meant expensive. Paramount distribution head Charles M. Reagan claimed that top films sold by auction had the potential to earn twice the amount earned through more traditional methods, and that the most costly pictures had the strongest potential of all: "I would rather go out now and sell one picture that costs $3,000,000 than two pictures that cost $1,500,000 each. I know that if the quality is in keeping with the cost, I'll get more income out of my single $3,000,000 production than the two which cost less."[76] Michael Conant has observed that relatively few releases were offered for auction bidding, as it was a time-consuming process that inconvenienced both exhibitor and distributor.[77] It was therefore generally reserved for those big pictures on which competition could be expected to be fierce. Although they could no longer dictate ticket price scales, distributors could fairly ask what prices exhibitors intended to charge:

If an exhibitor responded with an admission price that the distributor's agent considered too low, he was refused the license. If he stated one admission price and upon receiving the film charged another that was lower, he jeopardized his chances of being able to license later popular pictures from that distributor. One technique of suggesting that admission prices be increased for costly roadshow pictures was for the film distributor's salesman to tell the exhibitors what higher price other exhibitors were charging for that film.[78]

Following appeals from all sides, the Supreme Court's verdict on the case against Hollywood was handed down on May 3, 1948.[79] The majors were found guilty of maintaining a monopoly blatantly in restraint of trade. The district court's findings on price fixing and unreasonable clearances were upheld, but competitive bidding was considered an inadequate remedy that would involve the judiciary too heavily in arbitration. Instead, the high court recommended full divorcement of production and distribution from exhibition, leaving the lower court to work out the details via new consent decrees. The studios' reaction was pithily expressed by one of their defense lawyers: "We've been hit with a baseball bat."[80] RKO was the first to sign a consent decree in 1948, followed by Paramount in 1949, and Loew's, Warner Bros., and Fox in 1950. These decrees involved the corporations' selling off of about half of their theater holdings to independent exhibitors (divestiture), and the setting up of new, separate companies to control the remainder (divorcement). Because of RKO and Paramount's "prompt 'surrender' and negotiations with the court . . . these studios received more favorable terms than the other Big Five companies," who had to consult with the court before acquiring more theaters.[81]

Although the decrees came into immediate effect, they took the next decade to be put into practice. Because of the postwar box-office decline, eager buyers for theaters were hard to find. Indeed, it has been argued that the majors were lucky to be prevented from engaging in exhibition when they were, as that sector suffered more heavily than distribution in the coming recession.[82]

Blitz Exhibitionism and the Sex Western

Despite David O. Selznick's earlier defense of traditional roadshowing for *Gone with the Wind,* his western spectacle *Duel in the Sun* was released (through a new company, Selznick Releasing Organization [SRO]) in a new pattern the producer himself had devised. Selznick realized that, whereas *GWTW* had been presold through the tremendous success of the book, the casting search, and other free publicity, *Duel* (though based on a novel by Niven Busch) was a relatively unknown quantity that required intensive local advertising to create public awareness and stimulate interest. However, he was concerned that the expensive advertising would not be economic if the film was playing in only one theater per territory, even at advanced prices. He therefore proposed opening *Duel* in several downtown theaters per territory at once, along with simultaneous engagements in a larger number of suburban and outlying areas, all playing at continuous performances with advanced prices. Such multiple first runs would make possible a greater number of admissions in a shorter space of time than with an exclusive engagement. Play-off would be quicker, as would amortization of costs, an essential consideration for an independent producer funded directly by bank loans. Selznick explained his idea of saturating release territories with advance exploitation in a memo of July 22, 1946, when the film was still in postproduction:

I have been working on advertising plans . . . based upon enormously and unprecedent-edly heavy newspaper and radio advertising by territories in the eight or ten weeks before we go into each area, and during the first weeks that we are in each area . . . instead of spending our money nationally, with a staggered release, and thereby wasting a large part of the money, we will be able to flood an area just before we go into it. But this flooding is only good if there are an enormous number of seats available for the customers whom we will reach.[83]

Duel in the Sun opened in Los Angeles, for the purpose of attracting Academy Award nominations, on a reserved-seat basis in two theaters in late December 1946, with a third house added in January.[84] Some one hundred simultaneous play dates were then set for California and Texas in February, but these were delayed while SRO made arrangements for the shipping of prints and for the promotional appearances of the stars, Gregory Peck and Jennifer Jones (though there was much trade specula-tion that the delay was in fact caused by the objections of the Legion of Decency to the film's sexual content). *Duel* did not open widely until early May, with fifty-three simultaneous engagements in Greater New York, fifty-five in California, and a like number in other key territories. While the total box-office gross of these bookings (all on a grind basis with prices raised to an average $1.25 top) was an estimated $2.5 mil-lion, a record for a single week, few of the shows sold out. Attendance at the Capitol on Broadway, for example, was lower than expected because of the drain on patron-age by competing neighborhood houses. Nevertheless, it was claimed in trade press advertisements that some three million people had seen the film in only seven days. With 370 Technicolor prints in circulation and around seven hundred dates played (many in small towns and what would ordinarily have been late-run houses), *Duel* was reported to have earned $3 million in rentals in its first six weeks of wide release.[85]

Selznick dubbed his strategy "blitz exhibitionism" and planned to release another expensive production, Alfred Hitchcock's *The Paradine Case* (1947), in the same way. *Variety* pointed out that multiple day-and-date runs had been used for many years in Los Angeles, which was "particularly suited to it because it is so geographically spread out."[86] The policy was sometimes known as the "Los Angeles system" for that reason. But *Duel* proved to be highly influential in reviving and extending the area-saturation policy. In a telegram, Selznick claimed: "Entire film trade here regards this as tre-mendous milestone in motion-picture merchandising and exhibition, and as mark-ing revolution in picture business for handling big pictures."[87] In fact it caused some controversy in the industry. Exhibitors protested at the "discriminatory" practice of increasing the number of first-run engagements, while others saw their competing pictures benefiting from consumer resistance to *Duel*'s raised prices.[88] Some distribu-tors felt the policy "might seriously injure the reputation and prestige of the first-run," while others regarded it as "the best way to boost the number of first-runs without building more theatres."[89] Selznick may also have been influenced by his desire to limit the damage from negative word of mouth and poor reviews, which the advertising itself may even have helped to attract. He later expressed regret at some of the excessively vulgar promotional hype, costing around $1 million, used to attract audiences. In a memo of August 17, 1947, Selznick remarked that the "ballyhoo . . . was damaging . . . a complete contradiction of our former Tiffany standards," and regretted his personal loss of "prestige" and "position."[90]

Duel in the Sun was widely compared at the time with another controversial "sex western," made by another independent producer, which had also encountered censorship problems. Howard Hughes completed *The Outlaw* in early 1941, and received a Seal of Approval from the Production Code Administration (PCA) after making a number of cuts. But local censorship boards in six states, including New York, forbade the exhibition of the film without further editing, which Hughes was reluctant to perform. After the film had remained on the shelf for nearly two years, Hughes decided to roadshow it (his provisional distributor, Fox, having withdrawn), but with the wartime boom keeping movie houses fully occupied he was only able to make a single booking, at the Geary in San Francisco. The film's three weeks there, and a further four on moveover at the Tivoli, were hugely successful, but no other engagements followed for another three years. Hughes then ran into problems with the Motion Picture Association of America (MPPA, the trade body formerly known as the MPPDA), which held his advertising campaign to be unduly salacious and threatened to withdraw the film's PCA seal, and with exhibitors when, in April 1946, he authorized a trade press advertisement carrying box-office figures for the first six key-city engagements, thus contravening an unwritten industry rule against revealing actual grosses (it subsequently became extremely common in trade ads).

Now being distributed by UA, *The Outlaw* opened at four theaters in Los Angeles, gradually followed by multiple bookings in other territories (all well before the blitzing of *Duel in the Sun*). The film performed exceptionally well in most of its engagements, but continuing censorship difficulties, including the opposition of church groups and the police, limited its theater bookings.[91] By September 1948, *The Outlaw* had earned $3,019,700 from 6,153 play dates, about half the number that would normally be expected of a major release; accumulated costs were also around $3 million. In 1950, after Hughes's new acquisition RKO had taken over the film's distribution, it was reissued to a further domestic gross of $2,165,000. Successive cuts had reduced it from 121 minutes to 115 and finally to 103.[92]

Publicity for *The Outlaw* went out of its way to defy public morality and industry authorities. In addition to the famous poster images of a disheveled Jane Russell appearing "Mean, Moody, Magnificent," Hughes's chief publicist Russell Birdwell took out a full-page press article headlined "'The Outlaw' Proves Sex Has Not Been Rationed."[93] By contrast, Selznick's advertising stressed his willingness to comply with the Production Code. To obtain clearance from the Legion of Decency, and thereby forestall a Catholic boycott of *Duel in the Sun,* he reportedly had to make forty-six cuts, with the resultant loss of two to three minutes of footage. Some advertisements testified that the film had been made "in strict conformity with the morals code of the

Motion Picture Assn. and has received its seal of approval."[94] Of course, though this caption was a sop to the Legion, it was also an inducement for patrons who sought out scandalous material.

Duel and *The Outlaw* were, along with Paramount's *Kitty* (1945) and Fox's *Leave Her to Heaven* (1945) and *Forever Amber,* among a small group of high-cost films in the mid-1940s that earned critical condemnation for their alleged immorality, vulgarity, and suggestiveness. In this respect, all five ran counter to the dominant trends of wartime and postwar big pictures, which tended to favor romanticized repression and noble self-sacrifice over the brazen eroticism and wanton self-indulgence flaunted by these films' protagonists (compare them with, for example, *For Whom the Bell Tolls, The Song of Bernadette,* and *Since You Went Away*). All five amplify one element of *Gone with the Wind:* its heroine's driving sexual and material ambition, manifested in her pursuit of illicit passions and willingness to use her sexual charms to achieve wealth and position. The theme is differently modulated in each: Rio, the main female character of *The Outlaw,* is considerably more passive than her counterparts in the others, and her role is the least central to the narrative. Censor-baiting films such as these lost any air of prestige that might otherwise have been conferred by their upscale production values. All five were overlooked by the Academy Awards, which suggests that the industry largely shared the dim view of them taken by moralists. The inference could be drawn that filmmakers themselves were making a distinction between the soft excesses of spectacle and sexuality and the hard disciplines of piety and social relevance, and had chosen to reserve their honors for the latter.

Among the most highly regarded films of its time was Samuel Goldwyn's *The Best Years of Our Lives,* directed by William Wyler, a three-hour, multistory drama about the problems of returning war veterans. It was also regularly compared to *Duel in the Sun,* albeit somewhat fortuitously. Both were made by leading independent producers; both were in circulation simultaneously and often in direct competition for theater venues; both were in contention for the title of top earner of 1947; and each represented a wholly different kind of "special" production. In each and every instance, Goldwyn's film seemed to get the better of Selznick's. *Best Years* beat *Duel* to occupy the Astor, Broadway's most sought-after "run" house; screen for screen it out-ran and out-grossed its rival (the Astor engagement lasted thirty-eight weeks for a box-office gross of $1,312,000 and a rental to Goldwyn of over $800,000); and with laudatory reviews as well as seven Oscars it was an undisputed prestige picture, whereas *Duel* was regarded by most contemporary observers as downmarket pabulum. *Best Years* was also considerably cheaper, costing only $2.1 million, and therefore vastly more profitable.[95]

However, Goldwyn subsequently chose a "modified" blitz release for his next picture, the Danny Kaye vehicle *The Secret Life of Walter Mitty* (1947), using five or six theaters each in selected territories. Fox also adopted a saturation policy, starting with *Forever Amber* and the epic *Captain from Castile.* For the 1949 general release in Greater New York of Walt Disney's part-animated feature *So Dear to My Heart,*

Saturation opening in New York and New Jersey: trade press advertisement for
Mighty Joe Young (1949) (*Variety*, August 24, 1949, 12).

RKO followed its Broadway premiere run at the Palace with bookings in 113 suburban theaters, followed by two further day-and-date "waves," each separated by only seven days' clearance. Both Paramount and Universal-International adopted a general policy of multiple-theater, multiple-city bookings, having found that pictures suited to the strategy could earn twice their usual expected grosses and amortize their costs more quickly. Other companies, including MGM, Columbia, UA, and Allied Artists, preferred mass releasing on a national rather than a regional basis, with simultaneous openings in up to four hundred theaters located in key cities and towns across the country. All these were part of an increasing postwar trend toward wide, rapid releases designed to take advantage of intensive advertising campaigns.[96]

Both the regional and national saturation strategies called for an increased number of prints in circulation. Fox released *Forever Amber* with 475 prints, both *Prince of Foxes* (1949) and *The Black Rose* (1950) with 500, and used as many as 542 for *Father Was a Fullback* (1949).[97] Both strategies also had the negative effects of devaluing downtown theaters used to exclusive first runs, limiting the choice of program open to local filmgoers, and restricting the spread of positive word of mouth, as a picture's release was often over too quickly for it to benefit from customer recommendations.[98] But they nevertheless played a useful part in what became a desperate drive to reverse the trends of declining attendances and shrinking revenues. The next chapter will examine some of the other measures the industry adopted as it sought to adjust to a rapidly changing theatrical market.

Colossals and Blockbusters, 1949–1959

In what *Variety* called a "giant step back toward normality," the period 1949 to 1951 saw a rise in major studio output but a substantial reduction in operating costs.[1] With the box office now in recession, budgets and shooting schedules were cut. Careful advance planning helped eliminate wasted footage. Overheads were reduced by laying off permanent staff at all levels. Even executives and "above-the-line" talent (directors, producers, and stars) took pay cuts, often in return for profit or gross participation. In these three years combined, only eight films cost more than $3 million to produce, and of these only one more than $4 million.[2] According to one theater manager, "Super-dupers . . . are not worth the playing time, and film costs are too high in comparison to admission charges. Exhibitors have lost enthusiasm [for them] because there is a negligible profit."[3] Paramount president Adolph Zukor conceded that the industry still needed films with "abnormal staying power" to attract a more discriminating public, but added that "big, outstanding pictures [did not] necessarily mean very costly ones. Pictures need brains, not money. The talk that high-cost pictures attract the public is not correct. Give me brains and I'll make good pictures."[4] But it was not long before the lessons of the box office forced a return to bigness.

While the domestic market was depressed, the overseas market gradually returned to a more stable basis as agreements were reached with each of the major European countries that had imposed currency restrictions. However, considerable sums in film revenues were still prevented from being converted into dollars for remittance to the United States. With the availability of these blocked funds for local use, location shooting abroad came to seem a desirable option (see the next chapter for more detailed discussion). In advocating "Global Production," Darryl Zanuck stated: "Hollywood makes pictures for the whole world and therefore should consider the whole world as a shooting location. This, I believe, will be a stimulus to the box-office both here and abroad."[5] Zanuck claimed, with some justice, that his studio was in the forefront of this development. Fox had recently produced a number of location-shot films, including the period epics *Prince of Foxes* (filmed in Italy) and *The Black Rose* (filmed in Britain and Morocco). However, the devaluation of European currencies, especially the British pound (whose dollar exchange value fell by one-third), threatened to reduce the value of overseas earnings.[6] To recoup costs as quickly as possible, *Prince of Foxes* was premiered simultaneously in fifteen countries. According to *Variety* this was "one of the fastest playoffs ever accorded a top-budgeted film" and "the first time any picture [had] been given such a worldwide sendoff."[7]

Prince of Foxes and *The Black Rose* were also in the vanguard of a revival of the costume adventure, a genre that was to remain a staple of both Hollywood and international production for the next two decades. *The Black Rose* was one of a number of large-scale films that had been intended for production several years earlier, but were postponed because of the costs involved. Planned for shooting in Britain in 1947, it was canceled because of the ad valorem tax dispute and concerns over its budget, initially projected as high as $5 million. Adaptations of the pseudo-biblical best sellers *Quo Vadis?* and *The Robe* had been announced for production during the war, but shortages of materials and manpower led to their cancellation also.[8] The postwar recession posed similar problems for big pictures, and most costume films of the early 1950s were modestly produced by the standards of recent years. In 1950, Warners' *The Flame and the Arrow* and Disney-RKO's *Treasure Island* were each made for less than $2 million, while MGM's *Kim* and *King Solomon's Mines* each came in at under $2.5 million despite extensive overseas location work. (In contrast, MGM's *The Three Musketeers* [1948] had cost $4,474,000.)

While this period produced few films with superbudgets, there were also few superhits. George Gallup's Audience Research Institute estimated that the average A-picture of 1949 was seen by three million fewer Americans than in 1946. *Variety's* annual box-office charts showed no films with domestic rentals exceeding $5.5 million for the years 1948 and 1949, and only one in each of 1950 and 1951.[9] These two films, *Samson and Delilah* (1949) and *David and Bathsheba* (1951), seemed to be exceptions to the pattern of steady decline. They established a recurrent tendency whereby a small number of films each year would bring disproportionately large earnings, while the majority of releases failed to break even. They also gave renewed conviction to the long-held belief that big pictures meant big box office.

In common with many of the industry's leading figures, Cecil B. DeMille was now an independent producer-director with his own company. But he was still based on the Paramount lot and the studio continued to provide finance and distribution facilities for his pictures. *Samson and Delilah* had first been announced for production as early as 1934 and had frequently been postponed. Opening at Christmas 1949 in a dual Broadway engagement at the Paramount and the Rivoli (both on grind at slightly raised prices of $1.80 top),[10] the film became the highest grosser in the studio's history to date, with domestic rentals of $7,976,730 by 1955 and a further $6,232,520 overseas.[11] Its success provided a direct stimulus for the production of other biblical films, including Fox's *David and Bathsheba,* which *Variety* named the box-office leader of 1951. The journal adopted the term *colossal* (as both adjective and noun) to describe this and other upcoming big pictures, including Warners' British-based naval adventure *Captain Horatio Hornblower* (1951) and DeMille's circus melodrama *The Greatest Show on Earth* (1952), which it identified as heralding the industry's return— "on a limited scale, at least—to the multi-million-dollar epic."[12] Such films were said to justify their costs because they benefited the business as a whole, by drawing public attention to the cinema as a mass entertainment medium and away from competing leisure pursuits.

Both *Samson* and *David* were initially exhibited at advanced prices, but, in keeping with the dominant trend of the 1940s, neither was presented on a traditional reserved-seat, two-a-day roadshow basis. While their distributors were now forbidden to set admission prices in theaters they did not own or lease, they demanded such high rental terms—up to 70 percent from the first dollar—that exhibitors claimed they were virtually forced to raise their prices in order to guarantee themselves a profit. The same strategy was also used for such prestige pictures as Universal-International's *Harvey* (1950), Columbia's *Born Yesterday* (1950) and *Death of a Salesman* (1951), Paramount's *A Place in the Sun* (1951), and Warners' *A Streetcar Named Desire* (1951)— all based on literary or theatrical properties for which large sums had been paid for the film rights—while MGM offered a 10 percent profit guarantee to any exhibitors playing its musical *An American in Paris* (1951) with increased prices.[13]

For all their spectacle, *Samson* and *David* were quite economically produced, costing $3,097,563 and $2,170,000 respectively. They were made largely on their studios' home lots, with minimal use of locations, thus enabling close supervision of expenditure.[14] For its own religious epic, MGM sent cast and crew to Rome's Cinecittà studios to make the first sound version of *Quo Vadis* (1951). Production costs totaled a record $7,623,000, the bulk of which was financed by frozen lira and sterling (most of the principal cast being British).[15] In order to maximize revenues, the company used the system of auction selling much disliked by exhibitors for driving up rental prices: "It is clear to all who understand our business that with the customary methods of distribution, and at regular admission prices, there could not be a chance for us to recoup our investment, much less to earn a profit or produce an appropriate profit for the exhibitors . . . there is no course but to pre-release this great production on a competitive bidding basis for first run showings in suitable theatres."[16]

MGM required, in addition to offers on the sharing of the gross, guarantees from exhibitors on a minimum length of run, holdover control figures, the amount to be spent on advertising, and the minimum admission price at which tickets would be sold. Mindful of the prohibition on price fixing, the company requested the "voluntary" disclosure of such information in order for it to assess the value of competing offers. Despite scattered complaints, the company reported little resistance on the part of exhibitors. An extravagant marketing campaign stressed the single word "colossal" (or "Quolossal"). To coordinate international exhibition, a publicity conference for

Trade press advertisement for *Quo Vadis* (1951) (*Variety*, February 27, 1952, 12).

eighty-two delegates from thirty-seven countries was held in Rome, "the first global convention ever held by a motion picture company for a single film."[17] Such conferences subsequently became the standard launchpad for superproductions. *Quo Vadis* premiered simultaneously in two Broadway theaters, the Astor, playing separate performances, and the Capitol, playing continuously: the same two venues, with the same exhibition policies, used for *Gone with the Wind* in 1939. Throughout the country, *Quo Vadis* was mostly exhibited on grind with advanced prices (typically $1.25) and without an intermission, despite its three-hour running time. Worldwide rentals totaled $21,037,000, almost half of which came from the foreign market.[18]

The success in 1952 of *Quo Vadis, The Greatest Show on Earth,* MGM's British-produced medieval epic *Ivanhoe,* Samuel Goldwyn's costume musical *Hans Christian Andersen,* and Fox's Hemingway adaptation *The Snows of Kilimanjaro* demonstrated that a considerable audience still existed for films "of super-scale proportions," and that the potential earnings of such exceptional attractions were now proportionately far greater than when the market had supported a larger number of routinely profitable films.[19] Competitive bidding helped to increase potential revenues, as exhibitors fought one another to offer the best deals for top product. MGM's sales policy for *Ivanhoe* closely followed the pattern set by *Quo Vadis,* as did Columbia's for *Salome* (1953).[20]

Variety's review headline for *Quo Vadis* described it very simply: "A box-office blockbuster."[21] Borrowing a term from World War II—the name once used to describe a heavy bomb, one of the Allies' key weapons in the carpet bombing of Germany—the journal reintroduced it into another context of conflict: between studios and exhibitors, between the cinema and television, and between the film industry and declining audience interest. This new "blockbuster"—a film designed to make a big impact on the box office, one capable of generating exceptionally large revenues partly by virtue of its exceptional production values—came to be seen as the industry's principal weapon in this peacetime "war," and the term quickly passed into trade and public vocabulary to become all but ubiquitous by the mid-1950s.[22]

The renewed trend toward size and spectacle was not regarded with universal enthusiasm in the trade. Producer Stanley Kramer, in a self-penned *Variety* article headlined "Pix Can't Live By Bigness Alone," asserted that Hollywood

couldn't long survive just producing blockbusters, which I assume mean pictures that are replete with thousands of plunging horses and plunging necklines, plus gigantic, lavish situations and expenditures of millions of dollars. In the final analysis we are a story-telling medium, and our success depends directly upon our ability to tell stories well. If we must substitute size for all of the other well-tested elements that comprise expert story-telling, we belong in the circus business instead of motion pictures. It is possible that a wave of the super-colossal will engulf the industry.[23]

However, the industry's growing obsession with upgrading production values and upscaling budgets continued for nearly two decades. It was a tendency accentuated and accelerated by the appearance in the next few years of a range of new technologies and new techniques in cinematography, sound recording, and theatrical presentation.

A New Era Begins: Cinerama

In 1948, at the beginning of the postwar box-office decline, Universal-International's William Goetz had suggested that in order to appeal to an increasingly discriminating public, "our business will either have to come up with some new development as startling as sound, or refine its processes, both artistically and commercially, to the point where subject matter will count for the basic box-office value."[24] As we have previously noted, the introduction of synchronized sound in the 1920s was sufficient at that time to recapture the interest of audiences and increase attendance. Further technological developments in the form of wide-screen and large-screen processes had then been capped to prevent additional disruption to the industry at a time of economic instability. Whereas there had been no incentive to innovate in the boom years that followed the Depression, by the 1950s the industry was prepared to refresh a stagnant market with additional technological attractions.

Early fears that broadcast television might prove damaging to the motion picture business were largely dismissed. Trade papers even speculated that a nationwide TV link-up might actually prove advantageous to Hollywood, providing it with a source of publicity and promotion for its own products as well as a healthy source of competition.[25] However, by 1952 the film industry no longer regarded TV as a negligible threat. Al Lichtman claimed that 99 percent of the recent box-office decline could be laid at its door. He argued, in common with many in the industry, that the installation of large-screen television in theaters might help draw people away from domestic viewing. But this proved a dead end; other new photographic and presentational technologies prevailed instead.[26]

Color, which had been a feature of many of the big hits of the 1940s, was one weapon in the cinema's arsenal. The number of major-studio pictures in color had risen from an average of 4 percent of releases in 1939 to 21 percent in 1951. In each successive year thereafter, the proportion rose in increments of around 10 percent to reach 61 percent in 1955. There followed a slight dip, but by 1968 the film industry had effectively converted to total color production.[27] However, after Technicolor's virtual monopoly was overturned by antitrust legislation and by the introduction of cheaper processes such as Eastmancolor and its derivatives, color became too common to constitute a major commercial attraction by itself (television, too, had converted to color by the 1960s).

Outside the mainstream of the industry, several new screen processes were developed and demonstrated by independent filmmakers, inventors, and entrepreneurs. Cinerama, the first of the new systems to make a significant public impact, was devised by Fred Waller, former head of the photographic research and special effects department at Paramount. Waller claimed that his twin inspirations for the process were the apparent three-dimensional effect created by wide-angle lenses, and his observation that human depth perception is partly determined by peripheral vision. His first attempt to capitalize on these insights was the invention of a multiple-lens camera that captured eleven separate images; when projected inside a sphere they produced a single composite picture. This was first developed for, but not exhibited at, the 1939 New York World's Fair. The technology was adapted for the military during World War II as an aerial combat simulator for gunnery practice. After the war, Waller attempted to market a scaled-down version using three camera lenses and three projectors as an entertainment medium, initially under the name Vitarama. For several years Waller and his business partner, sound engineer Hazard E. Reeves, tried to interest Hollywood in the process, now renamed Cinerama. Having failed to do so, they instead found private funding for a holding company to market the technology. Its principal investors included journalist and adventurer Lowell Thomas, film producer Merian C. Cooper, and Broadway showman Michael Todd. Thomas, Cooper, and Todd collaborated on a "demonstration film" for the new process, which was completed shortly before Todd left the company.[28]

Cinerama involved three strips of 35 mm film (each frame six sprockets high, compared to the four of standard 35 mm) interlocked in photography and projection to provide a single vast picture spread across a deeply curved screen made from hundreds of vertical strips designed to refract stray light away from the image. Seven channels of stereophonic sound were carried on a fourth 35 mm reel coated with magnetic oxide. Because each frame-third was slightly taller than it was wide, the aspect ratio for the whole composite image was approximately 2.6:1, compared to the industry standard of 1.37:1, though the deep curvature of the screen appeared to exaggerate its breadth as well as suggest an illusion of optical depth.[29] Unveiled to the public on September 30, 1952 at the Broadway Theatre in New York under the title *This Is Cinerama,* the pilot film played to packed houses and an enthusiastic press. Trade response was equally favorable. *Variety* reported the commonly held view that Cinerama heralded "a new era in the film industry, and promises to hypo biz as did the advent of sound and color—and even to possibly a greater extent in view of the fact that Cinerama enthralled customers despite absence of story or characters."[30]

There is little attempt in *This Is Cinerama* to link sequences with any kind of narrative or thematic continuity. Lowell Thomas argued that in it,

nothing should be done to take the spotlight away from Cinerama. If, to take an extreme example, in our first picture we had some tremendous attraction, let's say Charlie Chaplin doing Hamlet, the focus of attention would be either on the great clown or on the new approach to Shakespeare. . . . We didn't want to be judged on subject matter. This advent of something as new and important as Cinerama was in itself a major event in the history of entertainment. The logical thing to do was to make Cinerama the hero.[31]

141

Thomas narrates the show, introducing it with a thirteen-minute prologue in standard-screen, monochrome, monaural 35 mm in which he gives a potted history of pictorial representation. Theatrical, fairground, and travelogue spectacle dominate the rest of the program. The first three-panel sequence is a roller-coaster ride with the camera positioned on the front car (the roller-coaster image came to symbolize the whole wide-screen era). The opening half also includes extracts from a production of *Aida* at La Scala, Milan; performances by Spanish toreadors and flamenco dancers, the Long Island Choral Society, and the Vienna Boys' Choir; and scenes filmed on the Venetian canals and at the Edinburgh Military Tattoo. The second half concentrates on American landscapes, natural and otherwise. A protracted visit to Cypress Gardens, a holiday theme park in the Louisiana Everglades, is followed by an aerial tour of American landscapes filmed from the nose of a B-52 airplane. The final shots unspool to a vocal performance of "America the Beautiful" by the Mormon Tabernacle Choir, which reportedly moved President Eisenhower to tears.[32]

The principle of showcasing the technology extends to the soundtrack as well as the image. In an aural prelude to the second act (played over closed curtains), a series of distinctly separated sounds of the orchestra is reproduced from speakers placed at strategic intervals around the auditorium, as Thomas's voice explains the soundtrack's power and range. Cinerama's was not the first stereophonic sound system. Western Electric's Bell Laboratories had demonstrated stereo at Carnegie Hall in 1940, the same year that Disney had experimented with Fantasound. In the late 1940s Hollywood studios had begun recording sound on magnetic tape (first introduced in Germany in 1945) rather than on celluloid film.[33] But neither motion pictures nor domestic record players yet offered multichannel playback. Not only was Cinerama's stereo fully directional, placing the sources of sounds in a three-dimensional aural space, it could also, according to publicity, "create a better musical balance than if the orchestra itself were present."[34]

With ticket prices set at $2.80 and two or three separate performances daily, *This Is Cinerama* ran thirty-five weeks at the Broadway before transferring to the Warner for a further eighty-seven weeks. This was the longest New York first run on record. The Stanley Warner Theatre Corporation (Warner Bros.' former theater chain, now a separate company following divorcement) was contracted to coproduce and exhibit films in the process on an exclusive basis for five years (an arrangement that had to be approved by the Department of Justice). After the first two years of exhibition in only thirteen U.S. cities, *This Is Cinerama*'s total box-office receipts were $14,767,535, including $3,599,722 from New York alone, and admissions numbered 8,081,461.[35] The second film in the process did not emerge until 1955, partly due to the need to obtain maximum mileage from the first (initial projections had been for six to eight pictures per year).[36] *Cinerama Holiday* followed the exchange visits of an American and a Swiss couple to each other's continents. *Seven Wonders of the World* (1956) and *Search for Paradise* (1957) visited a variety of exotic locations, while *Cinerama South Seas Adventure* (1958) followed an ocean voyage to the Pacific Islands. A rival three-

Roller Coaster Sequence Courtesy Rockaways' Playland Amusement Park, New York

3rd Year on Broadway!

The most fabulous story telling medium in the history of entertainment!

THIS IS CINERAMA

All other productions come and go, but THIS IS CINERAMA—one production—outlives a whole studio program: continuing month after month in the great cities of the nation!

Only CINERAMA'S three-eyed projection, seven-voiced sound and wrap-around screen can put YOU in the picture!

★

And the astounding figure of over 9 million viewers in only 13 CINERAMA theatres acclaims CINERAMA as the only really new wonder of the entertainment world!

★

Completed: Louis de Rochemont's
"CINERAMA HOLIDAY"
In Production: Lowell Thomas'
"SEVEN WONDERS OF THE WORLD"
In Preparation: Warner Bros. Studios
"LEWIS AND CLARK EXPEDITION"

As of Today, this is CINERAMA'S record:

New York, Warner Theatre	105 weeks	Minneapolis, Century	23 weeks
Boston, Boston Theatre	39 weeks	San Francisco, Orpheum	50 weeks
Chicago, Eitel's Palace	61 weeks	St. Louis, Mo., Ambassador	33 weeks
Detroit, Music Hall	79 weeks	Washington, D. C., Warner	41 weeks
Hollywood, Warner Theatre	78 weeks	Dallas, Melba Theatre	13 weeks
Philadelphia, Boyd	51 weeks	Cincinnati, Capitol	14 weeks
Pittsburgh, Warner	42 weeks	...and every run continues unbroken!	

Never has there been motion picture entertainment with this kind of impact! And now CINERAMA has its first overseas showing—opening September 30, 1954 at the CASINO THEATRE, in LONDON, ENGLAND!

STANLEY WARNER CINERAMA CORPORATION; DIVISION: STANLEY WARNER CORPORATION

Trade press advertisement marking the two-year anniversary of *This Is Cinerama* (1952) (*Variety*, September 29, 1954, 21).

strip process, Cinemiracle, backed by another exhibition chain, National Theatres, resulted in only one production, *Windjammer* (1958), before Cinemiracle was bought out by Cinerama, Inc., and several of its technical features were incorporated into Cinerama. This film also traced an ocean voyage, from Norway to America and the West Indies.[37]

The principal attraction Cinerama (and Cinemiracle) offered was a feeling of "engulfment" in the image due to the size and curvature of the screen, the use of wide-angle lenses (producing both extreme depth of focus and a distended sense of spatial depth), the clarity and high resolution derived from the large frame size, and the high-fidelity, multichannel directional sound.[38] Hence the logic of the travelogue form, taking the audience on vicarious journeys. John Belton has suggested that the successful marketing of Cinerama as a participatory event, rather than merely an entertainment, was keyed to an era encouraging more active forms of leisure and recreation than the "passivity" of regular motion-picture viewing. He argues that, in the absence of narrative, "Cinerama and other multiple-screen systems constitute the most extreme instances of cinema as pure spectacle, pure sensation, pure experience."[39]

Various announcements were made for three-strip narrative features to be made in collaboration with one or other of the majors.[40] Yet none resulted until two MGM co-productions, *The Wonderful World of the Brothers Grimm* (1962) and *How the West Was Won* (1963). The long delay is partly explained by the refusal of Cinerama's license holders to permit alternative versions of the films to be shot in 35 mm for subsequent general release, or to adjust their technical specifications to allow "printing down" to conventional, single-strip 35 mm (Cinerama ran at a speed of 26 frames per second [fps], so reduction prints could not be made for regular screen projection at 24 fps). Stanley Warner also held to the principle that travelogues were less costly and therefore commercially less risky than dramatic features, which involved heavier financial commitments, including stars as well as stories. There was also the problem of adapting the format to the requirements of narrative. The visibility of the lines dividing the three panels of the projected image was never satisfactorily corrected, and objects crossing between panels tended to bend at odd angles. Aside from its technical complexity, any attempt by the Hollywood studios to convert their production programs to the new format would have rendered their entire existing backlog of features obsolete. They therefore refrained from using the three-strip formats until their corporate owners were prepared to compromise. By 1962, Cinerama's frame speed had been changed to 24 fps, permitting reduction prints for general release. The change was necessary due to the diminishing box-office returns of the later travelogues; the demands for more, and more varied, product for the fifty-eight Cinerama theaters then in existence around the world; and the apparent reaching of saturation point for domestic installations (the first closure occurred in 1957).[41]

Cinerama was never intended for wide adoption as either a photographic medium or an exhibition format. The expense of installing and operating the cumbersome equipment (which required three separate projection booths and a full-time projection staff of up to seventeen operators) and the few communities that could profitably sustain the year-long runs needed to make the installations economically viable (estimated to be no more than twenty cities in the United States) meant that it was necessarily limited to a small number of carefully selected roadshow situations.[42] The commercial success of the five Cinerama travelogues, which earned an aggregate worldwide box-office gross of $120 million by 1962 (including $82 million in the United States and Canada), nevertheless demonstrated to the mainstream industry the market value of special screen formats.[43] *Variety* correctly predicted shortly after its debut that the industry's positive reception of Cinerama would lead to an "engineering binge" in a bid to revive the cinema box office and compete with television.[44] The new formats Hollywood adopted can broadly be divided into two types: those designed for wide distribution in regular motion-picture theaters operating on a general-release basis, and those designed for specialized exhibition in designated roadshow houses.

Upgrading General Release: 3-D, CinemaScope, and VistaVision

The first attempts to compete with Cinerama (which was regularly described in the trade press as a "three-dimensional" process) came with the adoption of various stereoscopic, or 3-D, systems. Efforts to market stereo vision in motion pictures before the 1950s had earned only limited success, being confined mainly to novelty short subjects such as MGM's *Audioscopix* (1935). The revival of commercial interest in 3-D was directly stimulated by the threat of television. Independent producer Sol Lesser acquired the American rights to Tri-Opticon, a process developed in Britain by Stereo Techniques, and planned to roadshow a program of five stereoscopic shorts that test-screened at the Academy Theatre in Hollywood in October 1952. However, Lesser was outpaced by another independent production, a feature made in Natural Vision.[45]

Bwana Devil (1952) premiered in two Los Angeles theaters in November 1952, within two months of Cinerama's New York opening. Like Tri-Opticon, Natural Vision involved dual projectors synchronized to show overlapping images representing left-eye and right-eye records of the subject. This produced an illusion of spatial depth that could only be perceived by viewers equipped with polarized spectacles. When *Bwana Devil* proved unexpectedly successful, UA purchased world distribution rights from its producer, Arch Oboler, for $1,750,000. The picture ultimately earned some $3 million in domestic rentals, although, according to Tino Balio, UA had paid so much for the rights and so overspent on the manufacture of ten million pairs of plastic glasses that it lost $200,000 on the release. Despite seven hundred prints having been ordered (twice the usual A-picture inventory), the film played only five hundred dates in its first six months of release due to the slow rate of theater conversions.[46]

Bwana Devil nevertheless prompted several studios to begin making 3-D productions. The most successful of these was Warner Bros.' *House of Wax* (1953), a remake of the studio's last two-color Technicolor feature, *Mystery of the Wax Museum*. Unlike *Bwana Devil*, which had a monaural magnetic soundtrack, *House of Wax* employed a

Trade press advertisement promoting the novel screen and sound technologies of
House of Wax (1953) (*Variety*, April 15, 1953, 21). The phrase "new era"
became ubiquitous in this period of innovation.

four-channel magnetic stereo soundtrack using a process developed by RCA, Warner-Phonic. Trade advertising called the film "the screen's first complete electronic merger of dimension-camera and dimension-microphone."[47] It earned worldwide rentals on first release of $7,387,000, an extraordinary sum for a horror film. But from the outset the trade was skeptical about the long-term value of 3-D; it was widely regarded as a cheap gimmick even before *House of Wax* opened, and its reputation was soon harmed by its association with low-budget "exploitation" pictures. It was not generally considered a suitable medium for prestige pictures. MGM's film of Cole Porter's stage musical *Kiss Me Kate* (1953) was one of several notable exceptions. Test engagements demonstrated that the film performed better in its 3-D version, but it was mostly shown "flat" and grossed only $3,117,000 worldwide.[48]

While distributors successfully demanded 50 percent rental terms from exhibitors for the first few 3-D releases, they were soon forced to make concessions as business dropped off. Although Jack Warner boldly claimed that "there is no inconvenience of any kind in wearing polaroid viewers," press reports suggested otherwise. There was also little interest in 3-D from overseas exhibitors, except in Britain.[49] As early as June 1953 a *Variety* headline suggested that "3-D's Gimmicks Aren't Enough"; in May 1954 the journal noted that "3-D Looks Dead in United States"; and at the beginning of 1955 it declared with finality that "3-D has had it."[50] What the industry needed, said one exhibitor, was "a simple process which can be mass-produced and easily adaptable to the average theatre, preferably without the audience having to use glasses."[51]

Anamorphosis—the use of a specially constructed taking lens to "squeeze" an image during photography, and a companion lens to unsqueeze it in projection—was employed in motion pictures as early as 1898. An anamorphic device was patented by French inventor Henri Chrétien as the Hypergonar lens in 1927 but failed to find much use in films on either side of the Atlantic. In late 1952, Twentieth Century-Fox's Research and Development Unit, charged with finding a wide-screen system to rival Cinerama, located Chrétien and bought an exclusive option on his lens. When used with 35 mm film, the lens (actually an attachment bolted onto prime camera or projector lenses) resulted in a picture with an aspect ratio of 2.66:1 (i.e., twice the full-aperture silent ratio of 1.33:1).[52]

Initially dubbed Anamorphoscope, the process was announced as CinemaScope in the first week of February 1953, when Fox declared that its entire future output would be filmed in the new format, beginning with *The Robe*. Long planned for production, the Roman epic was based on a best-selling 1943 novel by Lloyd C. Douglas, and was initially set to begin shooting in the standard Academy ratio. To take full advantage of CinemaScope's panoramic possibilities, shooting was delayed for the sets to be redesigned and rebuilt, adding $500,000 to the eventual $4.1 million budget. *The Robe* premiered on Broadway at the 5,717-seat Roxy on September 17, 1953. Playing on a continuous-performance basis with a top ticket price of $3, an all-time high for a grind engagement, it earned a world record box-office gross of $267,000 in its first week. The following month the film opened in forty-four key-city theaters, and at Christmas in a further 254 situations nationwide, including eighty-four in Greater New York. It ultimately returned domestic rentals of $17.5 million and $25 million worldwide, placing it second only to *Gone with the Wind* in *Variety*'s annually updated chart.[53]

Compared with Cinerama, CinemaScope was both more practicable and more economical. Fox's engineers had tried to "design CinemaScope in such a way that it could satisfy the needs of the conflicted motion picture marketplace for a dramatically new entertainment form while making it conform as much as possible with existing exhibition standards and practices."[54] However, optical distortions and lack of clear focus were among the most commonly remarked-upon flaws of early CinemaScope films. Improved lenses were first used for *Broken Lance* and *The Egyptian* (both 1954), but the basic defects of the lens construction (including limited depth of field and a tendency to horizontal distension in the center and outer edges of the image) were never satisfactorily overcome. The curvature of the studio's patented "Miracle Mirror" screen was at least partly an attempt to compensate for the distortion incurred by projecting a very wide picture from one lens.[55]

Perhaps the most innovatory aspect of CinemaScope was its sound format. Fox's sound department created a four-channel magnetic stereo sound system that, unlike those of Cinerama, Fantasound, and WarnerPhonic (all of which involved discrete soundtracks on separate reels played in interlock with the picture), was carried on the same strip of film as the image. To make room for the four magnetic "stripes" the picture aspect ratio was reduced from 2.66:1 to 2.55:1 (no space was left for an additional mono optical track). The sound-on-film format greatly simplified playback in theaters, but it nevertheless proved the major sticking point for cash-strapped exhibitors. Some were inclined to opt instead for an alternative sound system called Perspecta. In this process a three-channel mix encoded in a standard optical track could be reproduced with relatively inexpensive equipment, giving a "traveling" sound effect without the full range of directional stereo offered by multichannel magnetic. Introduced with the UK release in 1954 of MGM's first CinemaScope picture, *Knights of the Round Table* (1953), Perspecta was widely used by several of the studios, especially on overseas distribution prints, up to 1960.[56]

Although Fox at first insisted that theaters purchase its whole "package" of projection lenses, Miracle Mirror screen, and magnetic stereo reproducers, resistance eventually obliged it to compromise. The decision, in May 1954, to allow exhibitors not to install its approved screens and stereo sound substantially increased the number of CinemaScope installations. But it also downgraded the special status of the process and increased distribution costs, as Fox now had to produce both stereo and monaural prints (as other studios did already). In a further concession, from 1956 the studio agreed to supply "MagOptical" prints, combining both stereo and mono soundtracks on one strip. These prints further reduced the aspect ratio of the CinemaScope image to 2.35:1.[57]

Having patented the trade name, Fox stood to make further profits by licensing the CinemaScope brand and camera lenses to other producers. Seeking to undercut this, a number of companies adopted various alternative 35 mm anamorphic processes. The most important of these were SuperScope (introduced in 1954), Technirama (1956), Panavision (1957), and Techniscope (1960).[58] The Panavision anamorphic lens was a self-contained unit rather than an additional attachment and had greatly improved optics and a wider range of focal lengths than did CinemaScope. Under the sponsorship of MGM, Panavision quickly came to be Hollywood's anamorphic process of choice, a position it has retained to this day. Paramount, the only major studio not to embrace CinemaScope, was the leading advocate of a method of enhancing existing product without need for any changes in photographic technology. The unnamed "process" simply involved attaching a wide-angle lens to projectors, masking (or "matting") the image to an aspect ratio wider than the 1.37:1 Academy standard, and projecting onto a large screen masked to a similar aspect ratio. This "ersatz" wide-screen format (in John Belton's apt phrase) was already being widely used several months before the public debut of CinemaScope.[59] Aside from its simplicity, it offered protection for the studios' extensive backlog of unreleased product (valued at up to $350 million) and for the reissue potential of older titles. With refinements in film stock the loss of focus and increased visible grain caused by magnification were soon reduced. Early problems with unnaturally cropped compositions were resolved when the industry's technical branches agreed on a range of standard ratios and a "safety area" outside of which no essential visual information would be framed. The aspect ratios most commonly used were 1.66:1, 1.75:1, and 1.85:1.[60]

Paramount also introduced another wide-screen process, VistaVision, which used 35 mm film fed horizontally though the camera rather than vertically, each frame occupying the space of two standard frames. This enlarged negative area gave exceptional visual clarity and definition when printed down to regular 35 mm, especially when processed in Technicolor's dye-transfer imbibition method. (A number of films were also projected in the horizontal format in selected situations.) VistaVision was first used for the musical *White Christmas* (1954), which *Variety* named the top grosser of its year with anticipated domestic rentals of $12 million. As well as using the process for its own A-pictures, Paramount licensed it to other studios for a small number of films, including MGM's *High Society*, Warners' *The Searchers*, Universal-International's *Away All Boats* (all 1956), and UA's *The Pride and the Passion* (1957). It was also briefly adopted by the Rank Organisation in Britain. VistaVision required an extreme amount of light during shooting and used up film stock twice as rapidly as regular vertical-feed cameras. However, most audiences were apparently unable to distinguish VistaVision from "ordinary" non-anamorphic wide screen (it used the same range of relatively narrow aspect ratios). The additional production expense therefore seemed unwarranted when there was so little marketable differentiation from other formats, and VistaVision was discontinued from use in principal photography after 1961.[61]

Having achieved its goal of converting the industry to CinemaScope, with 13,175 out of 15,783 U.S. cinemas equipped for anamorphic projection within two years of its introduction, Fox had also paradoxically reduced the value of its own asset.[62] As a new norm, used for about one-third of all releases from 1955 onward, CinemaScope could be taken for granted by cinemagoers relatively soon after its appearance and ceased in itself to be a mark of "specialness." The studio attempted to reinstate its prestige in 1956 by introducing CinemaScope 55. This involved shooting on 55 mm film stock but retaining the same 2.55:1 aspect ratio as regular CinemaScope. As with VistaVision, the larger negative produced great visual clarity when printed down to 35 mm. Only two features, *Carousel* and *The King and I* (both 1956), were completed in this format before it was abandoned as too expensive (it added $200,000 each to their respective budgets) and insufficiently differentiated from regular CinemaScope. Although both films were shown only in 35 mm on their first release, Fox had originally intended to use 55 mm prints for roadshow purposes. This suggests that the studio's inspiration was less a desire to improve CinemaScope as a general release medium than to compete with other new wide-gauge systems that had recently been developed for special situations.[63]

Reinventing the Roadshow: Todd-AO, Camera 65, and Technirama 70

Despite having severed his links with Cinerama, the theatrical impresario Michael Todd remained enthusiastic about the notion of a special large-screen process for roadshow exhibition. In 1952 he commissioned the American Optical company to create a new single-camera system, which was announced the following year as Todd-AO. This process used 65 mm film stock in photography and 70 mm for release prints, the extra positive space being used for six channels of stereophonic sound carried on magnetic stripes in the manner of CinemaScope (unlike 35 mm MagOptical prints, all 70 mm copies had magnetic soundtracks only). The lens technology and wide film gauge produced extreme image clarity even on a vast screen (curved, like those of Cinerama and CinemaScope, to minimize distortion and to suggest an illusion of depth). The film ran at a speed of 30 frames per second to increase picture steadiness, and its projection aspect ratio was 2.2:1.[64]

Todd-AO was conceived as a synthesis of Cinerama's spectacular scale, VistaVision's superior image resolution, and CinemaScope's flexibility. Todd, who had produced a number of stage spectacles on Broadway and had described Cinerama as a "parlay between the legitimate theatre and the motion picture,"[65] was (like roadshow managers of the past such as J. J. McCarthy) concerned to appeal to the upmarket audience that patronized the legitimate stage, and which would be willing to pay Broadway prices for films sold as special attractions. Like Cinerama, it was envisioned that films shot in Todd-AO would initially be exhibited on a limited roadshow basis in theaters equipped for 70 mm projection. However, by shooting an additional 35 mm,

24-fps version of each title simultaneously with the Todd-AO one, the films could (unlike the Cinerama travelogues) also enjoy a regular general release after their road-show engagements were played out. Thus, Todd-AO aimed to embrace both mass and class markets for maximum revenues.[66]

To demonstrate its competitive edge over Cinerama, early Todd-AO test footage screened for press and the trade included scenes on Venetian canals and in a Spanish bull ring, and an inevitable roller-coaster ride—the very same roller coaster that had appeared in *This Is Cinerama*. The test screenings also demonstrated the more versatile 65/70 mm technology: not only did the film emerge from a single projection booth, operated by a standard projection crew, but also the projectors were capable of handling 35 mm prints as well as 70 mm. The Magna Theatre Corporation was formed to produce and release films in the process. Its board of directors included composer Richard Rodgers and lyricist Oscar Hammerstein II. Screen rights to their highly successful 1943 stage musical *Oklahoma!* had long eluded motion picture producers (including Cinerama's), and this was chosen as the first Todd-AO production.

Oklahoma! premiered at the Rivoli in New York on October 10, 1955, with tickets priced at up to $3.50 (which became the new standard price for Broadway roadshow engagements). Thereafter it was exhibited in a single United Artists theater in each of thirty other U.S. and Canadian cities, hired by Magna on a four-wall basis to allow the film to play indefinitely extended engagements (the Rivoli run lasted fifty-one weeks). In February 1957 it was reported that 4,672,184 tickets had been sold for a box-office gross to date of $8,970,087. The subsequent U.S. general release in the CinemaScope version was handled by Fox and foreign distribution, in 35 mm only, by RKO.[67]

Mike Todd had not been directly involved in the making of *Oklahoma!* The second Todd-AO film, however, was personally produced by Todd himself. He attempted to finance and distribute *Around the World in Eighty Days* (1956) independently, but when money ran out midway through production he approached UA, which supplied additional funds to make up the final cost of around $6 million in exchange for world distribution rights and 10 percent of the profits. The film combined the travelogue format of early Cinerama productions with a loose narrative structure derived from Jules Verne's classic novel. It boasted a series of spectacular attractions, including forty-four guest stars in brief "cameos" (a use of the word apparently coined by Todd). Two 65 mm negatives were produced, one running at 30 fps, the other at 24 fps, which were used to generate both 70 mm copies and 35 mm reduction prints for superior resolution.[68] The 30 fps reduction process was named Cinestage, in which the film played all its initial overseas engagements; like *Oklahoma!* it was not seen outside America in 70 mm until later reissues. Unlike the CinemaScope version of *Oklahoma!* the Cinestage prints of *Eighty Days* were also used for roadshow engagements as well as for subsequent general release.[69]

Several innovations in exhibition were also introduced with the picture. Rather than adhere to the traditional two-a-day roadshow performance schedule, Todd ordered matinees on selected days only (one on Saturdays, two midweek) for ten

Todd-AO's wide-angle "bug-eye" lens brings the spectator into the
spectacular scenery of *Around the World in Eighty Days* (1956).

performances weekly. In addition to ensuring full houses during off-peak hours, this
policy brought exhibition of the film even closer to legitimate theater practices. Todd
also negotiated a block "buy" of four hundred tickets nightly with the New York Theatre Ticket Brokers Association—another practice associated with the Broadway stage,
not used for motion pictures since the early 1920s.[70]

To describe the production Todd preferred the word *show* to *movie*. Reviewers and
columnists willingly adopted the same term, associating the film with the live stage
and the circus rather than the cinema. Consistent with this approach, Todd pursued
an advertising policy directly contrary to David O. Selznick's on *Duel in the Sun.*
Very little ad space was purchased in newspapers and magazines. Instead, Todd relied
on "free" publicity (such as editorial press and media coverage) and allowed word of
mouth to do the rest. He also sought advance guarantees from exhibitors. The first
five U.S. theaters to play the film paid a total of $1 million as an advance on antici-
pated rentals. After two years *Eighty Days* had earned a rental of $17.7 million from
1,569 domestic engagements, plus $4,552,000 from only 280 overseas bookings. It
remained in circulation on a roadshow basis for several more years. Having severed
relations with Magna (in a repeat of his Cinerama experience), Todd then set about
developing an alternative 70 mm format for other planned features, including a version of *Don Quixote.* However, he did not live to produce another film; he was killed
in an airplane crash in May 1958.[71]

Seeking once again to reclaim lost ground, Fox entered into a production and
distribution deal with Magna to use Todd-AO for its own future roadshow produc-

tions.[72] Fox's first picture in the format was another Rodgers and Hammerstein musical adaptation, *South Pacific* (1958). From this film onward, the format's principal advantage was its compatibility with existing cinema technology. In order to facilitate wider distribution without the cost of shooting a second version, the film speed was reduced to 24 fps without appreciable loss in visual quality. *South Pacific* was filmed only in Todd-AO, with 35 mm general release prints produced by reduction printing from the single 65 mm negative. Domestic exhibition followed the pattern set by *Eighty Days,* but *South Pacific* was the first Todd-AO film to be exhibited overseas in 70 mm. Within three months of its March opening there were forty engagements running worldwide. *South Pacific* also became for a time the most successful film ever released in the United Kingdom, where it earned a box-office gross three times its negative cost of $5,610,000. Anticipated global rentals after three years were $30 million.[73]

Like anamorphic photography, the 70 mm format could easily be imitated, and Todd-AO was also followed by competitor processes, most notably Super Panavision (1959) and Dimension-150 (1966).[74] Mike Todd's son, Michael Jr., developed Todd 70 for a single film, *Scent of Mystery* (1960), which in early roadshow engagements was presented with a special olfactory process, Smell-o-Vision.[75] Although there were slight technical differences between these formats, their 70 mm release prints were in most respects identical to Todd-AO's. Panavision was involved in the development of another wide-gauge system, sponsored by MGM, whose prints differed somewhat from the Todd-AO standard. MGM Camera 65 combined 65 mm film stock in photography with an anamorphic taking lens, producing an image with the same resolution as Todd-AO's but a potential aspect ratio of 2.75:1. As with Todd-AO its trade marketing hook was flexibility; prints of various gauges, formats, and aspect ratios could be struck from the wide negative, including three-strip, 35 mm, and 70 mm, depending on the requirements of exhibitors. MGM even claimed the process (which it promoted as "The Window of the World") to be "adaptable to whatever future variations of screen size or aspect ratio that may develop in the future."[76]

Camera 65 was first used to shoot *Raintree County* (1957), a $5,474,000 Civil War epic clearly intended to emulate *Gone with the Wind*. Release prints were, however, in 35 mm anamorphic format only. This was partly due to the scarcity of 70 mm–equipped theaters (those with Todd-AO already installed were still engaged with the long runs of *Around the World in Eighty Days*), and partly to MGM's loss of confidence in the roadshow potential of *Raintree County* after mixed reviews and disappointing box office in five reserved-seat situations. Alfred Hitchcock's *North by Northwest* (1959) was announced as MGM's second film in Camera 65, but it was instead filmed in VistaVision.[77] The only other film presented under the Camera 65 trade name was *Ben-Hur* (1959). Anamorphic 70 mm prints were utilized, but *Ben-Hur* was also made available in 35 mm prints for those theaters unable or unwilling to install the new equipment. MGM stated, "It is the film that is important, not the system."[78] Of the film's first sixty-five North American engagements, only fifteen were in 70 mm.[79]

When the company next used the process, on *Mutiny on the Bounty* (1962), it had been renamed Ultra Panavision. It was then adopted as a single-camera replacement for Cinerama. *The Wonderful World of the Brothers Grimm* and *How the West Was Won* were principally shot in the three-strip format, but both also used Ultra Panavision for second unit, special effects, and process work. (*How the West Was Won* also incorporated brief action footage from *Raintree County* and *The Alamo* [1960], the latter shot in Todd-AO.) It was used thereafter for six other films, five of which were exhibited under the Cinerama banner, beginning with *It's a Mad, Mad, Mad, Mad World* (1963).[80] Non-anamorphic Super Panavision was also used for several Cinerama presentations, including MGM's *Grand Prix* (1966) and *2001: A Space Odyssey* (1968). The switch to single-strip projection resulted in a far greater number of theater installations than with the three-strip format. By 1968, 230 Cinerama theaters in thirty-seven countries had converted to the "completely redesigned and re-engineered system."[81]

Between 1959 and 1970, thirty-five U.S.-produced features were filmed wholly or partly on 65 mm negatives. One other format is worth mentioning because its advent marked a move away from the exclusive association of wide-gauge presentation with roadshows. Technirama 70, subsequently renamed Super Technirama, was the trade name given to 70 mm prints struck from negatives filmed in Technirama, a process introduced by the Technicolor Corporation in 1956. Like VistaVision, it involved 35 mm stock fed horizontally through cameras, exposing a double-sized frame, but with an additional anamorphic "squeeze" to increase the image width. The process was designed to facilitate the striking of both 35 mm anamorphic prints (to CinemaScope specifications) and 70 mm prints (to Todd-AO specifications). It had the advantage of being cheaper to use than 65 mm negative stock but produced comparable image quality. Between 1956 and 1967 more than fifty films were shot in Technirama, of which perhaps half were exhibited in 70 mm.

Technirama 70 prints were first used in 1959 with two independent productions: Walt Disney's animated feature *Sleeping Beauty,* released through Disney's distribution arm Buena Vista, and Edward Small's biblical epic *Solomon and Sheba,* released through UA. Although these films played a small number of reserved-seat engagements (mostly abroad, though *Solomon and Sheba* was also roadshown in selected U.S. cities, including Boston, Milwaukee, and Minneapolis), they were more often presented on grind with raised prices. This caused some consternation in the industry, especially as *Sleeping Beauty* ran only 75 minutes and therefore seemed likely to cause public resentment at the steep admissions Disney insisted upon (as a nonparticipant in the antitrust consent decrees the company was entitled to set its own prices). At $6 million, *Sleeping Beauty* was by far Disney's most expensive animated feature (his others in the 1950s averaged $3 million to $4 million, still among the more costly films of the decade). It proved a commercial disappointment, but the value of Technirama 70 as a release format was successfully established.[82]

Finally, in 1963 Panavision developed a method of "blowing up" films shot in conventional 35 mm formats (flat or anamorphic) to 70 mm. With this facility, even

more economical than Super Technirama, producers and distributors could now postpone decisions about how to release their film to the postproduction phase without
having to invest up-front in any type of large-format negative. Panavision 70, as the
blow-up process was dubbed, was first tested with the London premiere run (apparently its only roadshow engagement) of UA's Cossack epic *Taras Bulba* (1962), and
was subsequently used for literally hundreds of films through the 1990s.[83] It fell into
disuse only when other new technologies for encoding stereo sound on 35 mm release
prints rendered 70 mm unnecessary.

New-Era Economics and Aesthetics

The new cycle of historical and spectacular subjects inaugurated by *Samson and Delilah, David and Bathsheba,* and *Quo Vadis,* the new screen and sound technologies
launched by *This Is Cinerama, The Robe,* and *Oklahoma!,* and the revival of roadshow
distribution and exhibition with the Cinerama and Todd-AO films marked the arrival
in stages of what trade press editorials and advertising repeatedly referred to as a "new
era" in cinema. The trends they represented had wide-ranging consequences, both
financial and aesthetic, for every area of the industry. Despite Fox's decision to film all
its pictures in CinemaScope (and in color), there was some debate in the industry over
its suitability for all subjects. Darryl Zanuck thought that CinemaScope's main value
lay "in the production of large scale spectacles and big outdoor films."[84] The qualities
of size and scale partly determined his selection of story properties, and Zanuck was
wont to cancel or reject any that did "not take full *advantage* of the new dimensions."[85]

In order to exploit the opportunities afforded by wide-screen formats, budgets
were increased at all the major studios. Fox reduced general overheads but raised direct
spending on film production. The average cost of one of its standard-screen releases in
1953 was $1,788,000; in 1954, Fox's first all-CinemaScope program had an average
unit cost of $2,354,000, or $3.5 million including prints and advertising.[86] As costs
went up, output went down. Between 1951 and 1953, the majors in total released
around 300 features a year. The number fell to 225 in 1954, and below 200 for the first
time in 1959. Despite this, revenues rose, a phenomenon partly attributable to ticket
price rises (both for individual films and on a permanent basis) and rental increases.
Average film length also increased, with two-hour-plus running times common by
1954 and several films running three hours or more in 1956.[87] Thus the "fewer but
bigger" pattern of the war years was repeated on an even larger scale. Among the big-
budget spectacles, costing $4 million and above, produced in just the first three years
of CinemaScope were Fox's *There's No Business Like Show Business* (1954), Disney's
20,000 Leagues under the Sea (1954), Goldwyn-MGM's *Guys and Dolls* (1955), UA's
Alexander the Great (1956), RKO's *The Conqueror* (1956), and Warners' *Helen of Troy*
(1956). These were far from uniformly successful, and profit margins on even the
most popular were small, fueling industry fears that too many superspecials flooding
the market would be self-defeating.[88]

While the extraordinary grosses achieved by early wide-screen films were cheering to those exhibitors able to take best advantage of them, they also had the effect, as John Belton has noted, of reaffirming, "in a legal way, the system of runs and clearances that had been outlawed as a result of the 1948 consent decree."[89] In fact, the wide-screen and especially the wide-gauge processes not only perpetuated this system but also enlarged it, in some instances increasing the gap between runs—or between pre-release and general-release phases—by years rather than months or weeks. Many theaters were forced to make structural alterations to accommodate wider and larger screens. With so many new technologies entering the market, exhibitors were faced with the problem of achieving standardization. Theaters could not afford to install every system, and their investments were jeopardized by the threat of obsolescence for those systems that did not take on (as happened in the case of 3-D, for example).[90]

The aesthetic impact of wide-screen formats on Hollywood films has often been addressed by critics and scholars. The vast majority of critical comment following their introduction was characterized by hostility at the disruption of stylistic codes that had governed a half-century of cinema, and at the apparent loss of subtlety in favor of mere elephantiasis and of cinematic specificity in favor of staginess.[91] Subsequent analyses have often sought to overturn these negative judgments, producing a number of classic accounts of the wide-screen work of favored auteur directors such as Elia Kazan, Vincente Minnelli, Otto Preminger, and Nicholas Ray.[92] But the facility of even the widest of screens for both spectacle *and* subtlety (sometimes simultaneously) can also be observed in blockbusters made by now-unfashionable craftsmen.

William Wyler's *Ben-Hur,* photographed by Robert Surtees, uses the extreme width of the MGM Camera 65 frame for just such dual purposes. In establishing shots showing marching columns of Roman soldiers advancing across Judea, lines of ships arrayed for battle, a triumphal entry into Rome, and the massive arena hosting the chariot race, the screen is fully taken up by great numbers of extras, large architectural structures, lavish costumes and props, expansive land- and seascapes, and furious action. But Wyler's talent for long takes and composition in depth, frequently celebrated in earlier films such as *The Best Years of Our Lives,* is also evident in more intimate scenes, where they are matched by his skill with composition in breadth. Although Camera 65, in common with other processes utilizing anamorphic lenses, had limited depth of field, Wyler's staging successfully exploits its aptitudes and overcomes its weaknesses. There are several examples from late on in the film.

As the mortally injured Messala (Stephen Boyd) awaits a visit from Judah (Charlton Heston) following the chariot race, his head and arms are positioned at frame left. While he struggles at being strapped down in preparation for surgery, the camera travels the length of his body to take in Judah's presence at the hospital door in the extreme right background, out of focus. This image is held for several seconds before the lens rack-focuses to shift attention to Judah, while Messala remains in shot at left and in the foreground, the surgeon and his assistants filling the middle ground. In the following sequence, when Judah and Esther (Haya Harareet) go to the Valley of

Breadth and depth in the wide-screen compositions of *Ben-Hur* (1959).

the Lepers, he hides behind a large rock to avoid being seen by his afflicted mother, Miriam (Martha Scott), and sister, Tirzah (Cathy O'Donnell), as they emerge from the mouth of a cave. Judah and the rock fill the foreground, screen left; Miriam, Tirzah, and the cave entrance occupy the background, screen right, with Esther in the middle center. This composition, which resembles a split-screen effect, is held for almost a full minute with only a brief cut-in to a close-up reaction shot of Judah. In both these instances the viewer must scan and absorb different areas of the image simultaneously to register the salient visual information.

The film's most extreme instance of this foreground/background, left/right dynamic is achieved in the scene of the Sermon on the Mount. A high-angle shot shows the congregation assembled on the slopes, with Judah barely discernible in the distance, across a small stream. The film cuts to a reverse angle of Judah stopping by a tree to gaze up at the multitude and the figure of Jesus above. A close-up of Judah is followed by a cut back to the first shot, as Christ enters the foreground at screen right. After we return to Judah by the tree, beginning to walk off screen left, a further cut back to the crowd frames Christ and Judah in the center of the image, but separated by a vast distance (with Esther again placed in the middle ground, among the crowd). This, the countermovement of the two figures, and their crisscrossing on the screen embodies the central narrative premise of Judah's destiny interweaving with and being influenced by Christ's destiny.

Finally, as Judah brings his family into Jerusalem to find the streets deserted, the group encounters a blind beggar. After asking directions, Judah drops a coin into his outstretched cup. In the background, a small crowd gathers to protest at the presence of the lepers, throwing stones to drive them away. The beggar remains in shot at the extreme left, and as the family group moves on in the background at screen right, he gently, sadly up-ends the cup to discard the (possibly contagious) coin. No reframing or editing draws attention to this; there is no close-up of the beggar, his cup, or the coin to make the point more forcibly. Instead, the tinkle of the coin is captured by the outer left stereo channel, the sound emerging from the speaker positioned behind that part of the screen. Here again Wyler's composition requires the spectator to exercise vigilance in registering the significance of action at the outer edges of the screen.

Although the wide-screen revolution seemed to reverse the slide in attendances for a brief period (average weekly domestic admissions rose from 42 million in 1953 to 50 million by 1956), they fell back again thereafter. Spyros Skouras's claim that "1954 marked the end of the threat of television" was therefore premature.[93] Richard Maltby has suggested that the problem with Hollywood's innovation of new screen technologies was that they were a short-term solution to a long-term problem; that the various formats provided a novelty or gimmick whose appeal quickly wore off.[94] This certainly explains the rapid abandonment of 3-D, the short "honeymoon" of CinemaScope, and the disappearance within little more than a decade of VistaVision. However, this is arguably not true of the wide-gauge formats, which continued to be an attraction in their own right for many years.

The advent of 70 mm exhibition led to trade speculation that Hollywood would soon deal exclusively in blockbuster productions, perhaps using wide film for all first-run engagements, with 35 mm reserved only for general release.[95] Wide-gauge production was simply too costly to permit its use on every A-feature. But Todd-AO and the other 70 mm processes retained much of their original impact precisely because they never achieved the wide diffusion of the 35 mm general release formats; they instead came to be associated with premium standards of presentation. By 1961, there were 606 70 mm theater installations worldwide, a tiny number by comparison with CinemaScope but sufficient to form, as Belton puts it, an elite "super-circuit" of top-tier theaters for a select few pictures designed for long roadshow runs.[96] The roadshow pattern came to dominate Hollywood's conception of the first-run, pre-release market in the 1960s, and will be considered in detail in the next chapter.

ROADSHOWS, SHOWCASES, AND RUNAWAYS, 1956–1970

In its year-end box-office summary for 1959, the British trade paper *Kinematograph Weekly* singled out five films as belonging in a distinct category separate from "ordinary" releases. These five—*The Ten Commandments, South Pacific, Around the World in Eighty Days, Gigi* (1958), and *The Nun's Story* (1959)—were labeled "hard ticket giants," a rubric at once indicative of their roadshow presentation, their large scale, and their enormous success.[1] The extraordinary grosses of *Around the World in Eighty Days* and *The Ten Commandments,* in particular, made it inevitable that Hollywood would seek to capitalize on a distribution and exhibition policy that had enabled these two films to take in "more rentals from fewer theatre engagements than any pictures in history."[2] While the box office generally continued to decline, their earnings reached levels scarcely imaginable even when business was at its height. *Variety* speculated on the possibility of an entirely revised exhibition structure: "many see roadshowing of big films as the start of an evolution that, eventually, will see only a couple of thousand key houses surviving with top product. Around them, there will be a satellite layer of convenient suburban locations, and then there will be drive-ins. The run-of-the-mill pix will be shown on tv in the homes."[3]

No film did more to entrench the roadshow policy than *The Ten Commandments.* While the success of *This Is Cinerama, The Robe,* and even *Eighty Days* could be attributed, at least in part, to their respective photographic and projection formats, that of DeMille's film (which cost a record $13,266,491) could not.[4] Although it was one of the first titles Paramount announced for production in VistaVision in 1954, *Commandments* did not premiere until two years later. The VistaVision trade name was played down in advertising in favor of the theme ("the birth of freedom"), size, and prestige of the picture itself.[5]

After its New York world premiere at the Criterion Theatre on November 8, 1956, fifteen other U.S. engagements of *Commandments* opened by the end of the

The Exodus of the Israelites, re-created in Egypt for *The Ten Commandments* (1956).

year, with thirty-six more in early 1957. All of these were on an exclusive, reserved-seat basis. In its first twelve months, the film played nearly one thousand domestic roadshow engagements.[6] The first twenty-four overseas openings, beginning almost one full year after the world premiere, included eight in Italy, four each in Germany and Switzerland, and one each in Australia, Britain, France, India, Japan, Peru, and Venezuela. Regular U.S. "pre-release" engagements, with continuous performances but still at advanced prices, began on March 19, 1958. Paramount's distribution plan involved a series of "wave" bookings, opening at a small number of theaters in each area for limited runs of several weeks each, with new waves building as the older ones broke. The goal was to keep the picture in circulation for as long as possible in order to tap its maximum box-office potential. Across the country, cities and towns that had never been able to sustain long runs enjoyed extended engagements. Paramount's press office claimed that the film had "reawakened interest in motion pictures among many segments, with marked attendance by whole family groups and large attendance by many industrial, fraternal, youth, religious and social groups."[7] General release at normal prices began in 1959 and continued until the end of the following year, when the film was temporarily withdrawn (the first of several reissues came in 1966). The worldwide rental by this time was around $60 million. In the domestic market, it dislodged *Gone with the Wind* from the number one position on *Variety*'s list of All-Time Rentals Champs. *GWTW* had hitherto maintained its lead through several reissues (and was soon to regain it through another in 1961). *Commandments,* however, had achieved its "monumental amount of coin in a single trip to market," a feat hitherto considered impossible.[8]

Variety identified thirty-six U.S. and Canadian cities that provided the bulk of domestic revenue for roadshows. Although it was possible for a picture to achieve a measure of commercial success just from these situations, the true test of a blockbuster, the journal claimed, was its ability to "continue the reserved-seat technique down to the smaller communities," as was the case with *Commandments*.[9] In the late 1950s, various studios tentatively experimented with placing selected prestige pictures in a limited number of roadshow engagements (sometimes only one, usually in New York). At least some of these films had not been produced with that purpose in mind, including Fox's *The Roots of Heaven* and Warners' *The Old Man and the Sea* (both 1958). Other films planned from the outset for roadshow exhibition included MGM's *Raintree County,* Buena Vista's *The Big Fisherman* (1959), Fox's *The Diary of Anne Frank* (1959), and Samuel Goldwyn's *Porgy and Bess* (1959), released through Columbia. In most situations they were rejected by exhibitors, the critics, and the public alike, leading to a rapid climb-down to a regular general-release policy after only a few big-city roadshow dates.

Eight more major-studio roadshows appeared in 1960, including UA's *Exodus* and *The Alamo,* Universal-International's *Spartacus,* and Columbia's *Pepe.* These four, all over three hours long in their initial presentations, were heavily criticized for overlength. Opening on October 24, *The Alamo* ran 202 minutes (including overture, entr'acte, and exit music). Following disappointing hard-ticket runs in Todd-AO, the film was sent into general release the following spring cut by a half-hour, earning a total domestic rental of $7,918,776 (including later reissues) on a budget reported as $12 million. John Wayne blamed the "reserved-seat thing" for failing to attract the right audience, though it was he who had insisted on it over the objections of UA executives.[10] Exhibitors in turn blamed several of the films as unsuited to roadshow presentation, bearing out fears that the potentialities of the policy would be squandered on inappropriate or inferior product.[11]

There were, however, a small but significant number of exceptions to this pattern of failure. Columbia's Anglo-American war film *The Bridge on the River Kwai* (1957) opened on a roadshow basis in selected U.S. cities (including New York, Chicago, Boston, and Los Angeles) and in London. Costing only $2,840,000 to produce, it grossed $30.6 million worldwide on first release.[12] MGM producer Arthur Freed had been advocating the presentation of film musicals on Broadway in the manner of stage shows since at least 1949 ("These films should be sold as entertainment on special runs. They should not go first-run then promptly be played at half-price."[13]). At his insistence, *Gigi* opened at the Royale, a legitimate Broadway theater hired on a four-wall

161

basis, along with seventeen other U.S. roadshow situations.[14] *Gigi* became the studio's most-successful-ever musical. Costing $3,319,335, its global rentals had reached $13,208,725 by 1966, following one reissue.[15] In addition to their financial riches, both *Kwai* and *Gigi* were amply rewarded by the industry, receiving a total of sixteen Academy Awards between them, including Best Picture in their respective years.

Once regarded as the industry leader, in 1957 MGM had, for the first time in its history, registered a corporate loss (only $500,000, but the 1958 profit was a mere $800,000). It had recently undergone several management changes, with long-time president Nicholas Schenck replaced first by Arthur Loew in 1955, and then by Joseph R. Vogel in 1956. For the company to embark at such a time on a project costing three times as much as its next most expensive picture might have looked like foolhardiness or desperation. *Ben-Hur* had been in planning since 1953 and was eventually filmed over ten months in Rome's Cinecittà Studios at a cost of $15,175,000. Yet studio executives stressed several factors that made the film a sensible business judgment rather than a reckless gamble. The success of *Quo Vadis, The Robe,* and *The Ten Commandments* had indicated that "there was a waiting market for a well-made spectacle."[16] This and the ongoing popularity of General Lew Wallace's original novel (second in all-time sales only to the Holy Bible, according to publicity), which was reprinted by five different publishers in tie-in editions, made the film seem a safe bet. Its massive budget was also not the problem it might have appeared. Although industry rules of thumb suggested that a picture had to earn twice its negative cost in order to turn a profit, this was not the case with "super expensive spectacles"; advertising and distribution expenses did not rise proportionately with the budget, even allowing for the greater costs incurred by roadshow publicity and 70 mm prints. The break-even point on *Ben-Hur* was estimated at $20 million in rentals, a sum that *Commandments* had comfortably recovered in under two years.[17]

The world premiere engagement, at Loew's State on Broadway (which had been renovated at a cost of $1 million for the occasion), began on November 18, 1959; it lasted seventy-five weeks and earned a box-office gross of $3 million. *Ben-Hur* also ran ninety-eight weeks in Los Angeles and 125 weeks in London (the latter run split over two theaters). The film earned back its production, sales, and advertising costs within one year, before even opening in most European territories, and almost single-handedly returned MGM to profitability (though not for long, as it turned out).[18] By February 1962, after just over two years in global distribution (still prior to full general release in some territories, including Britain), it was estimated that its total audience had exceeded 55 million and would top 90 million by year's end. *Ben-Hur* ultimately grossed $36,992,088 in the United States, and another $39 million overseas.[19] It also established a long-held record with an unprecedented eleven Academy Award wins and, unlike *The Ten Commandments,* was generally well received by critics.

Ben-Hur and *Commandments* did have a number of things in common, however. Both were religious epics. Both starred Charlton Heston. Both were successively the most expensive film yet made. And both were remakes of roadshow hits from the silent period, distributed by the same companies that had released the earlier versions. MGM's silent *Ben-Hur*, which opened at the end of 1925, had out-grossed all the other pictures released by the company in 1926 combined. With worldwide rentals of $9,386,000 on first release it was, with the sole possible exception of *The Birth of a Nation*, the highest-earning film of the entire silent era. (At a negative cost of $3,967,000, it was also the most expensive.) DeMille's own 1923 version of *Commandments* had been produced at a cost of $1,475,837 and had grossed $4,169,798 worldwide.[20] Such statistics were a powerful inducement for undertaking remakes.

The sound-era versions, while retaining the story outlines and recreating key scenes from their forebears (in some instances almost in facsimile), nevertheless have significant differences of emphasis. The biblical story in the silent *Commandments* had formed only an extended prologue to a modern story about the perils of breaking God's law. The modern parallels in the 1956 version are implicit rather than overt, and political rather than moral. DeMille made its relevance to the Cold War clear in his speech when accepting an award from the U.S. Chamber of Commerce as a Great Living American:

I know I could not have made *The Ten Commandments* in the Communist world where God is regarded as an enemy alien.

But here, where no government area restricts artistic freedom, where corporation executives . . . are willing to invest 13 and a half million dollars in the negative of a single picture, because they believe in its message, where management, talent and labor work together freely and share in the fruits of free enterprise, here it has been possible to produce this story of the birth of freedom and give it to the world.[21]

William Wyler later claimed also to be drawn to *Ben-Hur* for its contemporary relevance, seeing in its story of Jews suffering under the occupation of their homeland an allegory of the Zionist struggle for Israel (though apparently he missed the irony in his interpretation).[22]

These two films were not the only large-scale remakes of past hits made in the 1950s and early 1960s. Aside from the already mentioned *Quo Vadis*, MGM's many other remakes included *Show Boat* (1951, previously made by Universal in 1929 and 1936), *The Prisoner of Zenda* (1952, previously made by Metro in 1922 and by Selznick in 1937), *Scaramouche* (1952, made by Metro in 1923), *Beau Brummell* (1954, made by Warners in 1924), *Rose-Marie* (1954, made by MGM in 1928 and 1936), and *Kismet* (1955, made four times previously, including by Warners in 1930 and by MGM in 1944). Four of the six films MGM intended for release on a roadshow basis between 1960 and 1963 were also remakes. The studio's aim was to plan this "most profitable form of exhibition for [a] certain type of product" in a more orderly way than had prevailed hitherto, and thereby to justify the conversion costs of those theaters that had installed special projection and sound equipment.[23] But none of the six came up to expectations in terms of either profit or prestige.

Cimarron, a remake of RKO's 1931 Oscar-winning western, opened in only six reserved-seat engagements at Christmas 1960 before going quickly into general release. *The Four Horsemen of the Apocalypse,* updating Ibáñez's original story and Metro's 1921 film to a World War II setting, was set to open as a roadshow at Christmas 1961, but production delays led to its being released on grind in February 1962. Costing nearly $12.5 million between them, these two films (both in CinemaScope) were expected to earn no more than $9 million in aggregate rentals; $3 million was written off on *Four Horsemen* alone.[24] *King of Kings* (1961), which took the title of DeMille's 1927 life of Christ, was set up independently by the Spanish-based producer Samuel Bronston and sold to MGM shortly after the start of shooting. Opening in 70 mm roadshow engagements, it was continually compared to *Ben-Hur* in publicity statements but earned only $6,520,000 domestically, far below anticipations when production costs had amounted to around $8 million.[25] These major disappointments were as nothing, however, compared to the 1962 debacle of *Mutiny on the Bounty,* a reworking of MGM's 1935 Oscar winner (based on a book by Charles Nordhoff and James Hall). Problems with location shooting, which extended to nearly two years, and the erratic behavior of the film's star, Marlon Brando, caused production costs to rise to an all-time high of $19.5 million.[26] With ultimate domestic rentals reaching only $7,409,783 and the overseas figure about the same, the studio lost a fortune. In 1963 MGM declared a massive corporate loss of $17.5 million, directly attributing this to the failure of *Bounty.*[27]

The studio's two other roadshow pictures in 1962–63 were the fruit of its co-production arrangement with Cinerama. To ensure that the two films were not in direct competition with each other they opened at distinct intervals on both sides of the Atlantic. *The Wonderful World of the Brothers Grimm* premiered in August 1962 in America. *How the West Was Won* had its world premiere in London in November 1962, and opened in the United States the following February. *Grimm* cost $6.25 million; its domestic rentals totaled $4,832,038. *West* cost $14,483,000; although it earned $35 million worldwide in just under three years, with ultimate domestic rentals totaling $20,932,883, high distribution costs severely limited its profitability.[28] With these six would-be blockbusters all opening within the space of less than eighteen months, MGM did not release another full-scale roadshow until the end of 1965. Vogel was replaced as president by Robert H. O'Brien, who imposed an upper limit of $6 million on production budgets except in "extraordinary" circumstances.

Until the mid-1960s, most other studios released roadshows only on rare occasions, and with mixed results. Paramount launched no more while *The Ten Commandments* was still in circulation, in order to avoid direct competition. Universal continued to operate a traditional production-line policy, in which blockbusters were produced only rarely. Aside from *Spartacus,* its first roadshow since Laurence Olivier's *Hamlet,* the studio released none until 1967. Warner Bros. marketed most of its prestige productions of the late 1950s and early 1960s as "Special Engagements," which played at advanced ticket prices but on a grind basis. *Giant* (1956), *Sayonara* (1957),

Auntie Mame (1958), *The Nun's Story*, and *The Music Man* (1962) were all released in this way. Warners was nervous of roadshows because of the high publicity costs they entailed, the slow rate of returns, and the high risk of failure. Explaining the studio's decision not to roadshow its enormously over-budget ($7 million) Charles Lindbergh biopic *The Spirit of St. Louis* (1957), producer Leland Hayward stated: "If you miss with a roadshow, then you're really in trouble. . . . Your chances of making a genuinely great motion picture are small; and the public is fickle."[29]

There were, however, disadvantages to presenting extra-length, big-budget films on a general-release basis. Warners' *Giant* and Paramount's *War and Peace* (1956), each running around 200 minutes, opened with neither reserved seats nor intermissions. Exhibitors in first-run situations found problems with "turnover" not only of shows (with no more than three or four screenings per day), but also of patrons, many of whom stayed in their seats to see the films a second time, thus limiting seat availability for incoming audiences.[30] Opening at 182 minutes, Warners' musical remake of *A Star Is Born* (1954) was subsequently cut by half an hour to increase the number of daily showings. Had it been roadshown with twice-daily performances, the cuts might not have been necessary. Higher ticket prices might also have helped pay off the $5,017,770 negative cost; worldwide rentals amounted to only $6,913,000.[31]

From 1964 both Warner Bros. and Paramount began releasing a small number of roadshows each year; the former beginning with John Ford's western *Cheyenne Autumn* and the Lerner and Loewe musical *My Fair Lady*, the latter with Hal B. Wallis's British production *Becket* and Samuel Bronston's *The Fall of the Roman Empire* and *Circus World*. All of these were initially shown in 70 mm (*Circus World* as a single-strip Cinerama presentation). United Artists enjoyed considerable success in roadshowing both *West Side Story* (1961) and Stanley Kramer's epic Cinerama comedy *It's a Mad, Mad, Mad, Mad World* in 70 mm, but failed with Kramer's courtroom drama *Judgment at Nuremberg* (1961), filmed in standard wide-screen format and black-and-white. Columbia released the $13.8 million biopic *Lawrence of Arabia* (1962), filmed in Super Panavision 70, exclusively on a hard-ticket basis, but opened *Barabbas* (1962), *The Cardinal* (1963), and the $12 million Joseph Conrad adaptation *Lord Jim* (1965) as 70 mm roadshows in selected territories only.

After cutting its CinemaScope film of Grace Metalious's best-seller *Peyton Place* (1957) from 200 minutes to 157, Fox decided on an exhibition policy of four screenings daily without reserved seats, while still referring to the film as a roadshow.[32] Aside from *South Pacific* it was the studio's sole major hit of the late 1950s and early 1960s. Due to a run of expensive failures, including another $5 million Todd-AO musical, *Can-Can* (1960), Fox suffered corporate losses of $2.9 million in 1960, $22.5 million in 1961, and a record $39.8 million in 1962.[33] This situation led to Darryl Zanuck replacing Spyros Skouras as president and installing his son, Richard D. Zanuck, as head of production. Since 1956 the Zanucks had operated as independent producers, using Fox for finance and distribution. Darryl's most ambitious independent production was *The Longest Day* (1962), a three-hour reconstruction of D-Day filmed in black-and-white CinemaScope at a cost of $8 million. It grossed over $30 million worldwide as a roadshow followed by general release, thereby helping the studio regain stability during its period of reorganization.[34]

One of the films most responsible for Fox's financial difficulties was another epic remake. The escalating production problems (through three years of on-again, off-again shooting) and ballooning budget of *Cleopatra* (1963) had contributed substantially to the company's huge losses.[35] Fox set about recovering its investment by requiring theaters playing Todd-AO roadshow engagements to guarantee a minimum length of run (in the case of New York's Rivoli, seventy-five weeks, though in fact it ran only sixty-four) and to remit both 70 percent of advance ticket sales and a substantial portion of their anticipated box-office gross, calculated on the basis of revenues derived from previous roadshows, to the distributor as an advance on rentals (including $1,275,000 from the Rivoli alone). With top tickets set at an all-time high of $5.50, *Cleopatra* had amassed as much as $20 million in such guarantees from exhibitors even before its premiere. Fox claimed the film had cost in total $44 million, of which $31,115,000 represented the direct negative cost and the rest distribution, print, and advertising expenses.[36] (These figures excluded the more than $5 million spent on the production's abortive British shoot in 1960–61, prior to its relocation to Italy.) By 1966 worldwide rentals had reached $38,042,000, including $23.5 million from the United States. This was far short of original expectations (producer Walter Wanger had predicted a world gross of $100 million), but it was also far from the disaster often assumed. Fox's executive vice president Seymour Poe claimed that "by handling *Cleopatra* as a 'roadshow,' [the studio] earned millions more than it might otherwise."[37] But the film ultimately went into profit not from its theatrical release but from a sale to television.

The major studios had begun selling or leasing their old pictures to the television networks in 1956, at just the same time that they began marketing major new theatrical releases as roadshows. Before then, most of the films available for TV broadcast were foreign or independent productions, some of which had been released through the majors (especially UA), but the majority from Poverty Row. The majors preferred to hold on to their inventories because their theatrical reissue value initially seemed to outweigh their likely TV rental value. Ironically, it may have been the advent of wide-screen cinema formats that was a decisive factor in the studios' decision to release their pre-1949 backlogs to the networks, as these movies were no longer compatible with the new-shape screens and were therefore mostly unsuitable for reissue (some older films that *were* re-released were reformatted for wide-screen projection, as we shall see). An alternative possibility—the domestic TV broadcast of a new feature prior to or coincidental with its theatrical release as a form of promotion—was largely rejected when the telecasting of Laurence Olivier's *Richard III* (1956) on the day of its opening on a roadshow basis in New York was seen to have adversely affected the film's box-office performance. That same year, *Variety* reported that 4,169 feature films were being shown every week to the 36.5 million American homes now equipped with

Like other roadshows in the 1960s, press advertisements for *The Sound of Music* (1965) often included a reserved-seat order form for advance bookings (*Variety*, November 18, 1964, 19).

TV sets. The majors' offerings typically fetched between $20,000 and $75,000 each, depending on whether they had been sold outright to a subdistributor (in the case of RKO, Warners, and Paramount) or leased for a fixed period of time (the latter being the more lucrative option). By the early 1960s, more recent releases were becoming available (including films made in color and CinemaScope) and the networks were paying from $150,000 to $210,000 per title to show major features in prime-time schedules; by 1965 annual revenues from the lease of films to television approximated $400 million, compared to total domestic theatrical rentals of $315 million.[38]

The following year, in a deal that *Variety* called "the birth of the big picture TV special," *The Bridge on the River Kwai* was leased to the ABC network by Columbia for a record $2 million for two showings.[39] Its first broadcast, on September 25, 1966, achieved the highest audience rating for any film shown on television to date, with an estimated 28,490,000 homes tuning in.[40] Also in 1966, Fox made a deal with ABC for the telecasting of seventeen pictures, which brought the studio $19.5 million. Four films in the package were roadshows, accounting for $12.25 million of the total, including $5 million for *Cleopatra* alone.[41] These deals demonstrated that blockbuster status in theatrical exhibition (even failed blockbuster status) would drive up the price of a picture in its eventual TV sale, and that this might make the difference between profit and loss. Henceforward, all the studios would anticipate revenues from sale to television in their estimation of profit potential.

While all the studios increased their production of blockbusters in the second half of the 1960s, with the safety net of TV sales to offset the risk, Fox and MGM became most heavily identified with roadshows. In October 1963 Darryl Zanuck had announced a program of six roadshow pictures, to be made at a combined cost of $42 million, enabling Fox to dub itself "the roadshow company" in the trade press for several years thereafter.[42] In 1967, by which time the whole industry had been won over to the hard-ticket strategy, MGM's UK chairman and managing director, Michael Havas, pointed out:

Long-run roadshow attractions are a reality and will absorb more and more playing time in both 70 mm and 35 mm. Individual long runs prove that this type of attraction is wanted and enjoyed by the masses and has helped to create a new kind of movie-going habit. . . . This does not mean the conventional film will suddenly cease to be available to the world's cinemas, but certainly the bigger film, the long run, the hard-ticket engagement will become more and more the prime attractions.[43]

Barnstormers, Freak Pictures, and Instant Releases

Although the postwar film industry as a whole experienced a general downturn, certain sectors saw contrary patterns of growth. The intellectual and cultural elites, on the one hand, and the teenage and young-adult population, on the other, came to play far more important roles in the Hollywood economy than at any previous time.

Neither was the ideal target audience for the sort of expensive big pictures with which this book is primarily concerned, which depended upon finding the largest possible audience to meet their costs. Indeed, the very fact that such special-interest groups can be identified testifies to the fragmentation of the formerly homogeneous mass public that was one cause of Hollywood's state of crisis. Nevertheless, the forms of entertainment provided for these sectors, and the manner of their theatrical distribution and presentation, inevitably had an impact on the mainstream. Some of them were designed as an alternative to the fare offered by the major studios; others pioneered marketing strategies that would come to be taken up on a larger scale by the majors.

While a return to traditional reserved-seat roadshow presentation was not fully embraced by the studios until the advent of Todd-AO and *The Ten Commandments*, it had previously been revived in a small-scale but significant way for a select few specialized releases. In 1946, UA had engaged a legitimate theatrical press agent to promote Laurence Olivier's British-made Shakespeare adaptation *Henry V* as if it were "a touring company of the play."[44] Rather than attempt to integrate the film into regular exhibition patterns, as it did with only moderate success in the case of the Rank Organisation's $5 million superproduction *Caesar and Cleopatra* (1946), UA devised an innovative distribution strategy that aimed to treat the film "more like a legit show than any pic ever released in this country."[45]

All the initial engagements of *Henry V* were booked on a four-wall-hire basis, with UA paying theater publicity costs and staff and operating expenses. Outside the key cities, the film was mainly booked in college towns for limited twice-daily runs of between one and four days, depending on the size of the population, with reserved-seat tickets set at $2.40 top. This deliberately slow "barnstorming" release method meant scant distribution, print, and advertising costs. After more than two years and eight hundred roadshow engagements, *Henry V*—which according to publicity had cost Rank £475,708, or about $2 million, to make—had earned over $3 million in the United States, with a profit to UA of $1,620,000.[46]

Other British productions released in similar fashion included Olivier's *Hamlet* and *Richard III*, Michael Powell and Emeric Pressburger's *A Matter of Life and Death* (1946, released in the United States as *Stairway to Heaven*), *The Red Shoes* (1948), *The Tales of Hoffman* (1951), and Jean Renoir's *The River* (1951). American films roadshown in the same manner included RKO's *Mourning Becomes Electra* (1947), UA's *Cyrano de Bergerac* (1950), the independent release *Martin Luther* (1953), and MGM's version of Shakespeare's *Julius Caesar* (1953). A small number of European-produced films were also roadshown in the United States, most notably Federico Fellini's *La dolce vita* (1961) and a dubbed, reedited version of Sergei Bondarchuk's four-part, five-hundred-minute *War and Peace* (1968). Pictures such as these demonstrated the existence of an "art" market composed substantially of people who did not go regularly to the movies (those who had never done so or who had stopped doing so). They showed that many such patrons could be attracted by the right kind of product, marketed without traditional Hollywood ballyhoo, and presented amid suitable surroundings. The growing art-house circuit was described by *Variety* in 1951 as "TV-proof," as the audience attending such cinemas—many of which were nabes that had found it more profitable to alter their booking policy than to compete for new studio releases—was largely composed of people who scorned television as much as they did standard Hollywood product.[47]

Robert Sklar has claimed that the major studios had traditionally failed to capitalize on this audience because they persisted in the belief that "'the intellectuals' were their antagonists and 'the people' their friends."[48] The 1950s and 1960s saw increasing attempts by Hollywood to appeal to the intelligentsia as well as to the masses. In New York, many films were booked into off-Broadway and East Side art houses, often day-and-date with main-stem picture palaces, in order to reach as wide an audience as possible.[49] Prestige films were often used to test new exhibition policies, even in regular "de luxe" theaters. Fox's theatrical drama *All about Eve* (1950) was initially exhibited at the New York Roxy in "scheduled performances." Tickets were sold (at normal prices) for a specified show time and a seat was guaranteed, though the performances were continuous and no specific seats could be reserved. Designed to ensure that patrons saw the film from the beginning and without interruption (latecomers were not admitted), the policy was abandoned after only four days because of lower than expected business and the reluctance of other exhibitors to adopt it.[50] But it was later adapted by Alfred Hitchcock for his horror thriller *Psycho* (1960). To preserve the surprise of its shock twists, Hitchcock insisted that show times be clearly advertised and that latecomers be refused admission once the picture had begun. The scheduled-performance policy adopted by Hitchcock for *Psycho* enlarged its audience beyond that which normally visited such movies, became a talking point, and helped propel the film to a domestic rental of over $9 million, more than ten times its production cost and far more than any other horror film to date.[51] "Scheduled performances" (or "reserved performances") were subsequently taken up as an intermediate stage between the hard-ticket and grind release phases of major-studio roadshows.

Although it was released through Paramount, *Psycho* was the most successful instance of a type of film often referred to by the collective rubric "exploitation pictures." *Variety* defined these in 1946 as "films with some timely or currently controversial subject which can be exploited, capitalized on in publicity and advertising." The journal's choice of examples—including *The House on 92nd Street*, *Back to Bataan*, *Ziegfeld Follies*, *The Stork Club* (all 1945), and *The Beginning or the End* (1947)—indicates that the term was not originally associated with any particular genre or production category. But because most so-called exploitation films were by definition "marketed for their idea or subject-matter," rather than for their stars or production values, they were "more propitious for studios with shorter budgets."[52] The term subsequently became identified with films that were "exploitative" of their subjects (and their audiences) in the more common everyday sense, including pseudo-educational dramas and semidocumentaries about drug abuse or sex hygiene such as *Tell Your Children* (a.k.a. *Reefer Madness*) (1936), *The Birth of a Baby* (1937), and *Mom and Dad* (1944).

These films were produced outside the Hollywood mainstream by independent film-makers working on shoestring budgets. They were usually released on a literal road-show basis, their peripatetic producer-distributors hiring theaters and other venues and exhibiting them to adults-only (sometimes sexually segregated) audiences when permitted by local licensing laws.[53]

As we have seen, in the wake of *Duel in the Sun,* territorial "blitz" bookings had been used for a number of films of all kinds, from costume adventures to family comedies. But throughout the 1950s they came to be associated primarily with low-budget horror and science-fiction films and pop-rock musicals aimed at teenagers and young adults whose interests were more regularly addressed by independent producers and distributors.[54] These films too were often described as exploitation pictures, primarily because of their colorful promotional campaigns. RKO opened its gorilla thriller *Mighty Joe Young* (1949) simultaneously "in some 358 theaters in New England and upstate New York," accompanied by intensive press, radio, and even television advertising, to considerable success (see illustration on page 133).[55] The studio followed it in 1952 with the third re-release of the nearly twenty-year-old *King Kong,* using the same marketing methods and distribution pattern, designed by its head publicist, Terry Turner. To the industry's amazement, the reissue grossed a reported $1.6 million, more than twice its original domestic gross.[56] As a freelancer, Turner went on to use the same tactics on a number of other "creature features," including Paramount's *The War of the Worlds* (1953) and Warners' *The Beast from 20,000 Fathoms* (1953) and *Them!* (1954).[57] Turner noted as late as 1959 that television advertising had thus far been limited "to only this type of 'freak' picture or cheap melodramas," and that the industry had "made very little effort to find the right technique to apply it to the so-called 'big' pictures and get bigger and better results."[58]

"Freak" films and their like did not typically play downtown picture palaces. They could often be found, double- or triple-billed, in the open-air drive-in cinemas that had been appearing in ever-increasing numbers since the end of the war. Drive-ins apparently originated in New Jersey in the early 1930s (the first to appear in Los Angeles opened in 1934). At the beginning of 1949 there were reported to be around 750 "ozoners" in the United States; by mid-1952 there were 3,835, making up one-quarter of all exhibition sites but providing only 10 percent of domestic rental revenues. Most were independently owned. Being dependent on the weather, the average drive-in stayed open only eight months of the year. These factors, together with their discount pricing (tickets were often sold by the carload rather than to individual patrons), led the majors initially to regard drive-ins as second-class venues and to relegate them to lower-run status, especially for blockbusters. But with a national seating capacity of over five million, they were notably successful in attracting and retaining the regular patronage of both teenage and family audiences.[59] Exhibitor Robert Lippert claimed that "TV has reduced first-run grosses by 20 percent, neighbourhoods as much as 50 percent, drive-ins only 10 percent."[60] A number of independent companies prospered by supplying films directly to them and to those "hard-top" situations unsuited to roadshows and other prestige, first-run bookings. One such company was Joseph E. Levine's Embassy Pictures Corporation.

Levine, who started out as an art-house exhibitor in New Haven, Connecticut, first tried saturation booking when he bought the New England reissue rights to *Duel in the Sun* for $40,000, making a half-million-dollar profit on the deal. He made his name by importing the Japanese creature feature *Godzilla* (1956) and the Italian epic *Attila the Hun* (1958), and spending several times their acquisition costs on promotional campaigns orchestrated by Terry Turner. Two further low-budget Italian spectacles he acquired, *Hercules* (1959) and *Hercules Unchained* (1960), were released through Warner Bros., but Levine supervised their publicity campaigns. He claimed to have spent over $1 million apiece on intensive print, radio, and TV advertising for the two pictures, putting six hundred prints of each into domestic circulation. *Hercules* earned $4,396,000 in U.S. rentals on a cost to Warners of only $350,000. *Hercules Unchained* cost $500,000 to acquire and earned $3,646,000 in America and Britain. In the next few years several major and minor studios invested substantial sums from their frozen foreign accounts in coproducing or acquiring European-produced muscleman epics, none with quite the same impact as these two. American International Pictures, another independent company noted for low-budget "action" pictures, planned to roadshow its Italian pick-up *Sign of the Gladiator* (1959) until the success of *Hercules* persuaded it to switch to saturation instead. Levine also began to apply his mass-booking strategy to big-budget productions, most successfully with *The Carpetbaggers* (1964), based on Harold Robbins's salacious best-selling novel. Costing $3.3 million and released on seven hundred prints through Paramount, the film reportedly grossed $15.5 million domestically.[61]

A more venerable independent producer, David O. Selznick, further developed his *Duel in the Sun* release pattern with (in theory) a more prestigious property, the CinemaScope remake of Ernest Hemingway's World War I love story *A Farewell to Arms* (1957). Distributed through Fox, the film opened simultaneously, in what trade-paper advertisements described as "unreserved-seat roadshow engagements," with raised prices and continuous performances in eight Los Angeles theaters (seven suburban houses plus Grauman's Chinese).[62] Selznick believed this policy might "aid the 'fringe' exhibitor who would otherwise have to mark time while a big picture played itself out on a hard-ticket, or two-a-day, basis."[63] The "Selznick pattern," as it became known, was followed in other key-city openings of the film, though not in New York, where normal clearances were observed.[64] But the same year, a number of medium-budget films, including Columbia's *The Garment Jungle,* Fox's *Bernardine,* and Paramount's *Loving You,* went straight into mass neighborhood release in cities including New York, Detroit, and Chicago, bypassing downtown first-run theaters entirely. As *Loving You* was an Elvis Presley vehicle, and as other Elvis pictures, including Fox's earlier *Love Me Tender* (1956) and MGM's later *Jailhouse Rock* (1957), were released in much the same way, this policy became known as the "Presley pattern."[65]

One of Terry Turner and Joseph E. Levine's intensive exploitation campaigns is announced in this trade press advertisement for an imported European epic (*Variety*, July 13, 1955, 23).

In a bid to sever the association of quick release methods with "freak" and youth-appeal pictures, UA experimented with mass territorial bookings, accompanied by intensive media advertising, of its western *The Magnificent Seven* (1960), beginning in the South and Southwest where "outdoor pictures [did] proportionately better" than elsewhere.[66] Warners had adopted a similar policy for *The Hanging Tree* (1959) the previous year and had claimed a record 651 simultaneous openings with *The Boy from Oklahoma* (1954), while Universal had also established precedents for the regional saturation release of westerns and other grassroots attractions earlier in the decade.[67] *The Magnificent Seven* was not particularly successful in the United States; but it performed exceptionally well in Britain, where it was used to try out another "instant release" policy, in which selected suburban cinemas in Greater London played the picture concurrently with its West End premiere run.[68]

UA then adopted this strategy for the release in New York of *The Road to Hong Kong* (1962), a belated entry in the Bing Crosby–Bob Hope musical comedy series. The film opened day-and-date in thirteen theaters, including "an eastside Manhattan house and selected theatres in the four boroughs and neighboring communities in Long Island, New Jersey and Westchester," as well as on Broadway.[69] Subsequent runs encompassing up to seventy more theaters followed four weeks later. UA justified this precedent-setting move, which was at first strongly resisted by the major circuits, on the grounds that exclusive Broadway runs had become uneconomic because the cost of advertising and theater operation absorbed all box-office takings.[70] UA announced that the policy, now called "Premiere Showcase," "would be adhered to not only for the one film but for all of the [company's] product for the rest of the year, including roadshow films."[71] It gave the example of *Taras Bulba* as one film initially planned for roadshowing that would be released on Premiere Showcase instead.[72] "Golden Showcase," a further variation used for stronger films, was introduced with the Billy Wilder comedy *Irma la Douce* (1963). This policy involved delaying the neighborhood breakout for several weeks after the start of a regular Broadway and East Side pre-release, which continued while the picture spread to the nabes.[73]

Although it was particularly suited to New York because of the city's dense population, showcase releasing was soon used in other domestic keys, as well as overseas. It was said to be necessitated by "efforts to find a formula for breaking away from a progressively more difficult problem in the merchandising of films: the creeping obsolescence of the Broadway movie theaters and the rising costs of opening a film in one of them for an exclusive first run."[74] Showcase alleviated the logjam caused by lengthy roadshow and other pre-release engagements, which tied up downtown theaters for months at a time, and allowed new pictures to move out into general release more quickly (thereby returning revenue faster than the slow-earning roadshows). It also addressed the frequent complaints made by subsequent-run exhibitors that, by the time roadshow pictures reached them, they were "old and stale."[75] The pattern effectively came to be an adjunct to roadshowing rather than a mere alternative. When its eight-month Broadway reserved-seat engagement ended, *Judgment at Nuremberg* began its regular New York first run with simultaneous grind engagements in two downtown and thirteen neighborhood theaters, as per the showcase pattern.

The showcase plan upgraded many nabe theaters to first- or second-run status, while squeezing out many of the lesser later-run houses. As a by-product, it also persuaded exhibitors to share advertising expenses with the distributors. As *Variety* commented, while drawing some business away from Broadway, showcase releasing also "had the effect of attracting patrons who were not going to the Broadway outlet anyway."[76] Showcase releasing, with or without initial downtown pre-releases, was successful enough at attracting big audiences in a relatively short span of time and at increasing ticket sales overall for it to be taken up (under a variety of trade names) by all the major distributors and exhibition chains from the 1963–64 season onward. It remained standard policy for many years thereafter.

The films that particularly demonstrated the vast potential revenues from show-case, and especially its rapid speed of returns, were the early James Bond pictures. The success of the first two in the series, *Dr. No* (1963) and *From Russia with Love* (1964)—both of which opened on a regional-saturation basis in most of the country and on Premiere Showcase in New York—led to an escalation in the production and promotional budgets UA assigned to the third, *Goldfinger* (1964). The company suggested to the series' producers, Albert R. Broccoli and Harry Saltzman, that it should be released as a roadshow.[77] They opted instead for Golden Showcase. *Goldfinger* opened in two New York theaters, the DeMille on Broadway and the Coronet, an East Side art house, followed one month later by a thirty-theater break and a subsequent general release in ninety-four nabes. Most other key cities opened the film simultaneously with New York, with 485 prints (from a worldwide total of 1,100) circulating in the U.S. market. Breaking records in almost every situation it played (the DeMille stayed open twenty-four hours a day to accommodate the crowds), *Goldfinger* grossed nearly $23 million domestically. The fourth Bond film, *Thunderball* (1965), performed even better and the fifth, *You Only Live Twice* (1967), did almost as well. Only with the sixth series entry, *On Her Majesty's Secret Service* (1969), the first not to star Sean Connery, did a Bond picture significantly underperform by comparison with its predecessors.[78]

Between the appearance of each new episode (which invariably cost more than the one before) the earlier films were reissued in double-bill combinations, commanding first-run rentals even from theaters playing them for the second or third time. The first six pictures grossed in aggregate $220 million worldwide. The Bonds also generated massive revenues from spin-off merchandise such as toys and other commercial tie-ins. Over $50 million was earned in 1966 alone from more than one hundred licensed products. The success of the Bond "franchise" (as it would now be described) was reflected not just in the prolific 1960s spy cycle that imitated it, but also in the re-generation of the feature-length series picture, a generic concept that had largely been dormant since the advent of the filmed made-for-TV series in the 1950s. UA was in the forefront of this development, sponsoring not only the Bonds but also the various sequels spawned by *The Magnificent Seven, The Pink Panther* (1964), and *Fistful of Dollars* (1967).[79] But serial form is also a characteristic feature of the Bond films individually; they are typically constructed around a series of cliff-hanging encounters and relatively self-contained set pieces that are often only loosely motivated by their narrative placement. In all these respects the Bonds recalled the serial chapter plays and B-features of the 1920s, 1930s, and 1940s, and also anticipated the action-adventure blockbusters of the 1980s, 1990s, and 2000s.[80]

Despite these innovatory distribution strategies, the most widespread simultaneous bookings of any films before the 1980s were for two video records of live stage performances. John Gielgud's staging of *Hamlet* at the Lunt-Fontanne Theatre in 1964, with Richard Burton in the leading role, achieved the longest theatrical run (136 performances) of any Shakespeare production in Broadway history to that date. Over three consecutive performances in late June 1964, the play was recorded before live audiences by fifteen video cameras, and the edited material was transferred to 35 mm film. This tape-to-film process was dubbed Electronovision and the result, a Theatrofilm presentation.

Hamlet was picked up for U.S. distribution by Warners, which devised a plan for over one thousand simultaneous two-day engagements across the country of four performances each (two matinees, two evening shows) on September 24 and 25, 1964. Tickets were sold in advance on a reserved-performance (rather than reserved-seat) basis. This policy was intended to preserve the aura of live theater and to emphasize the exclusivity of the limited engagements. Even though more than one theater per territory was allowed to book the film, it was immediately withdrawn from circulation after the two-day runs and never re-released. The filmed record stood in for an out-of-town tour of the stage production (which had closed the month before), covering a larger number of play dates than any road company could or would, and had something of the ephemerality of live theater (the strict four-screening limit even ruled out advance trade and press previews). Warners aimed for 1,060 bookings and achieved 971, for a gross rental of $1,781,000. The total cost of the film, including prints and advertising (which made up the bulk of expenses), was reported as $1.1 million.[81]

Warners and other companies subsequently used similar distribution methods for a number of other filmed records of stage performances (ballet and opera productions as well as Shakespeare), including *Othello* (1965), based on Olivier's Royal National Theatre presentation in London, as well as for Joseph Strick's adaptation of James Joyce's *Ulysses* (1967), cofinanced by the Walter Reade Organization and British Lion. But the second Electronovision Theatrofilm presentation was distinctly more downmarket: a pop-music revue titled *The T.A.M.I.* [Teenage Music Awards International] *Show* (1966), for which a record 2,200 prints were struck for worldwide Christmas holiday bookings.[82]

Blockbuster Cycles and the International Market

In the broadest sense of the term, almost all the blockbusters of the roadshow era might be said to fall into the category of "epic." Given a big budget, wide-screen or wide-film format, and protracted running time, even the most intimate of subjects could be turned into an epic (precisely the objection reviewers made to Fox's three-hour CinemaScope film of *The Diary of Anne Frank*). As Kristin Thompson and David Bordwell have remarked, the 1950s and 1960s saw the "upscaling" of several genres through the "new commitment to big pictures."[83] Each genre produced distinctive cycles of large-scale films in this period. For example, *Around the World in Eighty Days* provided the model for several epic comedies with the episodic narrative structure of a chase or race. They included *The Great Race, Those Magnificent Men in Their Flying Machines* (both 1965), and *Those Daring Young Men in Their Jaunty Jalopies* (1969). The spectacular stunts, ornate period settings, and slapstick humor of these films easily crossed national boundaries, while their star-filled casts and cosmopolitan locations built in additional appeal for different markets. This was an increasingly pressing consideration.[84]

The domestic audience, traditionally large enough to enable a majority of films to break even from their American release alone, had declined to the point at which this could no longer be guaranteed. A majority of films now struggled to recover their costs from just the United States and Canada, and overseas income was often essential to profit margins. According to figures presented before a U.S. Senate Select Committee on Small Business in 1956, fifty-one out of seventy-one films released by Paramount between 1950 and 1952 failed to recoup their production costs in the domestic market.[85] Moreover, the balance of income from the two sectors had shifted. In the 1930s and 1940s, approximately two-thirds of all revenues were generated from the United States and Canada. Between 1958 and 1967, a little more than half of Hollywood's gross rental income came from foreign sources, with the biggest contributors being Britain, Italy, France, West Germany, and Japan. Because many of these and other territories, with the notable exception of Britain, had not suffered the same decline in theatrical attendance as the United States, they became crucial sources of revenue.[86] Between 1946 and 1960, annual ticket sales in America slumped from some 4,400 million to 2,129 million, and in Britain from 1,635 million to 501 million. In the same period those in Italy rose from 411 million to 745 million, and in France they remained approximately level at 419 million in 1960, compared to 417 million in 1946.[87]

Aside from their audiences, there were other economic advantages to be derived from the overseas markets, advantages that favored foreign location shooting, multinational coproductions, and the setting up of subsidiary companies to make films abroad. Such pictures were designated "runaway" productions, a derogatory term in common use from about 1960 onward, particularly with the American labor unions who saw work being taken away from their Hollywood-based members. As U.S. costs spiraled upward, European countries offered lower expenses for labor, raw materials, and technical facilities. Their governments often set limits on the amount of revenue that could be converted into foreign currency and remitted overseas, leading to the formation, as we noted in chapter 7, of large pools of "frozen" funds. However, these countries also sought to encourage their own film industries by making available various types of state subsidy. Such subsidies could be extended to foreign producers via coproduction deals or by working through subsidiaries whose products could be officially registered as non-American despite being financed by U.S. capital. Thomas Guback has identified two "waves" of overseas production in the 1950s and 1960s: "While blocked earnings were responsible for the first wave of runaway production, the availability of subsidization was the cause of its perpetuation and development into a second wave which cannot be attributed to unremittable revenues."[88] This second wave involved deeper involvement in foreign film industries, to the extent that by the end of the 1960s a large majority of, in particular, British production capital came from American companies, via their local subsidiaries.[89]

While the financial incentives described above were available to pictures in any budgetary range, they proved particularly useful to those at the more expensive end of the spectrum. Italy and Spain, especially, proved to have the right combination of studio facilities, scenic locales, and cheap, sometimes nonunion labor to attract numerous large-scale epics as well as more modest outdoor action pictures. Stanley Kramer claimed that *The Pride and the Passion,* filmed in Spain for $3.7 million, would have cost an additional $3 million to shoot in America. William Wyler claimed that *Ben-Hur* would have cost $7 million more to make in Hollywood than at Cinecittà in Rome. Anthony Mann estimated that *El Cid* (1961) would have cost as much as $20 million to make in Hollywood, rather than the $6 million he claimed it had cost in Spain.[90] According to Ted Richmond, producer of *Solomon and Sheba,* "for hiring an army . . . there is no place like Spain. . . . You go to the Minister of Defense," he said, "and tell him you need 3,000 soldiers a day. He tells you that you'll have to pay their salaries, plus cost of transportation and food. The army cost us a total of $80,000. The same number of extras here in Hollywood would have cost us $1,600,000." Richmond added that a Hollywood sound stage would have cost $750 a day for an independent company to rent, exclusive of maintenance and technical assistance. This compared to the five stages he rented in Spain for a total of $500 per week, inclusive of technicians' fees: "You just could not make a picture like *Solomon and Sheba* in Hollywood. The cost would be prohibitive. Who would make a picture these days in Hollywood if he knew he had to pay nearly $2,000,000 for extras? . . . The choice is simple. Either you make these spectacle pictures abroad or you don't make them at all."[91]

Of the biblical and ancient-world epics that proliferated in the wide-screen era, *Demetrius and the Gladiators, King Richard and the Crusaders, Prince Valiant, The Silver Chalice* (all 1954), *The Prodigal* (1955), *The Conqueror, Spartacus,* and *The War Lord*

(1965), along with *The Robe,* were made largely in America (in several instances, second-unit work or battle scenes were filmed abroad). *Knights of the Round Table, Alexander the Great, Helen of Troy, The Vikings* (1958), *Sodom and Gomorrah* (1963), and *The Long Ships* (1964) were all made in Britain (in the case of the first-mentioned) or Europe, and in the cases of *Land of the Pharaohs* (1955) and *Taras Bulba,* even further afield (Egypt and Argentina, respectively).[92] Although, as we have seen, several ancient-world epics were among the most successful films of the period, the vast majority performed poorly, especially in relation to their high costs. In some instances, disappointing domestic earnings were partly offset by superior performance abroad, where action and costume spectacle found an especially ready audience. In the case of *Spartacus,* overseas earnings to 1969 amounted to $12,462,044, while U.S. and Canadian rentals (even including a million-dollar TV sale) were only $10,643,181. But the film failed to show a profit on production costs of $10,284,014 because of distribution charges and expenses amounting to an additional $15,308,083.[93]

Later epics proved far more disastrous for their backers. Samuel Bronston's *The Fall of the Roman Empire,* filmed in Spain, cost $17,816,876 and grossed only $1.9 million in America.[94] George Stevens's long-gestating life of Christ, *The Greatest Story Ever Told* (1965), which had been in planning since 1954 and in production since 1962, earned domestic rentals of $6,962,715 on a $21,481,745 negative cost, the largest amount yet spent on a production made entirely within the United States.[95] *The Bible—in the Beginning . . .* (1966) was financed by the Italian producer Dino De Laurentiis from private investors and Swiss banks. He then sold distribution rights outside Italy jointly to Fox and Seven Arts for $15 million (70 percent of which came from Fox), thereby recouping the bulk of his $18 million investment. Although *The Bible* returned a respectable world rental of $25.3 million, Fox was still left with a net loss of just over $1.5 million. It was the last biblical epic to be released by any major Hollywood studio for nearly twenty years.[96]

Bronston and De Laurentiis were among several independent producers stationed in Europe who supplied Hollywood with large-scale pictures. (Others included the Italian Carlo Ponti and the British-based Sam Spiegel.) Bronston raised money for his productions by preselling world distribution rights on a territory-by-territory basis. An internationalized version of the old states rights system (albeit in advance of production rather than after completion), such global preselling was not new, but his *El Cid* was claimed to be "the first time it ha[d] been applied to a high-budget production destined to be launched as a road-show attraction."[97] Distribution of both *El Cid* and *55 Days at Peking* (1963) in the United States (as well as in Japan and the Near East) was handled not by a Hollywood major but by Allied Artists, a company generally known for exploitation movies and B-pictures. Other territories were taken by up to a dozen locally based distributors, including the Rank Organisation in Britain.

Internationalism was the keynote of Bronston's operation. Publicity claimed that Bronston, who was born in Bessarabia in the Russian Empire and spoke five languages, employed "key personnel representing just about every nation on earth."[98] Before his

179

The slaves' revolt in *Spartacus* (1960), filmed largely on Universal's back lot.

company's collapse in 1964, in a flurry of legal actions, he maintained offices in New York, London, Paris, Rome, Beverly Hills, Buenos Aires, and Tokyo.[99] This international dimension is manifested in the subjects of Bronston's films as well as in their packaging and distribution. *55 Days at Peking* dramatizes the Boxer Rebellion, in which the embassies of America, Britain, Japan, and Europe endured a fifty-five-day siege during an uprising of Chinese nationalists. The film begins by establishing its setting: the Chinese imperial capital city Peking (now Beijing) in the summer of the year 1900. The presence in the city of the foreign powers is introduced in a series of crane shots showing each of the occupying armies, in an array of different uniforms, playing their respective national anthems to the raising of their flags. Shot transitions are cued by the appearance in the outer left or outer right stereo channels of each successive anthem, as the camera establishes the locations of each of the foreign legations in relation to one another and to the Forbidden City, the seat of the Chinese Empress, in the distant background. The sequence also establishes the size of the production: the city and its surrounding walls were built full scale by art directors John Moore and Veniero Colasante at Las Matas outside Madrid, and serve constantly as a source of spectacle in their own right throughout the ensuing action.[100] Costing around $9 million to produce, *Peking* was reportedly "a winner around the globe, except for the US where it . . . performed unspectacularly," with rentals of $5 million.[101]

Replacing the epic after the mid-1960s was a type of historical drama marked less by scale than by the prestige conferred by literary or theatrical origins, and by an emphasis on dialogue rather than on action. This "intimate spectacle" cycle included Hal B. Wallis's *Becket, Anne of the Thousand Days* (1969), and *Mary, Queen of Scots* (1971), Columbia's *A Man for All Seasons* (1966) and *Cromwell* (1970), and Avco Embassy's *The Lion in Winter* (1968).[102] All of these used predominantly British actors, technicians, and studio facilities, and most were made at much less cost than the ancient-world epics. Several were released as roadshows, though their model was more *Henry V* than *The Ten Commandments*. As *Variety* noted of the most successful of them, *A Man for All Seasons*, the idea was "to market 'class' rather than 'bigness.'"[103] MGM's *Alfred the Great* (1969) fell problematically between the stools of prestige picture and action film. Following its premiere run as a roadshow in London to mostly dismal reviews and disappointing business, the studio attempted to market the film in the United States as an epic adventure rather than a character study. *Alfred*'s showcase opening in New York led most local reviewers to dismiss it as a "genre exercise," in a genre that, moreover, had little commercial credibility by the late 1960s, and the picture predictably failed.[104]

More popular than any of these, however, was MGM's *Doctor Zhivago* (1965), adapted from Boris Pasternak's Nobel-Prize-winning novel. A love story set in and around the Russian Revolution, it was produced by Carlo Ponti in Spain and Finland at a cost of $11.9 million. Opening to mixed reviews, it gradually built large audiences, and eventual world rentals were in the region of $100 million; $60,954,000 of this came from the United States, but the film set many all-time records in territories such as Italy and Spain.[105] For overseas release, MGM prepared "22 foreign language versions of the film, the greatest number for a single film in the studio's history."[106] In the wake of *Zhivago*, it released a number of other prestige costume dramas produced in Britain and Europe, including *Far from the Madding Crowd* (1967), *The Fixer* (1968), and *Mayerling* (1969), all of which failed in the United States. The studio's only new roadshow remotely to approach the success of *Zhivago* came from the same director/writer team of David Lean and Robert Bolt. Lean claimed, "I don't want an epic and I don't want a 'little gem.' I want something that has size and that size must be emotional."[107] At a cost of $13.3 million and with a fifty-two-week shooting schedule and a two-hundred-minute running time, the size of *Ryan's Daughter* (1970) was judged by most reviewers to be inappropriate to the slight story. The film did less than half of *Zhivago*'s business, but earned enough from the world market eventually to turn a profit.

MGM's most lucrative picture of the late 1960s besides *Zhivago* was yet another re-release of its most reliable property, *Gone with the Wind*. In 1954 and 1961, reissues of *GWTW* had been shown cropped to an "ersatz" wide-screen format. In 1967 the film was reframed and reprocessed for projection in 70 mm, losing nearly half its image composition in the process, with the soundtrack re-recorded in six-track stereo. The reissue grossed some $41 million domestically and a further $27 million overseas, more than any other re-release in industry history.[108] It was even more unusual in being on a roadshow basis; hitherto, reissues had invariably been offered at regular prices in general release. (MGM's attempt to follow it up with a roadshow reissue of *Ben-Hur* in 1969 failed, however.)

Before the 1960s, westerns had with few exceptions generally been regarded as a safe, reliable, and relatively inexpensive type of bread-and-butter product. But the cost of maintaining large crews on location drove up the cost of making such pictures, which traditionally appealed more to audiences in the South and Midwest of America than in the more populous and prosperous northern and eastern states.[109] The size, seriousness, and expansiveness of *The Big Country* (1958), *Cimarron,* and *Cheyenne Autumn* marked them as attempts at national epics, hence notionally of more interest to upscale audiences, though all performed disappointingly. Far more successful around the world was *How the West Was Won.* With three directors and an all-star cast, this was designed to be the definitive western. Its episodic narrative, linking a number of self-contained scenarios and spectacular action sequences shot in three-camera Cinerama, encompasses the broadest possible span of both U.S. history and generic conventions.[110] Either in spite or because of their specifically American themes, westerns generally found strong support overseas, where they often performed better than in the domestic market. Indeed, from the early 1960s many were actually made abroad, both by American companies—including Cinerama, which filmed *Custer of the West* (1968) in Spain—and by European filmmakers, such as the West German director Harald Reinl with the Karl May *Winnetou* series (filmed in Yugoslavia), the Italian Sergio Leone with the *Dollars* films and *Once upon a Time in the West* (1969), and the British producer Euan Lloyd with *Shalako* (1968) and several other films derived from the novels of Louis l'Amour.

War films, especially those set during the Second World War, more obviously had in-built appeal for overseas audiences. Blockbuster war films of the late 1950s and 1960s involved a number of distinct cycles. Military biographies included *Lawrence of Arabia, Cast a Giant Shadow, Khartoum* (both 1966), and *Patton* (1970). Reconstructions of battles and other large-scale military actions included *The Alamo, The Longest Day, Zulu* (1964), *Battle of the Bulge* (1965), *Is Paris Burning?* (1966), *The Charge of the Light Brigade* (1968), *Battle of Britain* (1969), and *Tora! Tora! Tora!* (1970). *The Bridge on the River Kwai* set the pattern for two further cycles. Its first half, set in a prisoner-of-war camp in Burma, revolves around the British Colonel Nicholson (Alec Guinness) and his refusal to permit officers to do manual work in the construction of the eponymous Japanese railway bridge. The second half concerns an Allied commando mission to blow up the bridge. (The transition between the two halves is marked by an intermission inserted in British reissue copies of the film.) Although both the prison-escape drama and the special-mission adventure had many antecedents, *Kwai* was the first film to set them on such a large scale and indeed to combine them. Subsequent large-scale POW films included *The Great Escape* (1963), *King Rat,* and *Von Ryan's Express* (both 1965). Later examples of the special-mission cycle included *The Guns of Navarone* (1961), *Operation Crossbow* (1965), *The Heroes of Telemark* (1966), *The Dirty Dozen* (1967), *Where Eagles Dare* (1969), and *Too Late the Hero* (1970). *Kelly's Heroes* (1970), in which a platoon of GIs robs a German bank of gold bullion, burlesques some of the latter cycle's conventions while also using them as the opportunity for action and spectacle. Many of these were filmed in Europe, where they tended to be roadshown, often in 70 mm; in the United States most were distributed on a general-release basis.

Jeanine Basinger has argued that the "Epic Recreation of Historical Events" constitutes a specific late stage in the evolution of the war film. Like *How the West Was Won* in relation to the western, several such films rework genre conventions as modern mythology. Of *Battle of the Bulge,* Basinger remarks: "it's as if the approach to history is to draw together all the movies into one long story from December 1944 to the end of the war."[111] She cites *In Harm's Way* (1965), with its many characters, multiple narrative strands, massive combat scenes, and "wide range of the war's iconography," as resembling "a complete miniature war in one movie."[112] *In Harm's Way,* along with other large-scale war and military films including *From Here to Eternity* (1953), *The Caine Mutiny* (1954), *The Young Lions* (1958), *Exodus,* and *The Victors* (1963), was adapted from a best-selling novel. So too were the films derived from the massive tomes of, for example, Edna Ferber (*Giant, Cimarron*), Irving Stone (*The Agony and the Ecstasy* [1965], *The Shoes of the Fisherman* [1968]), and James A. Michener (*Sayonara, Hawaii* [1966]).[113] In their dramatization of history and popular fiction, such films manifest the increasing dependence of Hollywood throughout the 1950s and 1960s on "presold properties"—a tendency most clearly demonstrated in the musical.

The success of MGM's *Annie Get Your Gun* (1950) and *Show Boat* (1951), both taken from stage plays, pointed the way to the genre's future development. Broadway shows promised prestige as well as presold songs and titles. Adaptations of them became the dominant mode of musical production in the latter part of the 1950s and throughout the 1960s. As Rick Altman points out, where once Hollywood had merely used the titles of stage properties and freely rewritten the books, the cost of acquiring movie rights for hits by the likes of Rodgers and Hammerstein or Lerner and Loewe, as well as the realization that audiences would expect to see the shows transferred to the screen intact, now often obliged filmmakers to remain scrupulously faithful to their sources.[114] Although original screen musicals continued to be made, the majority were vehicles for pop stars such as Elvis Presley and Connie Francis, aimed at the teenage market.

From 1955, the number of musicals, including stage adaptations, began to decline severely. "To understand the magnitude of the drop-off in production," remarked Altman in 1989, "it is perhaps helpful to consider that the production of the war years alone matches the entire production of the last three decades."[115] One reason for this decline was the downsizing of payrolls due to the high overhead costs of maintaining a fully staffed studio. More than other genres, musicals had traditionally depended on the existence of a large pool of talent and technical expertise being kept under permanent contract. A further reason was the generally poor performance of musicals in overseas markets, with the exception of Britain. The difficulties of dubbing or sub-titling song lyrics into different languages (they were sometimes cut out altogether, as happened with *The King and I*) meant that the majority of musicals earned the bulk of their rental income from domestic distribution. Even a European-themed picture such as *Gigi* earned only one-third of its worldwide gross from the foreign market. An American-themed musical like *The Music Man* fared even worse, grossing only $600,000 abroad compared to $7,242,000 in the United States. *West Side Story* was a partial exception; it set roadshow records for both earnings and length of run in Japan and ran for 218 weeks at the George V in Paris. Samuel Goldwyn's production of George Gershwin's black folk opera *Porgy and Bess,* which flopped in the United States, actually performed better overseas, though not well enough to bring a profit on its $7 million cost.[116]

Big-budget musicals nevertheless remained scarce until three hit films of the mid-1960s suggested that the genre might be the ideal form to attract back to cinemas the "lost audience" of adults with families. Bucking the trend of the genre, these three films were almost as successful abroad as they were in the domestic market. *Mary Poppins* (1964), which cost $5.2 million, was neither a stage adaptation nor a roadshow. But by the end of its first release, it had grossed nearly $50 million worldwide. In addition to its theatrical revenues, Disney enjoyed millions more from licensed merchandise, including soundtrack albums, books, toys, and commercial tie-ins.[117] *My Fair Lady* cost Warners $17 million to make, including a record $5.5 million just for the film rights to the Alan Jay Lerner and Frederick Loewe stage show and a million-dollar fee for star Audrey Hepburn. By 1967 it was reported to have grossed $55 million from roadshowing worldwide.[118]

But more than any other film, the benchmark for blockbusters in the second half of the decade was set by Fox's *The Sound of Music* (1965). Adapted from yet another Rodgers and Hammerstein property and filmed in Todd-AO on location in Austria, it cost $8,020,000 to produce. Estimates of worldwide rentals by the time of its withdrawal in 1969 ranged from $115 million to $125 million, either way making it the highest grossing film to date. As much as $50 million of the total came from the foreign market, around half of it from Britain alone, where the film more than tripled the take of the previous all-time record-holder, *South Pacific*.[119] *Music*'s phe-nomenal repeat business, which led to reports of many patrons seeing the film dozens, even hundreds, of times, stunned the industry. Many theaters racked up attendances higher than their local community populations; at least seventy-four North American roadshow engagements and twenty-one overseas ran for a full year or more, including sixteen that ran for two years or more.[120] Fox's head of UK distribution, Percy Living-stone, described the film as having appeal "on the widest possible front, suitable for all

Cecil Beaton's lavish costumes and Gene Allen's stylized set design are on display
in the Ascot sequence of *My Fair Lady* (1964).

the family, young and old, highbrows and lowbrows. . . . It is unique in the extent to
which all these qualities combine to make the perfect commercial movie."[121]

Hollywood quickly put other big musicals into production in the hope of repeat-
ing this success. At least sixteen were reported to be in preparation by January 1967.[122]
While *Camelot, How to Succeed in Business without Really Trying* (both 1967), *Funny
Girl, Half a Sixpence, Oliver!* (all 1968), *Hello, Dolly!, Paint Your Wagon, Sweet Charity*
(all 1969), *On a Clear Day You Can See Forever*, and *Song of Norway* (both 1970) were
all stage-derived, the studios were also now emboldened to commission a few screen
originals, including *Doctor Dolittle, The Happiest Millionaire, Thoroughly Modern Mil-
lie* (all 1967), *Chitty Chitty Bang Bang, Star!* (both 1968), and *Darling Lili* (1970).
Most of these films were designed for release on a roadshow basis, often in 70 mm.
Many were also among the most costly and lavish productions of the period, a fact
often seized upon by contemporary reviewers who regularly criticized them as "over-
blown," "overproduced," and so on.

Nevertheless, scale and spectacle are among the qualities most impressively exploited in *Hello, Dolly!* by director Gene Kelly and choreographer Michael Kidd.
"Put on Your Sunday Clothes" brings to a climax the first movement of the narrative. The song begins as a solo for Cornelius (Michael Crawford), watched and then

accompanied by Barnaby (Danny Lockin), in the cellar of the store where they work (they are about to desert their jobs in rural Yonkers and set off on a pleasure trip to New York City). As they don their hats and coats and strut outside, the film cuts to Dolly (Barbra Streisand) picking up the refrain as she collects her charges, Ermengarde (Joyce Ames) and Ambrose (Tommy Tune). They move from an upper room out onto a balcony and down a stairway, to be joined by other performer-spectators. The camera returns to Cornelius and Barnaby, themselves now accompanied by a chorus of dancers, and cuts back and forth between the two groups. Over one hundred other singers and dancers, in several other locations, are gradually introduced as the entire community seems to join in with Cornelius and Barnaby's anticipation of freedom and romantic fulfillment. The whole vast ensemble meets at the railway station where, led by Dolly, the song continues as everyone boards the train and concludes with the Todd-AO camera pulling out to a distant overhead shot of the station, railway, and surrounding landscape. The sense of boundlessness this sequence achieves is clearly available only to a production with immense financial and technical resources. The number is characterized by a series of backward-tracking camera movements, sometimes involving crane shots and culminating in the final helicopter shot, which progressively reveal more of the opulent production design and respond to the performers' own dynamic forward movement. Having begun in the darkness of a cramped cellar, the song ends in the bright open air with Cornelius and Barnaby integrated into communal activity, the performance space seeming to expand into something like infinity as individual joy becomes spectacularized.

Following the failure of most of its major musicals in the late 1950s and early 1960s (*Gigi* excepted), MGM made only one in the late 1960s, another remake of one of its past successes. Like Fox's *Doctor Dolittle*, *Goodbye, Mr. Chips* (1969) was produced by Arthur P. Jacobs' APJAC and had an original score by Leslie Bricusse. Unlike the expansive production numbers of *Hello, Dolly!* many of its songs are performed as voice-over soliloquies that express the contained emotion of the central character, a strait-laced English schoolmaster played by Peter O'Toole. The film still managed to cost $8 million and barely registered at the box office, even in Britain. Indeed, with the notable exceptions of *Funny Girl*, *Oliver!*, and *Thoroughly Modern Millie*, almost all the musicals mentioned here were box-office failures that hastened the end of the roadshow era and the start of a temporary hiatus in the regular production of big-budget films of all kinds. In 1970, MGM's recently appointed vice president in charge of production, Herbert Solow, remarked pointedly that henceforward "the company will not become involved in any 'epic' budget productions and definitely no musicals."[123] The next chapter will examine some of the other causes of this industry-wide crisis, and some of its consequences for Hollywood in the early 1970s and beyond.

MULTIPLE JEOPARDY, 1965–1975

In April 1965 *Variety* described "what might be called the 'new' picture business, a prevailing modus operandi which took a decade to evolve from five separate industry crises." That modus operandi included: "profitable (hence peaceful) coexistence with television"; the predominance of "studio-packager coproduction deals"; the aftermath of theater divorcement; the arrival of overseas production as something "here to stay"; and the development of "new compensation formulas" for talent (such as gross- and profit-participation deals) as well as "new production-distribution methods."[1]

The same article also noted the remarkably high number of films in the preceding five years—forty-three in all—that had earned domestic rentals of $6 million or more. The current season in particular had produced a sequence of massive hits, with *Goldfinger, Mary Poppins, My Fair Lady,* and *The Sound of Music* all having opened in the preceding six months, and *Thunderball* and *Doctor Zhivago* both to appear by the end of the year. The portrait *Variety* painted of Hollywood was one of achieved stability and prosperity. The proportion of profitable releases overall might have been small, but there seemed to be no limits to the earning power of the most successful films. A boom in suburban cinema building, particularly in shopping malls enclosing two, three, or more modestly sized auditoria under a single roof, and increasing numbers of drive-ins compensated for closures of traditional hard-top picture palaces and suggested a healthy, expanding exhibition sector.[2] The studios' revenues had also stabilized and annual profits were rising steadily, though this was due more to ticket price increases and windfall earnings from the lease of films to television than to any rise in theater attendance.

But still there were danger signs. Addressing the International Alliance of Theatrical Stage Employees (IATSE) labor union convention in 1966, the newly appointed head of the Motion Picture Association of America (MPAA), Jack Valenti, claimed that the average Hollywood picture now cost $3 million, a 50 percent increase in five years. Among the consequences of this, he pointed out, had been a further reduction in output as a way of limiting risk and an ongoing trend to produce films more cheaply overseas. If this situation continued, Valenti foresaw "the slow extinction of what we know as the motion picture industry in the United States."[3] Unions' demands for minimum wages and minimum crews were among the reasons often given for the runaway tendency. Exorbitant payments for leading actors also accounted substantially for increased budgets. The negative cost of Warners' adaptation of Edward Albee's play *Who's Afraid of Virginia Woolf?* (1966)—filmed in standard wide screen and black-and-white, largely set in domestic interiors, and with a cast of only four principal actors—amounted to $7,613,000, in part because stars Elizabeth Taylor and Richard Burton received up-front fees of $1 million and $750,000, respectively, against 10 percent of the gross apiece.[4] (Their participation was presumably added to the budget.)

Valenti might have been speaking of *Virginia Woolf*'s neophyte director, Mike Nichols, when he told his IATSE audience that "a new breed of movie makers are moving in," filmmakers who were "breaking away from old traditions" and "looking to the future." This new breed was being encouraged, he said, by the existence of a more sophisticated audience, the product of President Lyndon B. Johnson's "revolutionary educational legislation [that] has literally awakened a whole new world of potential and promise for film-making."[5] When Darryl Zanuck referred the following month to a "new wave of filmmaking," he had something different in mind. He was referring to roadshows—in particular, to his own studio's current reserved-seat attractions *The Sand Pebbles, The Blue Max* (both 1966), and *The Bible,* as well as the still-running *The Sound of Music.* Zanuck took pride in having instilled in Fox a commitment to this "new production concept" [*sic*], consisting of "advance-sale promotion of a prestige product with an in-bred guaranteed income."[6] The commercial philosophy embodied in Zanuck's policy was one that, to a greater or lesser extent, all the studios shared. As we have seen, roadshows were released in increasing numbers throughout the second half of the decade. The spread of 70 mm–equipped theaters (727 in the United States by 1968, or 5 percent of the estimated total) guaranteed more space for big-screen spectacles, even in smaller communities that traditionally had not been able to support long runs or high ticket prices.[7]

Zanuck himself was part of the ancien régime, the last of his generation of "moguls" to retain his position as active leader of a major studio. The mid-1960s saw a series of changes in ownership and management among the majors. As well as Zanuck's assumption of the presidency of Fox in 1962, new management teams at MGM and Columbia brought in policies aimed at limiting risk and improving profitability. Former talent agency MCA completed its takeover of Universal in 1963; the conglomerate Gulf + Western purchased Paramount in 1966; the Canadian company Seven Arts acquired control of Warner Bros. in 1967 to form Warner–Seven Arts (W-7 was sold again to conglomerate Kinney National Services in 1969); and the finance company Transamerica Corporation bought UA the same year. In 1968 Joseph Levine sold his Embassy company to another conglomerate, the Avco Corporation, while remaining in charge of its film production and distribution activities. However, neither these structural changes nor the influx of young executives, including Richard D. Zanuck, brought significant departures from the basic assumptions and practices of their predecessors. Among them was a cautious attitude toward the youth audience.

Youth Appeal, Sleepers, and the End of the Roadshow

It had long been known that the majority of the audience was composed of "young adults," particularly between the ages of sixteen and twenty-four. A report commissioned by the MPAA in 1967 found that 48 percent of the adult audience fell into this category.[8] Regular attendance fell off after age thirty as people married, had families, and spent more time at home. Older age groups were the hardest to attract and formed the bulk of the so-called lost audience (lost, that is, to television and other forms of recreation).[9] The MPAA report pointed out that almost half the national population either never visited cinemas at all or did so only rarely. Regular moviegoers, responsible for 76 percent of ticket purchases, represented a mere 18 percent of the population.[10]

Precisely because they could be relied upon as frequent attendees, younger patrons were taken for granted by the majors. Although the studios still groomed young actors as potential stars and made a number of films each year with teenage and young-adult audiences in mind, such films were typically low in prestige, moderate in cost, and modest in revenues. They were not, in other words, high-end productions expected or required to generate vast sums. Instead, the studios concentrated their greatest efforts on drawing back to theaters the older, married audience that they continued to see as the main source of revenue for an occasional special picture. "I believe that there is an error in appealing only to the young," stated the thirty-six-year-old Richard Zanuck in 1971 following his departure from Fox. "By far the largest potential audience lies in the group not now attending films. They can be brought back through showmanship."[11]

This was the audience at which roadshows were aimed. Younger viewers, it was assumed, would enjoy these films as well, and indeed the evidence seemed to suggest this was so. *The Sound of Music* was regarded as entertainment suitable for all ages and *Doctor Zhivago* was "acclaimed by teenage America as 'the most enjoyed movie of 1967,'" according to a survey conducted by *Seventeen* magazine.[12] On the whole, though, most roadshows appealed especially "to family audiences or, less frequently, 'serious' adults."[13] The relaxation of censorship with the introduction of the advisory warning "Recommended for Mature Audiences" in 1966 resulted in a growing number of films specifically intended for an adult viewership. However, the MPAA's 1967 report observed that "the more 'adult' films have become, the more they appeal to teenagers and the less they appeal to their elders."[14] This tendency was accelerated with the abandonment the following year of the thirty-eight-year-old Production Code in favor of a rating system. But as *Variety* observed, the narrowing of audience address with adult-oriented films kept many prospective patrons away, while others

DOCTOR ZHIVAGO

...ACCLAIMED BY TEENAGE AMERICA AS "THE MOST ENJOYED MOVIE OF 1967"*

*YOUNG AMERICA VOTES IT THE NUMBER ONE PICTURE OF THE PAST YEAR— ACCORDING TO A RECENTLY RELEASED SURVEY BY SEVENTEEN MAGAZINE.

Now this great love story...this great spectacle...this great box-office sensation returns for a Limited Engagement!

Launched by a powerful 1968 Advertising and Merchandising Campaign.

Full-scale promotion of the hotter-than-ever Academy-Award winning musical score from the MGM record album...featuring "Lara's Theme." A best-selling album for 95 weeks!

METRO-GOLDWYN-MAYER PRESENTS A CARLO PONTI PRODUCTION

DAVID LEAN'S FILM OF BORIS PASTERNAK'S

DOCTOR ZHIVAGO

GERALDINE CHAPLIN · JULIE CHRISTIE · TOM COURTENAY
ALEC GUINNESS · SIOBHAN McKENNA · RALPH RICHARDSON ·
OMAR SHARIF AS ZHIVAGO · ROD STEIGER · RITA TUSHINGHAM

ROBERT BOLT · DAVID LEAN

THERE'S NO LIMIT TO THE BOX-OFFICE POWER OF "DOCTOR ZHIVAGO"!

MGM

The success of *Doctor Zhivago* (1965) with young audiences is emphasized in this trade press advertisement (*Variety*, February 14, 1968, 12).

were alienated by the high prices charged for roadshows (up to $6 in New York for in-demand musicals like *Funny Girl*).[15]

Needing the widest possible audience to return the greatest possible revenues, most roadshows avoided restrictive ratings. One of the few that turned out to appeal more to the young adult audience than to the family trade was *2001: A Space Odyssey,* released initially in 70 mm Cinerama. MGM had announced the project early in 1965 as *Journey beyond the Stars.*[16] Over more than two years of filming amid great secrecy in British studios, producer-director Stanley Kubrick spent $10.4 million, twice the initial budget. On opening in April 1968 the 167-minute film received a mixed critical reception, and within two weeks Kubrick had removed nineteen minutes of footage. But it quickly became apparent that the qualities older viewers found problematic— sparse dialogue, an elliptical narrative, ambiguous meaning, and near-abstract visual orientation—were precisely those that most impressed younger ones. Unlike their elders, the film's fans did not bother to reserve their tickets in advance or sit in their allotted seats. Nor did they necessarily remain in the seats they chose to occupy: *Variety* reported that "a curious thing happened during most shows at most theatres" during the climactic "stargate" sequence, when viewers seated farther back in the auditorium would move down to the area in front of the screen "where they would lie flat on their backs in order to experience the episode in the most head-on manner possible." Partly in response to such incidents and to reports of "the smoking of marijuana in the balconies,"[17] MGM switched its marketing policy on the picture. Initially promoted along conventional generic lines as an "epic drama of adventure and exploration," the film was billed in later ads as "The Ultimate Trip" in acknowledgment of its hallucinogenic properties and countercultural resonance. *2001* eventually earned over $40 million in worldwide rentals.

The industry's perception of the youth market's potentialities began to shift with the appearance from 1967 onward of a number of films that vaulted to unexpected success on the strength of their apparent appeal to young, urban, college-educated audiences (precisely the demographic prized by Jack Valenti). These "sleepers" included Avco Embassy's *The Graduate* (1967); Warners' *Bonnie and Clyde* (1967), *Bullitt* (1968), and *Woodstock* (1970); Columbia's *Guess Who's Coming to Dinner* (1967) and *Easy Rider* (1969); Paramount's *Romeo and Juliet* (1968), *Rosemary's Baby* (1968), and *Goodbye, Columbus* (1969); Fox's *Butch Cassidy and the Sundance Kid* (1969) and *MASH* (1970); and UA's *Midnight Cowboy* (1969). None of these films was roadshown in the United States[18]; most were set in contemporary America or had a contemporary "take" on the past (the casting of genuine teenagers to play Romeo and Juliet, the urbane sophistication of the dialogue in *Butch Cassidy,* the antiauthoritarianism of *Bonnie and Clyde* and *MASH*); most were produced on modest or medium-sized budgets (as low as $450,000 for *Easy Rider* and no higher than $6,825,000 for *Butch Cassidy*); and all grossed upward of $10 million domestically.

The Graduate eventually earned U.S. rentals of $44,090,729 on a production cost of $3.1 million to become the most lucrative non-roadshow picture (and independent release) to date. Its executive producer, Joseph Levine, claimed that he had "made sure it would kick off in the modern shopping centre cinemas where the kids drive to; also that it would be in smaller houses, for longer runs and the attendant ballyhoo that 'you can't get in'."[19] At the outer edges of the mainstream, the exploitation market produced breakthrough hits in the form of "cult" films which found large young-adult audiences not only in drive-ins but at late-night screenings in regular movie houses, where semiunderground pictures like *Night of the Living Dead* (1968) earned grosses far in excess of their paltry production costs.[20]

These films were not, of course, the only major hits of their era. But they were conspicuously more profitable than many of the high-cost family blockbusters launched in the same period, most of which proved resistant to the tastes and viewing habits of the youth audience. As MGM vice-president Douglas Netter realized in hindsight, "high prices and reserved seats keep youngsters away since they want to see a show on the spur of the moment."[21] A further twist to the sleepers' popularity was the fact that most of them remained far longer in first run than was normally the case with non-roadshow releases. Several opened on multiple-run Showcase engagements then spread to wider saturation bookings in the now-standard manner. But they were frequently brought back for further play dates at first-run prices, often in the same theaters that had shown them previously. These were not reissues in the usual sense, as the films had not been withdrawn.[22] This suggested that exhibitors preferred to replay, and many audience members preferred to resee, established hits rather than take a chance on newer releases that were unknown quantities. This exacerbated the already existing tendency for a small number of films to dominate the marketplace, taking a disproportionately large share of the available patronage and resulting in negligible returns for the vast majority of pictures.

This situation was not caused by any shortage of new product, a complaint exhibitors had often made in the recent past. Indeed, by the end of the 1960s there were far too many films being released for the still-shrinking theatrical sector to support. The years 1967–68 saw the appearance of several new "instant majors" whose output intensified the competition for playing time and for revenue in an overstocked market. ABC Pictures and Cinema Center were formed as the respective production arms of the TV networks ABC and CBS. They used as their respective distributors the Cinerama Releasing Organization and National General, both offshoots of exhibition chains. Disney continued after its founder's death in 1966 to make films exclusively for the family audience, while Allied Artists and American International began varying their diet of exploitation product with pictures aimed at the mainstream market. All these "mini-majors" and major independents helped spread the available box-office income ever more thinly. In 1968 the seven majors collectively released 177 pictures, twenty more than the year before and the largest number since 1960, while all new releases totaled 454, about average for the decade.[23]

Oversaturation of the market was compounded by rising production costs. By the end of the 1960s, budgets of $4 million and above, once considered exceptional,

Film buffs.

These young people and thousands like them are doing their movie thing. They are all seeing the three motion pictures that have made their world more meaningful. And many are seeing these films again and again.

"GOODBYE, COLUMBUS," "ROMEO & JULIET" and "IF...." express everything that young people feel deeply about . . . like love and the establishment. You should see them, too, if you want to see the great change that is happening.

[*This ad appeared in the Amusement Section of the New York Times, Sunday, April 27.*]

The potency of the youth market is acknowledged by this trade press advertisement for a trio of Paramount releases (*Variety*, April 30, 1969, 16).

were commonplace. But of the ninety films listed by *Variety* as having earned upward of $1 million in the domestic market for 1968, only twenty-seven earned rentals of $4 million or more. Of the same number of pictures on 1969's chart, only twenty-five earned above $4 million. In addition, budgets far higher than the average were reached with greater frequency than ever before. *The Ten Commandments* had been the first picture with an eight-figure negative cost, a level subsequently reached by one film in 1959 (*Ben-Hur*), two in 1960 (*Spartacus* and *The Alamo*), and two or three a year from 1962 to 1967. But between 1968 and 1970, at least twenty pictures cost over $10 million, several of which cost over $20 million.

Al Howe, president of the Bank of America, one of the leading sources of loans for production funds, estimated the difference between the studios' actual outlay and the potential world market:

He calculated that the annual worldwide box office for film was worth perhaps $2,000 million. Of that, the cinemas kept $1,400 million, and the film companies took $600 million. Once the studios had knocked off their distribution fees, of perhaps $180 million, and their distribution costs, of perhaps another $180 million for making prints and advertising, there would be $240 million left, from all the world, to cover the cost of actually making the films. Howe thought even this figure was overly generous. Much of the worldwide take at the box office would stay with overseas distributors. His final calculation showed that American film companies could expect to bring back around $200 million from all their films in a year like 1967.[24]

The majors' aggregate production expenditure in this same year was about $350 million (with perhaps another $50 million by all other U.S. companies combined). All told, by 1969 the major studios had around $1.2 billion invested in unreleased or unamortized inventory.[25] *Variety* explained:

Until the over-production boom of 1966–68 the film industry, by accident or design, had kept feature film inventory levels at sensible proportions commensurate with the likely return from theatrical and free-tv markets. But Hollywood got caught up in its own blockbuster fantasy which, combined with a national inflationary boom, saw fiscal discipline disintegrate.

Amortization discipline gave way to wishful thinking; residual values ascribed to network licensing hopes skyrocketed (which helped to make the current balance sheets look good); above-the-line costs became ridiculous; film companies, with few exceptions, borrowed to the hilt and immediately spent to the hilt; everyone acted as though there were no tomorrow.[26]

The bubble finally burst in 1969, when virtually all the major studios began declaring corporate losses that over the next three years totaled over $500 million.[27] Of the seventy-four films Fox released between 1967 and 1970, at least fifty-two lost money. Losses on individual films ran in some instances to eight figures. In the case of *Hello, Dolly!*, the most expensive film of its year at a cost of $25,335,000, the shortfall after nearly eighteen months in release was reported as $13,702,000, nearly one-half of Fox's total loss for 1969 of $27.5 million.[28] This was not entirely due to uncontrolled extravagance. Completed almost a year before its premiere, the film had sat on the shelf because of the licensing terms of the studio's deal with David Merrick, producer of the live stage show still running on Broadway, who wanted to protect it from competition. During this time, and for the duration of the film's extended road-show release, Fox was obliged to pay stiff interest payments (estimated at between 10 percent and 13 percent) on the bank loans that had financed the production.[29]

Outsize budgets were not the only cause of the financial disaster. The obstacles to even an ostensibly successful film in the medium- to high-cost range making a profit can be seen from the example of Warners' *The Wild Bunch* (1969). The film's total revenues from seven years of worldwide release to 1976, including sales to television, reached $13,064,944. However, the balance sheet still showed a deficit of $5,826,871 from combined deductions totaling $18,891,815. These included the picture's negative cost ($6,240,000), Warners' distribution fee ($4,460,000) and distribution expenses including prints and advertising ($4,250,000), as well as its overhead charge ($1,240,000). In addition, cumulative bank loan interest amounted to $3,990,000.[30] In this way a moderately expensive, reasonably popular film was still left with a loss nearly equal to its actual cost. Projected across the whole industry, aggregate bank interest alone equated to "a single major company's entire world rental take" for one year.[31]

Thus a combination of overproduction, overspending, and overestimation of the market's value, along with the accumulation of hidden costs and the maintenance of production and release policies committed to making the most expensive items, most of them distributed in the slowest and most risky release patterns, for the smallest and least reliable audience sector, had led to what was perceived at the time as the downfall of the traditional studio system (or what little remained of it). Paramount executive Martin S. Davis commented, "the era of the majors, as we knew it in the so-called golden age of Hollywood, is over."[32] The industry-wide recession that resulted from this fiscal collapse lasted until 1973. During this time, several of the majors again changed corporate ownership or executive management, and all introduced drastic economy measures. MGM set a budgetary ceiling of $2 million on new pictures, a level most other studios accepted as sensible and at which they also aimed, whether or not they too imposed fixed spending limits. The majors also substantially reduced or even suspended production programs, sold off both fixed and moveable assets, and cut overheads wherever possible. Companies that still maintained their head offices in New York relocated them to the West Coast, while regional distribution exchanges were reduced in number, and staff at all levels and in all branches was downsized. Columbia sold its studio lot in Hollywood to share Warners' premises at Burbank, Paramount's senior management vacated its own headquarters for cheaper office accommodations off the lot, and MGM eventually pulled out of distribution to release its few new pictures through UA. Several companies merged their international distribution offices, reduced overseas production investments, and began concentrating their efforts on the home market. Reversing the trend of the previous two decades, from 1974 onward and for the next twenty years, domestic revenues exceeded foreign, sometimes by a substantial margin.[33]

One further change was the abandonment, yet again, of roadshowing. After reserved-seat releases reached a numerical peak in 1968, a large number of films in 1969 and 1970 that had been planned as roadshows were sent out instead on a grind basis, often after substantial reediting to reduce their running times.[34] Others intended for production were postponed or canceled altogether. Fox sharply limited the reserved-seat engagements of *Patton* and *Tora! Tora! Tora!* After *Ryan's Daughter*, MGM's only roadshow was yet another remake of a vintage title. A modestly budgeted biopic of Johann Strauss II, *The Great Waltz* (1972)—a remake of the 1938 film—was made independently in Europe by Andrew L. Stone as a follow-up to *Song of Norway*, his Edvard Grieg biography made for Cinerama. *The Great Waltz* was blown up to 70 mm from 35 mm Panavision and exhibited in only a handful of large-screen venues. Although MGM entered into an agreement to produce more films in association with Cinerama, this came to nothing, and the Cinerama company was liquidated a few years later.[35]

Only UA and Columbia remained committed to roadshows; the former with the musicals *Fiddler on the Roof* (1971) and *Man of La Mancha* (1972), the latter with the historical dramas *Nicholas and Alexandra* (1971) and *Young Winston* (1972). Each costing between $8 million and $11 million, these were among the most expensive pictures of their respective years, but only the first was successful. The last major-studio release to be extensively roadshown was far from the big-budget, family-entertainment epics of the previous two decades. Bernardo Bertolucci's erotic drama *Last Tango in Paris* (1972), a Franco-Italian coproduction financed and distributed by UA, was budgeted at $1,250,000. It grossed $37 million in worldwide rentals, nearly half of which was earned in the United States. The film broke box-office records for an art-house picture (it was filmed in English and French) thanks to UA's careful negotiation of the censorship furor caused by its graphic sex scenes featuring Marlon Brando. Its $5-top ticket price on Broadway was the most expensive for any film in town except hardcore pornographic shows.[36]

A low-budget action film about a half-breed Native American defender of liberal causes also broke through to blockbuster earnings thanks to a distribution policy borrowed from the independent sector. Produced for under $1 million and sold to Warners for $1.8 million, *Billy Jack* (1971) was considered a sleeper hit when it earned $9,725,000, mainly thanks to its success in midwestern territories. But its star and pseudonymous director Tom Laughlin was dissatisfied and claimed that its release had been sidelined in favor of the distributor's in-house product. He sued for loss of income and Warners settled out of court by agreeing to a reissue supervised by Laughlin's company Taylor-Laughlin. The re-release was supported by intensive press, radio, and TV advertising precisely targeting a number of different demographic groups, as well as by point-of-sale publicity leaflets addressing the various social issues the film raised. After test runs in March 1973, the reissue began in earnest in May with up to sixty-six Los Angeles theaters hired on a four-wall basis for one or two weeks each. This was followed in October with 389 simultaneous theater hires in New York, Philadelphia, Detroit, and Chicago.[37] Further reissues extended over the next two years, helping the film to an ultimate domestic rental of $32.5 million.

As we have already seen, neither saturation releases nor four-wall bookings were new. Both were frequently used in the 1970s in rural areas by independent producer-distributors of family-oriented outdoor adventures and nature documentaries, while four-walling was also used for some roadshow engagements and for potentially controversial pictures, including *Last Tango in Paris*. But *Billy Jack* proved that these methods could work equally well with seemingly unsophisticated product in urban situations when used in conjunction with media advertising that reached the surrounding environs as well as the cities. The industry took note and several other, more expensive films that had proved disappointing on initial release were reissued in similar fashion, including Warners' *Jeremiah Johnson* (1972) and Avco Embassy's *The Day of the Dolphin* (1973). MGM also released its science-fiction film *Westworld* (1973) in a four-wall saturation pattern. The majors' four-wall hires ran into opposition from exhibitors—who saw themselves being excluded from potentially lucrative releases, as the bulk of revenues from such arrangements went directly to the distributors—and from the Department of Justice.[38] But while it lasted, four-walling was one of a number of methods the studios employed as insurance against the sort of losses they had recently suffered with roadshows.

Best-sellers, Sequels, and Safe Risks

Each year between 1970 and 1975 *Variety*'s annual box-office charts were dominated by one or two films whose success far outstripped even their nearest rivals. Almost all these major hits were adapted from recent or current best-selling novels. They included Paramount's *Love Story* (1970) and *The Godfather* (1972); Universal's *Airport* (1970) and *Jaws* (1975); Fox's *The Poseidon Adventure* (1972); Warners' *The Exorcist* (1973); and *The Towering Inferno* (1974), which was released domestically by Fox and overseas by Warner Bros.[39] While, as we have seen, there was a long prior history of the success of big pictures owing something to the popularity (or notoriety) of the novels from which they were adapted, several of the early 1970s examples represent more deliberately calculated attempts at "synergy": the carefully planned cross-promotion of related products in more than one medium. Their success seemed to contradict a common assumption about the tastes of the youth audience, articulated by independent producer Aubrey Schenck: "the kids don't go to the plays or read the books. The best sellers in the bookstores are not always the best sellers on the campus."[40] The success of these films suggested either that Schenck was wrong (about these best sellers, at least), or that they owed their popularity to a much broader constituency than just "the kids," and that the long-standing imperative not to ignore the older audience was correct after all.

Erich Segal's *Love Story* and Mario Puzo's *The Godfather* had both been developed by Paramount from an early stage. Segal had written his novel at the studio's suggestion by adapting it from his original screenplay (as Alistair MacLean had previously done with MGM's *Where Eagles Dare*). The idea was that the book, published before the film was released, would become a form of advance promotion. The rights to Puzo's manuscript had been purchased before publication for $25,000, with a proviso for increases based upon the number of books sold up to a maximum of $85,000.[41] In neither case was the studio obliged to pay the sort of seven-figure fees that had recently been asked by other leading authors and publishers. Both *Love Story* and *The Godfather* went on to achieve enormous sales, but by this time the films were already in production. Their release while the novels were still on the best-seller charts enabled them to take advantage of intense want-to-see among their readerships; the films in turn stimulated further book purchases. The memorable themes composed by Francis Lai for *Love Story* and Nino Rota for *The Godfather* generated additional profitable spin-offs in their soundtrack albums. *Love Story* was one of the few soundtracks for a non-musical film to achieve over one million disc sales.[42]

Love Story was made for only $2,260,000 and, somewhat unexpectedly, earned nearly $50 million domestically. *The Godfather* had also begun as a comparatively inexpensive venture (at least one press report put its first budget at the same level as *Love Story*'s), with the novel's post–World War II setting updated to contemporary America.[43] But the decision by producer Albert S. Ruddy and director Francis Ford Coppola to retain the period setting for the gangster saga raised costs to $6.2 million, necessitating a more concerted marketing effort to ensure that the investment would be recovered. Announced for a Christmas 1971 premiere, the film's extended postproduction schedule led to its being postponed until March 1972. Paramount president Frank Yablans claimed that it was "the most pre-sold commodity on the market today," but that the studio would "not sacrifice one-tenth of 1% of the quality just to hit a release date."[44]

For its eventual release Yablans decided on a distribution policy that involved neither exclusive roadshow engagements nor regional saturation bookings. Instead, the film would be booked into a limited number of multiple runs in each major territory, generally two per community, though it was to premiere concurrently in five New York City theaters on March 15. One week later 322 other engagements opened in key cities across the country, further bookings spreading more widely as the release progressed. Ultimately more than eight hundred prints were put into domestic circulation. In New York, screenings at the five theaters were staggered so that patrons who were unable to get into one show would have time to get across town for the start of another. Performances were continuous and seats were unreserved, but prices were raised from the usual Broadway $3 top for non-roadshows to $4 for weekend evenings. Although it ran 175 minutes, Paramount strictly prohibited intermissions interrupting the film and allowed only five minutes between shows for the auditoria to be cleared.[45]

The speed with which *The Godfather* not only recouped its negative, distribution, and marketing costs but also broke the all-time box-office record took even Paramount by surprise. In its first full week, the film earned an exhibitors' gross of around $10 million, equivalent to rentals of over $7.3 million; within twenty-six days in 372 theaters it had grossed $26 million; and after eighteen weeks in 1,281 theaters, $101 million.[46] By the end of the year it had earned a domestic rental of $81.5 million, more than either *Gone with the Wind* or *The Sound of Music*. Undoubtedly Yablans's distribution plan had been partly responsible. So too had the deals with exhibitors, who had paid advance guarantees totaling over $13 million (including $1 million in New York alone). Rentals were calculated on a 90/10 basis: up to 90 percent of receipts after deduction of all theater operating expenses and publicity costs (the house "nut") were remitted to the distributor. In such deals, common on Broadway from the early 1950s and standard for first runs of major pictures by the 1960s, the rental

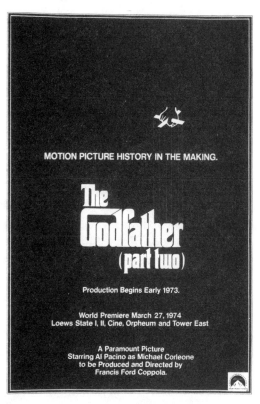

Paramount's campaign for *The Godfather, Part II* (1974) duplicated both the title logo and the distribution pattern of its 1972 predecessor (*Variety*, August 2, 1972, 10–11).

reduced in increments over successive weeks or months of a run, though usually with a minimum percentage of the gross specified as a "floor."[47]

Variety described the double impact of *The Godfather* on the trade: "(1) via an exhibitor willingness to go-along with a distributor with confidence (and cash up-front) never before enjoyed by a non-roadshow film, and (2), an enhancement of simultaneous playdates to achieve maximum penetration for maximum audience convenience."[48] Thus the combination of a presold picture that delivered on its promise and a distribution strategy that maximized its potential helped restore the industry's faith in its capacity to produce a record-breaking blockbuster. So confident was Paramount of being able to repeat history that five months after *The Godfather*'s premiere the studio formally announced that *The Godfather, Part II* would open in the same five New York theaters in March 1974. In fact, the sequel was also delayed (not opening until December 1974), but its nominal title remained unchanged. Other working titles such as *The Son of Don Corleone* and *The Death of Michael Corleone* were dropped in favor of the simple expedient of adding a number to the title of its forerunner, thus unambiguously announcing it as more of the same. Even the first film's poster design and title logo were retained for the second, to emphasize their continuity.[49] As further insurance, Paramount leased the original film to NBC TV for a record $10 million fee for one screening split over two nights in November 1974, the month before the sequel's release. Thus it became a three-hour trailer for the follow-up (which ended up grossing less than half as much).[50]

Sequels were common enough in the 1930s and 1940s, albeit mostly at the "B" level of series programmers. In the last chapter we noted UA's revival of the series film in the 1960s with its James Bond, *Magnificent Seven, Pink Panther,* and *Dollars* pictures, a model that other studios emulated. The spy cycle, for example, resulted in four pictures starring Dean Martin as secret agent Matt Helm (1966–69), three starring Michael Caine as Harry Palmer (1965–67), and two starring James Coburn as Derek Flint, released by Fox in 1966 and 1967. Fox also sequelized its $5.5 million science-fiction film *Planet of the Apes* (1968), which earned $20,825,000 worldwide on first release, beginning with *Beneath the Planet of the Apes* (1970) and continuing with three more follow-ups released on an annual basis in 1971, 1972, and 1973. They were also reissued in various combinations. Unlike the Bond films, each episode cost, and earned, less than the one before it, but all proved profitable. When its big-screen potential was exhausted, Fox exploited the *Apes* concept further with a live-action, prime-time television series in 1974, followed by a children's animated series in 1975. The *Apes* "franchise" also produced toys and other merchandise, along with a Marvel comic book.[51]

Among the few big hits of 1971 were a group of violent thrillers centered on unorthodox law enforcers: Warners' *Dirty Harry,* Fox's *The French Connection,* and MGM's *Shaft.* All were soon followed by sequels, as were two other entries, along with *Shaft,* in what *Variety* called the black action or "blaxploitation" cycle, *Super Fly* (1972) and *Cleopatra Jones* (1973). When *Walking Tall* (1973), the real-life story of a strong-arm small-town sheriff, proved a sleeper hit in southern and midwestern communities, it also received two follow-ups.[52] All these testified to the importance of capitalizing, as far and as fully as possible, on pictures with an identifiable and imitable commercial formula. This was another form of preselling and a hedge against risk, though in most cases the sequels failed to produce long-running series. The Bond films, in contrast, continued through the 1970s and 1980s with an average of one picture every two years until 1989. UA also successfully revived the bumbling Inspector Clouseau with its release of ITC's British production *The Return of the Pink Panther* in 1975. An unexpected smash hit worldwide, it was followed by two more pictures starring Peter Sellers as Clouseau and several more featuring a succession of other actors after Sellers's death in 1980.

As well as direct continuations of hit pictures, Hollywood in the 1970s developed a habit of following short-term generic cycles. Once again, there was nothing new in this; exhibitors in the 1930s had often complained of the bunching of a number of similar films released in close succession until their novelty wore off and a new cycle took their place. In the early 1970s most such cycles consisted of low-budget action films. As well as the vigilante cop and blaxploitation pictures there were gangster films inspired by *The Godfather,* martial arts films including Warners' *Enter the Dragon* (1973), and horror films inspired by *The Exorcist* (which we shall deal with shortly). These cycles particularly catered to the audiences that frequented downtown theaters in big cities. Located in areas now often given over to strip joints, sex shops, and cinemas showing both soft-core and hard-core pornography, many former picture palaces now tended to attract a predominantly male, working-class clientele rather than the family outings of the roadshow era.[53]

Most of the youth-oriented films made in response to the success of *The Graduate* and *Easy Rider* and to the failure of the roadshows proved also to be failures at the box office. The most expensive of them, MGM's *Zabriskie Point* (1970), directed by Michelangelo Antonioni at a reported cost of $7 million, was especially disastrous.[54] The only clear successes were a group of films about teenagers in past decades: the 1940s in Warners' *Summer of '42* (1971), the 1950s in Columbia's *The Last Picture Show* (1971), and the 1960s in Universal's *American Graffiti* (1973). All these were low- to medium-budget productions. But they can be related to another cycle of the period that was pitched to different demographic sectors, including women and older patrons, and involved more elaborate production values.

Nostalgia was not in itself a genre, but it took several generic forms with a common referent in the relatively recent past—the era of what was increasingly coming to be referred to as Hollywood's "golden age." On the one hand it embraced traditional genres given a contemporary spin: *Love Story* and *The Godfather* could both be considered exemplars of this trend, as could the musical drama *Cabaret* (1972), the screwball comedy *What's Up, Doc?* (1972), the romantic drama *The Way We Were* (1973), the crime caper *The Sting* (1973), and the private-eye thriller *Chinatown* (1974). So too could Mel Brooks's affectionate genre spoofs *Blazing Saddles* and *Young Frankenstein* (both 1974). All these were substantial hits. One group of films was concerned directly with the film industry and the social world of early Hollywood, including *The Day of the Locust, Hearts of the West, The Wild Party* (all 1975), *Gable and Lombard, The Last Tycoon, Nickelodeon,* and *W. C. Fields and Me* (all 1976). None of these was a box-office success. But one of the surprise hits of the decade was *That's Entertainment* (1974), a two-hour compilation of highlights from MGM musicals, presented in 70 mm with six-track stereo sound. Put together at a cost of just over $1 million, it grossed over $12 million domestically. *That's Entertainment* was released by UA after MGM's withdrawal from distribution and prompted recognition of the enduring commercial value of "vaulties" (old movies) beyond television.[55]

The most ambitious of the period-nostalgia films was *The Great Gatsby* (1974), which received Paramount's most intensive pre-release publicity campaign since *The Godfather.* The adaptation of F. Scott's Fitzgerald's classic novel was produced (mostly in Britain despite its American setting) by the Broadway impresario David Merrick and directed by Jack Clayton from a screenplay by Francis Ford Coppola. It was budgeted at $6 million, but Merrick complained publicly that studio interference had raised the eventual cost to $7.7 million. The film premiered at four New York theaters, one of which operated on a "semi-hard-ticket" (scheduled- or reserved-performance) basis, charging $6 top, the highest tab for a Hollywood movie since the roadshow era. Nationwide, 174 other engagements opened, for which record advances totaling $18.6 million had been paid. Paramount's marketing department arranged merchandising predicated on the white-themed "Gatsby look," with tie-in products ranging from Teflon cookware to Robert Bruce sportswear. Frank Yablans regarded *Gatsby* as the third corner of the studio's "Triple Crown," along with *Love Story* and *The Godfather.* Its box-office performance, however, did not live up to the hype, earning U.S. rentals nearly $4 million less than the exhibitors' advances.[56] *Variety* quoted Yablans's observation that "perhaps in the American mentality today, big and bigness is not enough [*sic*]. To gain attention something must be superbig."[57]

The shift in the balance of worldwide revenues back toward the domestic market can partly be accounted for by the thematic emphasis, in many of the films that characterized the "new Hollywood," on America itself. Although the work of filmmakers such as Robert Altman (whose *MASH* won the Palme d'Or at the 1970 Cannes Film Festival) found critical acclaim both at home and abroad and sparked claims of an American renaissance, the "antiheroic" tone of many films in this period did not meet the same kind of popular acceptance overseas as the epics of earlier years.[58] The exotic costume adventures that had once been the most popular product internationally were not made in the same numbers, or on the same scale, by Hollywood in the 1970s. Most of the historical pictures that did get made were initiated not by the U.S. majors, but in Britain and Europe. Following the lead of producers like Samuel Bronston and Dino De Laurentiis in the 1960s, figures such as Alexander and Ilya Salkind, Dimitri De Grunwald, and Michael Klinger, and companies such as Nat Cohen's EMI, Lew Grade's ITC, Alberto Grimaldi's PEA, and Robert Dorfmann's Corona raised funds for their pictures by preselling territorial distribution rights. Thus Paramount invested in the U.S. rights to De Laurentiis's *Waterloo* (1971), De Grunwald's *Murphy's War* (1971), and EMI's *Murder on the Orient Express* (1974); Allied Artists in those to Klinger's *Gold* (1974) and John Huston's *The Man Who Would Be King* (1975); Avco Embassy in ITC's *Moses* (1976); AIP in Klinger's *Shout at the Devil* (1976); Universal in PEA's *Casanova* (1976); and Fox in the Salkinds' adaptation of *The Three Musketeers* (1974) and its sequel *The Four Musketeers* (1975), and in what was claimed to be the first Soviet-American collaboration, a $10 million remake of *The Blue Bird* (1976).[59] International rights to Bernardo Bertolucci's five-hour-plus historical fresco *1900* (1976) were divided up between UA, Fox, and Paramount. Of these, only *Murder on the Orient Express* and the *Musketeers* films were hits in America, though most were, in varying degrees, popular in other markets around the world.

The biggest non-Hollywood production of the 1970s was probably *Mohammad, Messenger of God* (1977, also known as *The Message*). Produced and directed by Moustapha Akkad, a Syrian-born U.S. citizen, it was financed largely by Lebanese sources and staffed by a crew of roadshow veterans, including second unit director Andrew Marton and cinematographer Jack Hildyard, both of whom had worked on *55 Days at Peking*. Filming began in Morocco in 1974 but was halted by government intervention after protests from the Muslim community, even though Akkad had refrained from showing the subject of his biopic by using subjective point-of-view, with the camera representing the Prophet. Shooting resumed in Libya and was completed in 1976 at an estimated total cost of $17 million. The resulting three-hour film (or films, as Akkad shot two separate versions in English and Arabic), complete with overture and intermission, more closely resembled the roadshows of the previous decade than any recent American film except Stanley Kubrick's *Barry Lyndon* (1975).[60]

Filmed in Britain and Ireland, *Barry Lyndon* was wholly funded by Warner Bros. The studio had agreed to back the picture, without even knowing its title, setting, or source (an obscure eighteenth-century novel by William Thackeray), solely on the strength of Kubrick's reputation and his recent success with *2001* and *A Clockwork Orange* (1971). The latter had been made for Warners for $2 million and earned $17 million domestically. The budget for *Barry Lyndon* was $2.5 million, but Kubrick's meticulous period recreation and attenuated shooting schedule multiplied its eventual cost to $11 million. Although successful in Europe, the film earned just $9.2 million in the United States and received very mixed reviews.[61] Given such risks, most studios declined, or were forbidden by their shareholders, to finance productions beyond a certain amount. Even American-based independent producers were therefore obliged to put together their budgets from a number of different sources, unlike in the 1960s when they could generally secure total financing from one or other of the majors. Irwin Allen received only half of the $5 million cost of *The Poseidon Adventure* from Fox. When it turned out to be its most successful release of 1972, the studio had to share the proceeds with Allen's cofinanciers. Yet had the film flopped, the burden of loss would also have been shared.[62]

Additional sources of production funds included nonfilm companies such as Quaker Oats, which wholly financed David L. Wolper's musical fantasy *Willy Wonka & the Chocolate Factory* (1971), and Readers Digest, which coproduced musical versions of *Tom Sawyer* (1973) and *Huckleberry Finn* (1974) with Arthur P. Jacobs for release through UA. Berry Gordy's Motown record label coproduced several films for Paramount release, including the Billie Holliday biopic *Lady Sings the Blues* (1972). Until changes in tax laws closed the loopholes, a number of films were cofunded by private individuals and business consortia under "tax shelter" deals. Notable beneficiaries of this scheme included *Chinatown* and *The Great Gatsby*.[63] One further option was coproduction between two or more major companies. ABC Pictures and Allied Artists (AA) evenly split the costs of making *Cabaret*. AA distributed the picture in the domestic market, but overseas territories were sold off to Cinerama (ABC's regular distributor in Britain and elsewhere) and Fox. The profits of the very successful picture were shared between each of these companies. Two established majors, Fox and Warners, collaborated for the first time on Irwin Allen's *The Towering Inferno,* while MGM and Columbia subsequently partnered on John Milius's period adventure *The Wind and the Lion* (1975). Such collaborations, which would once have been anathema, have since become commonplace in defraying the risk of high-cost productions.

Incentives for producing expensive pictures remained in the potential revenues that could still be earned if they were successful. Not only were the early 1970s' superhits presold by their source material, most were also relatively high in cost, which reinforced the old association between big budgets and big grosses. Both the value of the blockbuster as a form of leverage, by which a distributor could control the market to its own advantage, and the hazards of large investments are demonstrated by *Papillon* (1973). The production was budgeted at $11 million, including $5.5 million in above-the-line expenses, exclusive of actual shooting costs; the total would eventually rise to at least $13 million and possibly as much as $15 million. To the consternation of its shareholders, Allied Artists paid $7 million to the film's French producer, Corona, for the U.S. distribution rights. This was the largest amount the independent distributor had ever invested in one film. Company chairman and president Emmanuel Wolf defended his decision, which flew in the face of all those lessons the industry had supposedly learned in the crisis of 1969, by arguing that a well-chosen blockbuster would enable AA to compete with the majors, cut better deals with exhibitors, and appeal more successfully to established audience preferences for big stars such as Steve McQueen and Dustin Hoffman and properties such as Henri Charrière's best-selling book. Although AA's investment had to be secured by a high-interest loan, much of it was recovered before the picture's release by exhibitor advances totaling over $8 million. Wolf's point seemed proven when *Papillon* went on to earn $22.5 million in domestic rentals, the company's largest ever take from any film. But according to David A. Cook, in the long term the cost of repaying its loan virtually crippled AA, which had far less luck with later acquisitions such as *Gold* and *The Man Who Would Be King* and finally declared bankruptcy in 1979.[64]

Disaster, the Devil, and the Deep Blue Sea

Airport opened in February 1970 and earned more money that year than any other film. It cost around $10 million to produce and ultimately grossed $45,220,118 domestically, making it the fifth-largest hit in industry history to date. *Airport* was the first film shot in Todd-AO not to be roadshown (in the United States, at least) and as such was a sign of things to come in blockbuster release patterns. It did not, however, produce any immediate successors in generic terms. *The Poseidon Adventure* opened in December 1972. In the interim, only MGM's airborne thriller *Skyjacked* (1972) could be said to share some of the characteristics of the cycle of "disaster" movies that did finally emerge as an identifiable trend in the fall of 1974. The key films were, in release order, *Airport 1975, Earthquake* (both released, like *Airport*, by Universal), and *The Towering Inferno*. All were among the biggest hits of the mid-1970s. In its review of *Airport 1975*, *Variety* also linked this first sequel to the 1970 film to two recent UA releases, *Juggernaut* and *The Taking of Pelham One Two Three*, labeling all three "Ark pictures."[65] Their common factor was a confined setting (an airplane, a cruise ship, an underground train) in which a set of otherwise unrelated characters meet and endure various threats. In that respect, the films were the descendants of a tradition that also included *Grand Hotel, The High and the Mighty* (1954, one of several 1950s dramas set on board a passenger plane), *The V.I.P.s* (1963, set in and around an airport lounge), *Ship of Fools* (1965, set on board an ocean liner), *Hotel* (1967, adapted from a novel by *Airport* author Arthur Hailey), and the various versions of the sinking of the Titanic, which included Fox's *Titanic* (1953) and the British *A Night to Remember* (1958).

Charlton Heston, who appeared in more disaster films than any other leading actor—among them *Skyjacked, Airport 1975,* and *Earthquake,* as well as *Two-Minute Warning* (1976), *Gray Lady Down* (1978), *Solar Crisis* (1990), and the TV movie *Crash Landing: The Rescue of Flight 232* (1992)—offered his own definition of the cycle's main features:

A more specific label would be "multiple jeopardy film." The basic situation always involves a disparate group of people, most of them strangers to each other, thrown suddenly into a life-threatening situation, usually (not invariably) a natural disaster. The movie explores the disaster as spectacularly as possible, and traces the reaction of the various characters to the common danger. The story structure requires as many as a dozen or so substantial roles in the film, though in two hours' running time, none of them can be very long.[66]

As Heston also points out, it was this profusion of characters that partly motivated the assembly of multistar casts: "Each [character] can have only a short introductory scene, then might not be seen again for another fifteen minutes. You have to be sure the audience can keep them all in mind as you move from story line to story line."[67] But it was the centrality of the disaster itself that most clearly distinguished the 1970s' films from the 1930s' disaster cycle, including *San Francisco, In Old Chicago, The Hurricane,* and *The Rains Came,* in which a natural catastrophe formed the climax to a multistrand narrative rather than its catalyst. Also unlike the 1930s' cycle, almost all the mid-1970s' examples had a modern, principally American, setting. (The major exception was *The Hindenburg* [1975], a $15 million flop that producer-director Robert Wise tried and failed to dissociate from the cycle.)[68]

A good deal of journalistic and scholarly writing has been devoted to speculative explanations for the resurgence and (short-lived) popularity of the disaster film in the mid-1970s. One is that the cycle was an expression of current societal and ideological anxieties regarding the economy (it coincided with a period of deep recession and high inflation), political institutions (this was the era of the Vietnam War and the Watergate scandal), the unreliability of technology, and threats to traditional values.[69] The films mostly offered a conservative response to these issues, dispensing reassurance that the system, the authorities, the experts, and the (mostly male) heroes could cope. A partial exception is *Earthquake,* whose hero, Graff (Heston), a construction engineer, dies in the climactic flood, leaving Los Angeles in ruins, its survivors in despair and without an obvious leader to head the reconstruction. However, in the television version of the film, expanded by Universal to fill a scheduled time slot by the inclusion of extra footage, an additional subplot features an architect and his wife who survive a hazardous airplane landing at LAX. This not only guarantees the film a happy ending it otherwise lacks but also provides it with an alternative hero who can help rebuild the city.

A variation of this account focuses on the audience's instinctive identification with enlarged versions of everyday experiences. Hence Richard Dyer's assertion that "the main source of the excitement" in *The Towering Inferno* is "that being trapped in a tower block on fire is the sort of thing that could happen to any of us."[70] However, as both Nick Roddick and Geoff King have stressed, the disasters in such films are shown mostly to affect unusually privileged people in (initially) luxurious surroundings, played by larger-than-life movie stars. Thus, while the audience may be vicariously distressed by the predicaments of the characters, they are equally comforted that the same things are unlikely to happen to them.[71]

A third explanation is that the films were an iteration of the industry's cyclical nature, driven purely by commercial opportunism (the repetition of a proven formula). They were therefore as much a source of reassurance for Hollywood as for the audience. Fred Kaplan argues that the disaster cycle appeared when it did as an answer to the failure of many of the post-*Graduate* youth movies and the urgent need to find forms of entertainment that would draw in older viewers.[72] The presence of major stars (including older stars in supporting roles, such as Fred Astaire in *Inferno* and Gloria Swanson in *Airport 1975*) was one way of appealing to this audience; the emphasis on spectacle, which had not been a conspicuous feature of the youth-appeal sleepers (and which was even thought to alienate many young adult viewers) was another. Richard Maltby has argued that the arbitrary motivation of spectacle in the disaster film represents a degeneration of narrative, thereby mirroring Hollywood's own decadence. He claims, with respect to *Inferno,* that the stars, including Paul Newman and Steve McQueen, "are the only sources of coherence in a film whose content is concerned with collapse, destruction and deconstruction."[73]

The disaster films were predicated on the capacity of special effects, albeit of a mostly traditional sort (miniatures, matte paintings, process work, and so forth), to create scenes of spectacular destruction. In addition to its visual effects, *Earthquake* also introduced a special sound process called Sensurround, the result of executive producer Jennings Lang's request for "some new dimension in film exhibition to make this motion picture a special event, one that could not be duplicated on television." Compatible with both 35 mm and 70 mm prints (the latter employed in overseas situations only), the system used "special audible and sub-audible effects, below the human hearing range," to create air movements "which vibrate against a person's body and ears with a sound pressure waveform comparable to that of an actual earthquake. As the vibrating sensation is airborne rather [than] structure-shaking, there is no physical danger to the audience."[74] The device was spotted in two tremors preceding the earthquake, in the main quake sequence (which begins inside a cinema, its first signs being the trembling, burning, and tearing of the film-within-the-film), and in two major aftershocks, for a total of about ten minutes of screen time. Sensurround decoders and amplifiers were made available to theaters by Universal for a rental of $500 per week, and were used in a relatively small number of the film's early engagements in larger first-run houses.[75]

The most successful entry in the disaster cycle was the $15 million *The Towering Inferno,* which earned over $48,650,000 in domestic rentals and about $40 million foreign.[76] No subsequent multiple-jeopardy film of the decade matched the popularity of the key 1974 releases, though *Airport '77* and *Black Sunday* (both 1977) were medium-sized hits. *Tidal Wave* (1975) and *Survive!* (1976), Japanese and Mexican imports respectively, performed as well as could have been expected. But *The Cassandra*

Elaborate model work and matte paintings portray the leveling
of Los Angeles in *Earthquake* (1974).

Crossing (1977), *Avalanche* (1978), *The Concorde: Airport '79, City on Fire, Hurricane,* and *Meteor* (all 1979) all flopped. So too did Irwin Allen's *The Swarm* (1978), *Beyond the Poseidon Adventure* (1979), and *When Time Ran Out . . .* (1980), after which the disaster film largely disappeared from the big screen, only to reemerge in different forms in the 1990s and 2000s. Until then, it became a staple of made-for-TV movies.

Two other films from this period that generated their own brief spin-off cycles (demonological and revenge-of-nature horror films respectively) are *The Exorcist* and *Jaws*. The latter is sometimes also linked to the disaster cycle through its emphasis on communal threat and public panic.[77] They are certainly comparable with each other, having a striking number of features in common despite one being set mainly in interior rooms, the other in outdoor locations on and by the sea. Where the disaster films proper are mainly concerned with crises affecting a diverse group of strangers or a generalized community, both these films feature a monster that attacks at the heart of the family unit: in *The Exorcist* a young girl, Regan (Linda Blair), is possessed by a demon; in *Jaws,* a giant shark preys on an island town, but its first victims are a teenage girl and a young boy, and it directly threatens the two young sons of the hero, police chief Brody (Roy Scheider). In both films the threat is countered by an all-male "group": two Jesuit priests in *The Exorcist;* Brody, a professional fisherman, and an ichthyologist in *Jaws*. In the course of the conflict, an older, more experienced combatant dies in the struggle; the hero is the one who successfully dispatches the monster, Father Karras (Jason Miller) by taking the demon into himself and then committing suicide, Brody by shooting a compressed-air cylinder he has thrust into the shark's mouth. The destruction of the monster leaves the family unit safe and confidence in the institution the hero represents (the Church, the law) notionally restored. But a vestige of doubt remains. Father Karras's death has served to expiate his guilt over the death of his mother, but Regan's family remains without a father figure (her mother is divorced and her father is in Europe). Although Brody has proven himself a worthy hero, the island community (whose main interest is its commercial welfare) and its corrupt administration (the mayor has risked the lives of people including his own family to keep the beaches open) continue unreformed. The films thus offer reassurance tempered with ambivalence.[78]

However, more telling than any critical reading are the reports of audience reactions at screenings. Both films engendered unusually intense emotional responses, expressed in vocal and physical terms, including fainting and vomiting at *The Exorcist* and cheering and applause at *Jaws*. The former was also widely protested by the very institution, the Catholic Church, it so prominently figured on the side of good, on the grounds of the possessed Regan's foul and blasphemous language and the disturbing imagery of her physical abuse (both by the demon that takes over her body and by Karras in the final confrontation).[79] Several of *Jaws'* most powerful scenes are structured around point-of-view and reaction shots that personalize the sense of terror, most famously the zoom-in/track-out on Brody's face following the killing of the child at the beach.[80] The film's climactic frisson is the blowing up of the shark (in Peter

Benchley's original novel it dies from exhaustion). The camera cuts between the encircling beast in the water and Brody as he climbs the mast of the sinking fishing boat and takes aim with his rifle. Having fired several shots to no avail he mutters under his breath, "Smile, you son of a . . . ," and at that instant (before he speaks the vulgar last word) the shark explodes as a bullet strikes the air cylinder, pieces of flesh scattering in a shower of blood and spume. As Andrew Britton has remarked, *Jaws* is at this point "a communal exorcism, a ceremony for the restoration of ideological confidence. The film is inconceivable without an enormous audience, without that exhilarating, jubilant explosion of cheers and hosannas which greet the annihilation of the shark, and which transform the cinema, momentarily, into a temple."[81] Such climactic moments were to recur repeatedly in future blockbusters that sought to recreate *Jaws'* impact.

Beyond their dramatic and thematic content, both films were at the center of a sociocultural phenomenon deriving from their extraordinary commercial success. Both were based on best-selling novels; the paperback editions, published by Bantam, ran to over nine million copies each by the time the films were in release. Warners collaborated with the publisher to help advertise *The Exorcist* more than two years before the film came out (the book's author, William Peter Blatty, also produced the film, though he ceded the right of final cut to director William Friedkin). The producers of *Jaws* participated in promotional activities for Benchley's novel, and Universal based the film's "high concept" poster image on its cover artwork.[82] Both films also ran heavily over schedule because of practical and technical difficulties. To allow the actors' breath to show on screen, *The Exorcist* was partly filmed in a refrigerated indoor set, which had to be repeatedly closed down and rechilled. Much of *Jaws* was shot at sea, in bad weather, with a defective mechanical shark and with constant intrusion by sightseers. As a result, their costs increased from reported budgets of $4 million for *The Exorcist* and $3.5 million for *Jaws* to $10,497,444 and over $8 million respectively. All this was widely publicized and undoubtedly attracted additional interest to the films.[83]

Their release patterns differed markedly, however. *The Exorcist* opened on December 26, 1973, in only twenty-four situations in twenty-two cities. Most of these were in relatively small, off-drag theaters in upmarket residential districts. When large numbers of predominantly young, working-class, and black spectators flooded into these areas, forming long lines and disrupting the neighborhood, Warners was obliged to open additional downtown engagements to cope with the demand for seats and relieve the local residents. Even so, wider release was withheld until the summer of 1974. In Greater New York, Warners booked 110 theaters, some hired on a four-wall basis, for the general release in June.[84] In its first week these theaters earned a box-office gross of $3,074,244. Before this, "in 24 weeks of exclusive runs in only 386 domestic playdates, [the film] generated gross film rentals of $46,968,800 from a cumulative boxoffice total of $65,487,022—for a 72% ratio of rental to b.o."[85] *The Exorcist* went on to earn $66.3 million in domestic rentals on first release and over $100 million worldwide.[86]

Jaws opened on 464 domestic screens (409 in the United States, the rest in Canada) on June 20, 1975. Unusually, in inviting bids from exhibitors, Universal

Backed by the Biggest T.V. Spot campaign in

National prime-time Motion Picture History!

The media advertising campaign for *Jaws* (1975) paid off at the box office
(*Variety*, April 9, 1975, 10–11).

stipulated that they would be required to contribute to the cost of national TV advertising (normally theaters only shared promotional costs at the local level). The
company bought thirty-second spots in twenty-three prime-time programs across all
three national networks on the three evenings preceding the film's opening and on the
first day itself (a Friday). Their effect was to earn box-office grosses of $21,115,354
in the first ten days, an industry record for so short a space of time. (That it was
not a foolproof method was demonstrated when Universal TV-advertised the John
Wayne–Katharine Hepburn western *Rooster Cogburn* [1975] even more heavily, to
disappointing results.) As the release widened, earnings reached a box-office gross of
$100,375,045 from 954 theaters in fifty-nine days, and $150,121,339 from 2,460
engagements over twenty-three weeks. By January 1976 *Jaws* had become the first film
to earn a domestic distribution gross of over $100 million (*The Sound of Music* having
been the first to reach that mark in exhibition gross). This represented the breaking
of an industry barrier as much psychological as it was fiscal, and set a new benchmark
for future blockbusters. *Jaws* went on to earn a total U.S. rental of $129,549,325.[87]

A great deal has since been written about the significance of the film's marketing
and release patterns, much of it inaccurate and overstated. It has been said, for example, that *Jaws* was the first big-budget, major-studio film to be given a wide saturation release, and that this was a distribution method formerly associated exclusively

with low-grade exploitation pictures. It has been called the first film to be intensively advertised in a national TV campaign, and even the first summer blockbuster.[88] As should be clear already from the preceding pages, none of this is strictly true. While a wide, rapid release was often used for films of doubtful quality to forestall negative word of mouth (Levine's *Hercules* epics being good examples), this was not always the case.[89] We have seen that saturation distribution was sometimes also used for specialized prestige pictures such as the 1964 Theatrofilm presentation of *Hamlet*. In the very week that *Jaws* was released, *Give 'em Hell, Harry!*, a filmed record of Samuel Gallu's play starring James Whitmore as President Harry S. Truman, was announced for simultaneous showing on 1,500 screens in September 1975, presented under the trade name TheatroVision.[90] UA had released the last three James Bond films—*Diamonds Are Forever* (1971), *Live and Let Die* (1973), and *The Man with the Golden Gun* (1974)—on around six hundred prints each in the domestic market, and had used 550 prints for the summer 1973 release of *Tom Sawyer*.[91] Among the reasons for such wide releasing was the desire to capitalize on intense want-to-see on the part of audiences, particularly in the case of heavily presold attractions, and to make the most of the availability of family audiences in holiday periods.

Universal had planned a similarly broad opening for *Jaws*, involving anything between six hundred and one thousand theaters depending on which account one reads; but following successful previews company president Lew Wasserman reportedly ordered the number of engagements cut back to give the film a degree of exclusivity in each area and thereby to increase its chances of an extended summer play-off, which it duly received (most bookings were for a minimum of twelve weeks).[92] In New York it opened on forty-six screens, in Los Angeles on seven, but in some other cities, such as Denver, Pittsburgh, and Kansas City, in exclusive single-theater engagements. Thereafter its release widened rapidly, as had that of *The Godfather* three years earlier, to capitalize on the publicity arising from the early engagements. By contrast, Tom Laughlin's sequel *The Trial of Billy Jack* (1974) had opened in 1,100 situations simultaneously, and in May 1975 Columbia released its Charles Bronson thriller *Breakout* (1975) in 1,325 theaters. Both these "saturation blitz" releases were supported by heavy TV advertising. The opening of Universal's *Airport 1975*, among others, had been preceded by national TV spots in peak-time slots, and TV advertising costing $2 million was credited with turning the independent release *Dirty Mary, Crazy Larry* (1974), a car chase movie that had cost less than $1 million to produce, into a smash hit with rentals of $13.7 million.[93] Roadshows of the 1960s such as *The Sound of Music* and *Doctor Zhivago* had also been heavily trailered on television, as had the Bond films.

None of this is to deny the watershed status of *Jaws* in the history of contemporary Hollywood or its undoubted significance in stimulating future attempts at calculated hits using the same marketing methods. But this status has nothing to do with its being the "first" blockbuster or the "first" film to be promoted or released in a particular way. Rather, it lies in its being by far the most successful film to date in taking advantage of multiple first runs, TV advertising, and so on. What can be said with absolute confidence about *Jaws* is that its distributors and promoters learned from all its antecedents and applied their lessons particularly well.

The recovery of the industry from depression and the arrival of another "New Hollywood" are usually dated from the release of *Jaws* in the summer of 1975. In fact, *Jaws* was the culmination to date of a revival that began much earlier, with the Christmas and New Year of 1973/74. This particular holiday saw an unusually strong line-up of new pictures, including *The Exorcist, The Sting, Papillon,* the police drama *Serpico,* Disney's animated feature *Robin Hood,* and the first *Dirty Harry* sequel, *Magnum Force. Variety*'s reports of key-city engagements rated it the best Christmas in five years. The summer of 1974 also set records, with a number of the year-end pictures, such as *The Exorcist,* going into wider release and newer hits including *Chinatown* and *That's Entertainment.* With the disaster films opening in the fall, *Variety* referred to the industry as now being "devoted to the 'blockbuster business' with 'blockbuster pictures' and 'blockbuster advertising campaigns.'"[94] The year as a whole earned the highest box-office receipts on record (without allowing for inflation) and the highest average weekly attendance in a decade. With the help of *Jaws* and other hits 1975 scored even better, though both earnings and attendances temporarily dipped again the year after. The revival was fueled by demographic change. Another audience survey commissioned by the MPAA suggested that cinema visits by unmarried over-eighteens were growing. With the 1960s' youth audience now aging but marrying later than in previous generations, married couples were also having children later, so they too kept up regular attendance in greater numbers than before.[95]

Thus *Jaws* was part of a new wave of blockbusters, but not the beginning of one. In December 1975 Columbia production head Mike Medavoy noted of the recent rise in big-budget productions that "the film industry is once again entering a very dangerous cycle. . . . And it's a very difficult thing to stop."[96] Addressing the audience at the San Francisco Film Festival two months earlier (where *Jaws'* director Steven Spielberg also took part in a public interview), veteran *Cleopatra* director Joseph L. Mankiewicz commented on the "apocalyptic" tendency in recent hits: "'Never has the film industry been more frantic to make the big, fast buck than it is now,' said Mankiewicz. 'The biggest current movie stereotype is the $100 million film that you'll all pay anything to see because it's about an apocalypse. And you of the audience will be happy because then you will be in on the destruction of yourselves.'"[97]

SUPER BLOCKBUSTERS, 1976–1985

As Mike Medavoy had warned, and as *Variety* noted in its review of 1975, the success of *Jaws* and other recent films had encouraged the majors to embark once again on a "'big picture' cycle with costs escalating accordingly."[1] Another wave of blockbuster productions was on the way. The most immediate successors to *Jaws* itself were Paramount's *King Kong* (1976) and *Orca—Killer Whale* (1977), Columbia's *The Deep* (1977), and Universal's *Jaws 2* (1978). *Orca, The Deep,* and *Jaws 2* all opened in the summer, and all three received what *The Deep*'s producer, Peter Guber, called "a wide, deep platform release."[2] *Jaws 2* and *The Deep* were box-office hits, the latter earning $31.2 million in domestic rentals, the former, $50.4 million. *Jaws 2* cost $20 million, but none of the three was as expensive as *A Bridge Too Far* (1977), *Hurricane, Meteor,* or the most expensive of the Roger Moore James Bond films, *Moonraker* (1979).[3] Of these, only *Moonraker* cost more than the $24 million it cost to produce *King Kong*.

King Kong ("presented," like *Orca,* by Dino De Laurentiis) was one of two projected remakes of the 1933 original.[4] It opened on 961 screens in North America on December 17 as part of a carefully planned "monster saturation premiere campaign" designed by Norman Weitman at Paramount. With a simultaneous saturation opening on over 1,200 additional screens throughout the world, it was the first of the 1970s blockbusters to be released in such a way on such a scale. The ambitions behind it were evident in the fact that Paramount insisted on booking terms in New York City that included a nonreturnable deposit of $100,000 and percentages of the gross prior to house nut deductions that ran from 70 percent in its first three weeks to 40 percent in its last three, terms that had not been demanded by Paramount since the release of the *Godfather* films.[5]

King Kong was similar to *Jaws* in several ways. It boasted a large and powerful animal protagonist (albeit a sympathetic one). It also contained traces of countercultural ideology, was accompanied by a massive merchandising campaign, and was heavily dependent on special effects. It went on to earn $36.5 million in domestic rentals and $80 million worldwide. However, as David A. Cook points out, because its ambitions had been so widely publicized, and because *Jaws* had set a new benchmark for box-office success, it was "widely perceived as a flop."[6] To add insult to injury, it finished behind the far less expensive *A Star Is Born* and the even less expensive *Rocky* (both 1976) in the box-office rankings for 1977.

Rocky was "the sleeper of the decade." Produced by UA and costing just under $1 million, it went on to earn a box-office gross of $117,235,247 in the United States and $225 million worldwide. A "sports inspirational," to use Cook's term, *Rocky* starred and was written by Sylvester Stallone. Stallone played "the ultimate underdog—a washed up boxer who gets a 'million-to-one shot' at a championship title."[7] Cook suggests that *Rocky* gave rise to other sports inspirationals, among them *Bobby Deerfield* (1977) and *Breaking Away* (1979). However, as he himself notes, the central characters in these other films are distinctly middle class, whereas *Rocky* stresses the proletarian origins, environment, and appeal of its major characters. This aspect of *Rocky* can be found in other late 1970s Stallone films, notably *F.I.S.T.* and *Paradise Alley* (both 1978). But neither of these was commercially successful, and while Stallone continued to play blue-collar characters in *First Blood* (1982) and in subsequent *Rocky* and *Rambo* films, the latter increasingly capitalized on the male action-body aspects of *Rocky* and the white-male, blue-collar rage that imbued so many action films in the 1980s and 1990s.[8]

UA opened *Rocky* on an exclusive basis at the 291-seat Cinema II in New York City on November 25, 1976. The decision to release the film in November was taken as a means of avoiding excessive competition from Christmas releases, a strategy UA had earlier adopted for the release of *Lenny* (1974) and *One Flew over the Cuckoo's Nest* (1975). Despite breaking Cinema II's opening day box-office record, *Rocky* widened extremely slowly. By the end of December, it was playing in only twenty-eight venues nationwide. In January 195 more were added and a further 230 in February. At this point, *Rocky* was being shown in second-run neighborhood venues as well as in regular showcase venues downtown.[9] In these ways, its pattern of release served to mark its status not only as a sleeper dependent on word-of-mouth recommendation, but as a low-budget feature with specific appeal to working-class audiences.

A Star Is Born, *Musicals, and Synergies*

A Star Is Born was released by Warners on December 25, 1976 on a relatively narrow basis. Following Christmas Day premieres in Los Angeles and New York, it went on to open in an additional 319 theaters nationwide the following week, breaking sixty-one house records during the course of its first nine days and eventually earning $37 million in domestic rentals.[10] An updated version of the 1937 original and its 1954 musical remake, *A Star Is Born* was a $7 million musical vehicle for Barbra Streisand, who was also the film's executive producer. Its story of showbiz success, failure, and bittersweet romance was set in the world of contemporary rock (Streisand's costar was Kris Kristofferson). In this and in other respects, it is possible to relate *A Star Is Born* not only to earlier rock musicals such as *Phantom of the Paradise, Stardust* (both 1974), and *Tommy* (1975), but also to subsequent ones such as *Saturday Night Fever* (1977), *Flashdance* (1983), and *Footloose* (1984). It shares with these films not just an emphasis on contemporary popular musical styles, nor just a tendency to root a capacity for musical performance in the everyday lives and careers of its characters. It also shares a tendency to eschew the artifice that had sustained traditional musicals and that had always been particularly evident in the transitions among moments of comedy, drama, pathos, and joy and the otherwise unmotivated sequences of musical performance that served to express them.

Many late 1970s and early 1980s musicals tend to set up sequences of this kind as rehearsals, as private acts of musical composition, or as public acts of performance within the fictional world of the films. They include *New York, New York* (1977) and *The Cotton Club* (1984), two particularly lavish musicals that set their production numbers on stage and their other performances in studios and nightclubs.[11] J. P. Telotte has written about the tendency in many musicals of this period "to depict a world whose prime expressive elements—music and dance—are clearly circumscribed." For him, the films articulate "a tension between the performers and a realm in which their singing and dancing seem almost out of place." As a result, "expressive activity" tends to be "channelled into arenas, stages and enclosed areas and repeatedly defined as 'performance.'"[12] Telotte contrasts musicals such as these with others such as *Grease* (1978), *Hair* (1979), *Annie* (1982), and *The Best Little Whorehouse in Texas* (1982). If by no means always traditional in musical style, these films tend to retain the artifice inherent in traditional musical films. Significantly, all of them were adaptations of long-running Broadway shows. Some were also the product of studio synergies, of studio investments in these shows, and in the theater more generally.[13]

Most of the musical numbers in these films appeared as singles or on soundtrack albums released by record companies owned by or allied to the companies that produced or distributed the films: Fox owned Twentieth Century-Fox Records, Warner Communications Inc. (WCI) owned Warner Bros. and Warner Bros. Records, and MCA owned Universal Pictures and MCA Records. Paramount Pictures was a subsidiary of Gulf + Western Industries, which sold Paramount's record label and music publishing company in 1974. However, it was Paramount that signed an agreement with Robert Stigwood's Stigwood Productions to cofund *Saturday Night Fever* in exchange for 60 percent of the profits three years later.[14]

Having founded the Robert Stigwood Organisation (RSO), Stigwood had entered into a partnership with agent Allan Carr to produce films in the United States. Carr owned the film rights to *Grease* and this was to be their first production. However, prompted by the vogue for disco music, Stigwood decided to feature John Travolta, who had appeared in *Grease* on stage, in *Saturday Night Fever* first. Stigwood arranged to release four singles from the film four months prior to the release of the soundtrack album, then the soundtrack album six weeks prior to the opening of the film, coordinating both with an escalating publicity campaign involving record retailers, radio stations, movie trailers, and video playback machines.[15] The album occupied the number one spot on *Billboard*'s album charts for twenty-six weeks, selling 35 million copies worldwide. The film opened wide at 726 theaters, breaking "*The Deep*'s domestic box-office record by earning $9.3 million in its first three days." *Grease* was an even greater success. Opening in 902 theaters, it became the box-office hit of 1978. The soundtrack album and the single, "You're the One That I Want," "were released before the film in a pattern similar to that of *Saturday Night Fever*," though as Cook points out, this pattern had in fact been pioneered by Jon Peters, producer of *A Star Is Born,* who had released the soundtrack album and "Evergreen" as a single two weeks prior to the opening of the film.[16]

Subsequent synergies emerged in the early 1980s with the advent of MTV. MTV was a cable music channel owned by WCI and American Express. As Jeff Smith explains, *Flashdance* "provided the initial model for film and video cross-promotion"; "Paramount followed the usual route of releasing the title track as a scout single succeeded by the release of the soundtrack album thereafter. Where Paramount deviated from the usual formula, however, was in its emphasis on MTV as a promotional vehicle for the film. Paramount released the video for Michael Sembello's 'Maniac' to MTV some four weeks before the film was released, which enabled it to play a key role in the cross-promotion of the film, album and single." As Smith goes on to point out, "several aspects of *Flashdance* made it particularly suitable for music video promotion, among them the film's slick visual style . . . and its modular narrative structure. As Paramount executive Dawn Steel notes, the film's plot was so designed such that sequences could easily be moved around during the editing process. Such modularity is significant in that it lays bare the film's structure as a series of discrete set pieces, any of which might be adapted to a music video format."[17]

Flashdance was exhibited in movie theaters in 35 mm with a Dolby Stereo soundtrack. Such soundtracks were relatively common by 1983 and were by no means confined to musicals. According to Cook, "almost 90 percent of all Hollywood films were being released in four-channel Dolby stereo" by the mid-1980s.[18] However, Dolby's sound systems had their origins in the music recording industry, so it is hardly surprising that musicals such as *A Star Is Born* pioneered Dolby Stereo in 35 mm, or that musicals such as *Grease,* and *The Wiz* (1978) helped pioneer Dolby Stereo in 70 mm (blown-up in these and other cases from 35 mm). Musicals helped prompt the development of other sound systems too.[19] But the films that created a new level of demand for Dolby were three record-breaking science-fiction films and comic book adaptations, *Star Wars* (1977), *Close Encounters of the Third Kind* (1977), and *Superman* (1978). Each of them contributed to what has been called "The Second Coming of Sound."[20] They also helped pioneer a new generation of special effects.

Star Wars, *Dolby Stereo, and Special Effects*

Dolby Stereo grew out of a noise reduction system (Dolby NR) developed for the recording industry in the late 1960s. The system reduced background noise and increased the response to wider sound frequencies. In 1973,

Eastman Kodak, RCA, and Dolby worked together to develop a simple two-channel stereo optical system that would have its left and right tracks running side-by-side in the area normally occupied by the monaural optical track . . . This meant that an unconverted projector could run a stereo optical track and still generate a mono-compatible signal. In the theater, Dolby stereo optical . . . reproduced its two stereo tracks through the left and right speaker, and a third channel—synthesized by a logic circuit in the "Dolby Cinema Processor" from different phase relationships between the left and right track—was sent to the center speaker.

The cost of conversion was about $5,000 per theater. "On the production side, it cost about $25,000 more to dub a film in Dolby stereo than in monaural and the conversion of an existing film-mixing studio to Dolby cost around $40,000." Although these were modest sums, conversion did not happen overnight. In the interim, Dolby

developed a way of adding surround information on the optical track at the mixing stage via "stereo matrix" circuitry that encoded the information onto the two-track signal; the matrix was then decoded by the Dolby Cinema Processor in the theater to create a fourth channel. The resulting surround signal was either sent to the rear speaker in existing four-speaker theaters, or could be distributed among new speakers positioned around the auditorium's side and back walls.[21]

During the course of these developments director George Lucas and producer Gary Kurtz approached Dolby to help design a soundtrack for *Star Wars*. Lucas and Kurtz were among a new generation of film personnel sensitized to the possibilities of sound not just by the culture of contemporary pop and rock music but also by postwar hi-fidelity sound recording and playback systems, the magnetic stereo soundtracks used to accompany most postwar roadshow films, the advent of the Nagra III magnetic tape recorder, and the more extensive use of Foley artists to create sounds in postproduction. By the mid-1970s, Sensurround had been pioneered by Universal, sound-conscious directors like Robert Altman were experimenting with radio microphones and eight-track recording systems, and sound editors like Walter Murch were working with other sound-conscious directors like Lucas and Francis Ford Coppola.[22] It is thus no surprise that Lucas and Kurtz approached Dolby to help with the soundtrack of *Star Wars* or that *Star Wars* showcased Dolby, both aesthetically and commercially, in ways that no other film had done before.

Opening with the old Fox fanfare (including its long-unheard CinemaScope extension), John Williams's main title theme, the roar of high-speed spacecraft, and the sounds of explosions and laser fire in space and in the interior of Princess Leia's spaceship, *Star Wars* underlines the importance of sound from its very beginning. The footsteps of troops in the spaceship's corridors are followed by the beeping and squeaking of R2-D2 (Kenny Baker), the metallic chattering of C-3PO (Anthony Daniels), the suspenseful silence as Leia's men await the boarding of their ship, and the asthmatic resonance of Darth Vader's breathing (as voiced by James Earl Jones). It is not until the initial exchange between Luke Skywalker (Mark Hamill) and Aunt Beru (Shelagh Fraser), some twenty minutes into the film, that we hear the sound of human voices unmediated by any form of on-screen technology—and even that is marked by the fact that the characters are some way away from one another and have to raise their voices in order to be heard.[23]

Based on an idea Lucas had been working on since 1973, *Star Wars* had been rejected by UA and Universal before Alan Ladd Jr. optioned the screenplay for Fox.[24] In the interim, while sound effects editor Ben Burtt had been gathering recordings, others had been working on the film's visual design and special effects. Special effects had been a key ingredient in *Jaws, King Kong,* and other horror, disaster, and science-fiction films. Most of the technologies involved—superimpositions, models, traveling mattes, and rear-screen projection—had been tried and tested for many years. Traveling mattes had been used extensively in *2001.* So too had front projection, in which the use of a beam-splitting mirror enabled live performers in a studio and a preshot background to be filmed simultaneously. Front projection was unusual, but otherwise most of the effects used in *2001* and in subsequent effects-driven films in the late 1960s and early to mid-1970s were fairly well worn. What changed with *Star Wars* was the introduction of "a computerized motion-control system designed by John Dykstra (patented as "Dykstraflex") to make traveling matte work cost-effective for the first time."[25]

Dykstra had helped found Industrial Light and Magic (ILM), a company dedicated to the use and development of special effects. At the heart of the Dykstraflex was a "motorized camera mount governed by a multi-track magnetic tape, which permitted the camera to pan, tilt, roll and track eight vertical feet or forty-two horizontal feet in precisely repeatable movements. Operators could program their cameras to execute complicated maneuvers one frame at a time, and the sequences could then be infinitely repeated through numeric control." Although preceded by an electronically driven tape system devised by Douglas Trumbull for *The Andromeda Strain* (1971), the computerized control of traveling matte photography "enabled the creation of special effects that were at once more complex and less expensive to achieve than ever before."[26]

Eventually costing $11,293,151, *Star Wars* was previewed at the Northpoint Theatre in San Francisco on May 1, 1977. At this point, the sound was still being mixed for different formats, theaters, and markets. There were four mixes overall: a 70 mm eight-track stereo mix, a 70 mm six-track stereo mix, a 35 mm two-track stereo mix, and a 35 mm monaural mix. The monaural version was designed for a wide release later in the summer. *Star Wars* was planned to widen gradually and the monaural mix was thus still incomplete when the film opened in 70 mm at thirty-two theaters on Wednesday, May 25, 1977, an additional nine on May 27, and one more each on June 1 and 3.[27] At the Chinese Theatre, the program began with

three trailers back-to-back on 35m film, projected monaural in 35m in lower screen center with conventional masking . . . At the end of the last trailer, the curtain closed while one could hear the sound system come alive in Dolby stereo. Then, lighting up a screen area probably six times that of the trailers, came the Fox logo and fanfare as the curtain and masking opened to its extreme dimensions: Applause. It never failed to happen.[28]

It was Lucas's idea to premiere the film in May: "I said I want my film to be released in May for Memorial Day weekend. And the studio said, 'But the kids aren't out of school'—and I said, 'Well, I don't want the kids out of school; I want the kids to be able to see the movie and then talk about it so we can build word of mouth.'"[29] A similar pattern of release was later adopted for *The Empire Strikes Back* in 1980.[30] In the meantime, the film industry "was stunned when *Star Wars* earned nearly $3 million in its first week,"[31] and as a result, Fox decided to accelerate *Star Wars*' release and to increase the number of theaters

to 362 on June 24; 504 by July 1; 585 on July 8; 628 on July 14; 811 on July 1; 959 on July 29; 956 on July 29; 1,044 on August 5; and 1,098 by August 19. After Labor Day, 1977, no new engagements were added, but existing runs continued for as long as they could play. Because certain runs terminated, the number reduced to about 700 theatres in October, 650 in November, and just short of 600 through the end of the year.[32]

By August, *Star Wars* had already broken some of the box-office records set by *Jaws*.[33] By the beginning of September, *Star Wars* "had grossed $100 million; it played continuously throughout 1977–78, and was officially re-released in 1978 and 1979, by the end of which it had earned $262 million in rentals worldwide to become the top-grossing film of all time—a position it would maintain until surpassed by Universal's *E.T. The Extra-Terrestrial* (1982) in January 1983."[34] These figures had been boosted by repeat attendances.[35] They had also been augmented by millions of dollars in income from the sale of tie-ins and merchandise.

By the 1980s Fox had made a profit of $88.5 million on top of its $75 million distribution fee. Aside from sales of the soundtrack album, which was released by Fox's subsidiary, most of the income from merchandise sales went to Lucas and Star Wars Productions. Lucas had negotiated the rights to tie-ins, sequels, and *Star Wars* as a brand early on; according to Michael Pye and Linda Myles, he had a line of action-figures, models, books, toys, games, T-shirts, and records in mind from the outset.[36] Tie-ins were not new, but it had not been uncommon, prior to *Star Wars,*

to give merchandising rights away for free publicity (as Fox had done with fast-food tie-ins in the 1970s); even when licensed for profit, as in the case of *Jaws* and *King Kong,* product tie-ins like T-shirts, jewelry and candy had little life or value apart from the film once its run was completed. But with *Star Wars* . . . merchandising became an industry unto itself, and tie-in product marketing began to drive the conception and selling of motion pictures rather than vice versa.[37]

Along with *Jaws, Star Wars* had ushered in a new era of what A. D. Murphy went on to describe as "super-blockbuster films," films designed not just to make millions of dollars, but to attain the status of what William Bates in *The New York Times* called "a national obsession."[38]

Close Encounters, *Science Fiction, and Seriality*

In developing the story of *Close Encounters of the Third Kind,* Steven Spielberg had drawn on his boyhood interest in space, an amateur film he had made as a teenager, his long-standing interest in UFOs, and a short story he had written in the early 1970s. With producers Michael and Julia Phillips, he took the idea to David Begelman at Columbia. Columbia was in financial straits and needed a box-office hit. The success of *Jaws* gave Spielberg the leverage to demand more for *Close Encounters,* and the budget was raised from $2.7 to $4.1 million.[39] Douglas Trumbull was put in charge of special effects and Rick Baker and Carlo Rambaldi were put in charge of creating the principal alien. The film was recorded in Dolby Stereo with the intention of releasing it on 70 mm with a six-track magnetic soundtrack in suitable venues.

Eventually costing $19,400,870, *Close Encounters* was previewed at the Medallion in Dallas on October 19 and 20, 1977.[40] Spielberg wanted to make further changes and to release *Close Encounters* the following summer, but Columbia was still in financial difficulties, and having initially planned to release it in the summer of 1977, the company insisted that the film be released in time for Christmas.[41] Preceded by a $9 million advertising campaign and demands for "unusually high advance guarantees from exhibitors," *Close Encounters* finally opened at the Ziegfeld in New York on November 16 and at the Cinerama Dome in Los Angeles two days later:[42]

At $4 per ticket, the film made approximately $21,000 on its first day at both theaters. These exclusive engagements ran until December 13, 1977, during which time the combined gross from both theaters was $1,076,927. The film went into general release on December 14, 1977 in 272 theaters in the United States and Canada, in a mixture of 35 mm and 70 mm engagements. By the end of the month, it had grossed $24,695,317; by the end of January 1978, it had grossed $62,033,815; and by the end of February, it had grossed $72 million and become the seventh-highest-grossing film of all time.[43]

In the interview in "Watch the Skies," a 1977 promotional documentary, Spielberg talks about "music, color and light" as the basic constituents of *Close Encounters.* Sound editor Frank Warner has discussed its use of silence.[44] As the sequences set at night in the environs of Los Angeles and in the Guiler household make particularly clear, movement in general, and the animation of objects in particular, plays a key part in *Close Encounters* too. In addition, the structure of alternation that marks the first half of the film is replaced by a linear one; horizontal human movements are increasingly replaced by vertical ones; patterns of colored light turn into views of the mother ship and other moving craft; and patterns of sound turn into music. In all these ways, the film draws attention not just to the sources of its audio-visual spectacle but also to the very ingredients that make it a film.[45]

Initially conceived by Spielberg in the era of Vietnam and Watergate, one of the most significant changes made to his earliest outline for *Close Encounters* was the removal of intimations of government conspiracy and governmental cover-up.[46] Occasional traces still remain, notably in the sequences in which the public is misled in being forced to evacuate the area around Devil's Tower. For the most part, though, government representatives, military personnel, and other figures of authority are eventually presented as wholly benign. So too are the aliens. In these respects, *Close Encounters* represents a departure from the conventions that had dominated science fiction in the late 1960s and early to mid-1970s. From *Planet of the Apes* to *Futureworld* (1976), corporate conspiracies, military imperatives, and the policies practiced by ruling elites had been depicted as responsible for all manner of social ills: the dominant tendencies were dystopian, the dominant tropes, suspicion and irony.[47]

Dystopian tendencies (and alien threats) were to return with a vengeance in *Alien* (1979), *Blade Runner* (1982), *The Thing* (1982), and other big-budget science-fiction and sci-fi horror films in the early 1980s.[48] In the meantime, alongside the benign *Star Trek—The Motion Picture* (1979) and the even more benign *E.T.,* the sequels to *Star Wars* continued to eschew what its *Variety* reviewer called "the cynicism that has in recent years obscured the concepts of valor, dedication and honor."[49] The same is

The appearance of the mother ship in *Close Encounters of the Third Kind* (1977).

true of *Flash Gordon* (1980), *Superman* and its sequels (1981–2006), *Raiders of the Lost Ark* (1981) and its sequels (1984–2008), and "sword-and-sorcery" films such as *Dragonslayer* (1981), *Legend* (1985), and *Willow* (1988). The sword-and-sorcery films drew on the knightly and quasi-mystical aspects of *Star Wars, Flash Gordon* on those aspects of *Star Wars* that derived from Hollywood serials of the 1930s and 1940s (not least *Flash Gordon* [1936] and its sequels). The tropes of seriality—episodic construction; cliffhanging crises; diverse settings; journeys, schemes, and threats of global or galactic import and scale—were to mark not only *Flash Gordon,* but *Superman* and *Raiders* too. In the case of *Raiders,* they were inspired by serials such as *Don Winslow of the Coast Guard* (1943) and *Blackhawk* (1952); in *Superman'*s case, by numerous *Superman* comic books, cartoon strips, and film and television serials.

Superman had been in planning since 1974. It was produced by Ilya and Alexander Salkind, who were based in Europe. Most of its studio-based sequences were filmed at Shepperton in the United Kingdom (as were sequences for *Superman II,* much of which was filmed back to back with *Superman*). As we have seen, the Salkinds (like De Laurentiis and Joseph E. Levine) raised money for their productions not only from U.S. distributors (Warners in this case), but also from the preselling of territorial distribution rights to a number of different distributors worldwide. *Superman* was one of several comic-book adaptations mooted for production at this time. Others included *Sheena,* which was eventually produced in 1984, and *Dan Dare* and *Captain Electric,* which were never made.[50] They also included *Popeye* (1980), a $20 million production that earned $24.5 million in domestic rentals. *Popeye* was widely perceived to be a failure. But *Superman* was a major, if even more expensive, box-office hit.

As was becoming de rigueur for big-budget blockbusters, *Superman* was selectively exhibited in four-channel Dolby Stereo optical in 35 mm and six-track Dolby Stereo magnetic in 70 mm. However, the focus of attention in most reviews, aside from the performances of Christopher Reeve as Superman and Margot Kidder as Lois Lane, was *Superman'*s special effects. One of the film's promotional tag lines was "You'll Believe a Man Can Fly," and its flying effects had been among the principal preoccupations of production personnel. A number of different techniques were used, among them a method patented as "Zoptic" by optical expert Zoran Perisic. Here, "the camera and the projector of a front-projection set-up were fitted with matching zoom lenses. . . . The lenses were both set at the same focal length and electronically linked to zoom in and out in unison." In this way, "any object placed in a fixed position between camera and screen would appear to be moving, rather than the other way round. . . . In this case, Superman was suspended in front of the screen, and as the projected image behind him shrank and the camera's zoom lens followed it, he appeared to fly toward the camera."[51]

Among the film's other effects was the production of "a glowing, ethereal look" for the opening sequence on Krypton and for the sequence in the icy setting visited by Superman as a young man.[52] Coupled with effects of other kinds (including the resonance produced by the recording and reproduction of the actors' voices), the design here serves to distinguish these sequences from others—Metropolis at night, Superman's adolescence in Kansas, the scenes set in Lex Luthor's apartment—all of which also possess a style of their own. A visual motif built around windows and glass links Lois and Superman throughout most of the film (from her first view of him through binoculars and the window of a train as a child, to the by-play involving glass partitions and doors in the *Daily Planet* offices, to her final view of him through the car window after her rescue at the end). But *Superman*'s seriality is nevertheless evident in its episodic structure and in the variations worked on its motifs and style.

Superman opened on 508 screens in the United States and Canada on December 15, 1978, "notching the third-highest opening weekend domestic boxoffice figures in film history."[53] Breaking numerous Warner Bros. records, it went on to earn $82.8 million and to feature on lists of big box-office earners ever since. It was followed by *Raiders of the Lost Ark,* which was to earn even more for George Lucas and Paramount. *Raiders* was a project conceived by Lucas in the early 1970s. According to Steven Spielberg, Lucas suggested it to him just prior to the release of *Star Wars.*[54] In the event, production had to wait until Spielberg completed *1941* (1979). In the interim, a proposal was put to Hollywood's distributors that

dared to assault standard Hollywood financial practices at several especially sensitive points. Chief among them was that while the distributor would be expected to put up the movie's budgeted $20 million negative cost, it would receive no distribution fee and take no overhead charge. Those items normally accounted for more than 50 percent of the gross film rentals (the amount returned to the studio after exhibitors take their share). Besides demanding large sums of money up front, Lucas and Spielberg also wanted enormous shares of the distributor's gross, a demand that was especially unusual for a director in that era. And while the distributor would be allowed to recover the entire negative cost of *Raiders* from gross rentals before Lucas and Spielberg started to receive their shares of the gross, Lucasfilm would eventually assume full ownership of the movie.[55]

Despite these conditions, a deal was eventually struck with Paramount.

According to Donald Mott and Cheryl Saunders, "Lucas gave Spielberg a very specific formula to follow: the screenplay was divided into sixty scenes, each two pages long, and it outlined the six dramatic situations that Indiana [Harrison Ford] would

The culmination of the glass motif in *Superman* (1978).

find himself in." They go on to quote Lucas himself: "Its a serialesque movie. . . . It's basically an action piece."[56] From its very beginning, the "action unfolds as a continuing series of exuberantly violent and deadly confrontations—with the Nazis, hired Arab assassins, thousands of venomous snakes that guard the ark, etc., in which Ford miraculously outwits the elements in approved comic strip fashion before fending off the next round of dangers."[57]

Eventually costing $20.4 million, *Raiders* was released by Paramount on June 12, 1981.[58] Opening on 1,078 screens, it grossed $8,305,823 in its first weekend. According to *Variety*, these were "less than the runaway blockbuster proportions Paramount had hoped for," particularly with *Clash of the Titans* (1981) opening at $6,565,347 on 1,125 screens and *Superman II* at $14,100,523 on 1,395.[59] However, playing on a constant number of screens into July then broadening to 1,140 in early August, it soon "regained its crown as the number one film in the market-place," helping, despite an overall drop in attendances, to contribute to a record summer at the box office.[60] It eventually garnered $115,598,000 in domestic rentals and grossed $363 million worldwide.[61]

Prior to directing *Raiders*, Spielberg had expressed a wish to direct a James Bond film.[62] Although their heroes differed in several ways (Indiana Jones was far less polished and far more vulnerable than Roger Moore's Bond), the Bond films shared a number of features with *Raiders*, not least their devotion to stunts and effects and their increasing deployment of serial tropes. Coincidentally, the then most recent Bond film, *For Your Eyes Only*, was released in the same month as *Raiders* and for a while provided stiff competition at the box office. As we have seen, the Bond films were one of the first manifestations of seriality in its sequel and franchise forms in the postwar era.[63] As we have also seen, they were among the first to pioneer showcase releasing as well. Their base in the United Kingdom, their international settings, and the fact that they were produced by international figures such as Harry Saltzman and Albert Broccoli (latterly Broccoli on his own) linked them to producers like De Laurentiis and the Salkinds and to many of the films they produced in the 1970s and 1980s. For *Variety*, it was these and other independents, the heirs of Sam Spiegel and Samuel Bronston, who led "the competitive craze to outspend one's competition" in the post-*Jaws* era, promoting the idea that "big investments can yield big returns."[64]

To some extent, they and the U.S. majors who followed their example proved to be right: "Of 10 films shot between 1976 and 1979, and playing off by 1979, five were profitable in the approx. $20,000,000 plus league. That is a far better batting average than the industry norm for an average film."[65] At the same time, as seriality in all its forms took increasing hold in the 1980s, and as films like *Superman II, Superman III, Return of the Jedi* (1983), *Star Trek—The Motion Picture*, and *Star Trek: The Wrath of Khan* (1982) broke more and more records for costs, box-office performances, or the number of screens on which they opened, it was accompanied by a further escalation in the scale of blockbuster budgets, record weekends, and what by now was coming to be called "wide releasing," as the following table of figures shows:

Title	Cost	Screens	Dates	W/E Gross
Star Trek: The Motion Picture	$42,000,000	857	12/7–9/79	$11,926,421
The Empire Strikes Back	$22,000,000	823	6/20–22/80	$10,840,307
Superman II	$54,000,000	1,385	6/19–21/81	$14,100,523
Star Trek: The Wrath of Khan	$11,000,000	1,621	6/4–6/82	$14,347,221
Return of The Jedi	$32,500,000	1,002	5/27–30/83	$30,490,619
Superman III	$35,000,000	1,759	10/17–19/83	$13,352,357

Sources: *Variety*, May 9, 1984, 522, and listings of costs in *Variety* and the Internet Movie Database. It should be noted that the dates and the number of screens listed here are for peak not opening weekends.

These, though, were not the only or in some cases even the widest or the most lucrative weekends in the late 1970s and early 1980s. As the same sources indicate, *Smokey and the Bandit II* was shown on 1,203 screens and grossed $11,149,285 over the weekend of May 15–17, 1980; *The Cannonball Run* was shown on 1,673 screens and grossed $11,765,654 over the weekend of June 19–21, 1981; and *Friday the 13th: The Final Chapter* was shown on 1,594 screens and grossed $11,183,148 over the weekend of April 13–15, 1984. *The Cannonball Run* cost $18 million, but the others were not big-budget productions.[66] Seriality and wide releasing were thus as manifest in low- to medium-budget comedy, horror, and country-oriented chase films as they were in expensive sci-fi and action-adventure films.

Releasing Wide: Comedy, Country, and Horror

In 1983, A. D. Murphy provided an overview of developments in production, distribution, and exhibition in the 1970s and early 1980s. He noted that ticket sales had risen by 4 percent "at an annual compounded rate" since 1971, and that the major companies were producing fewer films. He also noted that the average cost of a feature film was somewhere between $8 million and $10 million and that the majors were likely to spend in the region of $17 million per year on "prints, promotion . . . and participation costs."[67] Murphy noted too that there had been significant changes in the exhibition branch of the industry and that "the proportion of the nation's theatres that regularly enjoy key or subkey run status has doubled, from less than a quarter of all houses to a level that is steadily approaching half."[68] In other words, the social and industrial factors that had led to the growth of multiplex theaters, to the demise of roadshow releasing, and to the closure of downtown premiere venues had also led to an upgrading of suburban and neighborhood theaters, to a contraction in the number of distribution tiers, and to an increase in the use of showcase patterns for feature releases and in the the number of venues involved. In addition, rising production, publicity, and promotion costs had "combined to influence distributor marketing decisions so as to launch films from a wider base than the old single-screen exclusive run. . . . Suddenly, many older suburban houses and many brand new outlying theatres have become first-run situations."[69]

An additional factor here was the size and capacity of multiplex theaters; between 1972 and 1982 the number of screens had increased from 10,694 to 14,977, but the seating capacity had fallen from 6.1 to 5.12 million, thus placing a premium on showcase and wide releasing as a means of making maximum use of the seating capacity available during the course of a film's first run.[70] Figures such as these signaled the increasing importance of multiple engagements over exclusive runs and probably now represented "the best way to measure the true drawing power of an individual film, especially in large urban areas."[71]

There were several ways of launching films from a wider base in the 1970s and early 1980s. A showcase release was one way. A saturation release was another. Although the terminological distinctions are neither hard nor fast, a national or regional saturation release tended to involve skipping a premiere run altogether and opening either on a large number of screens across the country or on a large number of screens in specific locales. *King Kong* and *Star Trek* were released on a large number of screens nationwide. Along with the more marginal case of *Jaws,* they were among the first big-budget productions since the late 1940s to be released in this way. As we have seen, showcase releasing tended to be used for midrange productions with built-in commercial appeal, other forms of saturation as a means of distributing low- to medium-budget action, horror, and exploitation films, films with a specific regional appeal, or films adjudged to lack long-term commercial potential. This continued to be the case. Films like *The Return of the Pink Panther* were released by UA on a preplanned showcase basis, but *The Missouri Breaks* (1976) was released widely and rapidly because UA was unsure how it would perform: "in case anything goes wrong," as *Variety* put it, UA had over nine hundred prints available "for the biggest firstrun day-date saturation since *Breakout* a year ago."[72] *Breakout* "broke out in 1325 venues between May 23–25, 1975," as previously noted.[73] *Grizzly,* however, a low-budget animal-revenge film produced by Film Ventures International, was an archetypal exploitation film. Its costs were covered by presold guarantees; its release was preceded by a $2 million television advertising campaign; and it opened on 775 screens in the United States and Canada on May 12, 1976.[74]

Film Ventures International was based in Georgia. The South and the Southwest were distinctive regional centers for film production and distinctive markets for local saturation releases. In these areas, country-based settings, characters, and themes were particularly popular. *Smokey and the Bandit* was evidence of that. *Smokey* was one of the biggest box-office hits of 1977. It performed abysmally in its exclusive premiere run at the Radio City Music Hall in New York, but spectacularly well in a subsequent saturation run in the South.[75] Its success helped prompt other country comedies, rural chase films, and road films with country settings. Among them were *Convoy* (1978), *Smokey and the Bandit II, The Cannonball Run,* and a trio of Clint Eastwood films, *Every Which Way but Loose* (1978), *Any Which Way You Can* (1980), and *Bronco Billy*

(1980). The latter all drew heavily on country culture, and some broke wide-release records: *Bronco Billy* opened on 1,316 screens, *Every Which Way* on 1,273, and *Any Which Way* on 1,540.[76]

Country culture in the 1970s and early 1980s was spreading into the mainstream. In addition to the general popularity of country-oriented films, evidence can be found in the increasing popularity of country music and in the success in films of country music performers like Dolly Parton. Parton was paired with Burt Reynolds in *The Best Little Whorehouse* and with Jane Fonda and Lily Tomlin in *Nine to Five* (1980), another major box-office hit. *Nine to Five* was one among a number of successful female-oriented comedies and dramas in the late 1970s and early 1980s. Others included *The Other Side of Midnight* (1977), *Private Benjamin* (1980), *Tootsie* (1982), and *Terms of Endearment* (1983). Together they helped constitute a cycle of "grown-up movies," while overlapping with a trend toward comedy in all its major forms.[77]

Nine to Five opened on 912 screens and *Tootsie* on 964.[78] However, aside from the latter (which cost $25 million), the most expensive comedies and the most extensive wide releases tended to be big-budget action comedies and sci-fi-comedy hybrids like *1941, The Blues Brothers* (1980), *Ghost Busters* (1984), *Gremlins* (1984), and *Beverly Hills Cop* (1984). Many of these films featured a new generation of comedy performers, among them Dan Aykroyd, John Belushi, John Candy, Eddie Murphy, and Bill Murray.[79] Belushi came to fame in one of the biggest comedy hits of the 1970s, *National Lampoon's Animal House* (1978), which earned $70.9 million. At an estimated cost of $3 million, *Animal House* was inexpensive. But at $27 million, $30 million, and $32 million respectively, *1941, The Blues Brothers,* and *Ghost Busters* were among the most expensive films of the period. *Ghost Busters* earned over $130.2 million in domestic rentals and was a huge box-office hit. And, although they were both regarded as failures, *The Blues Brothers* earned over $32 million and *1941* over $23 million in domestic rentals. The biggest comedy failure of the period was *Ishtar* (1987), a $45 million vehicle for Warren Beatty and Dustin Hoffman that earned less than $8 million.[80]

Some of the effects in *Ghost Busters* derived from those pioneered in horror as well as in science fiction in the 1970s and early 1980s. Spurred on by the effects work of Rick Baker, Rob Bottin, and others, graphic violence, graphic mutations, and other corporeal effects had contributed to the emergence of new and spectacular forms of horror. Whether in slasher, rape-revenge, or supernatural form, whether in high-, low-, or medium-budget mode, the heirs to *The Last House on the Left* (1972), *The Exorcist,* and *The Texas Chain Saw Massacre* (1974) included *The Omen* (1976), *Halloween* (1978), *Dawn of the Dead* (1979), *The Amityville Horror* (1979), *Friday the 13th* (1980), *The Thing,* and *A Nightmare on Elm Street* (1984). In the late 1960s and early 1970s, low-budget horror films like *Night of the Living Dead* and *The Last House on the Left* had been produced independently and distributed to drive-ins, small- and often specialized big-city cinemas, and neighborhood theaters that had not been accorded first-run status.[81] However, the increasing scale of the new horror cycle, the sums of money earned by small- to medium-budget productions like *Halloween,* and the success of big-budget productions such as *The Exorcist* and *The Omen* led to wider patterns of release in mainstream cinemas. By the late 1970s, the opening of any film on five hundred to six hundred screens was regarded as a wide release; by 1981, this figure had risen to eight or nine hundred (with 1,500 screens or more now marked out as a "hypersaturation" release).[82]

Perhaps inevitably, horror films were as caught up in the revival of 3-D in the early 1980s as they had been in its introduction in the early 1950s and its brief revival in the mid-1960s and early 1970s. When *Friday the 13th, Part III* (1982) was released to 1,079 venues, 813 were equipped to show the film in its 3-D version. Earning $16.5 million in domestic rentals, it became the top-grossing 3-D film in cinema history. *Friday the 13th, Part III* was preceded by *Parasite* and *Rottweiler: Dogs of Hate* (both 1982) and followed by *Amityville 3-D* and *Jaws 3-D* (both 1983). Several different systems were involved, though they all necessitated the use of special spectacles and hence experienced the drawbacks associated with earlier ones. Most of the new systems used 35 mm film, cameras, and prints. But some used 70 mm and other large-gauge formats.[83]

The 70 mm 3-D systems were mostly used for specialized showings in venues such as Disney's EPCOT Center in Florida rather than in conventional commercial theaters. However, prompted by the advent of Dolby Stereo; by the surge in big-budget musical, sci-fi, and action-adventure spectacles; and by the corresponding demand for optimum visual and aural conditions in film presentation, there was a corresponding surge in the use of 70 mm for otherwise conventional commercial films in the late 1970s and early 1980s. Indeed, in the spring of 1982, *Variety* reported that "the coming summer will bring the greatest number of 70m films ever released at one time, with about a dozen new features bowing domestically in the wide-gauge format."[84]

Most of them equipped with six-track Dolby Stereo soundtracks, these new features included *Star Trek: The Wrath of Khan, E.T.,* and *The Thing,* films that followed in the wake of *Star Wars, Star Trek—The Motion Picture, Close Encounters of the Third Kind,* and *Alien.* However, they also included *Gandhi* (1982) and were soon to include *Amadeus, Greystoke: The Legend of Tarzan, Lord of the Apes* (both 1984), *Out of Africa,* and *Revolution* (both 1985), and other films that followed in the wake of *The Deer Hunter* (1978), *Apocalypse Now* (1979), and *Heaven's Gate* (1980). These were films with epic aspirations and adult appeal. They all opened exclusively rather than widely, which meant among other things that the limited number of 70 mm prints required for their initial release could easily be accommodated by the number of venues equipped to show them.[85] Along with *Reds* (1981), *Ragtime* (1981), and *Once upon a Time in America* (1984), which were all released in 35 mm only, they contributed to a cycle of large-scale prestige productions. Lying at the opposite end of the cultural spectrum to most sci-fi, comic-book, horror, and action-adventure films, they were nevertheless among the costliest films of the period. They served not only to perpetuate more exclusive patterns of release, but also in some cases to revive at least some of the traditions of the roadshow.

Epics, Exclusives, and Roadshows

During the late 1970s and early 1980s, reports in *Variety* pointed to a rise in the average age of filmgoers: the baby boom generation was now in its thirties, and as a result there was a growing audience for adult-oriented films.[86] This audience found itself catered for by the increasing number of films produced and distributed by art-house independents as well as by the "grown-up" comedies, dramas, and musicals referred to above.[87] It was also targeted by a number of other kinds of films.

Earlier on, in the mid-1970s, the term *adult* had tended to imply hard-core or soft-core pornography and the explicit depiction of sexual acts, and in 1976, Bob Guccione, owner and editor of *Penthouse* magazine, began production on *Caligula*, the era's only outright pornographic epic. Like *Fellini—Satyricon* (1970), an earlier adult art film, *Caligula* was set in Ancient Rome. It contained a number of large-scale sets and tableau shots, many of them showing simultaneous sexual acts, acts of violence, or instances of nudity. These and other sequences were interspersed with cut-in close-ups of sexual activity, some of them presumably performed by stand-ins. Either way, they were easily removable should censorship regimes in different countries so demand. *Caligula* remained unreleased (and possibly unfinished) for several years. Various versions were released in Europe in 1979. An unrated version was released in the United States in February 1980, and an R-rated one the following year. The unrated version was 156 minutes long. It opened exclusively at the Trans-Lux East in New York at a top ticket price of $7.50 on February 1, 1980. Guccione had hired the Trans-Lux East on a four-wall basis. He subsequently contracted Analysis Film Releasing to four-wall the film in other major cities. By the end of its initial run, the unrated version had grossed $13.5 million in approximately 250 theaters. The R-rated version was 117 minutes long and opened in 170 "class, first-run houses" in October 1981.[88]

The release of the R-rated version of *Caligula* had been preceded by a number of large-scale international coproductions and late 1970s Hollywood epics. The former included *1900, Mohammad, Messenger of God, Lion of the Desert* (1981), *Inchon* (1982), and *The Deer Hunter;* the latter included *Apocalypse Now* and *Heaven's Gate*. With the exception of *The Deer Hunter,* the former all failed at the box office in the United States. *Mohammad, Lion of the Desert,* and *Inchon* earned only $2 million, $1.4 million, and $5.2 million respectively.[89]

The Deer Hunter had been directed and cowritten by Michael Cimino, produced by EMI (a British company), and released by Universal.[90] Costing an estimated $15 million and part of an emerging cycle of films about the Vietnam War and Vietnam veterans, it was unusually long at 183 minutes. It was also highly distinctive. It consists of five different segments: the initial scenes in Clairton, the initial sequence in Vietnam, the second sequence in Clairton, the second sequence in Vietnam, and the third and final sequence in Clairton. These segments are all slowly paced and unusually lengthy (though they get progressively shorter). Within each of them, particular attention is paid minor, passing, or background characters. Within and across them, recurrent motifs—singing and dancing, communal rituals, acts of violence, fire and smoke, successful and unsuccessful acts of rescue—construct a set of contrasts between life and death and a set of evocations of Heaven and Hell.[91] Sounds as well as sights play a part here. *The Deer Hunter* was recorded and exhibited in Dolby Stereo. Cimino spent "six months shooting the film, and *five* months mixing the soundtrack."[92] The importance of sound is evident not just in the film's use of music, singing, and silence, nor just in its attention to accents, idioms, and languages, but also in the emphasis it places on the sounds produced by acts of human violence, the sounds made by machines, and the extent to which they contrast with the sounds and the silence of nature.

Although there was considerable controversy about the film's depiction of the Vietnamese, *The Deer Hunter* was generally well received and went on to win five Oscars and over a dozen other awards. It was initially accorded week-long premiere runs at the 1,112-seat National in Los Angeles and at the 600-seat Coronet in New York in December in order to qualify for Oscar nominations. At the Coronet it was shown on a twice-daily basis, and when it reopened there on February 2, Universal decided to continue roadshowing the film with two screenings on weekdays, three on Saturdays and Sundays, and prebookable $5 seats. It reopened in a more conventional manner at the Village in Los Angeles three weeks later and went on to open on an exclusive basis in theaters in other major cities. Of these, only seats at the Charles 1 in Boston appear to have been sold on an advanced-price, hard-ticket basis. As already indicated, *The Deer Hunter* was shown without an intermission both in these and in other venues, though when it opened on a wider showcase basis in April, thirty United Artists Theatre Circuit houses on Long Island introduced an intermission in order to increase income from the sale of candy.[93]

By the end of the year, *The Deer Hunter* had earned $26,927,000 in rentals. Meanwhile, after nearly a decade's work on the script, on production in the Philippines and the United States, and on postproduction in San Francisco, *Apocalypse Now,* the era's other Vietnam epic, had premiered on August 15, 1979.[94] Produced, directed, and coscripted by Francis Ford Coppola, funding for *Apocalypse Now* had been provided by UA in the form of a completion bond in return for domestic distribution rights. Production costs were initially estimated at $12–14 million, though they eventually rose to $30.5 million.[95] Coppola personally guaranteed the film's costs over and above the original budget and as a result found himself in debt for some years to come.

Various plans were devised for the film's distribution. In 1977, UA considered four-walling 70 mm prints of *Apocalypse Now* in New York and other major cities, charging as much as $7 per seat, then releasing 35 mm prints of the film more widely. However, problems of various kinds delayed the film's completion for nearly two years. Eventually, UA insisted that Coppola have the film ready for release in the summer of 1979. A 141-minute 70 mm version was finally premiered at the Ziegfeld Theatre in New York, the Cinerama Dome in Los Angeles, and the University Theatre in Toronto. Tickets were presold on a guaranteed-seat basis, and Coppola evoked the roadshow tradition by insisting that patrons each be provided with a sixteen-page brochure. The film was shown without an intermission, though there had earlier been plans to include one just prior to the French plantation sequence that was excised though eventually reinstated in the *Redux* version (2001).[96]

The four-walling plan had long been abandoned. The Ziegfeld, the Cinerama Dome, and the University Theatre had been booked in the usual way. They each did very well. By September 21, *Apocalypse Now* had grossed $1,951,334.21.[97] Some of the film's later engagements involved the use of the 35 mm version, which lacked the sound mix and stereo effects that marked the version in 70 mm. These had been key ingredients in *Apocalypse Now*.[98] They were key ingredients in *Heaven's Gate* as well. Indeed, *Heaven's Gate*'s sound mix became, along with its escalating costs and its catastrophic effect on UA, part of the tale of directorial self-indulgence and corporate timidity told by Steven Bach in his book, *Final Cut*.[99]

Heaven's Gate began life as an $11.6 million western about the 1892 Johnson County cattle wars and ended up as "a $36-million critique of frontier capitalism" that performed disastrously at the box office and resulted in a net loss of $44 million and the selling-off of UA to MGM by Transamerica.[100] Also directed and coscripted by Cimino, *Heaven's Gate* was as slowly paced as *The Deer Hunter*—and even more reticent about revealing the motivations of its central characters other than those of its villains. Built around large-scale scenes of communal activity, small-scale scenes of friendship and love, and scenes of confrontation that progressively escalate in scale, the film as a whole is marked by repetitious musical phrases, by sequences of dance, and by an overarching motif of circular movement.

Given more or less free rein, Cimino's initial cut was 219 minutes long. UA planned to roadshow the film at this length and with an intermission at the Cinema I in New York, at the University Theatre in Toronto, and at Plitt 1 and 2 in Los Angeles. A hundred theaters were to be added by the end of February, and the release was to widen further from there. However, dismal reviews, baffled reactions to the film at its New York premiere on November 18, 1980, and prebookings worth a mere $100,000, led UA to withdraw the film from Cinema I after only a week and from the University Theatre after only one screening. The Los Angeles bookings were canceled and the film was reedited. The following April, UA released a 149-minute 35 mm version and

The beginning and the end of the motif of circular movement in *Heaven's Gate* (1980).

a 153-minute 70 mm version (both with remixed soundtracks) on approximately 810 screens to grosses averaging a mere $1,605 per screen.[101] UA estimated the advertising and print costs for *Heaven's Gate*'s re-release at $8.5 million, *Variety*, its domestic rental income at $1.5 million. Nevertheless, *Variety* reported that the "Risky Megabuck Pic Trend" was "Still Ongoing," that among the other "mega-budgeted" films released in 1981 were *Ragtime* and *Reds,* and that among those forthcoming were *Gandhi* and *Once upon a Time in America.*[102]

Gandhi, Ragtime, and *Once upon a Time in America* had all been in gestation for many years. *Once upon a Time in America* was directed by Sergio Leone. In various stages of planning since the late 1960s, Leone finally secured the backing of Arnon Milchan, an Israeli millionaire, who acquired the rights to the source novel (Harry Grey's *The Hoods*) and set up a distribution deal with Warners and the Ladd Company. With several last-minute changes made to the script, Leone started filming on June 14, 1982. By the time filming had finished, Leone had gone over schedule and over budget (*Variety* estimated its cost at over $30 million). He also had ten hours of footage to edit, from which he produced a 229-minute cut.[103] With the precedent of *Heaven's Gate* fresh in the memory, Ladd and Warners were nervous. Their fears were fueled by the film's violence, its introspective tone, and what Leone described as its focus on "stasis."[104] They were exacerbated by negative reactions to a sneak preview held in Boston in February 1984. Shorn of its flashback structure, a 144-minute version was released widely, on 894 screens, in the United States on June 1.[105] "Catastrophe soon descended, as *America,* in its truncated version, made only $2.5 million in US rentals. The film was released in Europe in a 227-minute version approved by Leone, and it reopened in this form at the New York Film Festival on 12 October 1984," followed by a limited commercial run at the Gemini 2 in New York.[106]

There were fewer problems with *Ragtime* and *Reds.* Like much of *Once upon a Time in America,* both films were set in the early years of the twentieth century and focused on the contrasts between the era's youthful possibilities and its ultimate limitations. But where the tone of *Once upon a Time* was disillusioned and bitter and that of *Ragtime* sad and ironic, that of *Reds* was much more upbeat, ending as it did with images of survival and exuberant youth. *Ragtime* was produced by Dino De Laurentiis at a cost of $32 million, *Reds* by Warren Beatty at a cost of $52 million. Both were distributed by Paramount. *Ragtime* opened on a limited basis at the State and Coronet in New York, the Village in Los Angeles, the San Francisco Regency, and the Plaza in Toronto on November 20, 1981.[107] Despite being nominated for several Oscars and other awards, it earned only $10 million in domestic rentals. Starring Jack Nicholson and Diane Keaton as well as Beatty, *Reds* fared a good deal better. But *Variety*'s reviewer predicted that although its early business "in artier class sites could be brisk," *Reds* (a "socio-political drama" with a 200-minute running time plus an intermission), would "be very hard to sell broadly."[108] Sure enough, following a premiere on Thursday, December 3, it opened the following day on 396 screens, faring poorly "in the suburbs and the south" before spreading to 665 screens in January.[109] At this point, its earnings picked up and it went on to earn $21 million in domestic rentals. But this was less than half the amount it had cost.

Gandhi earned a similar amount in North America ($24.7 million), but because it had only cost $22 million it made a profit both from this and from other markets. *Gandhi* had been in gestation for at least as long as *Once upon a Time in America.* By 1980, its producer-director, Richard Attenborough, had been able to secure financial backing from the Indian government and from Goldcrest Film International (GFI) and International Film Investors (IFI). GFI and IFI were offshoots of Goldcrest Films, a British company that specialized in financing the development of projects and scripts. With *Gandhi,* they became major investors in a major production.[110] Shooting finally began in India in November 1980. By July 1981, GFI, IFI, and Attenborough were in a position to screen footage to potential distributors in the United States, and eventually to secure a deal in which, as GFI's Jake Eberts describes it,

Columbia acquired worldwide rights in all media, with the exception of India. Columbia paid an advance of $2 million against the domestic rights, but gave us 25 per cent of the gross rental from the first dollar. That percentage increased as the box-office receipts increased, to the point where we stood to take 65 per cent of the gross if the film was a smash hit. On the international side, the terms were similar, except that our share of the gross went up to a maximum of 80 percent.[111]

Gandhi opened on November 30, 1982. The film had been delivered in May, but "Columbia decided . . . to delay the opening until all the youth pictures that traditionally dominate the summer season at the US box office were safely out of the way."[112] Columbia devised a two-part strategy for the film's distribution; it "would be released at more or less the same time in as many different territories as possible, to take maximum advantage of the publicity that it was bound to attract, but within each territory it would open initially in a small number of . . . cinemas." Eventually, "if all went well, it would end up in the same place as a mainstream movie with well-known stars: a 1,000-print nationwide release."[113] At 188 minutes plus intermission, *Gandhi* opened with gala premieres in Delhi, London, Washington, New York, Los Angeles, and Toronto. It widened to sixteen venues in the United States in the New Year, then to 350 on January 21. It was on 805 screens by April 13, by which time it had already grossed $38,633,920 and won eight Oscars.[114]

The success of this and other Goldcrest films prompted GFI to invest in a series of expensive, anti-imperial epics and dramas, among them *Greystoke, Revolution,* and *The Mission* (1986). *Greystoke's* $23 million earnings were considerable, though they were outweighed by its $33 million production costs. *Revolution* and *The Mission* were box-office failures.[115] Other films with imperial settings, among them EMI's *A Passage to India* (1984) and Universal's *Out of Africa,* fared much better, though the former's earnings in the United States were insufficient to meet its production costs.[116] GFI's James Lee argued that the failure of GFI's films was due to the increasing number of films competing in what he called the "yuppie market" in the United States, as exemplified by films like *Kiss of the Spider Woman* (1985), *The Color Purple* (1985), *A Room with a View* (1986), and *Hannah and Her Sisters* (1986); James Ilott suggests that with more films requiring more screens, the number of play dates was simply insufficient to cope with demand.[117] Whatever the reason, the yuppie market (and adult-oriented films) were to prove important in the late 1980s and early 1990s too. By then, though, the U.S. film industry had undergone and was undergoing a series of transformations that were to change its structure and patterns of ownership and the nature of the media environment in which its films were produced and released.

Ancillary Markets, Globalization, and Digital Technology, 1986–2009

On January 2, 1986, *The Hollywood Reporter* predicted that "1986 will probably make entertainment history by marking the first time that home video revenues will exceed those of theatrical releases." According to *Variety,* it had already done so: "Consumer spending on the rental and purchase of videocassettes in 1985 skyrocketed to about $4.55 billion, a figure that soared above the '85 theatrical boxoffice total and nearly doubled the size of the video business in '84."[1] Along with cable and satellite television, video provided a new source of revenue that served not only to supplement the box-office earnings of the major film companies, nor just to provide them with the lion's share of their income, but also to enhance the commercial appeal of their films, increase the number of screens on which they could be shown, and encourage some of the companies to move (or move back) into theater ownership.

As we have seen, the TV networks had been a source of revenue for the major producers of feature films and TV shows since the late 1950s. However, the appearance of feature films on network TV was no longer the event it once had been. The ratings for features fell off markedly between 1975 and 1983. When the ratings for the screening of *Star Wars* on CBS in 1984 proved disappointingly low, sales to the networks weakened and those to syndication increased.[2] Paramount earned more than $1 million per title from syndication in 1985. In 1987, it earned more than twice that amount. By then, feature films provided the basis for syndicated TV programming in each of the country's top twenty markets. The networks continued to devote 20–25 percent of their primetime schedules to films, but their contribution to the studios' revenues declined from $430 million in 1980 to $100 million in 1990 while those from syndication rose from $150 million to $600 million.[3]

As the studios adjusted to the new media environment, adding cable and video to the growing number of "windows" through which their films could now be viewed, "network television was the big loser, and syndication, pay cable, and home video were the important new kids on the block."[4] Cable devices, systems, and services had been in existence since the late 1940s. They had been subject to strict regulation by the Federal Communications Commission (FCC), which sought, by and large, to protect the broadcast industry. However, by 1975, nearly 13 percent of U.S. households subscribed to cable, and a number of industry figures began to consider cable as an ideal carrier for pay-per-view services. In 1972, Home Box Office (HBO) had been set up by Time Inc. Following the successful launch of SATCOM 1 in 1975, it became the first cable company to exploit the commercial availability of satellite transmission. Viacom set up Showtime the following year. Two years later, the FCC relaxed its restrictions on the pay distribution of theatrical films. Previously, only films less than two years old

or more than ten could be shown on pay cable. Most films, especially the better ones, remained in theatrical release for first, second, and third run for more than two years, thus limiting pay TV's menu to very old or second-rate material. With the new three-year limit established in 1978, pay TV finally was able to provide movie fare sufficiently interesting to cable operators.[5]

Pay cable flourished and HBO began not only to produce its own made-for-TV films, but also to prepay film producers for the exclusive rights to screen their features.[6] By the late 1980s, 27.4 percent of U.S. homes subscribed to pay cable, and HBO had "become the largest financier of motion pictures in the world."[7] Along with Cinemax, Showtime, and The Movie Channel, it dominated the field of pay TV. Having sought and failed on antitrust grounds to enter the cable market in the late 1970s, the studios signed a number of distribution deals with the pay TV networks. In the mid-1980s, when the antitrust laws were interpreted in a more relaxed manner than they had been in the 1970s, Fox and MCA acquired cable stations as outlets for their films.

During the 1980s and early 1990s, synergies of a different sort became evident in the production of a number of TV shows based on feature films and a number of feature films based on TV shows. Among the former were *Private Benjamin* (1981–83), *Nine to Five* (1982–84), and *Starman* (1987–88); among the latter were *Dragnet* (1987), *The Untouchables* (1987), *The Fugitive* (1993), and *The Flintstones* (1994). The films were all expensive box-office hits: *Dragnet* cost $23 million and earned $30,234,468 in domestic rentals; *The Untouchables,* $30 million and $36,866,530; *The Fugitive,* $44 million and $92.6 million; and *The Flintstones,* $45 million and $70,753,383. In 1994, Ted Turner's cable company, TNT, released a 248-minute theatrical version of *Gettysburg,* a $25 million, 271-minute made-for-TV film that recalled the battle-reconstruction epics of the 1960s. By then the symbiosis between the film and television industries had been further cemented by a number of key corporate developments.

Unlike television, video was a new source of revenue, one that the majors approached with considerable caution. Video was an electronically based, analog technology devised initially for the recording of television programs. It worked by representing the images and sounds in an audio-visual field as electronic modulations and recording the results on magnetically coated tape. A number of formats were pioneered for professional use in the broadcasting industries in the United States in the 1950s and 1960s. In the 1970s, Telefunken in Germany, Decca in the United Kingdom, and MCA in the United States devised a series of disc systems, some founded on needle-based recording technology, others on the use of lasers. Discs proved popular with film devotees, but were only available in prerecorded form. By contrast, a number of the video systems introduced in the 1970s were specifically devised for recording and could thus be used to "time-shift"—to record televised shows and films for subsequent viewing. These systems included U-matic and Betamax, which were introduced by Sony in 1969 and 1975 respectively, and VHS (Video Home System), which was introduced by Matsushita and JVC (the Japan Victor Company) in 1978. Partly because of the four-hour capacity of its cassettes, VHS soon became the dominant system for home recording and for prerecorded programs and films.

The Hollywood majors were initially dismayed by the advent of video. Universal and Disney took Sony to court over the right to record off-air, and a rapidly expanding market for "adult" cassettes created an association between pornography and the prerecorded video industry that the members of the MPAA were keen to avoid. Nevertheless, between 1977 and 1982, each of them entered the market for prerecorded tapes. In 1977, Fox licensed Magnetic Video to distribute fifty of its films on tape. Among them were *The King and I, The Sound of Music,* and *Patton,* all of which had been blockbuster hits. Similar deals were struck by UA, MGM, and Orion. Warners, Paramount, Universal, and Disney established their own distribution arms, as did Fox when it bought out Magnetic Video in 1979. Columbia set up its own distribution arm, then went into partnership with RCA. According to Stephen Prince: "Between January 1979 and March 1980, the majors placed 477 titles into video release, an 854 percent increase over the 50 titles that had been available until then." Among them were *Alien,* which "reached the million dollar sales mark forty-five days after its home video release," and *9 to 5,* which was released on video less than two months after its initial theatrical run.[8]

Tapes were initially priced at between $50 and $70 and were sold directly to customers. The cost was high and the market was small. But thanks to the "first sale doctrine," owners of copyrighted works, including tapes of films, could sell or rent copies themselves. As a result, video stores began renting tapes. In 1979 there were seven hundred video stores in the United States. In 1989, there were 30,000, each serving an average of 1,943.33 households with VCRs (video cassette recorders).[9] By then the majors had devised policies that enabled them to increase video sales and to profit from the increase. They sought initially to do so by adding surcharges and license fees to the cost of tapes sold largely to renters. But the answer lay in lowering prices and increasing the number of tapes sold directly to consumers.

In the early 1980s, "Prices hovered around $80–90 per tape until Paramount, early in 1982, cut the nominal price of *Star Trek II: The Wrath of Khan* (as it was retitled for video) from $79.95 to $39.95 in an effort to encourage higher sales. The price reduction was enormously successful, generating sales of over 100,000 tapes." In 1983, it released *Flashdance* on video "a mere six months after its theatrical release," and "set new records by posting initial units sales of 500,000" when it released *Raiders of the Lost Ark* on video later that year.[10] By 1987 "about 60 million cassettes were sold to dealers for sell-through while 62 million units were sold to dealers for rentals."[11]

The biggest sell-through success that year was *Top Gun* (1986), which Paramount released at $26.95 per tape. A $14 million production about an elite group of pilots, *Top Gun* had been released on 1,117 screens in the summer of 1986 and had earned $79.4 million in domestic rentals during the course of its initial theatrical run.[12] According to Prince, Paramount sold 2.5 million video copies of *Top Gun* and earned an additional $40 million.[13] *Top Gun* was produced by Don Simpson and Jerry Bruckheimer and directed by Tony Scott. Bruckheimer and Simpson had previously produced the MTV-oriented *Flashdance;* Tony Scott had directed TV commercials in the United Kingdom. As Prince points out, these stylistic ingredients coalesced not just in the film and its video copy, but also in the advertisement for Diet Pepsi that preceded the film on the tape: "The ad shows a group of pilots returning to base after maneuvers. It is edited with quick, aggressive cutting and employs a rock music sound track like the film's." In this way, it "achieves a perfect synergy with the film, its style and thematic content blending seamlessly with the film's imagery . . . creating a symbiosis between the two products (Pepsi and *Top Gun*).[14] As such it was highly influential, creating a stylistic formula for subsequent Bruckheimer-Simpson hits such as *Days of Thunder* (1990) and *The Rock* (1996).[15]

In 1987, Universal sold over 15 million video copies of *E.T.* and earned over $175 million, nearly as much as the $187 million it had earned in domestic rentals during the course of its initial theatrical release.[16] By the end of the decade home video had emerged as the most important of the new ancillary markets, with income evenly split between rentals and sales. In 1980 video rentals and sales accounted for approximately $3 million in worldwide earnings for the U.S. film industry. By 1990 that figure had risen to $5.2 million, more than the $4.7 million earned from theatrical exhibition and pay TV combined.[17] By the end of the 1980s, "theatrical release accounted for only 30 percent of the studios' total receipts, while ancillary markets made up the other 70 percent. *Batman,* released in 1989, earned $250 million in the first five months of its theatrical release. When Warners released it on video, it earned another $400 million."[18] *Willow* "cost $55 million and grossed only $28 million in American theatres. But it earned an additional $18 million in video sales, and $15 million in television sales." Earnings such as these helped fuel a continuing rise in production costs:

During the second half of the 1980s, and allowing for inflation, the average Hollywood budget rose by 40 percent. In 1990, a major movie might be budgeted at $25 million, with additional marketing and distribution costs of $20 million. With overheads and interest charges, the studio that financed it would have to recoup more than $50 million to break even.[19]

These factors were to play an increasing part in the fortunes of the independents as well as the majors in the 1980s and 1990s.

Independents

While video technology began to be used in the shooting and editing of films such as *Star Trek—The Motion Picture* and *One from the Heart* (1982), the new ancillary markets generated increasing levels of demand and increasing sums of money, leading in the short term to an increase in the number of films produced and distributed by independent companies. Among these companies were Hemdale, Vestron, Miramax, and New Line. In an increasingly diverse market, all of them had hits on either a major or minor scale: Hemdale with *Platoon* (1986); Vestron with *Dirty Dancing* (1987); Miramax with *sex, lies, and videotape* (1989); and New Line with *Teenage Mutant Ninja Turtles* (1990).[20]

Written and directed by Oliver Stone at a cost of $6 million, *Platoon* had been picked up for release by Orion, a mini-major formed in 1982. Joining a group of Vietnam films such as *Uncommon Valor* (1983), *Missing in Action* (1984), and *Rambo: First Blood, Part II* (1985), it paved the way for Warners' *Full Metal Jacket* (1987), which cost $20 million and earned $22.7 million in domestic rentals, and Disney-Touchstone's *Good Morning, Vietnam* (1987), which cost $14 million and earned $58,083,108. The *Rambo* films had been produced by Carolco, an independent formed in 1975 to buy and resell foreign rights to domestic films and to form partnerships for financing low-budget productions. *First Blood,* the first of the *Rambo* series, had cost $14.5 million. But it had gone on to earn $22,947,561 in domestic rentals and to earn a box-office gross of $120 million worldwide. (Gross figures, it should be noted, were and are always higher than figures for rentals.) From that point on:

Carolco's strategy became set: rights in some foreign and ancillary markets were pre-sold to offset the initial budget; overhead was limited because the company did not require physical studio space or a distribution outlet for a steady stream of product (Carolco became increasingly focused on a small number of features); and production centered on action, "event" movies driven by star power.[21]

Sylvester Stallone was one of Carolco's stars, Arnold Schwarzenegger another. In both cases, spectacularly muscular male bodies and feats of endurance, strength, and power were showcased in stunts, fights, and action scenarios often allied to Cold War themes. *Rambo: First Blood, Part II* cost $25.5 million, earned $78,919,250 in domestic rentals, and grossed $300 million worldwide. *Rambo III* (1988) cost a then-record

$58 million. It earned only $28,508,000 in domestic rentals, but it performed well abroad and its costs had already been offset by nearly $80 million in presold guarantees for video as well as for domestic and foreign theatrical rights.[22] The 1980s *Rambo* series came to a temporary end in 1988; though having by then also featured in Cannon's $24 million *Cobra* (1986), Stallone continued his career as an action-body star with the $55 million *Tango & Cash* (1989), which earned $30.1 million for Warners, and *Rocky V* (1990), which earned $20 million for MGM/UA. Stallone returned to Carolco for the $65 million *Cliffhanger* in 1993. By then, though, Carolco was in trouble. *Cliffhanger* earned $43,306,664 in domestic rentals. With the addition of ancillary income it would have made a profit. But Carolco had been forced to sell domestic theatrical, video, and other ancillary rights to Tri-Star, its regular U.S. distributor, in return for a substantial portion of *Cliffhanger*'s budget. Carolco attempted to revive its fortunes with *CutThroat Island* (1995), a pirate adventure film. However, unable to secure a proven star, and having spent somewhere between $90 and 100 million, Carolco lost an estimated $50 million when *CutThroat Island* failed at the box office and soon found itself bankrupt.[23]

Arnold Schwarzenegger began his starring career with leading roles in the $21 million *Conan the Barbarian* (1982) and the $18 million *Conan the Destroyer* (1984), both of them produced by De Laurentiis. Feeding off the vogue for comic book heroes and pulp adventure, *Conan the Barbarian* earned $21,729,995 in domestic rentals and *Conan the Destroyer*, $14,292,546. Having established his reputation and his image by playing an almost indestructible killer robot in Hemdale's $6.4 million *The Terminator* (1984), Schwarzenegger went on to star in a series of big budget productions for Carolco, among them the post–Cold War *Red Heat* (1988), the dystopian *Total Recall* (1990), and *Terminator 2: Judgment Day* (1991). *Red Heat* cost $30 million and earned only $16 million in domestic rentals. But *Total Recall* cost $65 million, earned $63,511,000 in domestic rentals and grossed $260 million worldwide, and *Terminator 2* cost $94 million, earned $112.5 million in domestic rentals and grossed $490 million worldwide. By then, Carolco had invested in a video company, Live Entertainment. Live's guarantees helped fund these productions, and its partnership with Carolco allowed the latter to collect a higher-than-usual percentage of receipts from its video sales. In the meantime, Schwarzenegger capitalized on the increasingly self-aware and self-mocking qualities in his image by appearing in comedies such as *Twins* (1988) and *Kindergarten Cop* (1990), both of which were successes for Universal.[24]

For a time, Carolco was able to thrive in the new ancillary era. The fortunes of other large-scale independents, notably Cannon and Dino De Laurentiis, were much more uneven. Cannon sought to prosper by producing a mixture of low-budget art and exploitation films, none of which was commercially successful. Having initially set up a deal with MGM/UA for North American distribution, Cannon decided to upgrade its product and to distribute its films itself. However, this only exposed Cannon to further commercial risk. Its publicity budgets were on average only 36 percent of its films' negative costs. But with expensive failures such as *Pirates* (1986), which cost $31 million and earned less than $1 million in domestic rentals, they were still 27 percent greater than its domestic theatrical earnings. In 1987, Cannon produced the $35 million *Superman IV: The Quest for Peace* for release through Warners. The earlier *Superman* films had all been major box-office hits. But *Superman IV* failed dismally, earning a mere $8.1 million in domestic rentals. Cannon was in deep financial trouble. It was sued by the Securities and Exchange Commission (SEC) and was bought out in 1988 by Giancarlo Parretti.[25] Three years earlier, De Laurentiis had founded the De Laurentiis Entertainment Group (DEG) and embarked on a varied series of productions that included *Tai-Pan* and *King Kong Lives* (both 1986). These films cost $24 million and $21 million respectively. Neither was as expensive in relative terms as those produced by De Laurentiis in the 1960s, 1970s, and early 1980s. (*Dune* [1984], an epic science-fiction film, had cost $42 million.) But they were both box-office failures: *Tai-Pan* earned $2 million in domestic rentals, *King Kong Lives,* $1.7 million. Unsurprisingly, DEG declared itself bankrupt in 1988.

Other large-scale independents included Imagine Entertainment, Castle Rock Entertainment, and Morgan Creek Productions. These companies had a more stable and profitable history thanks largely to their commercial production policies and to a series of long-term deals with major distributors. Imagine was founded in 1986. It set up a long-term distribution deal with Universal. Universal distributed *Parenthood* (1989), a domestic comedy that earned $50,004,387 in domestic rentals, *Backdraft* (1991), an effects-driven action film that earned $40,260,678, and *How the Grinch Stole Christmas* (2000), which grossed $260,031,035 domestically. Castle Rock was founded in 1987. Its first film was *When Harry Met Sally . . .* (1989), which earned $41,790,000 in domestic rentals and helped reestablish romantic comedy as a major production trend. It was distributed and coproduced by Columbia. Columbia went on to coproduce and distribute a number of subsequent Castle Rock films, among them *A Few Good Men* (1992) and *In the Line of Fire* (1993). The former earned $71 million in domestic rentals, the latter $49 million. After that, a long-term distribution deal with Warners led to successes such as *Miss Congeniality* (2000) and *The Polar Express* (2004). Morgan Creek was founded in 1988. Its earliest films included *Young Guns* (1988), a teen-oriented western; *Major League* (1989), one of a number of films about baseball; and *Robin Hood: Prince of Thieves* (1991), an expensive costume adventure vehicle for Kevin Costner. *Young Guns* was distributed by Fox, *Major League* by Paramount, and *Robin Hood* by Warners. Fox distributed *The Last of the Mohicans* (1992), Morgan Creek's next film, in the United States. It earned $35,177,486 in domestic rentals. But *Robin Hood* had earned $86 million and its success set the seal on a long-term partnership with Warner Bros.

The success enjoyed by Imagine, Castle Rock, and Morgan Creek in the late 1980s and early 1990s was exceptional. The market share enjoyed by the independents as a whole had fallen substantially. While production costs had doubled between 1985 and 1989, domestic rentals for the independent companies had fallen by a third. The number of independent films released in the United States had risen from 156 in 1985 to 200 in 1987, then fallen to 142 in 1989 and a twenty-five year low of 126 in 1992.[26] Moreover, those films produced by independents but distributed by the majors (and by others abroad) were far less profitable than they might otherwise have been because so much of the money they earned was returned to those who had paid for the right to distribute them and because the video market was proving less of a panacea than initially hoped.

In the early 1980s, video had been a boon for independents specializing in sex comedies, horror films, and other low-budget productions. For companies like Crown International, "home video rights typically yielded 25 percent of the production costs."[27] Encouraged by these developments, Vestron set itself up as a video distributor and moved into film production from there. By the mid-1980s, however, it was becoming increasingly clear that "the key to a film's ancillary economic value is its theatrical release."[28] The bigger the release, the greater the degree of public awareness and the larger the likely market for video sales and rentals. But a bigger release necessitated a larger number of prints and screens, either in a film's initial launch or in the increasingly rapid process of widening that now marked the distribution of nearly all films, even those that opened on a limited or localized basis. Cable and video companies now monitored the scale of theatrical releases as a means of gauging the commercial potential of films in their respective ancillary markets. One of the former used five hundred prints as the benchmark for a wide release, one of the latter, eight hundred.[29]

By the end of the decade, "1500 to 2800-screen openings were common for commercial pictures."[30] The majors could afford to release the films produced by the likes of Carolco, Castle Rock, and Morgan Creek on this kind of scale. So, for a while, could DEG. But companies like Crown could not, not least because wide releasing had helped prompt a fivefold increase in print and advertising costs.[31] New Line launched *Teenage Mutant Ninja Turtles* on 2,006 screens. It widened rapidly to 2,337 and soon became "the most successful indie release in US history."[32] *Ninja Turtles* was a commercial project based on a comic book and a highly successful children's TV show. Yet New Line was only able to release the film this widely by doing so in March, a low point in the calendar for major releases. Although the number of available screens had risen from 17,675 in 1980 to 22,921 in 1989, the growth in the number of films and in the number and scale of wide releases meant that the opportunities for small-scale independents were increasingly limited.[33] In 1987 "approximately 37% of the annual production of indie US features received no US theatrical release at all"; of the 205 films that were released, sixty-four "were accorded only a marginal release or a test booking ahead of their ancillary use."[34]

By then, developments in the video industry were narrowing the opportunities for ancillary use as well. The introduction of "two-tiered pricing," of lower prices for sell-through cassettes of popular titles alongside the higher prices charged to video stores for rental releases, tended in both instances to favor "the few, big, high-profile films over the many medium-sized films financed by independent video pre-selling. It also gave a large amount of money to established studios with which to enhance their other marketing operations and increase their competitive edge."[35] By the early 1990s, video distributors knew that the number of copies they could ship was directly related to a film's initial box-office earnings:

if a film's domestic box-office over the first two months of release is between $1-million and $3-million, they can expect to ship between 50,000 and 80,000 units. . . . From $4–$10-million, one can ship between 80,000 to 120,000 units; if the box-office is $10–15-million, the range is between 100,000 and 150,000; at $20-million the range approaches 200,000. Of the four hundred pictures released annually, only about sixty pictures do this well.[36]

Most of these pictures were released by the majors.

By the early 1990s, Vestron and Media, the largest of the independent video distributors, were gone. So too were DEG, Hemdale, and Cannon. Only New Line, Miramax, and Live continued to prosper, thanks largely to their publicity skills, their knowledge of the independent market, and their unwillingness to invest more than they could earn. Following a fresh influx of capital in 1998, Live was renamed Artisan Entertainment. In 1999, it had a massive hit with *The Blair Witch Project,* a revamped example of a classic independent genre, the low-budget horror film. Costing a mere $35,000, *The Blair Witch Project* was accompanied by an innovative Internet marketing campaign that worked by creating a credible (but fictional) backstory and that thus helped establish the foundations of what has come to be called "viral marketing." It opened on twenty-seven screens in twenty-four cities on July 14, spread wide to 1,101 screens on July 30, and went on to gross "$28.5 million—a $25,885 per-screen average that far outpaced the $21,822 earned by *Star Wars: Episode 1—The Phantom Menace* in May. . . . By the end of November, *The Blair Witch Project* had grossed more than $140 million and became the most profitable independent film of all time (beside . . . *Deep Throat*)."[37]

Using its earnings from *Ninja Turtles* and the *Nightmare on Elm Street* films (1984–89), New Line set up Fine Line in 1990 to distribute art-house productions, while New Line itself began "to operate more like a major studio . . . especially in its commitment to the establishment of high-grossing mainstream franchise properties."[38] These properties included the *Lord of the Rings* films—*The Fellowship of the Ring* (2001), *The Two Towers* (2002), and *The Return of the King* (2003)—which were planned as a trilogy from the outset. Each cost over $93 million. They were released on 3,359, 3,622, and 3,703 screens respectively in successive Christmas periods in North America, and between them grossed nearly $3 billion worldwide.[39] By then New Line had been part of Time Warner for nearly a decade. The similarity between the *Lord of the Rings* films and the high-cost "franchise" properties produced and released on an ultrawide basis by the majors is therefore, perhaps, hardly surprising, though there are also parallels to be drawn between New Line's commercial policies and those adopted by Carolco and DEG in the 1980s. The differences here lie not in the scale or the commercial nature of the kinds of films produced, but in New Line's access to the financial resources and distribution facilities of a major conglomerate.

Aside from *sex, lies, and videotape,* the big breakthrough for Miramax came with the release of *The Crying Game,* a British art-house production, in 1993. *The Crying Game* earned $26,583,302 in North American rentals. It was followed by *Pulp Fiction* (1994), *The English Patient* (1996), and *Good Will Hunting* (1997), which earned $35.6 million, $41 million, and $61 million respectively. It was also followed by the *Scream* series (1996–2000), three self-referential slasher films that among them grossed $293,473,736. *Scream* and its successors were produced by Dimension Films, a genre-film label established by Miramax in 1992 and an equivalent to subsequent labels such as Sony's Screen Gems (1997) and Universal's Rogue Pictures (2004). In 1993 Miramax was acquired by Disney. From that point on most of the major companies set about acquiring or setting up specialist subsidiaries and classics divisions. Other examples included Sony Pictures Classics (1992), Fox Searchlight (1994), Paramount Classics (1998), Warner Independent Pictures (2003), and Universal's Focus Features, which was established via the acquisition and merger of Good Machine with USA Films (itself the product of a merger among October Films, Gramercy Pictures, and USA Home Entertainment) in 2002.[40] By then, the majors' specialized divisions had "practically abandoned the films they were created to release" and a new generation of independents began to emerge, among them Lionsgate (1997), IFC Films (1999), Magnolia Pictures (2001), Newmarket Films (2002), Freestyle Releasing (2003), The Weinstein Company (2005), and Picturehouse (2005).[41]

The setting-up of classics divisions had initially been prompted by the inability of the majors "to fight soaring costs on film sets" and by the fact that the majors were missing out on potential income from specialized markets.[42] But it was also a mark of their corporate power. Having themselves been involved in a series of realignments, mergers, and takeovers in the late 1980s and 1990s, the majors could now afford to acquire and fund independent expertise alongside their more mainstream commercial activities and alongside the production of ever more expensive blockbuster films. During the 1980s, they had profited from burgeoning demand and ancillary growth not by producing more films, but by distributing big-budget productions by the likes of Carolco and DEG. During the 1990s, as key components in multimedia conglomerates, they tended to cofund and distribute midrange productions by the likes of Morgan Creek and to diversify their portfolio by acquiring or setting up specialized classics divisions while producing more expensive films themselves or in partnership with other major companies. In these ways, financial risks were minimized and avenues of potential profit maximized.

The Majors

In 1980 the Hollywood majors—the eight members of the MPAA—were Fox, Columbia, Warner Bros., Universal, Paramount, MGM, UA, and Walt Disney. Columbia,

Fox, MGM, and Disney were stand-alone companies. UA, Warners, Paramount, and Universal were components in diversified conglomerates: Transamerica, WCI, Gulf + Western, and MCA respectively. Disney, UA, and MGM were struggling. In 1981, MGM acquired UA from Transamerica, and UA effectively "disappeared as a major, self-contained production and distribution company."[43] The following year Columbia was purchased by Coca-Cola and the year after that CBS, HBO, and Columbia set up Tri-Star as an instant major.

Coca-Cola's acquisition of Columbia was premised on its perception that

The entertainment business in general and the motion picture business in particular are undergoing significant changes, primarily due to technological developments which have resulted in the availability of alternative forms of leisure time entertainment, including expanded pay and cable television, video cassettes, video discs and video games. During the last several years, revenues from licensing of motion pictures to network television have decreased, while revenues from pay television, video cassettes and video discs have increased. However, the level of theatrical success remains a crucial factor in generating revenues in these ancillary markets.[44]

Coca-Cola's acquisition was a sign of things to come. From this point on, most of the major film companies sought or found themselves involved either in mergers and acquisitions or in programs of corporate reorganization designed to take advantage of new ancillary markets and new sources of ancillary income. Unlike Coca-Cola's acquisition of Columbia, though, most were premised on obvious synergies among and between the businesses, products, and markets in which the companies were already involved. It was on this basis that Gulf + Western shed more than fifty companies during the course of the 1980s and changed its name to Paramount Communications Inc. in 1989, that News Corporation acquired Fox and Metromedia Television in 1985, that Sony bought CBS records in 1986 and Columbia Pictures in 1989, that Matsushita bought MCA in 1990, and that WCI merged with Time Inc. to create Time Warner in 1989. Alongside them, Disney and the recently formed Orion were the only major companies to ride out the merger wave, though Orion created Orion Home Video and syndicated a number of television programs prior to its demise in 1992, and Disney expanded internally by setting up the Disney Channel and Touchstone (the latter to produce and distribute a wider range of theatrical features). Disney went on to acquire Capital Cities/ABC, a major broadcast television network, in 1995. A year earlier, the cable company Viacom had acquired Paramount Communications and Steven Spielberg, David Geffen, and Jeffrey Katzenberg had set up DreamWorks, the first new major Hollywood studio in sixty years. A year later, Time Warner acquired Turner Broadcasting.

Alongside these developments, synergies of another sort gave rise to the increasing involvement of at least some of the major companies in theatrical film exhibition. The late 1970s and early 1980s had seen record box-office figures for blockbuster hits and the release of more and more films on more and more screens. By the late 1980s and early 1990s,

Even when the majors sponsor an offbeat US film, its ultimate release pattern is increasingly forced to accommodate more screens and a faster playoff. This year, for example, Tri-Star's *The Freshman* [1990] bowed six screens to upbeat reviews, but instead of the usual platform release, it was on 1,040 screens in its second week with disappointing results.[45]

By the mid-1980s widespread theatrical exposure was increasingly viewed as a key ingredient in the profile and commercial potential of films in ancillary markets, as we have seen. Encouraged by the Reagan administration's laissez-faire attitude to business regulation, and prompted by a boom in theater construction and renovation, by a desire to control, simplify, and expedite the booking of films and the paying of rentals, and by the need to ensure theatrical outlets to showcase their films, a number of the major companies began to acquire (or to reacquire) theaters.

Although ticket sales remained relatively constant at approximately 1.06 billion per year throughout the 1980s,[46] ticket price inflation, the blockbuster earnings generated by a handful of ever more expensive wide releases, and the increasing demand for more and more play dates had already led exhibitors to upgrade their theaters and exhibition circuits to increase the number of screens: "Theater construction was up 14 percent in 1983, and by mid-decade exhibition was seeing the biggest yearly increases in total screens since the late 1940s. From 1980 to 1989, the nation's screen total jumped from 17,590 to 23,132," MCA had acquired a 30 percent stake in Cineplex-Odeon and Tri-Star, Gulf + Western and Warners had "all purchased major theater chains, marking their explicit return to classic vertical integration of production, distribution and exhibition."[47]

Alongside the opportunities for horizontal integration opened up by the new ancillary markets and the new media conglomerates in the late 1980s and early 1990s, vertical integration took its place in a new corporate system that was increasingly geared to "the creation of 'filmed entertainment' software, to be viewed through several different windows and transported to several different platforms maintained by the other divisions of diversified media corporations."[48] Theatrical exhibition sites were the first of these windows. Access to them remained a key corporate priority, especially in an era in which opening weekend performances and a logic of wide and instant impact increasingly governed the release of most major films. The major U.S. exhibition circuits all added to the number of screens in the early 1990s and a wave of "megaplex" theaters with up to twenty-four screens was inaugurated in 1994. By 1995 there were 29,613 screens in the United States and Canada. By 1999 there were 39,759.[49] As Charles Acland has pointed out, theater attendance grew in the United States in the mid-1990s, but patterns of attendance among and between different sectors of the population were distinctly uneven: in 1997 Caucasians made up 70 percent of the domestic audience, and in 1998 city dwellers outnumbered those who lived in small-town and rural areas. Those aged between sixteen and thirty-nine attended more often than older and younger people, and "avid" attenders, those who saw more than one film per fortnight, amounted to no more than 8 percent of the U.S. population but accounted for over 50 percent of ticket sales.[50]

The increase in the number of screens encouraged wider openings and wider and faster playoffs, even for films designed to open on a platform or limited basis. In 1992, D. Barry Reardon defined a wide release as the opening of a film on anywhere between 800 and 1,800 screens.[51] He cited the example of *Batman,* which opened even wider, on 2,194 screens, on June 23, 1989. By 1994, releases on 2,500 screens or more were becoming common and were often identified as "very wide" or "ultrawide" openings in the industry's press. Among those released that year were *Beverly Hills Cop III* (on 2,748 screens), *Star Trek Generations* (2,681), *Interview with the Vampire: The Vampire Chronicles* (2,604), and *Maverick* (2,537).[52] A decade later, Daniel Fellman defined a wide release as an "opening in between 700 and 3,000-plus theatres," citing *Ocean's Eleven,* which opened in 3,075 theaters on 7 December 2001, as an example.[53] His use of the term *theatres* should be noted. Given the nature of multiplex theaters, which permit a single print to service several adjacent auditoria simultaneously, the number of screens involved in a wide release is and was always higher than that; when *Harry Potter and the Sorcerer's Stone* opened in a then-record 3,672 theaters on November 16, 2001, it was actually shown on over 8,000 screens. However, it should also be noted that while the number of screens involved in wide openings increased during the late 1990s and early 2000s (2,000-theater releases were the norm rather than the exception by 1998), the number of wide releases fell from a high of 155 in 1996 to 139 in 2001.[54]

According to Fellman as well as to Reardon, a platform release entailed the launching of a picture "in single, exclusive openings in New York and Los Angeles, where it sits garnering reviews and word-of-mouth before spreading out . . . slowly."[55] Fellman cites *My Dog Skip* (2000). Reardon cites *Driving Miss Daisy,* Warners' adaptation of a Pulitzer Prize–winning play about the relationship between a Jewish widow and her black chauffeur. However, *Miss Daisy*

opened so strongly in four theatres in New York and Los Angeles that first weekend, mid-December 1989, that more theatres were immediately added in those cities through the Christmas period. . . . By Martin Luther King Day in January we were up to 277 screens in perhaps 100 markets; by January 31 we were up to 895 screens. . . . There was an intermediate step to 1,302 screens by February 14, 1990, increasing to 1,432 two weeks later, up to 1,668 by the end of March.[56]

So rapidly did *Miss Daisy* expand that it shared some of the characteristics of a limited release, one that "might open a picture in a few theatres in New York, Los Angeles and Toronto, then skip the platforms and move right to a wide release." Reardon cites *The Accidental Tourist,* "which opened exclusively at Christmas 1988, took advantage of good reviews and jumped to over 800 screens the first weekend in January."[57]

The use of limited and platform releasing for major productions and box-office hits has largely been ignored in accounts of post-1960s U.S. cinema. However, 1970s films such as *A Star Is Born, Close Encounters of the Third Kind, The Deer Hunter, Apocalypse Now,* even *Star Wars* could all be described as either limited or platform releases. So, too, could early 1980s films such as *Ragtime, Gandhi,* and *Once upon a Time in America.* Alongside Christmas comedies such as *Home Alone* (1990), *Kindergarten Cop, Hook* (1991), *Mrs. Doubtfire* (1993), and *The Santa Clause* (1994), all of which were widely released, Disney used platform releasing to launch a new generation of animated features in the post-Thanksgiving holiday period, among them *The Little Mermaid* (1989), *Beauty and the Beast* (1991), and *Aladdin* (1992).[58] This particular period had been used to launch adult-oriented, prestige productions, especially those designed to win Oscars, for many years. These too were often released on a platform or limited basis. Thus in addition to earning $50.5 million in domestic rentals, *Driving Miss Daisy* won Oscars for Best Picture, Best Actress, and Best Adapted Screenplay. *Glory,* a film about the first black regiment raised by the North in the Civil War, opened on three screens on December 15, 1989. It widened from six to eight then to 392 and 402 screens. By March, it was playing on 811 screens, and although it earned only $13 million in domestic rentals it won Oscars for Cinematography, Sound, and Best Supporting Actor. Later that year, *Dances with Wolves* opened on fourteen screens on November 9 following premieres in Washington DC and Los Angeles. It widened rapidly, in classic limited manner, to 1,048 screens a fortnight later. By the end of its run, it had earned $81,537,971 in domestic rentals and won seven Oscars, including Best Picture and Best Director.

Dances with Wolves was part of a cycle of westerns that emerged in the wake of *Silverado, Pale Rider* (both 1985), *Young Guns,* and the CBS network's enormously successful TV adaptation of *Lonesome Dove* (1989). Like all these programs and films, *Dances with Wolves* is marked by a particularly expansive sense of space in its frontier settings. As it follows its protagonist, John Dunbar (Kevin Costner), from east to west, "The tight close-ups and medium-distance shots of the opening section are replaced by a series of long shots." The film makes increasing use of the contours of the landscape and the Panavision frame to stage entrances and exits, appearances and disappearances, and unexpected encounters of various kinds, and Dunbar is increasingly "dwarfed by . . . panoramic vistas, particularly in a later section when Dunbar and the Sioux hunt a vast buffalo herd across the grasslands."[59]

In addition to *The Last of the Mohicans* and *Maverick,* the western cycle came to include *Far and Away* and *Unforgiven* (both 1992), *Tombstone* (1993), and *Bad Girls* and *Wyatt Earp* (both 1994). *Far and Away* was 140 minutes long, *Wyatt Earp,* 195, and *Dances with Wolves,* 181. All three films were marked by epic ambitions and in an earlier era might well have been roadshown. Indeed, the possibility of reviving roadshows had been discussed in the trade press and *Far and Away* was shot on 65 mm for release in Panavision Super 70 mm in select engagements.[60] But a roadshow run was never envisaged, and both *Far and Away* and *Wyatt Earp* were

Compositional width and depth in *Dances with Wolves* (1990).

widely released in the summer. *Dances with Wolves* was the only film in the cycle to receive a limited release.

Limited releasing itself, though, did not disappear. A series of lengthy and expensive biopics, among them *Born on the Fourth of July* (1989), *Bugsy* (1991), *J.F.K.* (1991), *Malcolm X* (1992), *Chaplin* (1992), *Schindler's List* (1993), and *Nixon* (1995), all received limited releases (and Oscars and Oscar nominations) in the late 1980s and early 1990s.[61] Most of these films cost more than they earned in domestic rentals. But the $18 million *Born on the Fourth of July* earned $36,803,148 and the $25 million *Schindler's List* earned $44,164,190. Along with a number of other, more obviously popular films aimed at adults, they were among the box-office hits of the period. Some were widely released. Some were released on a limited basis. Aside from *Dances with Wolves* and *Schindler's List,* the latter included *Rain Man* (1988), *Parenthood, Steel Magnolias* (1989), *Ghost, Pretty Woman* (both 1990), *Fried Green Tomatoes* (1991), *Unforgiven, Philadelphia* (1993), *Forrest Gump* (1994), and *Apollo 13* (1995).[62]

Despite the fact that platform and limited releases were increasingly regarded as a risk because they essentially involved "releasing a film several times," they continued and continue to be used to launch adult-oriented prestige fare in the post-Thanksgiving period.[63] In addition to musicals such as *Evita* (1996), *Moulin Rouge!* (2001), and *Chicago* (2002), examples include *Amistad* (1997), *The Thin Red Line* (1998), *The Hurricane* (1999), *Traffic* (2000), *The Royal Tenenbaums* (2001), *Million Dollar Baby* (2004), *The New World* (2005), and *Letters from Iwo Jima* (2006). Christmas-themed productions such as *The Santa Clause 2* (2002), family blockbusters such as the Harry Potter films (2001–7), and animated features such as *Toy Story* (1995) and *Toy Story 2* (1999) continued and continue to be released on an ultra-wide basis in the post-Thanksgiving period as well. They had by then been joined by *Titanic* (1997), the most expensive and successful of the 1990s blockbusters, and by *GoldenEye* (1995) and a number of later James Bond films.

Coproduced by Fox and Paramount and released by the latter domestically and the former abroad, *Titanic* had cost $200 million. It grossed $488,194,015 in North America and $1,209 million in foreign markets. Surpassing *Star Wars* as the highest grossing film of all time, its "combined worldwide box office, estimated retail video and soundtrack sales, and the sale of US broadcasting rights to NBC" amounted by

January 1999 to over $3.2 billion.[64] It thus established a new set of benchmarks for blockbuster films. But its Christmastime release was in this respect somewhat anomalous. Although there had been a 38 percent increase in weekly ticket sales in the Christmas season between 1968 and 1989, weekly sales in the summer (Memorial Day to Labor Day) had increased by 43 percent. By 1990, the latter had therefore largely displaced the former as the favored season for releasing "special effects extravaganzas" and other large-scale, high-cost productions.[65] Every year since then there has been a scramble for summer release slots and screens, fevered speculation has centered on the commercial potential of the majors' most expensive "tentpole" releases, and production, print, and publicity budgets have increased alongside the number of screens booked for opening weekends: "Production budgets rose 60% in real terms in the 1990s. In 1999 the major film companies spent a total of $2.55 billion on advertising. Only the automobile and retail industries spent more."[66]

Since 1990, the biggest blockbusters have generally been of four principal kinds: (1) Comic book adaptations and science-fiction films such as *Dick Tracy* (1990); the sequels to *Batman* (1992–97); *Alien³* (1992) and *Alien Resurrection* (1997); *Jurassic Park* and its sequels (1993–2001); *Independence Day* (1996); *Armageddon* and *Godzilla* (both 1998); *The Matrix* and its sequels (1999–2003); three more *Star Wars* films (1999–2005); *Planet of the Apes* (2001); *Spider-Man* and its sequels (2002–7); *King Kong* and *War of the Worlds* (both 2005); *Batman Begins* (2005) and *The Dark Knight* (2008); and *Superman Returns* (2006). (2) Action-adventure films with contemporary settings such as the sequels to *Die Hard* (1988) (1990–2007); *Lethal Weapon 3* (1991) and *Lethal Weapon 4* (1998); *True Lies* (1994); *Speed* and its sequel (1994 and 1997); *Mission: Impossible* and its sequels (1996–2000); *Con Air* and *Air Force One* (both 1997); and *The Bourne Identity* and its sequels (2002–7). (3) Historical action films and epics such as *Braveheart* (1995), *Saving Private Ryan* (1998), *Gladiator* (2000), *Pearl Harbor* (2001), and *Master and Commander: The Far Side of the World* (2003); *Pirates of the Caribbean: The Curse of the Black Pearl* and its sequels (2003–7); *King Arthur, Troy* (both 2004), and *Kingdom of Heaven* (2006). (4) A new generation of disaster films that included *Twister* (1996), *Volcano* (1997), *Deep Impact* (1998), *The Perfect Storm* (2000), and *The Day after Tomorrow* (2004).[67]

Nearly all these films have been characterized as prizing action and effects-laden spectacle over complex characterization and finely tuned drama. However, they are neither devoid of narratives nor of a capacity to generate involvement in the actions and fates of their characters. In favoring "moral polarization, emotional intensification, and sensationalism," and in using stock "situations" as the building blocks of their stories, they derive their aesthetic from nineteenth-century melodrama, as Scott Higgins and others have pointed out.[68] In the nineteenth century, situations "tended to be discrete moments, often moments of suspense or deadlock when characters are arranged in seemingly inescapable dilemmas. It was the playwright's charge to arrange, motivate, and resolve stock situations, a method that could yield plots of rather loose plausibility and with relatively broad latitude for coincidence." Among them were

"Loss of Loved Ones," "Crime Pursued by Vengeance," "Appearance of Rescuer to the Condemned," and "Disaster, a Natural Catastrophe," variants on which can be found in nearly all the films listed above.[69] Rather than creating a conflict between spectacle and narrative, situations like these "act as a bridge, a narrative element conceived independently as visually sensational."[70] Along with scene-setting sequences, they also often act as entry points for the deployment of special effects. Rather than characterize these films as examples of a new "Cinema of Attractions," a cinema akin to the earliest and shortest attention-grabbing films, it might therefore be better to characterize them as a "Cinema of Spectacular Situations."[71]

Mention should also be made here of animated features such as *The Lion King* (1994), *Pocahontas* (1995), *The Hunchback of Notre Dame* (1996), *Mulan* (1998), *Tarzan* (1999), and *Finding Nemo* (2003). These films also deploy spectacular situations and melodramatic narratives, often mixing them with comedy, and often using songs as additional sources of spectacle and as a means of stating their characters' dilemmas. They were all also summer releases. Costing an estimated $79.3 million, $55 million, $70 million, and $70 million respectively, the first four, which were produced and released by Disney, were accorded exclusive premieres or limited releases. Along with *Jurassic Park* and *Independence Day*, *The Lion King* and *Pocahontas* were among the biggest box-office hits of the 1990s. *Jurassic Park* grossed $357.1 million domestically and $556 million abroad; *The Lion King*, $289.9 and $341.4 million; *Pocahontas*, $141.6 and $176 million; and *Independence Day*, $306,169,220 and $510,800,000. Like the other summer extravaganzas listed above, and, indeed, like those released at Christmas and on occasion at other points in the year as well, they all served to consolidate the trend toward "ultra-high-budget" productions capable of exploitation as "events" on a global scale. They also served as vehicles for digital effects and other digital technologies.

Globalization

As we have seen, foreign markets, industries, companies, films, facilities, technologies, locations, and personnel have been important to the U.S. film industry in various ways since the 1890s. However, the late 1980s and the 1990s witnessed the advent of two key developments. The first was the acquisition and ownership of major U.S. film

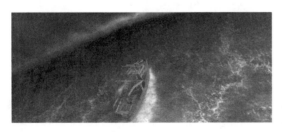

A spectacular situation in *The Perfect Storm* (2000).

companies by foreign corporations. The second was a reversal in the proportion of annual box-office income earned in foreign and domestic markets. The former began with the acquisitions made by News Corporation (an Australian-based company) and by Sony and Matsushita in the late 1980s and early 1990s. Time Warner restructured its film and cable operations in partnership with Toshiba and Itoh in 1992, and Matsushita sold MCA to the Canadian company Seagram in 1995. Seagram was taken over by Vivendi, a French conglomerate, in 2000, though MCA and most of its holdings were later acquired by NBC. Like the other takeovers, mergers, and instances of corporate reorganization since the mid-1980s, these were designed to take advantage of international synergies, distribution channels, and sources of income and capital as a means of generating profits on a global scale.

These profits were soon forthcoming. In 1989, foreign rentals yielded $1.35 billion. Japan was the leading foreign market for the fifth consecutive year, followed by Canada, France, West Germany, the United Kingdom and Ireland, Spain, Italy, Australia, Sweden, and Brazil. Two years later, foreign rentals yielded $1.44 billion. A year after that, U.S. Christmas blockbusters began to be released on a more internationally synchronized basis during the end-of-year and New Year holiday periods.[72] Then in 1994, for the first time since 1973, "offshore rental—the amount of box office coin returned to distributors—surpassed domestic rentals." That year, *Forrest Gump* grossed $298.1 million in the United States and Canada and $341.4 million abroad; *True Lies,* $146.2 and $208.1 million; *The Flintstones,* $130.5 and $211 million; *Schindler's List,* $91.1 and $209 million; and *Speed,* $121.2 million and $161.6 million. Overall, "*Variety*'s annual survey of top worldwide boxoffice champs totaled $8.34 billion."[73]

Fueled by an increase in "the worldwide demand for films" in the 1980s, "the result of such factors as economic growth in Western Europe, the Pacific Rim, and Latin America, the end of the Cold War, the commercialisation of state broadcasting systems, and the development of new distribution technologies," the majors had expanded their overseas operations and formed partnerships with foreign investors as well as their new overseas conglomerate owners.[74] Under pressure from the majors and their partners, a number of European countries began to upgrade their theaters. Here and in South America, there was an expansion in the number of screens and multiplex theaters, many of them funded, owned, or operated by U.S. exhibition chains and Hollywood conglomerates or their local partners.[75] By 1998, there were 22,252 screens in Western Europe and 3,640 in South America as compared to 20,400 and 3,382 a decade earlier. There was a decline in numbers elsewhere, but an increase in faster playoffs and in the synchronization of ultrawide summer releases in the United States with a wide release in the summer abroad.[76] From that point on, it became feasible to consider the possibility of opening some films "everywhere" at once. In this respect, as Acland points out, *The Matrix Revolutions* (2003), which was released in November 2003, "may be an extreme instance of wide international release, but is also a harbinger of a trend toward simultaneity. Within the first week of its release, its 10,013 prints had premièred in 107 territories, and on 18 IMAX screens. Reportedly, co-producers Warner Bros. and Village Roadshow [an Australian-based cinema chain] coordinated many of the premières to begin at exactly the same time."[77]

By 1995, ancillary earnings from abroad had grown to such an extent that they now outweighed foreign box-office earnings.[78] Income from video copies of films now outstripped income from theatrical exhibition both in domestic and foreign markets. A reconfiguration of the ratio and relationship between the private and public consumption of films had occurred on a global scale. The introduction of the DVD (Digital Video or Versatile Disc) in Japan in 1996, in the United States in 1997, and in Western Europe in 1998 brought a new technology into the equation, one that had already transformed film production and one that had begun to redefine the possibilities of film distribution, film exhibition, and, indeed, the very nature of films themselves.

Digital Technology

Digital technology works by sampling and/or assembling audio or visual fields in the form of mathematically coded units or "bits" of information. It was initially used in Hollywood for effects in science-fiction films. In *Westworld* it was used to represent a robotic gunslinger's point of view, in *Alien* to simulate the graphics on computer screens, in *Tron* (1982) to create the environment of a computer game peopled by electronic characters, and in *Star Trek: The Wrath of Khan* to represent the simulation of the effects of a device designed to transform dead moons into habitable environments. Although its use in *Alien* was not particularly marked, its use in all four films was thus as spotted as the initial deployment of sound, color, large-gauge, and large-screen technologies had been earlier on in Hollywood's history.

This was equally true of its use in subsequent science-fiction and fantasy films. *Willow, The Abyss* (1989), and *Terminator 2* used digital "morphing" to represent the generation or transformation of otherworldly beings; *RoboCop 2* (1990), the expressions on a cyber monster's face; and *Jurassic Park,* an array of different kinds of dinosaurs. Digital effects were also used to represent "feats impossible to achieve in the physical world," feats that were usually performed by alien beings or superheroes rather than by ordinary human characters.[79] In each case, digital spectacle was linked more to narrative actions and those who performed them than it was to the setting in

The "flocking" of planes in *Pearl Harbor* (2001).

which they took place, though some of the dinosaurs that inhabit the Park in *Jurassic Park* function largely as spectacular attractions in a particular on-screen environment, as animate beings to be gazed at in wonder as much by the film's on-screen visitors as by its own spectators.

The use of digital technology in animated features was spotted as well. In *The Lion King*, it was used in the wildebeest stampede. Here, in a sequence reminiscent of the one in *Snow White and the Seven Dwarfs* discussed in chapter 5, a computer program was used to group and to individualize the diverse movements of animated creatures. (Similar techniques were used to create the flocking and dispersal of airplanes, flies, and bats in *Pearl Harbor, The Mummy* [1999], and *Batman Begins,* respectively.) In *Beauty and the Beast,* digital technology was used in the ballroom scene to produce an effect of unusual spatial mobility as Beauty and the Beast dance round the room and as our view of them circles and swirls then swoops up to encompass them from a position high-up near the ceiling. This effect was produced by compositing the hand-drawn movements of the couple against a constantly changing background perspective produced by computer technology. It thus involved a virtual camera movement. Virtual camera movements were common in animated films, but hitherto they had been produced by traditional hand- or machine-drawn techniques. They were soon to feature extensively in live-action films as well, where they often also involved compositing digital characters with human actors in wholly or partly computer-created spaces. In these instances, as in purely animated films, motion parallax, the fact that large, fast-moving objects appear closer than smaller and slower ones, became key to perceptions of spatial depth and help to explain the ubiquity of real and virtual camera movements in so many contemporary blockbuster films.[80] They also account for the effects of spatial expansiveness produced by the computerized movements of characters like Tarzan, Spider-Man, and Superman as they swing or fly through trees or between buildings. A variant was produced in *The Matrix* by digitizing a set of simultaneous still images taken by an array of cameras in different positions and processing them in a computer in order to produce an apparently continuous camera movement circling around characters who appear to be frozen in time, midair, and mid-action. Here, an effect of spatial and optical ubiquity is produced not by the real or apparent movement of objects or characters, nor by combining movements of this kind with those of a real or virtual camera, but by virtual camera movement alone. Elsewhere in the film, different rates of apparent camera movement, character movement, object movement, and stillness combine to produce highly distinctive forms of spatiotemporal organization, presentation, and perception. Aylish Wood calls these forms "timespaces" and stresses the extent to which they are capable of multiplying or redistributing the focus of spectators' attention.[81]

The use of CGI (Computer Generated Imagery) in animated films led to digital versions of the parting of the Red Sea and a chariot race in *The Prince of Egypt* (1998), each of them deriving from stunt- and effects-driven sequences in live-action epics (*The Ten Commandments* on the one hand, and *Ben-Hur* and *The Fall of the Roman*

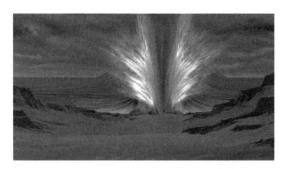

The parting of the Red Sea in *The Prince of Egypt* (1998).

Empire on the other). Two years later, the capacities of CGI enabled *Gladiator* to revive the epic in partial live-action form and on a scale that would have been prohibitively expensive had it not been for CGI sets, effects, and crowds. Like the CGI sci-fi, disaster, and action-adventure films, *Gladiator* and its successors were marked by an increasing use of "digital verticality": a pronounced use of height and of vertical movement in sets and settings, in virtual camera movement (the ballroom sequence in *Beauty and the Beast* is an early example), and in the actions of characters.[82]

By then, *Toy Story* had become the world's first computer-animated feature and *The Phantom Menace* had become one of the first films in which digital characters intermingled with human actors in an almost entirely synthetic environment, and in which digitally enhanced or generated shots far outnumbered those that were not.[83] From that point on, as CGI has been increasingly used to enhance or replace photographically recorded imagery, it has become increasingly difficult to distinguish among animated films, live-action films, and hybrids on either a technological or philosophical basis. ("Posthumous performances" by the likes of Oliver Reed, who died during the production of *Gladiator,* and by Laurence Olivier, whose voice and face were sampled for *Sky Captain and the World of Tomorrow* [2004], are evidence of that.) Disaster films still tended to operate an apparent distinction between their CGI ingredients and their more conventionally photographed ones by reserving the former for scenes in which computerized "natural" phenomena function as spectacular antagonists to conventionally photographed human characters. Science-fiction, fantasy, and comic-book films still tended to mark many of their digital effects as "special" and many of their digital characters as non- or super-human. But digital technology was not the sole province of high-cost productions, and distinctions like these were hard to maintain in films that used CGI to represent ordinary, everyday worlds and their inhabitants as well as extraordinary, historically distant, or otherworldly ones.

Since the early 1990s, digital technology had also been used to enhance and synthesize the sounds as well as the sights of features like these. Although sound recording and mixing had involved digital techniques for a number of years, and although CDs (compact discs) had been available since the early 1980s, the first digital soundtracks and the first digital sound systems did not appear until the advent of CDS in 1990,

Dolby Digital Stereo (DDS, originally SR-D) in 1992, and Sony Dynamic Digital Sound (SDDS) and Digital Theatre Systems (DTS) in 1993. CDS was a short-lived format in which six-track digital sound information could be encoded on both 35 mm and 70 mm prints, but without standard 35 mm optical soundtracks for cinemas unable to play digital.[84] DDS involved "six discrete channels of sound, digitally encoded and optically printed onto the actual film soundtrack"; SDDS "eight discrete channels: five behind the screen, two stereo surrounds and a sub-woofer"; and DTS, an "audio system that is separate from the film strip, having been recorded onto digital compact disc, and replayed on a CD-Rom machine that reads an optical timecode track on the film strip in order to keep sound and image in synchronization."[85] Like DDS, DTS was cheaper to install than SDDS. It was used to premiere *Jurassic Park* and thus also had the advantage of showcasing the film's sonic density and the system's dynamic range:

In the scene in which the T-Rex attacks the truck containing two children, the soundtrack begins simply with the sound of pouring rain. This sparseness helps build suspense. The soundtrack is then broadened by the dull, resonant thud of the T-Rex's footsteps as they disturb the surface of a glass of water. The noises become increasingly layered as the fence wires begin to snap and its frame creaks under pressure from the dinosaur. When the dinosaur eventually attacks, the soundtrack reaches its fullest complexity: the roars of the T-Rex, the screams of the children, squelching of mud, occasional snatches of dialogue and the continual pouring rain are clearly discernible from one another, while simultaneously combining to form a dense body of sound that complements the visuals.[86]

As with digital visuals, digital sound was not restricted to "special" moments and scenes. In general, digital sound systems allow for more ambient sound and facilitate greater sonic detail and texture, even in ordinary settings or conversation scenes, than analog soundtracks. They facilitate the fabrication and mixing of sound in a manner and to a degree that echoes the synthetic nature of many contemporary image tracks, while generating an all-enveloping sense of space of their own:

Digital reverb units . . . allow engineers both to simulate the sound of prescribed spaces (types of room, qualities of texture) and to localise sound within a 360 horizontal and limited vertical, location . . . to dismantle the sense of audio as a "surface" projected from stereo speakers by creating, instead, the sensation that it is "all around."[87]

By the late 1990s, the advent of DVDs, digital television sets, and domestic cinema systems allowed this sensation to be experienced at home as well as in public auditoria.

Unlike laser discs and prerecorded videos, DVDs were an instant success, adding an important new tier of release and an important new source of ancillary revenue. One of the reasons for this was that the industry's major conglomerates owned or controlled the "home entertainment" industry by the time DVDs were launched. Another was that the studios made their libraries available on DVD very quickly. In addition, despite the fact that DVD necessitated the purchase of a player, and despite the fact that players were initially unable to record and therefore to time-shift, DVDs were more compact and durable than video and were initially priced at between $14 and $20 in the United States in order to encourage sell-through sales—and thus put larger portions of the proceeds in the majors' coffers. In 1999, "DVDs represented 11 percent of the studios' home entertainment revenues, and videos represented 30 percent. By 2003, DVDs represented 76 percent of the studios' home entertainment revenues and video rentals only 6 percent."[88] By 2002, sales of DVDs had overtaken sales of videos; by 2003 there were an estimated 189.6 million DVD households worldwide;[89] and by 2004, "90 percent of all US households owning TV sets had a VCR (98.9 million) and 60 percent had DVD players. . . . In that same year they spent $27 billion on DVD software while overseas consumers spent $24.6 billion. Meanwhile consumer spending on the box office was roughly half that amount."[90]

The revenue added by the sales of DVDs to the income earned by films soon became significant. According to Philip Drake, the production and publicity costs of *Spider-Man* amounted to $289 million; its worldwide box-office gross to $821.7 million; its earnings from the sale of U.S. TV rights to $60 million; its domestic video earnings to $89.2 million; and its DVD earnings to $338.8 million.[91] DVD also added to the windows of release (theatrical, pay cable and satellite television, video, and network television) and helped speed up the rate at which most films moved from window to window. This rate had already been on the increase, largely because video releases were heavily dependent on theatrical publicity campaigns and on initial theatrical impact. DVD has increased the rate still further, partly as a means of increasing sales of players and discs, and partly because its digital base made it particularly prone to Internet piracy. *Terminator 3: Rise of the Machines,* for instance, "opened in theaters in early July 2003 in the United States and Canada and in other major markets around the world in July and August—and was released on video and DVD on November 4, 2003."[92]

By then, digital video games had become a further source of ancillary revenue (as well as a source of material for major productions such as *Lara Croft: Tomb Raider* [2001] and *Resident Evil* [2002]), and digital projection had already been used in the theatrical exhibition of films like *The Phantom Menace* and *Toy Story 2.* Digital TV sets and high-definition DVD formats had also been introduced, and the majors had begun to explore the possibility of using the Internet as a means of distributing features. All the while, the capacities of DVD have been increasingly used for additional features such as commentaries, extended or alternative versions, and documentaries about the making of the film, its historical significance, or its place in the careers of its personnel. These features are often available in multidisc special editions, and these editions generally cost more than standard ones. As such they feed into a culture of cinematic connoisseurship, as Barbara Klinger has pointed out.[93] They also introduce an element of differentiation into an otherwise standardized market and as such recall the differentiations in format, length, and cost associated in previous eras with roadshowing and other modes of exclusive exhibition. Unsurprisingly, past roadshow productions such as *Gone with the Wind, Ben-Hur, Cleopatra,* and *The Sound of Music* have been among the films to be recycled on DVD in this way. More recent films have also revived or recalled the roadshow tradition on DVD. When a much longer version of *Kingdom of Heaven* than was released in movie theaters was released with extensive extras in a special four-disc box-set edition in 2007, the first half of the film was preceded by an overture, the second by entr'acte music, and the set was sold in the United States as the "Roadshow Edition." It remains to be seen whether DVD will be replaced by its apparent successor medium, Blu-ray, a high-definition disc system developed by Sony and first introduced in Japan in 2002. After winning out in the format war against Toshiba's rival HD system in 2008, Blu-ray quickly came to compete with DVD for dominance of the high-end home video market.

Another kind of differentiation has been introduced theatrically with the presentation of large-format versions of a number of major Hollywood features on IMAX screens. First developed as an exhibit at Expo '70 in Osaka, Japan, in 1970, IMAX uses 70 mm film stock running at 24 fps but with each frame fifteen perforations tall (compared to the five-perf height of standard 70 mm frames), giving an image area three times larger than that of Todd-AO. It has since been used for the production and presentation of many specially produced films, mostly documentaries running under an hour, at dedicated sites around the world, often in museums and science institutions, using vast screens far larger than those in any conventional cinema. For thirty years IMAX (and its cousin, OMNIMAX, in which IMAX films are projected on a concave rather than a flat screen) formed a wholly separate and distinct branch of film production and exhibition.[94]

But on January 1, 2000, Buena Vista released an IMAX version of *Fantasia 2000,* its successor to the 1940s animated concert movie. This had been preceded in December 1999 by the film's world premiere in 35 mm at Carnegie Hall (Disney's intended venue for the original film), accompanied by a live symphony orchestra. (Other such events took place in London, Paris, Tokyo, and Los Angeles.)[95] Other mainstream Hollywood films were subsequently converted for IMAX projection, among them Disney's *Beauty and the Beast* and *The Lion King,* as well as *Apollo 13, Star Wars, Episode II: Attack of the Clones* (2002), *Spider-Man 2* (2004) and *Spider-Man 3* (2007), *The Matrix Reloaded* (2003) and *The Matrix Revolutions.* The last-named was the first IMAX edition to open simultaneously with the standard 35 mm version. Similar dual-format day-and-date releases were accorded by Warners to *Harry Potter and the Prisoner of Azkaban* (2004), *The Polar Express,* and *Batman Begins,* among others, and this seems likely to become a regular occurrence with future special-effects blockbusters.[96] *The Dark Knight,* the most successful film since *Titanic* with a worldwide theatrical gross of nearly $1 billion, was partly filmed in IMAX and seems likely to give rise to further such hybrids.

Finally, 3-D has seen a resurgence in both IMAX and digital formats. *The Polar Express* and *Beowulf* (2007) are among the feature films that have been released in

IMAX 3-D. In regular theatres, digital 3-D has been used to present mainly animated films, such as *Bolt* (2008); family adventure films, such as *Journey to the Center of the Earth* (2008); horror films, such as *My Bloody Valentine* (2009); and concert movies, such as *U2-3D* and *Hannah Montana & Miley Cyrus: Best of Both Worlds Concert* (both 2008). However, by far the most successful 3-D film to date has been James Cameron's science-fiction fantasy *Avatar*.

Premiered in London on December 10, 2009, and opening in the United States and fifty other countries one week later, *Avatar* was widely reported to have earned a global box-office gross of more than $1 billion within its first month of release. Much like the raising of prices for roadshows and other top attractions in previous decades, theaters exhibiting the film in its digital 3-D version imposed a surcharge on ticket sales, as well as a nominal fee for the purchase of plastic polarized spectacles. *Avatar*'s special effects, "using a combination of computer animation and motion-capture technology,"[97] are employed to represent a forested planet, the race of humanoid beings and other creatures that inhabit it, and the scientific installations and military vehicles that visit it from Earth. In its construction of an extraterrestrial habitat, *Avatar* is as much marked by multiplanar depth arrays as the forest scenes of *Snow White and the Seven Dwarfs*. In the transparent observation ports, holographic viewing monitors, and windowed doors and partitions that characterize its human settings, it features a glass motif as prominently as does *Superman*. In both environments, 3-D is used less to project weapons and other objects outward into the auditorium than to deepen the apparent space enclosed by the screen and to envelop the spectator in a richly detailed, color-saturated fictional world. In this respect, *Avatar* is representative of a renewed attention to visual depth and three-dimensional space that, following several decades of dominance by the shallow focus of telephoto-lens composition, may well come to characterize the digital age.

At the time of writing (January 2010), both Steven Spielberg and Peter Jackson are engaged in planning a trilogy of 3-D movies about the Belgian comic-book hero Tintin, and other studios have pledged to produce films in 3-D formats for both conventional digital and IMAX exhibition, including "instalments of the *Toy Story*, *Ice Age* and *Shrek* franchises."[98] Thus the tradition of special theatrical presentations for the contemporary equivalent of superspecial productions continues into the new technological era.

Conclusion

We have sought in this book to detail the history and characteristics of large-scale, high-cost film productions in the United States from the 1890s to the 2000s. In doing so, we have also noted the scale and the characteristics of a number of major box-office successes. Drawing principally on the trade press and on archival sources, we have sought to relate them to the industrial contexts from which they emerged, into which they intervened, and which some of them, at least, helped to modify. Insofar as these contexts were conditioned by wider social, political, or cultural trends, events, or policies—among them the two world wars, the Great Depression, the advent of radio in the 1920s, and home video in the late 1970s, the spread of television and the diversification of leisure in the 1950s, the restrictions placed on the export of foreign earnings in Western Europe in the late 1940s and 1950s, the history and application of antitrust legislation in the United States from 1910s to the 1980s—they too have been discussed. Attention has also been paid to vaudeville, the legitimate theater, the music and publishing industries, the television and video industries, and other institutions of commercial entertainment, all of which have acted as key sites, models, or sources for the production, distribution, exhibition, presentation, or promotion of films at a number of points in U.S. film history. However, the emphasis has been as much on the deployment of audio-visual technologies and on policies and practices of film production, distribution, and exhibition as on broader contextual factors.

The attention paid to distribution and exhibition is, we would argue, one of the innovative features of this book. The history of roadshowing, a set of practices central in all its various forms to the history and circulation of high-cost productions from the 1910s to the 1970s, has never been told in full before. Nor has the history of what is now called wide or saturation releasing, a set of practices that has hitherto been associated almost exclusively with Hollywood since the mid-1970s, but that has in fact been deployed on an occasional and localized basis since the 1910s, and which came to be used more and more in the postwar era for occasional special productions, routine releases, exploitable imports, and series and sequels such as the James Bond films. As we have seen, the costliest prestige productions were either roadshown or released in other exclusive ways in the 1950s and 1960s. Roadshowing more or less disappeared in the 1970s, to be revived only with the use of IMAX for the exhibition of a number of high-cost Hollywood features in the late 1990s and early 2000s. But while many high-cost films were widely released in regular cinemas from that point on, it was *King Kong* (1976) and *Superman* rather than *Jaws* or *Star Wars* that led the way, and alongside films like these, prestige productions, including high-cost ones, continued and continue to be released on a platform or limited or exclusive basis, as the examples provided by *A Star Is Born* (1976), *The Deer Hunter, Apocalypse Now, Ragtime, Gandhi, Dances with Wolves, Schindler's List, The Thin Red Line,* and *Chicago* make clear.

Roadshowing and exclusive releasing have nearly always been used to pioneer new technologies, especially those that have challenged the prevailing norms of film production and film exhibition. These include IMAX films or IMAX versions of films, which have necessarily been exhibited in specialized cinemas. But they also include films that pioneered a number of sound technologies in the 1900s, 1910s, and 1920s; additive color films; the films made or shown in various large-gauge, large-screen, and wide-screen formats in the late 1920s and early 1930s and in the 1950s and 1960s; the films released with magnetic, Dolby, or digital stereo soundtracks in the 1950s, 1960s, 1970s, and early 1990s; and the films released in 3-D in the early 1950s and the early 1980s. Some of these processes were successful on a long-term basis; others were short-lived. In the broadest sense, most of them have been used to produce or showcase a sense of aural or visual spectacle.

As is well known, the U.S. film industry's output is cyclic. As is also well known, and as we have detailed, the industry underwent a major series of shifts in the 1910s, the late 1920s, the late 1940s and 1950s, the late 1960s and 1970s, and the late 1980s and 1990s. Overall, the history of high-cost films has been variously, sometimes repeatedly, dominated by historical epics, adventure films, and romances; by musicals, war films, disaster films, and westerns; by occasional large-scale comedies; and, more recently, by science-fiction films, action-adventure films, comic-book adaptations, and family-friendly features, many of them animated by hand-drawn or digital means. It has also been littered by record-breaking box-office failures as well as by major box-office successes.

As detailed at various points in this volume, the successes include *The Birth of a Nation, The Covered Wagon, Snow White and the Seven Dwarfs, Gone with the Wind, The Ten Commandments* (1956), *Ben-Hur* (1959), *The Sound of Music, The Exorcist, Jaws, Batman, Jurassic Park, Titanic, Gladiator,* and the *Star Wars, Harry Potter, Pirates of the Caribbean,* and *The Lord of the Rings* series.[1] The failures include a number of often very similar kinds of films, among them *Intolerance, Greed, The Big Trail, Romeo and Juliet* (1936), *Wilson, The Fall of the Roman Empire, The Greatest Story Ever Told, Hello, Dolly!, Heaven's Gate, Ishtar, CutThroat Island, Treasure Planet* (2002), and *The*

Alamo (2004).[2] They also include those whose earnings were considerable, but whose production, distribution, or promotional costs meant that they failed to make a profit when initially released. Among these were *Joan the Woman, Ben-Hur* (1925), *Lost Horizon* (1937), *The Wizard of Oz, Fantasia, A Star Is Born* (1954), *Spartacus, The Bible . . . in the Beginning, A Bridge Too Far, Apocalypse Now, Reds, Annie,* and *Willow.*[3]

It is important to note as well that many of the most successful films have been produced in the low- to medium-budget range or at a cost lower than has otherwise been the norm for major productions. These include *The Kid, The Singing Fool, The Broadway Melody, The Life of Emile Zola, The Bells of St. Mary's* (1945), *The Best Years of Our Lives, Psycho, The Graduate, Love Story, Rocky, Smokey and the Bandit, Driving Miss Daisy, Home Alone, Teenage Mutant Ninja Turtles, There's Something about Mary* (1998), *The Sixth Sense* (1999), *The Blair Witch Project,* and *My Big Fat Greek Wedding* (2002).[4] Unsurprisingly, the generic range of these films is probably broader overall than the range for bigger-budget productions, including as it does a number of unspectacular dramas and comedies as well as a number of low-budget horror films. Equally unsurprisingly, despite the success of films like this, and despite the fact that there has never been an exact correlation between cost and profit, the U.S. film industry has nearly always been tempted to spend more and more on its top-range productions, even in or soon after periods of stagnant growth or recession.

In its earliest decades, high spending was a means of demonstrating representational prowess; representational prowess was seen as a means of making higher-than-average profits; and higher-than-average profits were seen as a means of gaining or retaining industrial power. In the postwar era, representational prowess was seen as a means of reaching adult patrons and regaining higher-than-average profits in a period of audience decline. In more recent years, high spending has been driven not just by the anticipation of high earnings from theatrical screenings, nor just by the prowess provided by the spectacular use of digital technologies, but by the anticipation of even higher earnings from global markets and ancillary sources. These sources now make it much more likely that domestic box-office failures might make a profit, though it is worth pointing out that foreign earnings were rarely recorded systematically in the industry's press from the 1940s to the 1990s, so the extent to which they may have affected the cost-to-earnings ratios of apparent failures prior to that is in many cases hard to determine. The same is true of international productions whose financing depended on the sale of territorial distribution rights, and, for that matter, of productions of any kind whose distributors owned the rights to income from television screenings and video rentals and sales.

Whether as stand-alone entities or as components in corporate conglomerates, Hollywood's principal companies have all contributed in various ways and at various points in time to the history of high-cost productions and box-office hits. However, as we have also seen, independents of various kinds, some of them based in the United States, some abroad, have often played major roles as well. They include D. W. Griffith, Charles Chaplin, Walt Disney, Samuel Goldwyn, David O. Selznick, Sam Spiegel,

Samuel Bronston, Dino De Laurentiis, Harry Saltzman and Albert R. Broccoli, and Alexander and Ilya Salkind. They also include Orion, Carolco, Imagine Entertainment, Castle Rock, and Morgan Creek. In addition, although Cecil B. DeMille was based at Paramount for most of his career, and although George Lucas and Steven Spielberg have worked with Fox and Universal respectively (and Paramount jointly) for lengthy periods, all three were or are relatively autonomous producer-directors, and all three have had a particularly major impact on the nature, history, and scale of big-budget production and of box-office success. Less well known, but worth underlining here, have been the contributions made to the early history of the large-scale roadshow by Pliny Craft, George M. Kleine, and J. J. McCarthy, and to the early history of wide saturation releasing by Selznick, Terry Turner, and Joseph E. Levine.

We have sought throughout this book to relate exceptional productions of one sort or another to the industrial, technological, and aesthetic norms that prevailed in the U.S. film industry at the time these productions were made. We have often been surprised by the lack of consistent or detailed information both on these norms and on their exceptions. We have also been surprised by the lack of published research not just on distribution but also on exhibition. For all the welcome attention that has been paid to specific rural, small-town, or big-city cinemas and their audiences in recent years, we still know very little about the day-to-day operation of domestic theater chains, the booking practices of unaffiliated and overseas theaters, or the specific nature and make-up of the blocks of films offered to theaters by the principal production and distribution companies in the United States in the 1930s and 1940s. There now exist a number of excellent period-based or overview accounts of U.S. film history. In writing this book, we have sought to approach this history from a relatively unexplored angle in order to fill in a number of gaps. In doing so, we also hope to have opened up a number of new ones.

Notes

The following abbreviations for periodical titles have been used in the notes:

FD	*Film Daily*
HR	*The Hollywood Reporter*
KW	*Kinematograph (Kine.) Weekly*
MP	*Motion Picture Herald*
MPW	*The Moving Picture World*
NYDM	*New York Daily Mirror*
NYT	*The New York Times*

Notes to Introduction

1. King, *Spectacular Narratives;* Wood, "Timespaces in Spectacular Cinema," 370–86.
2. Sobchack, "Surge and Splendor," 24–29.
3. Higgins, "Suspenseful Situations"; Neale, *Genre and Hollywood,* 196–202; Brewster and Jacobs, *Theatre to Cinema,* 19–29.
4. Brewster and Jacobs, *Theatre to Cinema,* 8.
5. Hovet, *Realism and Spectacle in* Ben-Hur, passim.

Notes to Chapter 1

1. There is a huge amount of writing on early film in the United States and elsewhere. The most detailed account of early films and early film production, distribution, and exhibition in the United States is Musser, *The Emergence of Cinema.* The best summary accounts are in Abel, *Encyclopedia of Early Cinema.*
2. Singer and Keil, "USA: Production," in Abel, *Encyclopedia of Early Cinema,* 656.
3. Hendricks, "The History of the Kinetoscope," in Balio, *The American Film Industry,* 48.
4. Quinn, "USA: Distribution," in Abel, *Encyclopedia of Early Cinema,* 659; Balio, "Part 1: A Novelty Spawns Small Businesses, 1894–1908," in Balio, *The American Film Industry* (1985), 16.
5. Allen, "Vitascope/Cinématographe," in Fell, *Film before Griffith,* 146–47.
6. Quinn, "USA: Distribution," in Abel, *Encyclopedia of Early Cinema*, 659.
7. Ibid., 660.
8. Fuller, *At the Picture Show,* 5–27; Hollyman, "The First Picture Shows in Austin, Texas,"

9–22; Lowry, "Edwin J. Hadley: Traveling Film Exhibitor," in Fell, *Film before Griffith,* 131–43; Musser, with Nelson, *High-Class Moving Pictures;* Pryluck, "The Itinerant Movie Show and the Development of the Film Industry," 11–22; Thomas, "From Page to Screen in Smalltown America," 3–14.

9. Musser "Itinerant Exhibitors," in Abel, *Encyclopedia of Early Cinema,* 141.

10. Pryluck, "Industrialization of Entertainment in the United States," in Austin, *Current Research in Film,* 117–35.

11. Gomery, *Shared Pleasures,* 12–13; Musser, "Itinerant Exhibitors," in Abel, *Encyclopedia of Early Cinema,* 342; Swartz, "Motion Pictures on the Move," 1–7; Stones, *America Goes to the Movies,* 11–13; Waller, "Robert Southard and the History of Traveling Film Exhibition," 2–14.

12. Gunning, "The Cinema of Attractions," in Elsaesser, *Early Cinema,* 56–62.

13. Streible, "Boxing Films," in Abel, *Encyclopedia of Early Cinema,* 80.

14. Musser, *The Emergence of Cinema,* 198.

15. Ibid., 199.

16. Niver, *Klaw and Erlanger Present Famous Plays in Pictures,* 5.

17. Musser, *The Emergence of Cinema,* 210.

18. Niver, *Klaw and Erlanger Present Famous Plays in Pictures,* 1–2.

19. Musser, *The Emergence of Cinema,* 213, 218.

20. Ibid., 297.

21. Singer and Keil, "USA: Production," in Abel, *Encyclopedia of Early Cinema,* 656–57.

22. Abel, *The Red Rooster Scare,* 1, 3–6.

23. Abel, "Look There! It's an American Subject!" in Quaresima, Raengo, and Vichi, *La nascita dei generi cinematografici,* 381.

24. Ibid.

25. Musser, *The Emergence of Cinema,* 366.

26. Alvarez, "The Origins of the Film Exchange," 431–35.

27. Musser, *The Emergence of Cinema,* 367.

28. Quinn, "USA: Distribution," in Abel, *Encyclopedia of Early Cinema,* 660.

29. Musser, *The Emergence of Cinema,* 371–413; Abel, *The Red Rooster Scare,* 42–46.

30. Musser, *The Emergence of Cinema,* 299.

31. Abel, "Nickelodeons," in Abel, *Encyclopedia of Early Cinema,* 478–79.

32. Ibid., 479.

33. Gomery, *Shared Pleasures,* 19. Elements of Gomery's description are more likely to have applied to big cities than to small towns. He discusses both later on in his book.

34. Musser, *The Emergence of Cinema,* 428–29.

35. Abel, "Nickelodeons," in Abel, *Encyclopedia of Early Cinema,* 479.

36. Musser, *The Emergence of Cinema,* 430.

37. Ibid., 433.

38. Abel, *The Red Rooster Scare,* 52.

39. Ibid., 64, 65.

40. Ibid., 59.

41. Ibid., 61.

42. Ibid.

43. Some give the date of the formation of the MPPC as 1909. The MPPC was incorporated in law on September 9, 1908. It was activated as a corporation on December 18, 1908. Its rules took effect from January 1, 1909, the date on which it signed its agreement with Eastman Kodak.

44. Abel, *The Red Rooster Scare,* 87–140.

45. Irwin, *The House That Shadows Built,* 128.

46. Anderson, *The Motion Picture Patents Company,* 213.

47. Quinn, *Early Feature Distribution and the Development of the Motion Picture Industry,* 56.

48. Ibid., 47–50, 55–59, 64–67. Similar points are made in Quinn's subsequently published articles, "Paramount and Early Feature Distribution," esp. 99–102, and "Distribution, the Transient Audience, and the Transition to the Feature Film," esp. 35–47. It could be argued that he occasionally overstates the nature of and the difference between the practices of audiences for programs in the late 1900s and early 1910s and those for films in subsequent eras. His argument assumes that individual films were the attraction in the late 1910s, the 1920s, the 1930s, and beyond, and that audiences went specifically to see particular films. Transient audiences in the earlier period would merely drop in to see a program of shorts. However, it could be argued that going to the movies, going to the local movie house to see whatever was playing, and even dropping in to see films on a whim was as much a mark of moviegoing in the era of the feature-length film as it was earlier on. Moreover, individual feature films were nearly always shown as part of a program, as we shall see. The individual feature-length film was most markedly the only or the principal attraction for audiences in the case of premieres and roadshows.

49. Indeed, an editorial in *MPW,* July 31, 1909, 151, is titled "The Charm of Variety." It notes complaints from exhibitors about the lack of variety in some of the programs packaged by distributors. See also "Balancing the Program" and "Letters to the Editor," *MPW,* June 10, 1911, 1303 and June 24, 1911, 1450, respectively.

50. Quinn, *Early Feature Distribution and the Development of the Motion Picture Industry,* 64–67.

51. For a discussion of "Coming Feature Films" and "Christmas Pictures," see *MPW,* December 17, 1909, 878.

52. Quinn, *Early Feature Distribution and the Development of the Motion Picture Industry,* 63. Uricchio and Pearson, *Reframing Culture,* discuss Vitagraph's quality films.

53. Brewster, "Multiple-Reel/Feature Films: USA," in Abel, *Encyclopedia of Early Cinema,* 456. These few feet were important. The $10^{3}/_{8}$-inch reels that were used on projectors could not accommodate a full 1,000 feet of film and in consequence footage at the beginning and the end of prints was often lost. See *MPW,* February 12, 1910, 212.

54. Brewster, "Multiple-Reel/Feature Films: USA," 455.

NOTES TO CHAPTER 2

1. The number of reels specified here and elsewhere in this and the following chapter are derived from advertisements, reviews and entries in *The Moving Picture World* (*MPW*), *Variety,* Hanson and Gevinson, *The American Film Institute Catalog of Motion Pictures Produced in the United States,* and from the online AFI Silent Film Database (http://afi.com/members/catalog). It should be noted that sources vary on the lengths of some of these films. Unless otherwise specified, Hanson and Gevinson and the AFI Database will be taken as authoritative.

2. Contemporary debates about the nature of features are discussed in Quinn, *Early Feature Distribution and the Development of the Motion Picture Industry,* 63–70.

3. *MPW,* June 8, 1912, 933.

4. Bowser, *The Transformation of Cinema,* 224.

5. Uricchio and Pearson, *Reframing Culture.*

6. Ibid., 17–64; Bowser, *The Transformation of Cinema,* 37–52; Grieveson, *Policing Cinema,* 11–32.

7. Unless otherwise specified, the release dates for these and for all the other foreign productions cited in this book are U.S. release dates.

8. Abel, "Look There! It's an American Subject!" 246–77, 311–16, 321–23; Bowser, *The Transformation of Cinema,* 218.

9. Brewster, "Periodization of Early Cinema," in Keil and Stamp, *American Cinema's Transitional Era,* 68.

10. Usai, "Italy: Spectacle and Melodrama," in Nowell-Smith, *The Oxford History of World Cinema,* 125.

11. *MPW,* July 15, 1911, 14.

12. Ibid., January 14, 1911, 7; April 18, 1911, 817.

13. Ibid., November 6, 1909, 648–49.

14. Uricchio and Pearson, *Reframing Culture.* 170.

15. Quoted in ibid., 171.

16. *MPW,* December 4, 1909, 791. See also January 15, 1910, 49; February 18, 1911, 359; March 25, 1911, 639; September 2, 1911, 606–7.

17. Ibid., May 20, 1911, 1124.

18. Singer, "Feature Films, Variety Programs," in Keil and Stamp, *American Cinema's Transitional Era,* 76–100.

19. Brewster, "Multiple-Reel/Feature Films: USA," 456.

20. *MPW,* July 11, 1914, 272–73.

21. *Variety,* August 23, 1912, 19.

22. Ibid.

23. *MPW,* April 16, 1910, 591.

24. *Variety,* February 21, 1913, 15.

25. Bowser, *The Transformation of Cinema,* 128.

26. Abel, *The Red Rooster Scare,* 61–63, documents the opening of a number of large nickelodeon theaters in 1907.

27. Bowser, *The Transformation of Cinema,* 121–36; Stones, *America Goes to the Movies,* 28–30.

28. Herzog, *Motion Picture Theater and Film Exhibition,* 73.

29. *MPW,* September 2, 1911, 633.

30. Ibid., March 1, 1913, 866.

31. Smith, "A Religious Spectacle in Theatre and Film," in Cosandey, Gaudreault, and Gunning, *Une invention du diable?* 312.

32. McNamara, *The Shuberts of Broadway,* 75.

33. Pearson, "The Menace of the Movies," in Keil and Stamp, *American Cinema's Transitional Era,* 316.

34. Ibid.

35. Bowser, *The Transformation of Cinema,* 106–19; deCordova, *Picture Personalities,* esp. 38–45; McArthur, *Actors and American Culture.*

36. Duckett, "Theater, Legitimate," in Abel, *Encyclopedia of Early Cinema,* 628; Pearson, "The Menace of the Movies," 317.

37. McLaughlin, *Broadway and Hollywood,* 34–55; Tibbetts, *The American Theatrical Film,* 53–110.

38. Quinn, "Paramount and Early Feature Distribution," 100.

39. Ibid., 101.

40. Ibid.

41. Quinn, *Early Feature Distribution and the Development of the Motion Picture Industry,* 156–220. It is worth noting here that the "advance showing" of films in order to gauge audience reaction and facilitate improvements prior to general release, a practice pioneered by Vitagraph, is theatrical in origin too. See *MPW,* April 11, 1914, 192.

42. *MPW,* May 3, 1913, 467.

43. Musser, "On 'Extras,' Mary Pickford, and Red-Light Filmmaking in the United States," 151.

44. *Variety,* June 27, 1913, 16.

45. Robinson, *From Peep Show to Palace,* 136; Bertellini, "Shipwrecked Spectators," 45.

46. *Variety,* May 8, 1914, 18.

47. "*Quo Vadis* Department, Profit and Loss Statement," George Kleine Papers (GKP), Library of Congress, Box 49.

48. Ibid.

49. *MPW,* February 7, 1914, 680.

50. Ibid., November 8, 1913, 598.

51. *Variety,* June 12, 1914, 18; August 7, 1914, 22. *Cabiria* was accompanied in Chicago, San Francisco, and Los Angeles by a score compiled and composed by Joseph Carl Breil. For details on this and other scores used to accompany *Cabiria,* see Marks, *Music and the Silent Film,* 104–8.

52. *MPW,* June 21, 1913, 1232; August 16, 1913, 712.

53. Musser, "On 'Extras,' Mary Pickford, and Red-Light Filmmaking in the United States," 157–59; *Variety,* August 29, 1913, 10; September 12, 1913, 13; March 20, 1914, 22, 26; June 5, 1914, 17.

54. Schaefer, "*Bold! Daring! Shocking! True!*" 18.

55. *MPW,* November 1, 1913, 521.

56. *Variety,* March 21, 1913, 13.

57. Hampton, *History of the American Film Industry,* 107.

58. "Memorandum of Agreement," April 24, 1913, GKP, Box 8; "Statement of *Quo Vadis* Engagements from April 21st, 1913 to October 4th, 1913," GKP, Box 49. This statement indicates that the split for regular showings in regular movie theaters tended to be higher for Kleine (as high as 70 percent) and correspondingly lower for the theaters themselves.

59. *MPW,* May 30, 1908, 11; November 13, 1909, 12; July 9, 1910, 82; Staiger, "Announcing Wares, Winning Patrons, Voicing Ideals," 8.

60. Horwitz, "George Kleine and the Early Motion Picture Industry" in Horwitz and Harrison, with White, *The George Kleine Collection of Early Motion Pictures in the Library of Congress,* xvii.

61. Rhodes, "Our Beautiful and Glorious Art Lives," 309–10, 317–20; Wyke, *Projecting the Past,* 41–47.

62. Tomadjoglu, "Rome's Premiere Film Studio," 268–70; Wyke, *Projecting the Past,* 35–37, 148–49.

63. Dennett and Warnke, "Disaster Spectacles at the Turn of the Century," 101–2; Malamud, "The Greatest Show on Earth"; Mayer, *Playing Out the Empire;* Tibbets, *The American Theatrical Film,* 25; Vardac, *Stage to Screen,* 76–82; Wyke, *Projecting the Past,* 14–20, 114–24, 149–65.

64. *NYDM,* April 30, 1913, 28; 65; *NYT,* quoted in an advertisement in *MPW,* May 3, 1913, 497.

65. Bowser, *The Transformation of Cinema,* 258.

66. *New York Telegraph,* quoted in *MPW,* May 3, 1913, 497.

67. There are a number of different versions of *Quo Vadis?,* each of different lengths, in a number of different archives. We have only been able to see the print in the BFI National Archive and the video version distributed in the United States by Movies Unlimited.

68. Bowser, *The Transformation of Cinema,* 258.

69. Hovet, *Realism and Spectacle in* Ben-Hur.

70. Brewster, "Deep Staging in French Films, 1900–1914," in Elsaesser, *Early Cinema,* 45–55, and "Multiple-Reel/Feature Films: USA" in Abel, *Encyclopedia of Early Cinema,* 606–7; Bordwell, *On the History of Film Style,* 175–98, and *Figures Traced in Light,* 43–82. It should be noted that Brewster and Jacobs, *Theatre to Cinema,* 14, caution against too rigid a distinction

between Europe and the United States: "pictorialism was part of both European and American filmmaking traditions, and . . . its relationship to changes in editing is complex."

71. Bowser, *The Transformation of Cinema*, 201.

72. It is worth noting here that the version of *The Last Days of Pompeii* released on video and DVD by Kino Video appears to be the Kleine-Ambrosio version and not the Pasquali version, as is claimed in the credits. As Maria Wyke points out, the Pasquali version "only survives in the British National Film Archive and is currently incorrectly listed as an Ambrosio film directed by [Mario] Caserini" (*Projecting the Past*, 209n47). As she also points out, the Ambrosio version was directed by Eleuterio Rodolfi, the Pasquali version by Giovanni Enrico Vidali (ibid., 161).

73. Usai, "*Cabiria*, an Incomplete Masterpiece," 259–72.

74. Nelson and Jones, *A Silent Siren Song*, 122–27; Schickel, *D. W. Griffith: A Biography*, 202–3.

75. *The New York American*, quoted in an advertisement in *NYT*, March 6, 1915, 18.

76. Carli, "*The Birth of a Nation*: Music," in Usai, *The Griffith Project*. Vol. 8, *Films Produced in 1914–15*, 88; Marks, *Music and the Silent Film*, 131–35.

77. Altman, *Silent Film Sound*, 293–94; Carli, "*The Birth of a Nation*: Music," in Usai, *The Griffith Project*. Vol. 8, *Films Produced in 1914–15*, 88–91; Gaines and Lerner, "The Orchestration of Affect: The Motif of Barbarism in Breil's *The Birth of a Nation* Score," in Abel and Altman, *The Sounds of Early Cinema*, 252–68; Marks, *Music and the Silent Film*, 135–66. According to *Variety*, October 12, 1918, 42, the two dollar admission price was Aitken's idea, and applied initially to boxes and several orchestra seats on opening night. After that, it was extended to include all the orchestra seats and a number of balcony seats as well.

78. Schickel, *D. W. Griffith: A Biography*, 271; *FD*, August 1, 1926, 4; *Variety*, March 5, 1915, 19. Schickel, *D. W. Griffith: A Biography*, 281, reports that by the end of 1917, the cumulative receipts from showings of *The Birth of a Nation* amounted to precisely $4,839,748.41. In common with most film historians, he estimates that *The Birth of Nation* cost "just a little more than $100,000" to produce (p. 244).

79. Bowser, "*The Birth of a Nation*: Production," in Usai, *The Griffith Project*. Vol. 8, *Films Produced in 1914–15*, 55, 62; Cripps, "The Reaction of the Negro to *The Birth of a Nation*," in Silva, *Focus on* The Birth of a Nation, 111–24; Gaines, *Fire and Desire*, 219–57, Kaufman, "*The Birth of a Nation*: Distribution and Reception," in Usai, *The Griffith Project*. Vol. 8, *Films Produced in 1914–15*, 91–98; Lang, "*The Birth of a Nation*: History, Ideology and Narrative Form," in Lang, *The Birth of a Nation*, 3–24; Lenning, "Myth and Fact," 117–41; Simmon, *The Films of D. W. Griffith*, 104–36; Williams, *Playing the Race Card*, 96–128, and, "*The Birth of a Nation*: Politics," in Usai, *The Griffith Project*. Vol. 8, *Films Produced in 1914–15*, 98–107.

80. Nelson and Jones, *A Silent Siren Song*, 125–27.

81. Ibid., 146–49; Schickel, *D. W. Griffith: A Biography*, 222–23, 239–42.

82. Abel, *Americanizing the Movies and "Movie-Mad" Audiences*, 141–67; Bowser, "*The Birth of a Nation*: Production" in Usai, *The Griffith Project*. Vol. 8, *Films Produced in 1914–15*. 55–58; Mayer, "*The Birth of a Nation*: Theatrical Sources," in Usai, *The Griffith Project*. Vol. 8, *Films Produced in 1914–15*, 81–87; Spears, *The Civil War on the Screen and Other Essays*, 11–54.

83. Keil, "*The Birth of a Nation*: Style and Technique," in Usai, *The Griffith Project*. Vol. 8, *Films Produced in 1914–15*, 63.

84. Ibid., 64.

85. Ibid., 65–69.

86. Elsaesser and Barker, "Introduction" to "The Continuity System: Griffith and Beyond," in Elsaesser, *Early Cinema*, 295.

87. Birchard, *Cecil B. De Mille's Hollywood*, 37.

88. Ibid, 90. Higashi, *Cecil B. De Mille and American Film Culture*, 119, claims that the roadshow version of *Joan the Woman* was thirteen reels long. She also notes that some states

rights distributors, with DeMille's agreement, subsequently cut the film to eight reels. For a detailed study of the production, distribution, promotion and reception of *Joan the Woman,* see DeBauche, *Reel Patriotism,* 5–28.

89. Birchard, *Cecil B. De Mille's Hollywood,* 100–102.

90. Ibid., 95.

91. Merritt, "*Intolerance:* Production and Distribution," in Usai, *The Griffith Project.* Vol. 9, *Films Produced in 1916–18,* 42, 46. Advertisements in the trade press doubtless exaggerated the film's box-office success, but it is worth noting that an advertisement in *Variety,* February 23, 1917, 18, claimed that the film played for five months at the Liberty Theatre and eight weeks at the Pitt Theatre in Pittsburgh, that twelve roadshow companies were touring America, that attendance records were broken at the Chestnut St. Opera House in Philadelphia, and that receipts for a three-day engagement at the Davidson Theatre in Richmond amounted to $4,950.

92. Ibid., 39–46; Merritt, "D. W. Griffith's *Intolerance:* Reconstructing an Unattainable Text," 337–75.

93. The credits for *Intolerance* in Usai, *The Griffith Project.* Vol. 9, *Films Produced in 1916–18,* 31, specify the release length as thirteen reels (per September 5, 1916 copyright records) or fourteen reels (footage as of October 16, 1916: 11,663 ft.).

94. Canjels, *Beyond the Cliffhanger,* 24.

95. Gunning, "*Intolerance:* Narrative Structure," in Usai, *The Griffith Project.* Vol. 9, *Films Produced in 1916–18,* 48.

96. Ibid., 49.

97. Ibid., 51.

98. Merritt, "On First Looking into Griffith's Babylon," 18.

99. Ibid., 18–19.

100. Keil, "*The Birth of a Nation:* Style and Technique," in Usai, *The Griffith Project.* Vol. 8, *Films Produced in 1914–15,* 58–61.

101. Grieveson, *Policing Cinema,* 193–98.

Notes to Chapter 3

1. Koszarski, *An Evening's Entertainment,* 63.

2. Gibson, with Firth, *The Original Million Dollar Mermaid,* 115–17.

3. *Variety,* September 29, 1916, 20; October 20, 1916, 22. According to *Variety,* August 4, 1916, 24, the rights to New England sold for $100,000, Jersey for $30,000, Illinois for $75,000, and "five western states" for $96,000. According to *Motography,* September 2, 1916, 526, Ince and his associates (who included A. H. Woods), initially intended to roadshow the film themselves. However, "It was found that at least sixty prints would be necessary to accommodate the demand and that an organization of vast proportions would have to be formed. Then, too, it was pointed out that Mr. Ince's best interest could be guarded by allowing individuals to continue to dominate their own territories rather than for him to enter direct competition with them where it was not necessary."

4. *Variety,* April 25, 1916, 21; March 18, 1925, 27.

5. Gibson, with Firth, *The Original Million Dollar Mermaid,* 122; Lahue, *Dreams for Sale,* 123.

6. *Motography,* July 29, 1916, 260. *Neptune's Daughter* and *A Daughter of the Gods* could both also be described as *extravaganzas.* Wilmeth, *The Language of American Popular Entertainment,* 87, defines extravaganza as a "confusing form of American and English entertainment especially popular in the nineteenth century. Basically, a light entertainment in dramatic form, with music, often improbable in plot, and spectacular in presentation."

7. *Variety,* March 18, 1921, 39; March 18, 1925, 27; March 5, 1920, 65; *MPW,* January 27, 1917, 449.

8. *MPW,* February 17, 1917, 987.

9. *Motography,* July 15, 1916, 141; *MPW,* April 28, 1917, 660; *Variety,* April 25, 1916, 21; August 4, 1916, 24. In its edition of May 5, 1916, 21, *Variety* noted that "'Big pictures' are in the class of the Griffith *The Birth of Nation* and the forthcoming William Fox picture, *A Daughter of the Gods.*" It went on to speculate that a number of films such as these "would be sufficient to supply a picture theater like the Strand or the Rialto with a 'big picture' feature weekly for a season, thereby dividing feature films into two classes, the big and the little picture. Exhibitors of the 'little picture,' as the present 4, 5 or 6 reeler is now known, would have a certain field at present occupied by many, the best money makers of which are said to be houses like Loew's New York theatre that changes features daily."

10. See, among others, Rob King, "Made for the Masses with an Appeal to the Classes," 3–33.

11. Higashi, *Cecil B. De Mille and American Film Culture,* 142.

12. Schickel, *D. W. Griffith: A Biography,* 340, 359–60. *Hearts of the World* is often listed as a states rights release, but as Schickel makes clear, it received a nationwide roadshow run before being released on a states rights basis and later on as part of the FPL program. According to an advertisement in the *MPW,* May 11, 1918, 814, seat prices at the 44th Street Theatre in New York were as high as five dollars; according to a report in the *MPW,* June 29, 1918, 1875, the price paid by states rights franchisees "exceeded all previous state rights purchase records."

13. Schickel, *D. W. Griffith: A Biography,* 355.

14. Ibid., 428–29. According to *Variety,* March 18, 1925, 27, *Way Down East,* which was thirteen reels long, cost $801,000 to produce, and netted $1,350,000 on its roadshow run. According to Brown, *Movie Time,* 54, it premiered at the 44th Street Theatre at "an unprecedented top price of $10 a ticket." (His source is not specified.)

15. Schickel, *D. W. Griffith: A Biography,* 404; *Variety,* May 30, 1919, 1.

16. Letter from D. W. Griffith to Albert Grey, November 9, 1918, quoted in Schickel, *D. W. Griffith: A Biography,* 377.

17. So widespread were some of these practices that the distributor of *The Italian Battle Front* (1917), William Moore Patch, was moved to complain about "forced and inflated runs" on Broadway "beyond the period of the natural drawing powers of a production in order to impress the trade" (*MPW,* September 29, 1917, 2015).

18. Hampton, *History of the American Film Industry,* 174.

19. *MPW,* February 3, 1917, 710.

20. Ibid., August 31, 1918, 1252, reported that over 1,000 bookings had been taken by the end of August, and that twenty roadshow companies were already touring the country.

21. Ibid., January 25, 1919, 479.

22. Ibid., March 15, 1919, 1479.

23. *Variety,* March 11, 1921, 39.

24. Ibid., May 19, 1916, 24; *MPW,* May 11, 1918, 875.

25. *Wid's Daily,* March 8, 1921, 1; *MPW,* March 12, 1921, 184. According to *MPW,* March 19, 1921, 266, sixty-five prints of *The Kid* were "booked solid for thirty days beginning March 7 in Greater New York. Twenty-five theatres along Broadway showed *The Kid* simultaneously during the week of March 7."

26. Cohen, *Silent Film and the Triumph of the American Myth,* 141–42; Golden, *Vamp: The Rise and Fall of Theda Bara,* esp. 83–86, 161–64, 171–72; Jacobs, *The Rise of the American Film,* 266–67; Koszarski, *An Evening's Entertainment,* 273–76.

27. *MPW,* December 29, 1917, 1974.

28. Ibid., September 22, 1917, 1802; October 6, 1917, 7; November 24, 1917, 1124.

29. Ibid., August 4, 1917, 771.

30. Ibid., October 6, 1917, 7.

31. Ibid., August 10, 1918, 821.

32. Unpaginated advertisement, *Variety*, August 1, 1919.

33. Quinn, *Early Feature Distribution and the Development of the Motion Picture Industry*, 162.

34. Ibid., 163–66.

35. Ibid., 168.

36. Ibid., 169–70; Whitfield, *Pickford: The Woman Who Made Hollywood*, 122–46.

37. Quinn, *Early Feature Distribution and the Development of the Motion Picture Industry*, 178.

38. Ibid., 171.

39. Lewis, *The Motion Picture Industry*, 8.

40. Quinn, *Early Feature Distribution and the Development of the Motion Picture Industry*, 203–6.

41. Brown, *Movie Time*, 53, 91. The figure for 1929, 95 million, is an all-time high. See p. 96. Other sources, such as Finler, *The Hollywood Story*, 288, give somewhat lower figures of around 80 million per week (see chapter 5, note 2 below).

42. *Variety*, October 13, 1926, 12.

43. Hall, *The Best Remaining Seats;* Herzog, *Motion Picture Theater and Film Exhibition*, 109–30; Stones, *America Goes to the Movies*, 35–61.

44. *Variety*, August 18, 1926, 46.

45. Ibid., November 4, 1925, 29.

46. Ibid., November 3, 1926, 3.

47. Hampton, *History of the American Film Industry*, 211.

48. Ibid., 211–12; *Variety*, February 24, 1922, 39; *MPW*, March 26, 1922, 362; *Variety*, April 14, 1922, 1, 3.

49. Lewis, *The Motion Picture Industry*, 17.

50. Koszarski, *An Evening's Entertainment*, 74; Hampton, *History of the American Film Industry*, 252–80.

51. Wasko, *Movies and Money: Financing the American Film Industry*, 21.

52. Balio, *United Artists: The Company Built by the Stars*, 63–64.

53. Ibid., 35–39; Aberdeen, *Hollywood Renegades*, 39–41.

54. Quinn, *Early Feature Distribution and the Development of the Motion Picture Industry*, 183.

55. *Variety*, February 4, 1921, 47.

56. Ibid., February 18, 1921, 1.

57. Ibid., April 1, 1921, 13; April 22, 1921, 43.

58. *MPW*, July 30, 1921, 473, 520. According to *Variety*, December 16, 1921, 36, Fox was "calling in" the companies involved in touring *The Queen of Sheba*.

59. Finler, *The Hollywood Story*, 37; *Variety*, September 5, 1928, 7; June 21, 1932, 62. It should also be noted here that *Orphans of the Storm* was released in the midst of the industry's downturn.

60. *Wid's Daily*, August 31, 1921, 4.

61. *Variety*, September 2, 1921, 61.

62. Balio, *United Artists: The Company Built by the Stars*, 42.

63. *Wid's Daily*, December 5, 1920, 3.

64. Studlar, *This Mad Masquerade*, 81.

65. Koszarski, *An Evening's Entertainment*, 270.

66. Studlar, *This Mad Masquerade*, 231; Koszarski, *An Evening's Entertainment*, 89; Schatz, *The Genius of the System*, 21–28. According to *MPW*, March 15, 1923, 181, *The Hunchback of Notre Dame* was one of the first films to promote the acceptance of roadshow ticket prices in ordinary picture theaters.

67. Koszarski, *Von: The Life and Films of Erich von Stroheim,* 340.

68. Ibid., 342. Canjels, *Beyond the Cliffhanger,* 18, notes that both before and after cutting *Greed* down to twenty-four reels himself, Stroheim proposed to MGM that it be shown in two installments on consecutive nights, with a break for dinner each night, as Griffith had planned with *Intolerance.* In the end, a ten-reel version was unsuccessfully released as a special.

69. *Wid's Daily,* April 17, 1921, 3.

70. *MPW,* November 5, 1921, 85.

71. Ibid., November 19, 1921, 294; Balio, *United Artists: The Company Built by the Stars,* 42; Koszarski, *An Evening's Entertainment,* 79. According to *Variety,* November 26, 1926, 18, UA withdrew *The Thief of Bagdad* (1924) from its roadshow run for similar reasons.

72. Slide, *The American Film Industry: A Historical Dictionary,* 125.

73. Basinger, *Silent Stars,* 271.

74. *Variety,* March 18, 1925, 27; June 21, 1944, 9; May 6, 1991, 100. According to the Eddie Mannix Ledger, the 1926 domestic reissue grossed $665,000.

75. *Variety,* February 18, 1921, 40.

76. Ibid., April 8, 1921, 1.

77. *Wid's Daily,* April 2, 1921, 1.

78. *MPW,* October 29, 1921, 1057.

79. Basinger, *Silent Stars,* 270–71; Leider, *Dark Lover,* 112–13; Walker, *Stardom: The Hollywood Phenomenon,* 143.

80. *NYT,* March 7, 1921, 8.

81. *Wid's Daily,* February 20, 1921, 3.

82. According to Birchard, *Cecil B. De Mille's Hollywood,* 45, 51, *The Ten Commandments* cost $1,475,836.93 and grossed $4,169,798.38, and *The King of Kings* cost $1,265,283.95 and grossed $2,641,687.21.

83. Eyman, *Lion of Hollywood,* 99–109; Hay, *MGM: When the Lion Roars,* 27–32; Soares, *Beyond Paradise,* 70–96.

84. Eyman, *Lion of Hollywood,* 109, Soares, *Beyond Paradise,* 97, 100.

85. Kenaga, "*The West before the Cinema Invaded It,*" 66–119.

86. Letter from Lasky to Zukor, April 19, 1923, quoted in ibid., 119.

87. Kenaga, "*The West before the Cinema Invaded It,*" 40.

88. Smith, *Shooting Cowboys and Indians,* 177–78.

89. *Variety,* May 3, 1923, 20; Kenaga, "*The West before the Cinema Invaded It,*" 119–30; *Variety,* May 7, 1924, 1.

90. Kenaga, "*The West before the Cinema Invaded It,*" 50–63.

91. Ibid., 101–2.

92. McBride, *Searching for John Ford,* 145–52.

93. *Variety,* December 29, 1926, 14.

94. Finler, *The Hollywood Story,* 123; *Variety,* August 18, 1926, 46; May 4, 1927, 4.

95. Suid, *Guts and Glory,* 25.

96. *Variety,* October 28, 1925, 34; 29 December 1926, 14.

97. Hampton, *History of the American Film Industry,* 313; Finler, *The Hollywood Story,* 123. In his autobiography, *A Tree Is a Tree,* 83, Vidor put the production cost at $245,000.

98. Vidor, *A Tree Is a Tree,* 82–83; *FD,* January 21, 1927, 1, 5. According to this report, *The Big Parade* "is also credited with the longest run of any American picture shown abroad. It was shown recently for 27 weeks at the Tivoli, London, in spite of some editorial opposition from a section of the British Press." *Ben-Hur* subsequently ran at the same theater for forty-nine weeks in 1926–27.

99. *MPW,* December 26, 1925, 761; May 7, 1927, 27; *Variety,* December 16, 1925, 31; April 28, 1926, 36.

100. Vidor, *A Tree Is a Tree,* 73.

101. Ibid., 77–78.

102. Quoted in Lewis, "Goldstein, Incorporated, Advertising, Maintenance of Broadway Exploitation Theater," 417–25, reproduced and edited by David Pierce (1999) at www. cinemaweb.com/silentfilm/bookshelf/31_rs_10.htm.

103. *Harrison's Reports,* June 9, 1928, 89, 92; July 7, 1928, 105, 108; July 14, 1928, 112; *MPW,* May 1, 1926, 35; *Variety,* December 2, 1926, 14, 23; January 26, 1927, 9; September 28, 1927, 9; November 2, 1927, 4; December 14, 1927, 22; January 4, 1928, 7; January 15, 1928, 47; April 25, 1928, 5.

104. Suid, *Guts and Glory,* 33; *Christian Science Monitor,* quoted in the *Wings* press book, Academy of Motion Picture Arts and Sciences (AMPAS).

105. *Wings* file, AMPAS; *Variety,* October 12, 1927, 18; August 22, 1928, 26.

106. DeBauche, *Reel Patriotism,* 179.

107. Ibid., 186.

108. Slide, *Silent Topics,* 79; *The Motion Picture News,* March 31, 1928, 1029; Crafton, *The Talkies,* 135. According to *Variety,* March 21, 1928, 15, each roadshow unit cost $10,000 to run and "travels with 47 pieces of baggage. . . . The extra baggage is necessitated by the effects and the sound devices used with the picture. A three-kilowatt motor generator is part of the excess equipment. Where formerly a picture road show arrived in a can, a brief case and a couple of crates and required no more than two hours to set up, *Wings* needs from five to seven hours."

Notes to Chapter 4

1. Usai, "Color," in Abel, *Encyclopedia of Early Cinema,* 139; Gunning "Colorful Metaphors," 253.

2. Usai, "Color," in Abel, *Encyclopedia of Early Cinema,* 139.

3. Salt, *Film Style and Technology,* 44.

4. Koszarski, *An Evening's Entertainment,* 128.

5. Enticknap, *Moving Image Technology,* 77–78.

6. Fulton, *Motion Pictures,* 109.

7. Theodore Huff, *Films in Review* 4 (June–July 1959): 314.

8. Koszarski, *An Evening's Entertainment,* 127.

9. Usai, "Color," in Abel, *Encyclopedia of Early Cinema,* 140.

10. Crafton, *The Talkies,* 12. It should be noted that spotting meant "spotlighting" as well as "in spots," and that it thus encompassed the drawing of attention to technologies as well as their intermittent use.

11. Kelley, "Natural Color Cinematography," 45, quoted in Koszarski, *An Evening's Entertainment,* 128.

12. Quinn, *Early Feature Distribution and the Development of the Motion Picture Industry,* 82.

13. *MPW,* December 17, 1909, 873.

14. Bowser, *The Transformation of Cinema,* 229.

15. Ibid.

16. *NYDM,* May 3, 1911, 34, quoted in ibid.

17. Grau in *MPW,* August 12, 1911, 61; September 30, 1911, 959.

18. Quinn, *Early Feature Distribution and the Development of the Motion Picture Industry,* 82.

19. Bowser, *The Transformation of Cinema,* 228.

20. Ibid.

21. Quinn, *Early Feature Distribution and the Development of the Motion Picture Industry,* 86.

22. Ibid., 81.

23. Slide, *The American Film Industry,* 110.

24. Koszarski, *An Evening's Entertainment,* 128.

25. Ibid.

26. Ibid.

27. Enticknap, *Moving Image Technology,* 86.

28. Koszarski, *An Evening's Entertainment,* 130.

29. Nowotny, *The Way of All Flesh Tones,* 215–16.

30. *Variety,* March 10, 1926, 40.

31. Ibid., April 7, 1926, 25, 30.

32. *NYT,* March 9, 1924, 21.

33. Koszarski, *An Evening's Entertainment,* 130.

34. Worldwide grosses are listed in Ramsaye, *The Motion Picture Almanac.* Finler, *The Holly-wood Story,* 281, tabulates the period's two-color films by studio, showing that Warner Bros. and its subsidiary First National released by far the largest number of all-color features from 1924 to 1933, with a total of twenty between them.

35. Finler, *The Hollywood Story,* 198; *Variety,* August 18, 1930, 3.

36. Nowotny, *The Way of All Flesh Tones,* 233–34.

37. *Variety,* April 17, 1929, 5; September 25, 1929, 7; October 23, 1929, 8; January 1, 1930, 11; April 8, 1930, 11; May 28, 1930, 4.

38. Nowotny, *The Way of All Flesh Tones,* 237–42.

39. *Film Daily Yearbook,* 1931, 883.

40. Paul, "Screens," in Abel, *Encyclopedia of Early Cinema,* 574.

41. Ibid., 575.

42. Belton, *Widescreen Cinema,* 36. According to Herzog, *Motion Picture Theater and Film Exhibition,* 150–51, screen sizes increased during the 1920s: "seventeen by twelve feet and eighteen inches was standard for a two thousand seat theater, and fifteen by twenty feet for thirty-five hundred seats and up." But the projected image itself was still relatively small: "In today's theaters of only one to two thousand seats, the screens are forty-eight or fifty feet wide; the movie palace had two or three times the number of seats and the screens were one-half to one-third the size of present day models."

43. *Variety,* April 23, 1924, 17.

44. Ibid.; *MPW,* January 30, 1926, 1, 4.

45. Carr and Hayes, *Wide Screen Movies,* 5. Sherlock, "*Widescreen Movies* Corrections," disputes Carr and Hayes's claim that the screening was at FPL's behest, but given the evidence of FPL's earlier interest in large-screen projection as well as in the lens and its possible uses, it seems likely that Carr and Hayes may, at least on this occasion, be right.

46. Crafton, *The Talkies,* 86; *Variety,* April 13, 1927, 4;

47. *MPW,* December 11, 1926, 422, 441.

48. *Variety,* May 19, 1926, 1, 23; October 13, 1926, 5; August 15, 1926, 4; September 22, 1926, 5. *Variety,* December 8, 1926, 16, finally estimated *Old Ironsides'* eventual production cost as "something like $2,400,000."

49. Belton, "The Rivoli."

50. *MPW,* December 11, 1926, 441.

51. Belton, *Widescreen Cinema,* 37.

52. Allvine, *The Greatest Fox of Them All,* 27–34. Allvine also claimed the credit for using Magnascope and for bringing del Riccio's lens to FPL's attention.

53. *Variety,* December 8, 1926, 16.

54. Ibid., October 23, 1929, 6.

55. Ibid., March 21, 1928, 9.

56. Ibid., March 28, 1928, 40. According to the Eddie Mannix Ledger, the negative cost of *The Trail of '98* was $1,538,000, though trade publicity claimed that it cost over $2 million. See the advertisement in *Variety,* January 2, 1929, 14.

57. *Variety*, March 28, 1928, 30.

58. Ibid., March 21, 1928, 9, 15.

59. Ibid., March 14, 1933, 14.

60. Ibid., January 22, 1930, 8.

61. Ibid., January 15, 1930, 14.

62. Ibid., May 29, 1929, 17; July 24, 1929, 4.

63. *NYT*, September 18, 1929.

64. Ibid.

65. *Variety*, January 15, 1930, 11.

66. Belton, *Widescreen Cinema*, 12–33. It is worth noting here that a format such as Veriscope, which used 63 mm film stock and a projector capable of throwing "almost 15/70 Imax-size pictures" was devised solely for the production and exhibition of a film of the Corbett-Fitzsimmons boxing match (see Lobban, "In the Splendor of 70 mm"). As we have noted in chapter 1, boxing films, like passion plays, were nearly always treated as special events.

67. *Variety*, January 8, 1930, 78, 93.

68. Ibid., February 26, 1930, 11.

69. Ibid., March 19, 1930, 16.

70. Ibid., March 5, 1930, 11.

71. Ibid., September 11, 1929, 5, 22.

72. Ibid., October 16, 1929, 7.

73. Ibid., October 9, 1929, 6.

74. Quoted in Solomon, *Twentieth Century-Fox: A Corporate and Financial History*, 11.

75. *Variety*, February 19, 1930, 21.

76. Ibid., February 12, 1930, 10.

77. Ibid., October 23, 1929, 21, 32.

78. Ibid., October 9, 1929, 6; Barrios, *A Song in the Dark*, 174.

79. *Variety*, July 24, 1929, 4; September 18, 1929, 12. Whereas Realife used a duplicate 35 mm negative to produce release prints, Magnifilm prints were struck directly from the original 65 mm negative.

80. With the exceptions of the Magnafilm and Realife specifications, which are cited by Sherlock, "*Widescreen Movies* Corrections," these aspect ratios are taken from www.in70mm.com/library/formats.htm.

81. *Variety*, January 22, 1930, 8; June 25, 1930, 103, 108.

82. Carr and Hayes, *Wide Screen Movies*, 6, 8; Limbacher, *Four Aspects of the Film*, 119–20.

83. *Variety*, May 7, 1930, 5, 12.

84. Carr and Hayes, *Wide Screen Movies*, 6, 8; Coles "Magnified Grandeur," 6.

85. *Variety*, August 27, 1930, 4; November 12, 1930, 11. Costing $611,000 and $647,000, respectively, *Kismet* and *The Lash* earned only $462,000 and $716,000 in worldwide rentals. *The Great Meadow* cost $439,000 and grossed $409,000.

86. Ibid., October 29, 1930, 8.

87. It is worth noting here that the 70 mm and 35 mm versions were shot by different cinematographers (Arthur Edeson and Lucien N. Androit, respectively). As Cossar, *Screen Space*, has pointed out, the 70 mm version in wide screen was marked by a greater use of medium two shots, a comparative absence of close-ups and "singles" (framings of single characters), a lower camera height, lower sets, and an absence of deep or vertically oriented compositions.

88. *Variety*, November 19, 1930, 8.

89. Ibid., August 13, 1930, 5; October 8, 1930, 4.

90. Ibid., October 22, 1930, 8.

91. Ibid., December 17, 1930, 3, 40.

92. Belton, *Widescreen Cinema*, 44–45.

93. Ibid., 52–64.

94. *Variety,* December 17, 1930, 3.

95. Enticknap, *Moving Image Technology,* 102.

96. Ibid. For details on each of these forms, see Abel and Altman, *The Sounds of Early Cinema,* and Altman, *Silent Film Sound.*

97. Enticknap, *Moving Image Technology,* 99.

98. Gomery, *The Coming of Sound,* 26.

99. Enticknap, *Moving Image Technology,* 106.

100. *Variety,* February 21, 1913, 7.

101. Enticknap, *Moving Image Technology,* 108.

102. Crafton, *The Talkies,* 23–61.

103. Ibid., 75–76; Gomery, *The Coming of Sound,* 11–13, 21–22; Koszarski, *An Evening's Entertainment,* 50–56. The spread of prologues, presentations, and "extra attractions" to supplement the showing of ordinary pictures in ordinary picture houses appears to have begun during the temporary slump of 1922 and taken off in earnest in 1923. See *Variety,* September 15, 1922, 5; October 20, 1922, 1, 43; March 15, 1923, 30; April 5, 1923, 30; April 12, 1923, 23, April 19, 1923, 1; May 10, 1923, 6; May 14, 1923, 17.

104. As early as 1921, Riesenfeld was a leading member of the Synchronized Music Company (later the Music Score Service Corporation), along with Carl Edouarde, music director of the Strand at that time; James C. Bradford, former director of musical synopses for FPL; and Joseph Carl Breil, composer and arranger of the score for *The Birth of a Nation.* The aim of the company was to provide standardized scores for theaters big and small. See *MPW,* May 21, 1921, 312.

105. Crafton, *The Talkies,* 67; Gomery, *The Coming of Sound,* 30.

106. Enticknap, *Moving Image Technology,* 111.

107. Gomery, "Writing the History of the American Film Industry: Warner Bros. and Sound," 40–53; Gomery, *The Coming of Sound,* 23–46.

108. Gomery, *The Coming of Sound,* 35.

109. Crafton, *The Talkies,* 80 (emphasis in original).

110. *FD,* August 16, 1926, 7.

111. Ibid., August 8, 1926, 3.

112. Gomery, *The Coming of Sound,* 94.

113. Gomery, *The Coming of Sound to the American Cinema,* 144 (emphasis in original).

114. Crafton, *The Talkies,* 82.

115. Ibid., 549; *Variety,* April 13, 1927, 13.

116. Crafton, *The Talkies,* 549.

117. Gomery, *The Coming of Sound,* 45.

118. Crafton, *The Talkies,* 273.

119. Ibid., 549.

120. Barrios, *A Song in the Dark,* 49.

121. Gomery, *The Coming of Sound,* 55–61.

122. Ibid., 48–49.

123. Crafton, *The Talkies,* 162.

124. *Variety,* October 24, 1928, 7. On October 3, 1928, 24, *Variety* noted that there was "No Film Road Show Now Out or in Sight Until January," and reported that "While the wired houses are now limited and under 1,000 currently . . . grosses from them especially as secured by Warners . . . reach so high they make road showing unnecessary." During the period of conversion, however, the roadshowing of sound systems, devices, and films in small towns and rural areas by small-scale independents was given a boost. See *Variety,* November 14, 1928, 7; November 21, 1928, 28; December 12, 1928, 20; January 30, 1929, 17; March 13, 1929, 18.

125. McLaughlin, *Broadway and Hollywood*, 63–67.

126. Ibid., 103–19; Crafton, *The Talkies*, 352–54; Hampton, *History of the American Film Industry*, 393–405.

127. Slide, *Silent Topics*, 88.

128. Sanjek, *Pennies from Heaven*, 47; *MPW*, February 22, 1919, 1057.

129. Slide, *Silent Topics*, 88.

130. Sanjek, *Pennies from Heaven*, 106.

131. Crafton, *The Talkies*, 106–7, 273.

132. Ibid., 195; Gomery, *The Coming of Sound*, 195; Sanjek, *Pennies from Heaven*, 55; Smith, *The Sounds of Commerce*, 30.

133. Hilmes, *Hollywood and Broadcasting*, 33–38, 53–55.

134. Gomery, *The Coming of Sound*, 123.

135. *Variety*, January 2, 1929, 9.

136. Crafton, *The Talkies*, 315 (emphasis in original).

137. Ibid., 315.

138. Sanjek, *Pennies from Heaven*, 107.

139. *Variety*, April 24, 1920, 57.

140. Ibid.; Barrios, *A Song in the Dark*, 69.

141. Barrios, *A Song in the Dark*, 60–65.

142. Ibid., 62.

143. Crafton, *The Talkies*, 294.

144. Thompson and Bordwell, *Film History*, 195.

145. Barrios, *A Song in the Dark*, 74.

NOTES TO CHAPTER 5

1. For an extensive survey of production trends in the 1930s, see Balio, *Grand Design*, 179–312. On big-budget productions in particular, see Smyth, *Reconstructing American Historical Cinema: From* Cimarron *to* Citizen Kane.

2. Finler, *The Hollywood Story*, 286, 288. Other sources give different figures, as noted above in chapter 3, note 41.

3. *Variety*, August 18, 1930, 3; August 27, 1930, 5.

4. Ibid., December 29, 1931, 6.

5. Birchard, *Cecil B. De Mille's Hollywood*, 252.

6. *Variety*, August 11, 1937, 1, 4; September 29, 1937, 3, 21; January 5, 1938, 5.

7. Ibid., December 23, 1936, 6; July 21, 1937, 3, 10; August 11, 1937, 1, 4; June 1, 1938, 2.

8. Ibid., June 25, 1930, 18.

9. Ibid., January 8, 1930, 87.

10. Ibid., January 22, 1930, 9; January 29, 1930, 8; March 12, 1930, 11.

11. Ibid., November 22, 1932, 16.

12. On the spread of percentage booking terms in the early years of sound, see Lewis, *The Motion Picture Industry*, 190–200; Hanssen, "Revenue Sharing and the Coming of Sound," in Sedgwick and Pokorny, *An Economic History of Film*.

13. *Variety*, May 14, 1930, 4.

14. Ibid., October 25, 1932, 26. One of Warner–First National's standard trade advertising slogans of the period was "Available to you NOW—Day and Date with Broadway." See, for example, *Variety*, February 26, 1930, 18–19.

15. Ibid., September 22, 1931, 5.

16. Ibid., July 1, 1936, 5.

17. Ibid., January 3, 1933, 34.

18. Ibid., October 11, 1932, 6; November 8, 1932, 4; December 6, 1932, 5; January 17, 1933, 27; January 24, 1933, 9; January 31, 1933, 35; March 7, 1933, 23.

19. Ibid., August 9, 1932, 4.

20. Ibid., January 31, 1933, 32, 35; March 14, 1933, 12; March 28, 1933, 24; April 18, 1933, 4.

21. Ibid., May 8, 1935, 6; May 22, 1935, 9; May 29, 1935, 9.

22. Ibid., July 31, 1935, 1; September 18, 1935, 6; October 16, 1935, 7; November 6, 1935, 9; November 13, 1935, 9.

23. Ibid., July 1, 1936, 2. Universal generally released its 1936 remake of *Show Boat* for similar reasons, taking out trade advertisements to explain, "Why we are not using *Show Boat* as a roadshow" (ibid., May 13, 1936, 28).

24. Ibid., July 1, 1936, 5.

25. Ibid., July 21, 1937, 4. Balio, *Grand Design,* 180, claims that "from six to ten prestige pictures were typically accorded this [roadshow] status each year" during the 1930s. In fact, aside from 1937, no more than four pictures were so presented on Broadway in any one year from 1935 to 1943.

26. *Variety,* September 1, 1937, 6; September 15, 1937, 3. Paramount subsequently demanded rentals of 40–50 percent on *Men with Wings* (1938) (ibid., July 13, 1938, 7; October 19, 1938, 7).

27. Ibid., July 28, 1927, 28.

28. Ibid., October 8, 1930, 4; December 18, 1934, 6; September 18, 1935, 21; October 9, 1935, 7, 56; August 18, 1937, 2; September 15, 1937, 3.

29. Ibid., January 6, 1937, 12.

30. Ibid., May 18, 1938, 1, 22.

31. The impression is often given by historians that all A-pictures were booked on percentages and all B-pictures on flat fees, but this was far from being the case. Many regular A-films were booked for fixed rentals, and exhibitors protested when percentage terms were asked for what they considered an excessive number of films.

32. *Variety,* September 25, 1935, 4; October 9, 1935, 4; March 9, 1938, 25.

33. Ibid., January 13, 1937, 5, 21.

34. Ibid., November 15, 1939, 5, 22.

35. Ibid., November 22, 1939, 8.

36. Ibid., December 14, 1938, 3, editorialized: "Blockbooking is the Moloch which consumes good, bad and indifferent output in its insatiable machinery. The wonder is not the scarcity of outstanding, smashing film hits, but that under the present system of operation there are any hits at all."

37. Ibid., January 14, 1931, 11; October 25, 1939, 2, 18.

38. Ibid., March 2, 1938, 5, 19; January 25, 1939, 3, 55.

39. Ibid., February 1, 1931, 19; November 20, 1935, 24; May 21, 1947, 22. There is some doubt as to whether all these engagements were concurrent: when UA's *History Is Made at Night* (1937) opened in 182 simultaneous play dates, this was claimed to be a record (ibid., March 31, 1937, 7).

40. Ibid., August 16, 1939, 5.

41. Ibid., March 2, 1938, 13.

42. Ibid., December 7, 1938, 4.

43. Ibid., July 24, 1935, 4; October 2, 1935, 7, 33; January 6, 1937, 6; November 16, 1938, 6. Selznick International seems consistently to have circulated a large number of copies of its releases through UA, including a remarkable 545 for *The Garden of Allah* (1936), 474 for *Little Lord Fauntleroy* (1936), and 494 for *A Star Is Born* (1937) (Schatz, *The Genius of the System,* 198).

44. *Variety,* March 20, 1940, 5. *Abe Lincoln in Illinois* was planned for roadshow engagements in legitimate theaters, but its unsuccessful early runs may have scotched this.

45. Ibid., November 29, 1932, 3.

46. Ibid., August 23, 1932, 5.

47. Birchard, *Cecil B. De Mille's Hollywood,* 251–52. According to Paramount production records the final cost of *The Sign of the Cross* was $655,949, including an overhead charge of $158,523.49 (AMPAS). Birchard, *Cecil B. De Mille's Hollywood,* 251, gives its world gross to 1937 as $2,738,993.35.

48. Wyke, *Projecting the Past,* 135, 137.

49. *Variety,* April 4, 1933, 5.

50. Birchard, *Cecil B. De Mille's Hollywood,* 275, 283, 292; Paramount Production Files, AMPAS.

51. Erb, *Tracking King Kong* 53–119.

52. *Variety,* April 11, 1933, 8. For details of *Kong*'s original release, see Erb, *Tracking King Kong,* 51–52.

53. *Variety,* January 4, 1939, 44; June 21, 1939, 7, 20.

54. Ibid., July 19, 1939, 1, 37.

55. Schatz, *The Genius of the System,* 90, 94; *Variety,* March 8, 1932, 5. According to the latter report, Universal's million-dollar gross for *Frankenstein* was "the maximum to be had under present conditions." *Dracula* had been intended for a roadshow premiere run but instead was obliged to fulfill an obligation to open on grind at the New York Roxy (*Variety,* January 28, 1931, 5; February 4, 1931, 6).

56. *Variety,* April 20, 1938, 7, 19. Balio, *Grand Design,* 311, expresses doubt that censorship and morality campaigns were behind the trend toward costume prestige pictures, stressing instead the budgetary constraints that prevented their production in significant numbers earlier in the decade.

57. The quotation is from an article Warners commissioned from I. Isaacs, a lecturer in English and Literature at King's College, University of London, which was circulated for use in publicity (in *A Midsummer Night's Dream* files, Warner Bros. Archives, USC).

58. *Variety,* July 24, 1935, 5; October 30, 1935, 4, 15; November 20, 1935, 4; December 4, 1935, 7; January 1, 1936, 27; March 4, 1936, 23, 74.

59. Sklar, "Hub of the System," 202–3. On Warner Bros.' prestige films of the 1930s, see Schatz, *The Genius of the System,* 199–227.

60. *Variety,* December 9, 1936, 25.

61. Ibid., August 26, 1936, 20.

62. Ibid., December 9, 1936, 3, 25.

63. Ibid., February 13, 1934, 3.

64. Ibid., January 29, 1935, 3.

65. Ramsaye, *The Motion Picture Almanac.* Solomon, *Twentieth Century-Fox: A Corporate and Financial History,* 16, claims *Cavalcade* earned $3 million domestically, a figure that is not supported by contemporary sources (this may be the worldwide figure instead). Ramsaye, *The International Motion Picture Almanac,* 834, reports domestic rentals of $750,000.

66. *Variety,* October 30, 1934, 13; December 30, 1936, 3, 15; November 17, 1937, 1, 2; September 14, 1938, 13; March 15, 1939, 14, 54; July 19, 1939, 11; September 6, 1939, 1, 6; September 13, 1939, 3, 16.

67. On Hollywood's attempts to appeal to the English-speaking foreign markets, see Glancy, *When Hollywood Loved Britain.* On the imperial adventure cycle, see Richards, *Visions of Yesterday.* On the "Merrie England" series, see Roddick, *A New Deal in Entertainment,* 235–48.

68. *Variety,* December 6, 1939, 12; January 3, 1940, 5.

69. Ibid., March 1, 1939, 5, 20. Most historians of the western cite 1939 as the crucial year in the genre's artistic development. For a discussion of its significance, see Stanfield, "Country Music and the 1939 Western," in Cameron and Pye, *The Movie Book of the Western,* 22–33.

70. Balio, *Grand Design,* 193–95; Schatz, *Boom and Bust,* 108. See also Roddick, *A New Deal in Entertainment,* 199–216.

71. *Variety,* October 4, 1939, 1, 18–19.

72. Hirschhorn, *The Hollywood Musical.*

73. MGM also released a trio of backstage musicals in 1933. At close to $1 million each, *Dancing Lady, Broadway to Hollywood,* and *Going Hollywood* were all considerably more expensive than Warners'. Only the first, which featured the screen debut of Fred Astaire, was successful.

74. *Variety,* October 3, 1933, 2. On Berkeley's career and his approach to choreography, see Rubin, *Showstoppers: Busby Berkeley and the Tradition of Spectacle.*

75. Independent producers Walter Wanger and Samuel Goldwyn cast themselves in the mold of White and Ziegfeld when they created their own self-named screen revues, respectively *Walter Wanger's Vogues of 1938* (1937) and *The Goldwyn Follies* (1938). Both were expensive; neither was successful. See Bernstein, *Walter Wanger: Hollywood Independent,* 126–27; Berg, *Goldwyn: A Biography,* 298–305.

76. On biopics, see Custen, *Bio/Pics: How Hollywood Constructed Public History.*

77. *Variety,* January 3, 1940, 32.

78. Ibid., March 31, 1937, 4; April 28, 1937, 16; May 19, 1937, 5. According to the last report, the *Revue* would "be played singly in a majority of cases." Gabler, *Walt Disney: The Triumph of the American Imagination,* 218–19, quotes a 1934 request from Roy E. Disney, when *Snow White* was already in the planning stages, to an exhibitor not to show a program of short cartoons as they might "take the edge off this feature idea and give people the impression that a cartoon feature is merely a hodgepodge of several connected subjects."

79. Gabler, *Walt Disney: The Triumph of the American Imagination,* 270. Other accounts of the film's production and reception are given in Bart, *Boffo!,* 257–66; Behlmer, *Behind the Scenes,* 40–60; Eliot, *Walt Disney: Hollywood's Dark Prince,* 81–103; Holliss and Sibley, Snow White and the Seven Dwarfs *and the Making of the Classic Film;* Holliss and Sibley, *The Disney Studio Story,* 26–32; Krause and Witkowski, *Walt Disney's* Snow White and the Seven Dwarfs.

80. Gabler, *Walt Disney: The Triumph of the American Imagination,* 262–63.

81. Behlmer, *Behind the Scenes,* 57; Holliss and Sibley, *The Disney Studio Story,* 31.

82. *Variety,* January 12, 1938, 5; January 19, 1938, 6; June 1, 1938, 4; July 13, 1938, 7. When *Snow White* was booked "by mistake" into a late-run double-feature house in Minneapolis in early 1939, RKO had to apologize to rival exhibitors who had been assured it would never play except as a single feature (ibid., March 8, 1939, 17; March 15, 1939, 23).

83. Ibid., April 27, 1938, 8; May 11, 1938, 23. Other roadshow engagements were reported in Southern California and Arizona, but in most of the country the film played on grind.

84. Ibid., June 14, 1939, 3.

85. Ibid., April 19, 1939, 4. Paramount's western *Wells Fargo* had received 13,200 bookings, the highest number for the 1937–38 season.

86. Ibid., July 19, 1939, 46.

87. Gabler, *Walt Disney: The Triumph of the American Imagination,* 327.

88. The C. J. Tevlin ledger (dated June 30, 1952) does not specifically indicate the 1940 and 1944 reissues, but Gabler, *Walt Disney: The Triumph of the American Imagination,* 277, reports the total gross to May 1939 as $6.7 million. We have therefore presumed that the balance of the figure given by Tevlin (Jewell, "RKO Film Grosses, 1929–1951: The C. J. Tevlin Ledger") derives from these later releases.

89. *Variety,* October 5, 1938, 3; July 19, 1939, 1, 46.

90. Gabler, *Walt Disney: The Triumph of the American Imagination*, 396; Holliss and Sibley, *The Disney Studio Story*, 39, 48. Ironically, in view of its extended exhibition life, *Snow White* was quickly considered by its makers "technically obsolete and unsuitable for revival" because of the advances made by its successors (*Variety*, April 8, 1942, 6).

91. Holliss and Sibley, *The Disney Studio Story*, 39. See also Sam Robins, "Disney Again Tries Trailblazing," *NYT*, November 3, 1940.

92. Gabler, *Walt Disney: The Triumph of the American Imagination*, 347. No Fantasound engagements took place overseas, where the film went straight into general release at regular prices.

93. *Variety*, September 4, 1940, 6; November 20, 1940, 4; Holliss and Sibley, *The Disney Studio Story*, 40.

94. Garity and Jones, "Experiences in Road-Showing Disney's *Fantasia*." For more on Fantasound, see Carr and Hayes, *Wide Screen Movies*, 239, 327–28.

95. *Variety*, June 4, 1941, 23.

96. Ibid., December 3, 1941, 5.

97. Ibid., March 11, 1942, 19 (emphases in original).

98. Ibid., April 22, 1942, 13. On the long history of *Fantasia*, see also Davis, "The Fall and Rise of *Fantasia*," in Stokes and Maltby, *Hollywood Spectatorship*; Luckett, "*Fantasia*: Cultural Constructions of Disney's 'Masterpiece,'" in Smoodin, *Disney Discourse*.

99. This figure excludes the roadshow engagements handled by Disney but probably includes income from a 1946 reissue.

100. Disney described the well-received *Dumbo* as "just one of those little things that we knocked out between epics!" (Gabler, *Walt Disney: The Triumph of the American Imagination*, 381).

101. Ibid., 328. This accounts both for the innovation of Fantasound and for the roadshow plans initially made, then abandoned, for *Bambi*. Max and Dave Fleischer's *Gulliver's Travels* (1939) and *Mr. Bug Goes to Town* (1941), both released through Paramount, were among the few non-Disney animated features made in the United States before the 1950s.

Notes to Chapter 6

1. *Variety*, October 18, 1939, 1, 54.

2. The final negative cost of *Gone with the Wind* (*GWTW*) has been variously reported between $3.9 million and $4.25 million. According to Haver, *David O. Selznick's Hollywood*, 299, the total cost was $4,085,790; according to Selznick himself, it was $4,073,000 (*Variety*, July 24, 1940, 4).

3. See, for example, Bridges and Boodman, Gone with the Wind: *The Definitive Illustrated History of the Book, the Movie, and the Legend;* Flamini, *Scarlett, Rhett, and a Cast of Thousands;* Harmetz, *On the Road to Tara;* Haskell, *Frankly, My Dear:* Gone with the Wind *Revisited;* Lambert, *GWTW: The Making of* Gone with the Wind; Turner, *A Celebration of* Gone with the Wind; and Vertrees, *Selznick's Vision:* Gone with the Wind *and Hollywood Filmmaking.*

4. Memo, David O. Selznick to Al Lichtman, October 20, 1939, in Behlmer, *Memo from David O. Selznick*, 223–26.

5. Sample questionnaires and responses are in the *GWTW* file, Vertical Files Collection, AMPAS.

6. *Variety*, November 29, 1939, 8. See also Thomas M. Pryor, "Listen, *The Wind*!," *NYT*, November 26, 1939.

7. Selznick to Lichtman, 226.

8. A copy of the booklet is contained in the AMPAS file previously cited.

9. Viewers who have only seen roadshow films in home video formats, which often include "Overture," "Entr'acte," and "Exit Music" screen captions to explain the additional music, tend erroneously to assume that these captions were also part of the films' theatrical presentation.

10. Schatz, *The Genius of the System,* 292.

11. *Variety,* December 13, 1939, 3; December 27, 1939, 4; March 6, 1940, 6. The only reported instances of MGM having to reduce its share to make good on the 10 percent profit guarantee were in Canada. Selznick estimated that the distributor's share of the total domestic box-office gross to May 1940 was 66 percent (ibid., April 10, 1940, 4, 16; May 15, 1940, 6).

12. Ibid., January 10, 1940, 4; February 7, 1940, 2.

13. Ibid., February 28, 1940, 3.

14. Ibid., April 3, 1940, 6.

15. Ibid., October 23, 1940, 7; November 13, 1940, 8; February 8, 1941, 7.

16. Ibid., July 24, 1940, 4.

17. Haver, *David O. Selznick's Hollywood,* 307, 329.

18. *Variety,* December 31, 1941, 20; August 18, 1943, 5; January 31, 1945, 1; Haver, *David O. Selznick's Hollywood,* 307, 329. The controversy over the film's British release is discussed in Eyles, "When Exhibitors Saw Scarlett," 23–32.

19. *Variety,* June 5, 1940, 6, 20.

20. Ibid., August 14, 1940, 1, 47; October 16, 1940, 4, 29; October 30, 1940, 6.

21. Ibid., October 21, 1942, 27; February 14, 1945, 7. Contrary to its reputation as a flop, *Citizen Kane* performed extremely well at regular prices in many of those theaters that played it. As a roadshow, however, it was described as "one of the season's worst" (ibid., May 28, 1941, 10). *Variety,* May 14, 1941, 4, reported the sage wisdom of the trade, that "Orson Welles is good, but he isn't Rhett Butler."

22. Ibid., September 10, 1947, 3, 22.

23. Ibid., May 8, 1940, 5, 18; August 28, 1940, 5, 20; December 4, 1940, 7; July 29, 1942, 5; September 16, 1942, 7; October 21, 1942, 5, 22; April 26, 1944, 7; May 26, 1943, 5; December 1, 1943, 7.

24. Ibid., May 7, 1941, 5, 22; August 13, 1941, 7; October 29, 1941, 10; November 12, 1941, 10; September 9, 1942, 7; February 17, 1943, 5. See also Roddick, *A New Deal in Entertainment,* 210–14.

25. *Variety,* July 28, 1943, 46; *MPH,* December 18, 1943, 16.

26. *Variety,* November 6, 1940, 20.

27. Ibid., February 12, 1941, 5. Oddly, all the films listed except *The Blue Bird* had American themes.

28. Ibid., September 2, 1942, 6.

29. Ibid., August 21, 1940, 3, 22; September 18, 1940, 3, 12; November 13, 1940, 1, 29; January 8, 1941, 73; January 22, 1941, 5.

30. Ibid., August 12, 1942, 27; September 23, 1942, 20; December 23, 1942, 7, 16; July 21, 1943, 5, 16; August 18, 1943, 7; August 25, 1943, 7; September 1, 1943, 7; November 17, 1943, 5, 25.

31. Ibid., February 25, 1942, 5, 47; May 20, 1942, 5; July 1, 1942, 7; November 4, 1942, 5, 53; December 30, 1942, 5; October 6, 1943, 5; October 27, 1943, 5; November 10, 1943, 3, 46; February 2, 1944, 5; June 21, 1944, 9.

32. Ibid., July 1, 1942, 21. In fact, the film had been given fifteen test engagements at advanced prices before MGM opted for regular distribution (ibid., June 24, 1942, 13). In latter-day interviews its star, Greer Garson, claimed that the prompt release of *Mrs. Miniver* was at the specific request of President Roosevelt.

33. Frank S. Nugent, in "How Long Should a Movie Be?" *NYT,* February 18, 1945, counted twenty-three films in 1944 running more than two hours.

34. Quoted in ibid.

35. *Variety,* October 4, 1944, 3, 38; *KW,* June 14, 1945, 5; July 19, 1945, 5; Haver, *David O. Selznick's Hollywood,* 342.

36. *Variety,* June 21, 1944, 3, 24.

37. Ibid., October 30, 1940, 20; November 6, 1940, 20; November 13, 1940, 3, 56; September 3, 1941, 13; December 2, 1942, 1; May 19, 1943, 6; July 24, 1943, 10; September 8, 1943, 8. As the first of these reports notes, the previous record price for screen rights to a novel had been the $110,000 paid by RKO for Edna Ferber's *Cimarron.*

38. Ibid., July 21, 1943, 22.

39. *For Whom the Bell Tolls* file, AMPAS; *Variety,* September 25, 1946, 5.

40. *Variety,* June 9, 1943, 19; July 21, 1943, 5; June 14, 1944, 7; June 21, 1944, 24; October 25, 1944, 3; *KW,* November 11, 1943, 36.

41. Behlmer, *Memo from Darryl F. Zanuck,* 78.

42. *Variety,* February 24, 1943, 1, 23; March 24, 1943, 5; December 29, 1943, 3; January 5, 1944, 1, 54–55; March 8, 1944, 7.

43. Ibid., April 17, 1946, 1, 70.

44. Ibid., September 25, 1946, 1, 5.

45. Ibid., January 8, 1947, 1, 8.

46. Ibid., January 7, 1948, 63.

47. *Variety,* January 7, 1948, 5–6.

48. Ibid., December 22, 1948, 3, 16. Other sources place the admissions peak slightly earlier in the year.

49. Finler, *The Hollywood Story,* 288. According to Finler's figures, weekly admissions bottomed out at 16 million in 1971.

50. For more detailed discussion of these developments, see for instance Belton, *Widescreen Cinema,* 69–84.

51. *The Emperor Waltz* file, AMPAS; *Variety,* January 5, 1949, 1, 53.

52. *Variety,* April 17, 1946, 25.

53. Ibid., August 7, 1946, 6.

54. Ibid., October 2, 1946, 5, 8.

55. Glancy, "Warner Bros. Film Grosses, 1921–51: The William Schaefer Ledger," microfiche supplement, appendices 2 and 3.

56. The cost of *Duel in the Sun* has been reported as both $5,255,000 (Haver, *David O. Selznick's Hollywood,* 361) and $6,480,000 (Thomson, *Showman: The Life of David O. Selznick,* 472); the latter figure may include distribution expenses. *Forever Amber* cost $6,375,000 (Solomon, *Twentieth Century-Fox: A Corporate and Financial History,* 243). The cost of *Arch of Triumph* was estimated by *Variety,* December 22, 1948, 4, as over $4 million and by Balio, *United Artists: The Company Built by the Stars,* 217, as over $5 million.

57. *Variety,* February 18, 1948, 1, 16; April 14, 1948, 5, 16; May 5, 1948, 3, 31; June 9, 1948, 7; July 14, 1948, 1, 5, 16, 47; July 28, 1948, 3, 17; September 29, 1948, 11; December 1, 1948, 1, 21; December 15, 1948, 3, 22.

58. Ibid., May 28, 1947, 6; June 4, 1947, 3, 49; February 4, 1948, 7, 25.

59. For further discussion of the antitrust proceedings, see Conant, *Anti-Trust in the Motion Picture Industry;* Conant, "The Impact of the Paramount Decrees," in Balio, *The American Film Industry* (1976); Borneman, "United States versus Hollywood: The Case Study of an Antitrust Suit," and Conant, "The Paramount Decrees Reconsidered," both in Balio, *The American Film Industry* (1985); Schatz, *Boom and Bust,* 19–21, 323–28.

60. Blind *buying* or blind *selling* (the purchase by exhibitors of films sight unseen, or without disclosure of their rental terms by distributors) should not be confused with blind *bidding* (the sale of pictures on an auction basis to exhibitors who submit competitive bids without knowing their rivals' offers).

61. Favorable rental terms were crucial to the profitability of even the most successful films. Selznick's *Rebecca* (1940)—which according to Haver, *David O. Selznick's Hollywood,* 324, cost

$1,280,000—was among the most popular films of its year; but because UA was unable to make more than 1,200 bookings on a percentage basis, the film's U.S. rental on first release was only $1.2 million (*Variety,* August 15, 1945, 18).

62. *Variety,* January 8, 1941, 28. See also *MPH,* December 18, 1943, 15–16.

63. *Variety,* August 2, 1944, 7, 38; December 27, 1944, 5, 18; March 7, 1945, 9.

64. "Findings of Fact," article 64 [1950], *Film History* 4, no. 1 (1990): 54.

65. *Variety,* October 16, 1946, 7.

66. Ibid., October 23, 1946, 3. Universal, Columbia, and UA eventually conceded the roadshow "ban" in 1949 (ibid., November 16, 1949, 7, 14).

67. Ibid., October 30, 1946, 3, 31; November 6, 1946, 11, 3; July 9, 1947, 3, 26. *Variety,* September 29, 1948, 10, observed that the term *roadshow* had now become so vague that it was being used to designate "any film given special distribution handling." It quoted a Fox executive as stating that *The Snake Pit* (1948) would be given "individual handling on a roadshow basis," though it was neither shown twice daily with reserved seats nor exhibited with raised admission prices.

68. Ibid., September 24, 1947, 5, 16. In contrast, Samuel Goldwyn believed there were too few such films; he saw raised prices as a sign of quality, which made exhibitors share the risk of expensive items with producers (ibid., October 29, 1947, 11, 22; March 17, 1948, 6).

69. Ibid., August 6, 1947, 6.

70. Ibid., January 7, 1948, 63; January 12, 1949, 5. Worldwide rentals for *The Best Years of Our Lives* amounted to $14,750,000. According to both Haver, *David O. Selznick's Hollywood,* 368, and Thomson, *Showman: The Life of David O. Selznick,* 472, *Duel in the Sun* earned around $10 million domestically. According to Solomon, *Twentieth Century-Fox: A Corporate and Financial History,* 66, *Forever Amber* earned $8 million worldwide, the amount *Variety* considered necessary for it to break even (November 26, 1947, 21). According to Birchard, *Cecil B. De Mille's Hollywood,* 329, *Unconquered* earned total gross rentals of $6,665,992, including "gross receipts" of $4,633,486; the film showed a loss to March 1951 of $1,717,979. According to the William Schaefer Ledger, total worldwide earnings for *Life with Father* were $6,455,000; its production cost was $4,710,000, Warners' highest to date.

71. *Variety,* April 7, 1948, 7, 20; April 14, 1948, 5, 16; June 9, 1948, 7; November 30, 1949, 3, 16.

72. Ibid., July 21, 1948, 3, 8; July 28, 1948, 5, 20; August 4, 1948, 5, 20; September 8, 1948, 7, 22; May 11, 1949, 5, 20; August 10, 1949, 3, 63; August 31, 1949, 4; December 21, 1949, 3, 9, 16. Costs and earnings figures for *Joan of Arc* are included in the Walter Wanger Collection, State Historical Society, University of Wisconsin–Madison, as well as the Tevlin ledger as excerpted in Jewell, "RKO Film Grosses, 1929–1951," and in Bernstein, *Walter Wanger: Hollywood Independent,* 237–46, 444. The film's disappointing performance in its October 1950 general release was partly attributed to negative publicity arising from star Ingrid Bergman's extramarital affair with the Italian director Roberto Rossellini (news of which broke in December 1949)—an issue that apparently did not affect its exceptionally strong foreign grosses.

73. *Variety,* January 4, 1950, 59.

74. Ibid., June 12, 1946, 1, 4; March 26, 1947, 6; April 2, 1947, 3, 18.

75. Ibid., July 17, 1946, 5; July 24, 1946, 9, 3, 26; July 31, 1946, 9, 16; August 28, 1946, 24–25; September 4, 1946, 11; September 11, 1946, 5, 62; September 18, 1946, 3, 22; September 25, 1946, 11, 29; October 30, 1946, 6; January 22, 1947, 3, 54; February 12, 1947, 7, 23; April 9, 1947, 5, 18.

76. Ibid., August 7, 1946, 1, 62.

77. Conant, "The Paramount Decrees Reconsidered," in Balio, *The American Film Industry* (1985), 559–60.

78. Conant, *Anti-Trust in the Motion Picture Industry,* 212.

79. *Variety,* September 11, 1946, 5, 29; October 9, 1946, 7, 14; April 2, 1947, 3, 18; April 9, 1947, 5.

80. Ibid., May 5, 1948, 1, 3, 18.

81. Holt, "In Deregulation We Trust," 24.

82. Monaco, *American Film Now,* 31.

83. Behlmer, *Memo from David O. Selznick,* 356–57.

84. Fox's *Gentleman's Agreement* and Universal's *A Double Life* (both 1947) opened in Los Angeles on a reserved-seat basis in late 1947 for the same reason.

85. *Variety,* February 26, 1947, 18; March 19, 1947, 4, 18; May 7, 1947, 20–21; May 14, 1947, 3, 20–21, 25; June 18, 1947, 3, 20.

86. Ibid., July 16, 1947, 5, 18.

87. Telegram, Selznick to Paul MacNamara, May 7, 1947, in Behlmer, *Memo from David O. Selznick,* 358–59.

88. *Variety,* May 21, 1947, 22.

89. Ibid., July 30, 1947, 6.

90. Selznick to MacNamara, May 7, 1947, in Behlmer, *Memo from David O. Selznick,* 359.

91. *Variety,* May 21, 1941, 4; July 23, 1941, 1, 48; December 31, 1941, 7; January 28, 1942, 5; February 4, 1942, 6; June 17, 1942, 2, 55; July 8, 1943, 7; November 18, 1942, 5; February 10, 1943, 16; March 17, 1943, 5; March 31, 1943, 15; April 21, 1943, 7; January–July 1946, passim; September 11, 1946, 4, 24; October 2, 1946, 9; October 16, 1946, 4; October 23, 1946, 4; October 30, 1946, 10; June 4, 1947, 6, 25; July 21, 1948, 2.

92. Ibid., September 1, 1948, 4; Tevlin ledger in Jewell, "RKO Film Grosses, 1929–1951"; McCarthy, *Howard Hawks,* 299, 679.

93. *Variety,* February 17, 1943, 21.

94. Ibid., May 7, 1947, 10.

95. Ibid., November 6, 1946, 3, 20; November 20, 1946, 4; February 19, 1946, 3; March 19, 1947, 5, 18, 25; May 7, 1947, 4; August 13, 1947, 20; August 27, 1947, 5; December 29, 1948, 7; Berg, *Goldwyn: A Biography,* 417. Only two U.S. theaters presented *The Best Years of Our Lives* on a reserved-seat basis: the Esquire, Boston, and the Beverly, Los Angeles.

96. *Variety,* February 2, 1949, 5; May 4, 1949, 15.

97. Ibid., October 8, 1947, 5; April 6, 1949, 3, 22; June 15, 1949, 4, 6; July 13, 1949, 7, 18; September 21, 1949, 5, 20; March 7, 1951, 5, 16; August 22, 1951, 20; December 7, 1951, 7, 22; September 28, 1949, 3.

98. Ibid., March 15, 1950, 3, 17; June 27, 1951, 5, 22; June 11, 1951, 5, 29. Fox later drew up a plan to limit the number of day-and-date engagements in a particular territory by splitting theaters into "A" and "B" houses that would play a given film on successive weeks, but this failed to win the cooperation of exhibitors (ibid., June 27, 1951, 5, 61; July 25, 1951, 5, 15).

NOTES TO CHAPTER 7

1. *Variety,* January 5, 1949, 3.

2. According to McCarthy, *Howard Hawks,* 461, Fox's location-shot comedy *I Was a Male War Bride* cost around $2 million, but Solomon, *Twentieth Century-Fox: A Corporate and Financial History,* 244, gives a figure of $3,330,000. If correct, this would make it the most expensive release of 1949.

3. *Variety,* June 21, 1950, 18.

4. Ibid., July 13, 1949, 1, 55.

5. Ibid., January 4, 1950, 6.

6. Ibid., March 16, 1949, 3, 10; March 23, 1949, 1, 14; July 6, 1949, 5, 23, 53; July 20, 1949, 5, 20; September 21, 1949, 3, 18; October 12, 1949, 7, 20; Clark, "Rome: New Directions," 12.

7. *Variety,* October 5, 1949, 9.

8. Ibid., December 22, 1943, 8; December 29, 1943, 1; November 1, 1944, 18; October 16, 1946, 7; May 28, 1947, 37; July 7, 1948, 14; April 26, 1950, 2, 24.

9. Ibid., February 23, 1949, 5, 20; March 12, 1952, 1.

10. Ibid., April 3, 1934, 4; December 16, 1936, 4.

11. Folder 358, Vertical Files Collection, AMPAS. Birchard, *Cecil B. De Mille's Hollywood,* 334, gives a net profit to 1969, following two reissues, of $5,564,925. *Variety* predicted an ultimate domestic gross of $11 million for *Samson and Delilah* and $7 million for *David and Bathsheba* (January 3, 1951, 58; January 2, 1952, 70). Its estimate for the latter was subsequently revised downward, to $4.72 million.

12. *Variety,* August 1, 1951, 1. See the case study of *Captain Horatio Hornblower* in Stubbs, *Inventing England.*

13. *Variety,* July 5, 1950, 3, 6; July 12, 1950, 5, 18; August 8, 1951, 15; September 5, 1951, 5; October 29, 1952, 5; November 12, 1952, 5.

14. DeMille claimed that avoiding excess footage kept his film's costs down: "I don't believe 200 feet of *Samson and Delilah* landed on the cutting room floor. . . . That's how closely it was watched" (ibid., November 16, 1949, 29).

15. Ibid., May 3, 1950, 5, 22; May 10, 1950, 5, 18. Unlike earlier versions, the 1951 *Quo Vadis* omits the question mark from the title.

16. Ibid., November 21, 1951, 16–17.

17. *KW,* March 27, 1952, 8.

18. *Variety,* August 1, 1951, 5; August 29, 1951, 5, 18; October 10, 1951, 5, 13; November 28, 1951, 3; April 30, 1952, 1, 54; May 21, 1952, 5.

19. *Variety,* January 7, 1953, 61.

20. Ibid., August 6, 1952, 3, 18; September 17, 1952, 16–17; January 21, 1953, 12–13.

21. Ibid., November 14, 1951, 5.

22. Compare the journal's earlier comment: "Hollywood will unleash its biggest guns in the 1950 fall season . . . to give one of the greatest mass attacks on TV yet provided" (ibid., August 9, 1950, 7).

23. Ibid., January 2, 1952, 7, 53.

24. Ibid., January 7, 1948, 5.

25. Ibid., March 9, 1949, 3, 4; April 6, 1949, 20. The potential publicity value of television for Hollywood movies was demonstrated this same year with live TV coverage of a number of film premieres, including *Samson and Delilah's* (ibid., December 28, 1949, 7).

26. Ibid., March 29, 1950, 5, 18; April 16, 1952, 4; December 31, 1952, 14. It was reported in *Variety,* March 11, 1953, 15, that 110 theaters in sixty-two cities had been equipped for large-screen TV projection.

27. See the figures in Finler, *The Hollywood Story,* 281.

28. *Variety,* December 28, 1949, 1, 47; May 26, 1954, 4, 18; February 22, 1950, 7; August 9, 1950, 4; July 11, 1951, 7, 29; December 5, 1951, 24; August 6, 1952, 4; January 1, 1958, 12. On the earlier triple-camera system used for Abel Gance's *Napoléon* (1927), see Carr and Hayes, *Wide Screen Movies,* 3–5; Sherlock, "*Widescreen Movies* Corrections," 4.

29. On the development of Cinerama, see Belton, *Widescreen Cinema,* 85–105, 164–65; Boyle, "And Now . . . Cinerama"; Carr and Hayes, *Wide Screen Movies,* 11–27; Erffmeyer, *The History of Cinerama;* Reeves, "The Development of Stereo Magnetic Recording for Film" and "This Is Cinerama"; Sherlock, "*Widescreen Movies* Corrections," 8–16; Swadkins, "Whatever Happened to Cinerama?"

30. *Variety,* October 8, 1952, 6.

31. *This Is Cinerama* Souvenir Program (London: Cinerama Exhibitors, Ltd., 1954, n.p.).

32. Belton, *Widescreen Cinema,* 90.

33. *Variety,* April 17, 1940, 4; January 8, 1941, 35; November 28, 1945, 11; October 14, 1953, 62; November 1, 1950, 15.

34. *This Is Cinerama* Program.

35. *Variety,* December 31, 1952, 13; August 5, 1953, 3, 18; January 13, 1954, 10; September 29, 1954, 20; January 3, 1955, 5.

36. Ibid., October 22, 1952, 3, 18.

37. Ibid., August 10, 1955, 7; January 1, 1958, 12; July 2, 1958, 5; September 24, 1958, 5, 18; December 20, 1961, 18. In 1963 a compilation feature, *Best of Cinerama,* was made by cutting up leftover prints of the five travelogues and editing the segments together.

38. The concept of "engulfment" is discussed in Erffmeyer, *The History of Cinerama,* 238–46, and Spellerberg, *Technology and the Film Industry,* 140–41, 208–14.

39. Belton , *Widescreen Cinema,* 76–84, 97.

40. *Variety,* October 29, 1952, 3, 20; January 14, 1953, 3, 61; May 13, 1953, 3; April 21, 1954, 13; December 4, 1957, 18.

41. Ibid., May 2, 1956, 24; January 16, 1957, 17; April 17, 1957, 22; July 24, 1957, 29; August 21, 1957, 10; March 26, 1957, 23; September 3, 1958, 3, 14; September 24, 1958, 13; August 12, 1959, 7, 10; December 16, 1959, 5; December 23, 1959, 5, 63; January 8, 1962, 3; July 11, 1962, 24; Erffmeyer, *The History of Cinerama,* 95–226.

42. A simplified version of Cinerama that could be installed in theaters on a temporary basis was tried in Atlanta in April 1956 but not repeated. Traveling Cinerama shows, involving the erection of inflatable tents in temporary locations on a circuslike basis, toured Continental Europe from 1961 and Britain from 1964. See *Variety,* February 15, 1956, 3, 20; March 28, 1956, 17; May 10, 1961, 3; September 13, 1961, 24; May 29, 1964, 22; *KW,* August 31, 1961, 9; April 30, 1964, 11; Erffmeyer, *The History of Cinerama,* 184–87, 230–31.

43. *Variety,* April 11, 1962, 3; September 19, 1962, 15.

44. Ibid., November 5, 1952, 1.

45. Ibid., June 22, 1927, 13; June 25, 1928, 18; May 14, 1930, 23; December 23, 1936, 5; February 26, 1941, 12; July 5, 1950, 1, 55. On the history of 3-D processes, see Hayes, *3-D Movies: A History and Filmography of Stereoscopic Cinema;* Morgan and Symmes, *Amazing 3-D;* Spellerberg, *Technology and the Film Industry,* 144–56.

46. *Variety,* October 22, 1952, 7; December 10, 1952, 15; January 14, 1953, 3; March 25, 1953, 3; April 29, 1953, 7; Balio, *United Artists: The Company That Changed the Film Industry,* 51. Natural Vision was coincidentally the same name as the 63 mm wide-gauge process used by RKO for *Danger Lights* in 1930.

47. *Variety,* April 1, 1953, 23; Carr and Hayes, *Wide Screen Movies,* 257–58; Morgan and Symmes, *Amazing 3-D,* 64. On the distribution and promotion of *House of Wax* and other 1950s 3-D films, see Heffernan, *Ghouls, Gimmicks, and Gold,* 16–42.

48. *Variety,* August 19, 1953, 5, 15; November 4, 1953, 4, 16; November 11, 1953, 17; November 25, 1953, 10. Morgan and Symmes, *Amazing 3-D,* 88, claim that *Kiss Me Kate*'s New York premiere run at Radio City Music Hall was in a flat version because of the management's perception of the "shady reputation of 3-D in the public's mind."

49. *Variety,* March 25, 1953, 27; March 18, 1953, 3; July 29, 1953, 7, 14; August 26, 1953, 7, 20; September 2, 1953, 3, 16; October 21, 1953, 11, 22.

50. Ibid., June 10, 1953, 5; May 26, 1954, 1; January 5, 1955, 59. Maltby, *Harmless Entertainment,* 58, argues that "3-D failed because of the purpose to which the studios put it."

51. *Variety,* January 7, 1953, 33.

52. Belton, *Widescreen Cinema,* 40–43. On the development of CinemaScope, see Belton, "CinemaScope: The Economics of Technology"; Carr and Hayes, *Wide Screen Movies,* 57–65;

Hincha, "Selling CinemaScope: 1953–1956" and *Twentieth Century-Fox's CinemaScope;* Sherlock, "*Widescreen Movies* Corrections," 20–22; Spellerberg, *Technology and the Film Industry* and "The Ideology of CinemaScope."

53. *Variety,* January 14, 1953, 3, 61; February 4, 1953, 1, 7, 20; May 6, 1953, 5; July 1, 1953, 5, 14; September 23, 1953, 6, 23; September 30, 1953, 4; November 4, 1953, 3, 16; December 30, 1953, 7, 15, 16; January 6, 1954, 5; January 13, 1954, 10; Thomas M. Pryor, "Fox Films Embark on 3-Dimension Era," *NYT,* February 2, 1953; Solomon, *Twentieth Century-Fox: A Corporate and Financial History,* 85, 88.

54. Belton, *Widescreen Cinema,* 137.

55. Belton, "CinemaScope: The Economics of Technology," 38–40; Belton, *Widescreen Cinema,* 146; Hincha, *Twentieth Century-Fox's CinemaScope,* 121–29, 189–95, 265–74.

56. *Variety,* January 13, 1954, 5, 22; March 24, 1954, 15; April 21, 1954, 4, 16; *KW,* January 20, 1955, 3; Belton, *Widescreen Cinema,* 133–35; Carr and Hayes, *Wide Screen Movies,* 244–46; Hincha, *Twentieth Century-Fox's CinemaScope,* 129–34, 195–221; Sherlock, "*Widescreen Movies* Corrections," 43–44.

57. *Variety,* May 5, 1954, 5, 15; May 26, 1954, 7; April 6, 1955, 16; June 15, 1955, 15; October 26, 1955, 22; November 2, 1955, 22; November 23, 1955, 22; June 13, 1956, 5; October 24, 1956, 4; January 30, 1957, 17; Hincha, "Selling CinemaScope: 1953–1956," 48–51; Belton, *Widescreen Cinema,* 136–37. Other companies had been using combined magnetic-optical prints since 1955. For an account of Fox's dispute with the Rank circuits in Britain over stereophonic sound and extended runs for CinemaScope pictures, see Eyles, "CinemaScope and the Fox Circuit."

58. See Carr and Hayes, *Wide Screen Movies,* 67–89, 152–55; Sherlock, "*Widescreen Movies* Corrections," 23–25, 28–29.

59. Belton, *Widescreen Cinema,* 116–17.

60. *KW,* February 3, 1955, 3; September 29, 1955, 3. These became the standard widescreen aspects ratios for, respectively, Continental Europe, Britain, and the United States. Some films were also recommended for framing at 2:1.

61. *Variety,* April 28, 1954, 3, 20; August 18, 1954, 5, 16; October 13, 1954, 10; January 5, 1955, 5, 59; *KW,* April 14, 1955, 38; Belton, *Widescreen Cinema,* 125–27; Carr and Hayes, *Wide Screen Movies,* 144–52; Sherlock, "*Widescreen Movies* Corrections," 27–29. On the development of VistaVision, see also Vincent, *Standing Tall and Wide.* Despite its discontinuance in principal photography, VistaVision was often used for special effects shots from the 1970s through the 1990s because of its superior resolution.

62. *Variety,* October 19, 1955, 3.

63. Ibid., September 1, 1954, 3, 22; September 29, 1954, 3; August 10, 1955, 5, 52; November 9, 1955, 4; October 26, 1955, 13; November 16, 1955, 5, 75; January 25, 1956, 5; Belton, *Widescreen Cinema,* 152–55; Carr and Hayes, *Wide Screen Movies,* 65–67; Sherlock, "*Widescreen Movies* Corrections," 22–23.

64. Belton, *Widescreen Cinema,* 165–73.

65. *Variety,* July 11, 1951, 29.

66. Ibid., March 25, 1953, 1, 20; December 9, 1953, 3, 26; May 19, 1954, 3, 23; June 30, 1954, 3, 16; January 19, 1955, 5, 18; April 27, 1955, 4; November 2, 1955, 5, 24; Thomas M. Pryor, "Hollywood Revelation: First Demonstration of Todd-AO Shows Process Is a Challenge to Cinerama," *NYT,* June 27, 1954; *KW,* September 29, 1955, Studio Review, iii. On the development of Todd-AO, see Belton, *Widescreen Cinema,* 158–82; Carr and Hayes, *Wide Screen Movies,* 164–72; Sherlock, "*Widescreen Movies* Corrections," 30–35.

67. *Variety,* November 24, 1954, 3, 16; October 19, 1955, 11; April 4, 1956, 4; October 10, 1956, 5; February 6, 1957, 3. The CinemaScope version of *Oklahoma!* was reportedly made at

the insistence of the Bankers Trust Company, which provided $1.5 million of its production cost (ibid., March 9, 1955, 4).

68. See the Web page "Two Different Camera Negatives—Four Different Prints," at the American Widescreen Museum, www.widescreenmuseum.com/widescreen/80daysformats.

69. *Variety,* September 22, 1954, 3; September 19, 1956, 15; *HR,* May 21, 1957, 1; August 23, 1957, 1, 4; Balio, *United Artists: The Company That Changed the Film Industry,* 129–32. In Britain, the 35 mm Cinestage prints were shaved by 1 mm to avoid both Entertainments Tax and the quota regulations applicable to standard-gauge films, which would have limited the length of runs (*KW,* July 4, 1957, 7; Carr and Hayes, *Wide Screen Movies,* 172).

70. *Variety,* March 7, 1956, 4; October 10, 1956, 25; *HR,* September 19, 1956, 1, 4.

71. *Variety,* October 24, 1956, 3, 70; June 31, 1957, 1, 4; March 26, 1958, 16; May 23, 1958, 1; November 12, 1958, 7; *HR,* October 16, 1956, 1; September 25, 1957, 1; November 18, 1957, 1.

72. Reporting the studio's "belief that the Todd-AO label is one which the public respects when it comes to roadshows," *Variety,* December 3, 1958, 14, also stated that Fox had "conceded that CinemaScope has been 'bastardized' to the point where it virtually means little any more at the boxoffice."

73. *Variety,* October 17, 1956, 23; February 20, 1957, 1, 54; June 7, 1961, 3; January 23, 1963; Solomon, *Twentieth Century-Fox: A Corporate and Financial History,* 227, 251.

74. Carr and Hayes, *Wide Screen Movies,* 157–59, 178–83.

75. *Variety,* July 1, 1959, 20; March 16, 1960, 19, 21. *Scent of Mystery* was later deodorized, reedited, retitled *Holiday in Spain,* and reissued in 1961. It was converted for three-strip Cinerama projection in some overseas situations (Carr and Hayes, *Wide Screen Movies,* 179–80, 221–23, 413–14).

76. *Raintree County* publicity brochure (MGM, 1957), 13.

77. *Variety,* December 12, 1957, 1, 4; *HR,* December 2, 1957, 2.

78. *KW,* April 23, 1959, 4.

79. *Variety,* August 17, 1960, 4, 6.

80. Carr and Hayes, *Wide Screen Movies,* 27–30; *Variety,* June 12, 1963, 3, 17.

81. *Krakatoa, East of Java* Souvenir Program (Cinerama, 1969, n.p.).

82. *Variety,* September 19, 1957, 17; December 10, 1958, 5; March 4, 1959, 7, 14; February 8, 1960, 3; Carr and Hayes, *Wide Screen Movies,* 152–63.

83. Belton, *Widescreen Cinema,* 179–82; Carr and Hayes, *Wide Screen Movies,* 196–206; Coate and Kallay, "Presented in 70 mm"; Lobban, "Coming in 70 mm"; Sherlock, "*Widescreen Movies* Corrections," 36–37. *The King and I* had earlier been blown up from 55 mm to 70 mm for a 1961 reissue, a process Fox named "Grandeur 70."

84. Zanuck to Skouras, 223. Fox in fact continued to release a few non-anamorphic and black-and-white films each year, but these were mostly B-movies made by independent producers rather than in-house productions.

85. Memo, Zanuck to All Producers and Executives, March 12, 1953, in Behlmer, *Memo from Darryl F. Zanuck,* 233–34 (emphasis in original).

86. *Variety,* April 21, 1954, 10; September 8, 1954, 18; December 8, 1954, 63.

87. Ibid., August 25, 1954, 5; October 6, 1954, 5.

88. Ibid., September 1, 1954, 10, quoted exhibitor S. D. Kane's observation, "If the market holds more big pictures than the buying public can digest there will be heavy losses on costly and meritorious pictures—losses that could easily wipe out profits on others."

89. Belton, *Widescreen Cinema,* 175.

90. Bosley Crowther, "Picture of Hollywood in the Depths," *NYT,* June 14, 1953.

91. See, for example, Kohler and Lassally, "The Big Screens." Producer John Houseman

argued that "successful widescreen production demands a director with an awareness of stage techniques" (interviewed in *Variety,* May 6, 1953, 20).

92. See, for example, Barr, "CinemaScope: Before and After," and Bordwell "CinemaScope: The Modern Miracle You See without Glasses."

93. *Variety,* January 5, 1955, 7.

94. Maltby, *Harmless Entertainment,* 56–59.

95. *KW,* November 24, 1955, 10.

96. Belton, *Widescreen Cinema,* 279, 175.

NOTES TO CHAPTER 8

1. *KW,* December 17, 1959, 6. *The Nun's Story* was released on a roadshow basis in Britain, but not in the United States.

2. *Variety,* January 8, 1958, 6.

3. Ibid., January 1, 1958, 12.

4. Birchard, *Cecil B. De Mille's Hollywood,* 351.

5. For further discussion of the film's marketing, see Cohan, *Masked Men,* 122–30.

6. Bosley Crowther, "Screen Phenomenon," *NYT,* November 10, 1957.

7. Press release, March 7, 1957 (*The Ten Commandments* file, AMPAS).

8. *Variety,* January 7, 1959, 48.

9. Ibid., December 28, 1960, 7.

10. Ibid., November 9, 1960, 4; January 11, 1961, 5, 15; February 8, 1961, 4; Clark and Anderson, *John Wayne's* The Alamo, 112, 139, 159.

11. *Variety,* August 3, 1960, 22; September 7, 1960, 1; November 9, 1960, 11; December 14, 1960, 17. The other four 1960 roadshows, all of which failed, were Fox's *Can-Can,* MGM's *Cimarron,* Warners' *Sunrise at Campobello,* and the independent release *Scent of Mystery.*

12. *Variety,* October 2, 1957, 11; December 26, 1962, 6; January 29, 1964. 5; *HR,* September 25, 1957, 1; November 29, 1957, 2; December 5, 1957, 1.

13. *Variety,* June 22, 1949, 1, 48.

14. Ibid., August 20, 1958, 16.

15. Fordin, *MGM's Greatest Musicals,* 493–95.

16. *Variety,* December 2, 1959, 13.

17. Ibid, 7.

18. Ibid., November 9, 1960, 1, 69; November 23, 1960, 4.

19. *KW,* February 1, 1962, 16; Eames, *The MGM Story,* 128.

20. Birchard, *Cecil B. De Mille's Hollywood,* 178; DeMille, *The Autobiography of Cecil B. DeMille,* 237.

21. Press release, April 30, 1957 (*The Ten Commandments* file, AMPAS).

22. See the comments made in the documentary *Directed by William Wyler* (Topgallant Productions, 1986, available on DVD from Kino Video), which contains an interview conducted a few days before Wyler's death in 1981.

23. *Variety,* November 18, 1959, 8, 86; December 21, 1960, 3.

24. *HR,* October 20, 1961; *Variety,* May 30, 1962, 24.

25. *Variety,* January 9, 1962, 61.

26. Ibid., January 8, 1964, 37; Manso, *Brando,* 514–55.

27. *KW,* April 25, 1963, 8; *Variety,* May 19, 1993, C-94.

28. *Variety,* January 3, 1962, 3; August 15, 1962, 14; August 8, 1963, 5; January 8, 1964, 13; October 14, 1964, 15; September 1, 1965, 5; May 19, 1993, C-90, C-108.

29. Ibid., February 27, 1957, 5.

30. Ibid., August 29, 1956, 7, 18.

31. Haver, A Star Is Born: *The Making of the 1954 Movie and Its 1983 Restoration,* 202–4.

32. *HR,* August 21, 1957, 1; December 9, 1957, 1, 8; advertisement, *Variety,* December 25, 1957, 15.

33. "Change in Policy Decided on at Fox," *NYT,* May 8, 1961.

34. Gussow, *Darryl F. Zanuck,* 243–44.

35. Solomon, *Twentieth Century-Fox: A Corporate and Financial History,* 140–53; Silverman, *The Fox That Got Away,* 91–115.

36. *Variety,* January 16, 1963, 5, 19; June 5, 1963, 1, 63; June 19, 1963, 4; October 30, 1963, 16; February 26, 1964, 4.

37. Vincent Canby, "Costly *Cleopatra* Is Nearing Its Break-Even Point," *NYT,* March 25, 1966. Canby notes that the film's break-even point had now been refigured at $41,358,000.

38. *Variety,* February 11, 1953, 21; November 2, 1955, 25; March 7, 1956, 4; March 28, 1956, 26; April 11, 1956, 13; May 16, 1956, 1, 3, 61; July 4, 1956, 1, 40; November 7, 1956, 1, 4; October 30, 1960, 31, 34; April 14, 1964, 1, 68; February 8, 1967, 11; July 15, 1970, 1. On the sale of theatrical features to television, see also Balio, "Part IV: Retrenchment and Reorganization, 1948–," in Balio, *The American Film Industry* (1985), 434–38; Segrave, *Movies at Home;* Leonard Sloane, "At the Movies: Big Costs, Revenues, TV Sales," *NYT,* October 23, 1966.

39. *Variety,* March 30, 1966, 27.

40. Ibid., January 3, 1973, 99.

41. Ibid., September 28, 1966, 1, 29, 68.

42. Ibid., October 16, 1963, 3, 13.

43. *KW,* June 24, 1967, 20; see also *KW,* June 8, 1968, 48.

44. Paul Lazarus Jr., UA's director of advertising and publicity, quoted in Knight, "The Reluctant Audience," 191. See also Griffith, "Where Are the Dollars?" and Street, *Transatlantic Crossings,* 96–106.

45. *Variety,* February 6, 1946, 3.

46. Note from Harold Auten, August 5, 1948; office rushgram from Auten, September 2, 1948 (*Henry V* file, United Artists Collection, Wisconsin State Historical Society, University of Wisconsin–Madison). Street, *Transatlantic Crossings,* 94, quotes an actual U.S. gross for *Henry V* of only $1,254,788, but gives no accounting date. Internal company correspondence suggests that total cumulative earnings were ultimately much greater. For example, a letter from Auten dated November 20, 1947 gives the net *profit* (not gross rental) for UA to that point as $1,282,744.17.

47. *Variety,* April 4, 1951, 1, 55; January 9, 1952, 7, 53. Knight, "The Reluctant Audience," 191, writing in 1953, claimed that "the number of 'art houses' . . . has jumped in the past six years from a scant dozen to over 450."

48. Sklar, *Movie-Made America,* 271–72.

49. *Variety,* September 9, 1964, 3, 25.

50. Ibid., September 27, 1950, 10, 22; October 18, 1950, 3, 16.

51. Ibid., July 20, 1960, 5; August 10, 1960, 13. Paramount used a similar policy, with less success, for the western *One-Eyed Jacks* (1961) and the Cold War drama *The Spy Who Came In from the Cold* (1965).

52. Ibid., January 9, 1946, 36.

53. See Schaefer, *"Bold! Daring! Shocking! True!"* for a comprehensive history of exploitation roadshows before 1959.

54. A 1949 Audience Research Institute survey confirmed its long-held belief that teenagers were "the most frequent and faithful theatregoers" and concluded that "profits do not lie in a producer's knocking himself out trying to get into the theatre that portion of the public that infrequently buys a ticket" (*Variety,* August 31, 1949, 5). Nevertheless, Hollywood preferred to do exactly that.

55. *Variety,* July 13, 1949, 7; July 20, 1949, 7.

56. Ibid., January 21, 1953, 20.

57. Ibid.; Heffernan, *Ghouls, Gimmicks, and Gold,* 35.

58. *Variety,* April 8, 1959, 17. On Turner's campaign for *The Beast from 20,000 Fathoms,* see Hayes and Bing, *Open Wide,* 145–50.

59. *Variety,* December 25, 1934, 2; March 17, 1948, 7, 18; January 5, 1949, 30; October 26, 1949, 3, 20; May 7, 1952, 5; June 4, 1952, 7, 22; July 23, 1952, 3, 23. See also the figures in Finler, *The Hollywood Story,* 288.

60. *Variety,* January 14, 1953, 17.

61. Ibid., June 18, 1958, 18; October 6, 1958, 15; December 10, 1958, 7, 19; April 1, 1959, 5, 18; August 5, 1959, 24; September 9, 1959, 7; October 14, 1959, 3, 18; November 18, 1959, 7; February 8, 1961, 10; June 24, 1964, 11; Robert Alden, "Advertising: Hard Sell for Motion Pictures," *NYT,* May 29, 1960. On Levine's life and work, see McKenna, "Joseph E. Levine: Showmanship, Reputation, and Industrial Practice, 1945–1977."

62. *Variety,* December 18, 1957, 14. Fox executive Alex Harrison explained that "we wanted to come as close to a hard ticket policy without going actually into hard tickets" (ibid., October 30, 1957, 24).

63. *Los Angeles Times,* January 14, 1958, 12.

64. *Variety,* January 1, 1958, 13; January 15, 1958, 16; *HR,* November 5, 1957, 3; January 10, 1958, 1; "'Farewell' Saturates Area," *Los Angeles Times,* January 14, 1958. On the making and marketing of *A Farewell to Arms,* see Behlmer, *Memo from David O. Selznick,* 423–43.

65. *Variety,* June 26, 1957, 5, 18. *Love Me Tender* opened in some five hundred theaters simultaneously in Thanksgiving week, 1956; its success "under-scored the need for the industry to develop players and subject matter to bring out the juvenile audience sector" (ibid., November 28, 1956, 4).

66. Ibid., August 31, 1960, 7, 62. Regional saturation was also used for the wide general release of *The Alamo* in the summer of 1961.

67. Ibid., June 15, 1953, 5; January 27, 1954, 21; February 24, 1954, 7; June 2, 1954, 5; April 15, 1959, 14.

68. *KW,* July 7, 1962, 8.

69. *Variety,* May 30, 1962, 3.

70. Ibid., May 16, 1962, 3, 11.

71. *KW,* July 7, 1962, 8.

72. *Variety,* May 30, 1962, 16. As this article points out, the Showcase plan had been pretested in New York the year before with UA's highly successful Greek import *Never on Sunday.*

73. Ibid., August 22, 1962, 7; July 24, 1963, 18.

74. Bosley Crowther, "New York's Movie Showcase: 2-Year Exercise in Frustration," *NYT,* July 7, 1964; see also Balio, *United Artists: The Company That Changed the Film Industry,* 210–12; Leonard Sloane, "For Film Makers, 2 Roads to Profit," *NYT,* June 15, 1969.

75. *Variety,* August 17, 1960, 15.

76. Ibid., October 10, 1962, 14.

77. Rubin, *The James Bond Films,* 55–57.

78. *Variety,* June 26, 1963, 26; April 15, 1964, 4; January 13, 1965, 1, 86; March 31, 1965, 3, 20; December 29, 1965, 5, 14; October 12, 1966, 1, 76; March 15, 1967, 5; October 4, 1967, 4; March 3, 1971, 6, 26; Balio, *United Artists: The Company That Changed the Film Industry,* 260–62; Chapman, *License to Thrill,* 112–14.

79. *Variety,* January 20, 1965, 4; February 24, 1965, 7; April 28, 1965, 17; May 5, 1965, 4, 16; September 15, 1965, 1, 90; February 16, 1966, 11; April 27, 1966, 29; May 18, 1966, 3; March 7, 1973, 22.

80. Chapman, *License to Thrill,* 20–21.

81. *Variety,* July 1, 1964, 3, 18; July 29, 1964, 1, 30; August 12, 1964, 1, 62; August 19, 1964, 7, 16; September 16, 1964, 11, 21; September 23, 1964, 28; September 30, 1964, 7, 26; Warner Bros. press release (n.d.), in *Hamlet* file, Warner Bros. Archives, USC.

82. *Variety,* November 25, 1966, 20. A thousand prints were made of UA's Beatles vehicle *A Hard Day's Night* (1964), but they do not appear all to have been used for concurrent national bookings: *Variety,* September 23, 1964, 5, lists 397 U.S./Canadian engagements in its first six weeks of release.

83. Thompson and Bordwell, *Film History,* 343.

84. Ironically, despite its international theme and cast, *Around the World in Eighty Days* was far more successful in the United States than abroad.

85. Segrave, *American Films Abroad,* 201.

86. *Variety,* April 30, 1952, 1, 54; January 6, 1954, 9; May 27, 1959, 7. See also the data in Segrave, *American Films Abroad,* 287–90.

87. Figures quoted by Wagstaff, "Italian Genre Films in the World Market," in Nowell-Smith and Ricci, *Hollywood and Europe,* 74. France's ticket sales had actually fallen slightly in the mid-1950s and then recovered, while those of Italy had risen still further before declining slightly; they reached 819 million in 1955 compared to France's 373 million in that year. Television eventually began to make inroads into these markets in the 1960s, though not as seriously as in Britain and America.

88. Guback, *The International Film Industry,* 166.

89. For more detailed discussion, see Murphy, *Sixties British Cinema;* Walker, *Hollywood, England.*

90. *Variety,* October 17, 1956, 15; March 4, 1959, 7; August 24, 1960, 7, 20; December 27, 1961, 3, 17; Fadiman, "Runaways."

91. In Murray Schumach, "Hollywood Stand: Case for Shooting in Spain Upheld by *Solomon and Sheba* Producer," *NYT,* October 4, 1959.

92. Among the many accounts of the biblical and ancient-world epic, see particularly Babington and Evans, *Biblical Epics;* Eldridge, *Hollywood's History Films;* Elley; *The Epic Film;* Richards, *Hollywood's Ancient Worlds;* Solomon, *The Ancient World in the Cinema;* and Suras, *The Epic in Film.*

93. Balance sheet in *Spartacus* file, Kirk Douglas Collection, University of Wisconsin–Madison. Of course, the film's distributor, Universal-International, enjoyed the benefits of the distribution and overhead fees levied on the independent production.

94. *Variety,* August 11, 1965, 11.

95. *The Greatest Story Ever Told* files, George Stevens Collection, AMPAS; *Variety,* May 10, 1993, C-88.

96. *Variety,* October 14, 1964, 7; June 28, 1965, 3, 18; October 6, 1965, 3; *Films and Filming,* December 1963, 46; Silverman, *The Fox That Got Away,* 325. Columbia released *King David* in 1985.

97. *KW,* December 1, 1960, 5.

98. *King of Kings* London Conference Brochure, 6.

99. *55 Days at Peking* Souvenir Program Brochure (London: Program Publishing, 1963), n.p. On Bronston's Spanish empire, see particularly Rosendorf, *The Life and Times of Samuel Bronston* and "Hollywood in Madrid."

100. "Director of Second Unit Operations" Andrew Marton has claimed the credit for devising and executing this opening sequence. See the accounts of the film's troubled production in D'Antonio, *Andrew Marton,* 413–23; Eisenschitz, *Nicholas Ray,* 380–89; Gordon, *Hollywood Exile,* 145–64; Heston, *In the Arena,* 273–96; Martin, *The Magnificent Showman,* 89–128; Rosendorf, *The Life and Times of Samuel Bronston,* 290–97.

101. *Variety*, January 15, 1964, 7.

102. The term "intimate spectacle" was used by *Cromwell* producer Irving Allen (ibid., November 5, 1969, 30), among others. Galbraith IV, *A History and Analysis of the Roadshow Mode of Motion Picture Exhibition*, 59–62, discusses "intimate epics." See also Murphy, *Sixties British Cinema*, 256–75.

103. *Variety*, September 28, 1966, 4.

104. Ibid., December 10, 1969, 5.

105. Eames, *The MGM Story*, 325; *Variety*, November 1, 1972, 24; May 9–15, 1994, 40. *Variety* had previously carried a domestic rental figure for *Zhivago* of $47,253,762 (e.g., May 10, 1993, C-84); the reasons for its alteration are unclear.

106. *KW*, February 24, 1966, 8.

107. Pratley, *The Cinema of David Lean*, 204; see also Brownlow, *David Lean*, 553–88.

108. *Variety*, January 5, 1972, 67.

109. New York's Radio City Music Hall, conscious of local antipathy toward the genre, insisted on billing the John Wayne vehicle *True Grit* (1969) as an "outdoor adventure picture" rather than as a western (ibid., April 23, 1969, 28).

110. See Coyne, *The Crowded Prairie*, 105–19; Hall, "*How the West Was Won*: History, Spectacle, and the American Mountains," in Cameron and Pye, *The Movie Book of the Western*; Kimble, "*How the West Was Won*—in Cinerama"; Shivas, "*How the West Was Won*."

111. Basinger, *The World War II Combat Film*, 197.

112. Ibid., 198–200.

113. See the tabulations of box-office performance by original author in *Variety*, February 28, 1962, 7, 16. The highest-grossing authors were, in order, Lew Wallace (for the two versions of *Ben-Hur*), Margaret Mitchell (*GWTW*), and Jules Verne. Michener was the most lucrative living writer.

114. Altman, *The American Film Musical*, 196–97.

115. Ibid., 198–99.

116. *Variety*, April 26, 1961, 20; August 9, 1961, 4; March 21 1962, 3, 21; April 24, 1963, 21; May 18, 1966, 18; Balio, *United Artists: The Company That Changed the Film Industry*, 177; Berg, *Goldwyn: A Biography*, 487.

117. *Variety*, April 28, 1965, 3, 20; Holliss and Sibley, *The Disney Studio Story*, 82–84, 194–95; Gabler, *Walt Disney: The Triumph of the American Imagination*, 600.

118. *Variety*, November 27, 1963, 5; January 1, 1964, 14; March 29, 1967, 3; interoffice memo, D. Knecht to Jack L. Warner, January 4, 1962, in *My Fair Lady* files, Warner Bros. Archives, USC. It is perhaps worth pointing out that there is no entry for *My Fair Lady* in the William Schaefer Ledger, which otherwise lists rentals for most Warner Bros. releases up to 1966, and that *Variety*'s estimates of its earnings have fluctuated considerably over the years. Rumors persist that it was in fact a flop, but it is the film's reputation as a success at the time that concerns us here.

119. Solomon, *Twentieth Century-Fox: A Corporate and Financial History*, 254; Silverman, *The Fox That Got Away*, 324; *Variety*, August 14, 1968, 23 (advertisement); May 3, 1972, 254.

120. Coate, "Roadshow: The Sound of Money."

121. *KW*, December 17, 1966, 9. See also Silverman, *The Fox That Got Away*, 116–23; Shipman, "The All-Conquering Governess"; Joan Barthel, "Biggest Money-Making Movie of All Time—How Come?" *NYT*, November 20, 1966.

122. *Variety*, February 1, 1967, 1, 78; May 3, 1967, 5, 78.

123. *Films and Filming*, February 1970, 24. In fact, the studio did make one more musical in the early 1970s. *The Boy Friend* (1971) was made in conjunction with MGM's British partner EMI for the comparatively modest amount of $2 million. For discussion of the compilation film *That's Entertainment*, see chapter 9.

NOTES TO CHAPTER 9

1. *Variety,* April 14, 1965, 1, 68. For discussion of the advent of the "new" Hollywood and the demise of the old, see, for example: Elsaesser, Horwath, and King, *The Last Great American Picture Show;* Harris, *Scenes from a Revolution;* King, *New Hollywood Cinema;* Krämer, *The New Hollywood;* Madsen, *The New Hollywood: American Movies in the '70s;* Toeplitz, *Hollywood and After.*

2. *Variety,* November 27, 1968, 5.

3. Ibid., July 27, 1966, 15.

4. Ibid., August 11, 1965, 23; May 4, 1966, 1.

5. Ibid., July 27, 1966, 15. Valenti had until recently been a speechwriter and aide to Johnson.

6. Ibid., August 10, 1966, 3, 15.

7. Ibid., April 24, 1968, 7.

8. Ibid., January 24, 1968, 28. Only over-sixteens were interviewed for the MPAA survey, so the proportion of children in the audience was not assessed. For an account of earlier audience research establishing the importance of viewers under thirty, see Ohmer, "The Science of Pleasure," in Stokes and Maltby, *Identifying Hollywood's Audiences,* 67–69.

9. *Variety,* November 12, 1969, 26, reported on the NATO (National Association of Theatre Owners) convention at which exhibitors insisted on the continuing importance of attracting older patrons: "they are our lost audience and we need them back at the boxoffice." See also Sklar, "The Lost Audience," in Stokes and Maltby, *Identifying Hollywood's Audiences.*

10. *Variety,* March 20, 1968, 78.

11. Ibid., January 20, 1971, 23.

12. Ibid., February 14, 1968, 12 (advertisement).

13. Ibid., August 14, 1968, 5.

14. Ibid., March 20, 1968, 78.

15. Ibid., February 12, 1969, 5.

16. Bizony, 2001: *Filming the Future,* 10–11.

17. *Variety,* January 29, 1969, 19. Avco Embassy's historical drama *The Lion in Winter* was also a roadshow that was seen to appeal to young-adult audiences by virtue of its "'contemporary' casting, camera angles, and . . . dialog" (ibid., December 4, 1968, 17).

18. *Romeo and Juliet* had been planned for roadshowing, but in the United States its distribution policy was altered in favor of regular release instead, precisely in order to appeal more to young people (ibid., August 14, 1968, 5, 26; September 11, 1968, 25; October 9, 1968, 24).

19. Ibid., April 3, 1968, 26.

20. Heffernan, *Ghouls, Gimmicks, and Gold,* 202–19.

21. *KW,* January 3, 1970, 3.

22. *Variety,* April 8, 1970, 5; June 16, 1971, 5–6.

23. Finler, *The Hollywood Story,* 280.

24. Pye and Myles, *The Movie Brats,* 39.

25. *Variety,* April 22, 1970, 3, 24, 93; July 1, 1970, 5; May 12, 1971, 6; September 1, 1971, 3, 60. The last report considered $450 million to be a "sensible" inventory level for the revenue available from the world market.

26. Ibid., May 2, 1973, 4. See also Londoner, "The Changing Economics of Entertainment," in Balio, *The American Film Industry* (1985), 606–8, 618–19.

27. *Variety,* September 29, 1971, 4; November 10, 1971, 5; April 12, 1972, 20.

28. Silverman, *The Fox That Got Away,* 326–29.

29. Solomon, *Twentieth Century-Fox: A Corporate and Financial History,* 164, 256; *Variety,* January 14, 1970, 30; April 28, 1971, 3.

30. Balance sheet in Folder 39, *The Wild Bunch* files, Sam Peckinpah Collection, AMPAS.

31. *Variety*, August 19, 1970, 28.

32. Ibid., October 29, 1969, 1, 24.

33. Ibid., March 11, 1970, 3, 5, 70, 78; April 29, 1970, 3, 25; June 24, 1970, 3, 26; August 26, 1970, 3, 6; January 27, 1971, 3; May 5, 1971, 3; May 19, 1971, 3, 28; June 9, 1971, 3, 24; January 26, 1972, 6; May 3, 1972, 3; Segrave, *American Films Abroad*, 231, 288.

34. *Variety*, June 24, 1970, 4; August 5, 1970, 5.

35. Ibid., March 28, 1973, 3. On the decline of roadshowing, see Galbraith IV, *A History and Analysis of the Roadshow Mode of Motion Picture Exhibition* and Hall, *Hard Ticket Giants*. It is worth pointing out that although roadshowing went out of fashion in the United States at the end of the 1960s, it remained common elsewhere, especially in Britain, Northern Europe, Australia, and Japan, for several years to come. Many more films were roadshown in these territories than in the domestic market.

36. *Variety*, November 29, 1972, 4; December 27, 1972, 3; February 7, 1973, 7, 22; August 22, 1973, 3. For further details of UA's hard-ticket exhibition policy for *Last Tango in Paris*, see Balio, *United Artists: The Company That Changed the Film Industry*, 293–301.

37. *Variety*, November 10, 1971, 4; February 9, 1972, 15; March 15, 1972, 4, 30; February 14, 1973, 5, 90; March 14, 1973, 3; May 23, 1973, 26; November 7, 1973, 1, 5, 63. For further details of four-walling and *Billy Jack*'s release, see Siminoski, "The *Billy Jack* Phenomenon: Filmmaking with Independence & Control" and Wyatt, "From Roadshowing to Saturation Release," in Lewis, *The New American Cinema*, 73–78.

38. *Variety*, November 7, 1973, 5, 36; April 3, 1974, 1, 26; April 17, 1974, 7; May 8, 1974, 3, 64; May 22, 1974, 3, 32; June 26, 1974, 7; September 11, 1974, 5, 22; November 13, 1974, 30.

39. The number-one hit of 1976, UA's *One Flew over the Cuckoo's Nest* (1975), was based on a book that had also been adapted into a play, though in this case the correlation between cinema success and source material seems less clear.

40. *Variety*, January 28, 1970, 7.

41. Ibid., March 24, 1971, 21; July 21, 1971, 5; May 3, 1972, 254.

42. See the chart of tie-in record albums that went gold in ibid., May 15, 1974, 59. Other nonmusical films whose soundtracks sold one million units or more included *Exodus, How the West Was Won, Doctor Zhivago, The Graduate, 2001: A Space Odyssey, Midnight Cowboy, Butch Cassidy and the Sundance Kid, American Graffiti*, Francis Lai's score for *A Man and a Woman* (1966), and Nino Rota's for *Romeo and Juliet*.

43. Ibid., January 6, 1971, 5; April 19, 1972, 4.

44. Ibid., July 21, 1971, 3.

45. Ibid., November 17, 1971, 4; February 16, 1972, 4; March 22, 1972, 5, 26; September 6, 1972, 60; Cowie, *The* Godfather *Book*, 66–74.

46. *Variety*, April 5, 1972, 22; April 12, 1972, 3; August 2, 1972, 1, 53; January 3, 1973, 7.

47. Ibid., July 26, 1972, 5. With a substantial hit, 90/10 deals worked greatly to the distributor's advantage, though in the case of a flop the provision for recovering the house nut could virtually wipe out profits on rentals. See Beaupré, "How to Distribute a Film," in Kerr, *The Hollywood Film Industry*, 196–201.

48. *Variety*, April 5, 1972, 3.

49. Ibid., February 23, 1972, 3; May 10, 1972, 5; August 2, 1972, 10–11 (advertisement). Hammer's science-fiction horror film *Quatermass 2* (1957), which had taken its title from the BBC TV serial *Quatermass II* (1955) from which it was adapted, had been renamed *Enemy from Space* for U.S. release. Of course, the title of Coppola and Puzo's sequel had other antecedents in Shakespeare's history plays, which they may well have had in mind. The cinema's earliest numbered sequel would seem to be Akira Kurosawa's *Sanshiro Sugata II* (1945), as Richard Chatten pointed out in the *Guardian* (*Notes and Queries*, September 13, 2001).

50. Ibid., July 31, 1974, 3. Fox used a similar ploy by arranging for a TV screening of *The French Connection* immediately prior to the theatrical release of *French Connection II* (1975). It was reported in *Variety*, September 13, 1972, 26, that Coppola planned ultimately to release (or re-release) both parts of *The Godfather* as a single five-hour roadshow. Although never shown theatrically, this instead became a television mini-series, *Mario Puzo's The Godfather: The Complete Novel for Television*, adding an hour of footage deleted from the two feature films. Broadcast by NBC on four successive nights in November 1977, the series drew an average 100 million viewers for each episode. See Cowie, *The Godfather Book*, 102–5.

51. *Variety*, July 29, 1970, 3; Greene, Planet of the Apes *as American Myth*; Silverman, *The Fox That Got Away*, 327.

52. *Variety*, August 1, 1973, 16.

53. Ibid., March 7, 1973, 5, 30.

54. Ibid., November 3, 1971, 1, 48; July 26, 1972, 5, 20.

55. On other musicals in the 1970s, see Cook, *Lost Illusions*, 209–20.

56. *Variety*, May 23, 1973, 39; September 12, 1973, 3; November 20, 1973, 5; March 6, 1974, 3; March 13, 1974, 5, 28; May 22, 1974, 5, 34; October 16, 1974, 5; January 8, 1975, 68; April 2, 1975, 4.

57. Ibid., June 19, 1974, 28.

58. Ibid., May 20, 1970, 5, 20; April 24, 1974, 3, 24.

59. Ibid., July 23, 1975, 4, 28. Paramount had previously put money into *The Red Tent* (produced 1969; U.S. release 1971) and Warners had been involved in, but withdrew from, *Tchaikovsky* (produced 1970; U.S. release 1972). There had also been a three-way coproduction among Italy, the United States, and the USSR in 1965, *Italiani brava gente* (a.k.a. *Attack and Retreat*).

60. Ibid., January 23, 1974, 1; March 27, 1974, 28; May 22, 1974, 37; May 29, 1974, 1, 60; August 7, 1974, 2; June 11, 1975, 7, 32; March 10, 1976, 26, 32.

61. Baxter, *Stanley Kubrick: A Biography*, 278–94; LoBrutto, *Stanley Kubrick*, 377–408.

62. *Variety*, December 27, 1972, 4; Solomon, *Twentieth Century-Fox: A Corporate and Financial History*, 173.

63. *Variety*, June 12, 1974, 3, 21; August 14, 1974, 5–6; September 10, 1975, 1, 86; September 17, 1975, 3, 30; October 29, 1975, 3, 40; November 5, 1975, 3, 6, 28, 30.

64. Ibid., April 25, 1973, 5, 24; May 30, 1973, 3, 27; June 20, 1973, 4; September 26, 1973, 3; October 21, 1973, 4; November 14, 1973, 20; Kim, *Franklin J. Schaffner*, 285–306, 447; Cook, *Lost Illusions*, 325–28.

65. *Variety*, October 16, 1974, 14. For discussion of generic definitions, the disaster film in historical context, and the 1970s' cycle, see Keane, *Disaster Movies*, 1–50.

66. Heston, *In the Arena*, 470.

67. Ibid.

68. *Variety*, December 31, 1975, 3. Nick Roddick, "Only the Stars Survive," in Bradby, James, and Sharratt, *Performance and Politics in Popular Drama*, uses a more inclusive definition of the disaster genre that incorporates postapocalyptic and dystopian science-fiction films such as *Fahrenheit 451* (1966), *THX 1138* (1971), *Logan's Run* (1976), and the Charlton Heston vehicles *Planet of the Apes*, *The Omega Man* (1971), and *Soylent Green* (1973). See also Yacowar, "The Bug in the Rug," in Grant, *Film Genre Reader III*.

69. See, for example, Roddick, "Only the Stars Survive," in Bradby, James, and Sharrat, *Performance and Politics in Popular Drama*; Rosen, "Drugged Popcorn"; Ryan and Kellner, *Camera Politica*, 52–57; Turner, "Quaking in the Stalls."

70. Dyer, "American Cinema of the '70s: *The Towering Inferno*," 31.

71. Roddick, "Only the Stars Survive," in Bradby, James, and Sharrat, *Performance and Politics in Popular Drama*, 251–52, King, *Spectacular Narratives*, 146.

72. Kaplan, "Riches from Ruins," 3–4. For a more general account of the cycle, see Cook, *Lost Illusions,* 251–57.

73. Maltby, *Harmless Entertainment,* 327.

74. *American Cinematographer* 55, no. 11 (1974): 1313. This entire issue is devoted to articles on the various production departments of *Earthquake,* mostly written by the chief crewmembers responsible (the section on Sensurround is unattributed). Many had been in the industry for decades and had worked on special effects for films as far back as *San Francisco.* Sensurround was used for only three or four more pictures, including *Midway* (1976), *Rollercoaster* (1977), *Battlestar Galactica* (1978), and possibly *Mission Galactica: The Cylon Attack* (1979). *Krakatoa, East of Java* (1969), a precursor of the 1970s disaster movies that had first been released in 70 mm Cinerama, was reissued in Europe in 1975 with Feelarama, a variant of Sensurround, under the title *Volcano.* See Carr and Hayes, *Wide Screen Movies,* 249–50; Sherlock, "*Widescreen Movies* Corrections," 44–45.

75. Cook, *Lost Illusions,* 389–90.

76. Solomon, *Twentieth Century-Fox: A Corporate and Financial History,* 233; *Variety,* December 17, 1975, 5.

77. Lev, *American Films of the 70s,* 45–49. *Jaws* has also been linked via the disaster cycle to *Nashville* (1975). See Hoberman, "*Nashville* Contra *Jaws,*" in Elsaesser, Horwath, and King, *The Last Great American Picture Show;* Man, "Movies and Conflicting Ideologies," in Friedman, *American Cinema of the 1970s,* 144–45; Wyatt, *High Concept,* 113–17.

78. Despite his involvement as producer, Blatty considered the film of *The Exorcist* to be a "downer," partly because he felt audiences did not understand that Karras takes the initiative to kill the demon inside him and not vice versa, and partly because an optimistic coda involving two subsidiary characters had been cut by Friedkin before release. See Kermode, *The Exorcist,* in which Blatty states his concerns over the original ending—"I don't want them to think that the devil won" (118)—and also his fear that if it were changed, "that power that's spoken of would disintegrate" (119). Contrariwise, the dedication of Travers and Reiff's making-of book, *The Story behind* The Exorcist, is to Blatty, "for instilling in his novel, his film, and in us the feeling that everything would finally be alright."

79. On the reception of *The Exorcist,* see Gateward, "Movies and the Legacies of War and Corruption," in Friedman, *American Cinema of the 1970s,* 111–15; Travers and Reiff, *The Story Behind* The Exorcist, 167–205.

80. On the use of POV in *Jaws,* see Buckland, *Directed by Steven Spielberg,* 96–99; King, *New Hollywood Cinema,* 106–8; Kolker, *A Cinema of Loneliness,* 272–76; Morris, *The Cinema of Steven Spielberg,* 60–61.

81. Britton, "American Cinema in the '70s: *Jaws,*" 27.

82. The notion of "high concept"—a simple, easily grasped premise that can be translated into a marketable image or brand—is discussed at length in Wyatt, *High Concept.*

83. *Variety,* September 22, 1971, 7, 48; February 6, 1974, 7; February 13, 1974, 4; June 26, 1974, 4; April 2, 1975, 5; June 4, 1975, 7, 26; November 19, 1975, 16; Gottlieb, *The* Jaws *Log;* McBride, *Steven Spielberg: A Biography,* 230–59; Pye and Myles, *The Movie Brats,* 232–28; Travers and Reiff, *The Story Behind* The Exorcist, 15–131. Other estimates of *Jaws*' final cost run as high as $12 million (Finler, *The Hollywood Story,* 217).

84. *Variety,* January 9, 1974, 12–13 (advertisement); February 6, 1974, 5; February 20, 1974, 3, 20; February 27, 1974, 5, 22; April 3, 1974, 4; June 12, 1974, 1, 54; November 19, 1975, 16.

85. Ibid., July 3, 1974, 5.

86. Ibid., August 20, 1975, 3.

87. Ibid., April 16, 1975, 3, 34; July 2, 1975, 37; August 27, 1975, 7, 26; January 21, 1976, 1, 102.

88. Among the many accounts of *Jaws'* place in Hollywood history, see for example Cook, *Lost Illusions,* 40–44; Gomery, "The Hollywood Blockbuster," in Stringer, *Movie Blockbusters.* 72–74; Hayes and Bing, *Open Wide,* 156–60; King, *New Hollywood Cinema,* 54–56; Morris, *The Cinema of Steven Spielberg,* 43–45; Schatz, "The New Hollywood," in Collins, Radner, and Collins, *Film Theory Goes to the Movies,* 17–19; Wyatt, "From Roadshowing to Saturation Release," in Lewis, *The New American Cinema,* 78–83.

89. *Variety,* December 8, 1971, 19, commented, "only a few multiple-type runs escape the snap-judgement, both by consumer press critics and the industry, that something is 'wrong' with the film in question. The conversion of attitudes by those inside and outside the industry will take a long time."

90. *Variety,* June 25, 1975, 16–17 (advertisement).

91. Ibid., December 15, 1971, 13; June 13, 1973, 4.

92. See, for example, Bruck, *When Hollywood Had a King,* 342–43; Hayes and Bing, *Open Wide,* 159–60.

93. *Variety,* August 28, 1974, 3, 27; October 23, 1974, 5, 76, 78; November 20, 1974, 1, 64; December 11, 1974, 1, 62; February 5, 1975, 32; May 7, 1975, 40 (advertisement); May 14, 1975, 6; May 21, 1975, 5, May 28, 1975, 6; Wyatt, *High Concept,* 111–12; Wyatt, "From Roadshowing to Saturation Release," in Lewis, *The New American Cinema,* 77–78.

94. *Variety,* October 16, 1974, 3.

95. Ibid., January 16, 1974, 1, 3, 39, 40; January 30, 1974, 3, 22; July 10, 1974, 1, 55; September 18, 1974, 3, 26; October 9, 1974, 1, 77; October 16, 1974, 7, 22; December 18, 1974, 3, 24; January 22, 1975, 1, 90; July 2, 1975, 1, 37; August 13, 1975, 1, 61; September 17, 1975, 5, 28; October 8, 1975, 3, 34; October 15, 1975, 5; December 17, 1975, 1, 70; January 14, 1976, 1, 86; Finler, *The Hollywood Story,* 288.

96. *Variety,* December 17, 1975, 3.

97. Ibid., October 29, 1975, 30.

Notes to Chapter 10

1. *Variety,* January 7, 1976, 50.

2. Quoted in Shone, *Blockbuster: How Hollywood Learned to Stop Worrying and Love the Summer,* 82.

3. *Variety,* January 5, 1977, 14.

4. Kezich and Levantesi, *Dino: The Life and Times of Dino De Laurentiis,* 218.

5. *Variety,* December 15, 1976, 3.

6. Cook, *Lost Illusions,* 44.

7. Ibid., 291.

8. King, *Heroes in Hard Times;* Lichtenfeld, *Action Speaks Louder;* Pfiel, *White Guys;* Tasker, *Spectacular Bodies.*

9. *Variety,* January 12, 1977, 5; advertisement in ibid., November 24, 1976, 9. Ironically, *Rocky IV* established a record for "the widest distribution of any film in history" when it widened from 1,332 screens to 2,232 in December 1985, thus beating records previously established by *Rambo: First Blood, Part II,* which was "screened in 2074 theaters at its height" earlier that year. See ibid., December 25, 1985, 3.

10. Ibid., January 12, 1977, 36, 46, 47, 70.

11. According to Cook, *Lost Illusions,* 214, *New York, New York* cost $9 million and earned $7 million in domestic rentals; according to Prince, *A New Pot of Gold,* 228, *The Cotton Club* eventually cost $47 million and returned only $13 million in domestic rentals. A detailed account of the evolution of *The Cotton Club* can be found in Parish, *Fiasco: A History of Hollywood's Iconic Flops,* 123–47.

12. Telotte, "The New Hollywood Musical," in Neale, *Genre and Contemporary Hollywood,* 48, 53, 55, 58.

13. *Variety,* November 29, 1978, 1, 98; January 3, 1979, 70; January 10, 1979, 1, 115; May 2, 1979, 1, 148; November 14, 1979, 3; January 16, 1980, 1, 112; September 3, 1980, 1, 83; December 16, 1981, 78.

14. Sanjek, *Pennies from Heaven,* 597.

15. Ibid., 598.

16. Cook, *Lost Illusions,* 55.

17. Smith, *The Sounds of Commerce,* 200–201.

18. Cook, *Lost Illusions,* 390.

19. According to Ioan Allen, who worked for Dolby, only six theaters were equipped to exhibit *A Star Is Born* in 35 mm optical Dolby Stereo. The film was also exhibited with a four-track magnetic soundtrack in 35 mm and a six-track magnetic soundtrack in 70 mm. See Sergi, *The Dolby Era,* 99, and *Variety,* January 27, 1982, 26.

20. Schreger, "The Second Coming of Sound," 34–37.

21. Cook, *Lost Illusions,* 387–89.

22. Ibid., 391–93; Monaco, *The Sixties,* 104–6; Schreger, "The Second Coming of Sound," 34–37; Sergi, *The Dolby Era,* 16–18; Whittington, *Sound Design and Science Fiction,* 19–30, 34–37, 75–90.

23. For further discussion of the use of sound in *Star Wars,* see Whittington, *Sound Design and Science Fiction,* 93–114.

24. Cook, *Lost Illusions,* 48. The most complete account of the evolution and production of *Star Wars* can be found in Rinzler, *The Making of* Star Wars.

25. Cook, *Lost Illusions,* 383–84.

26. Ibid., 384.

27. Rinzler, *The Making of* Star Wars, 290–93; 301; *Variety,* June 1, 1977, 1; June 8, 1977, 3.

28. *Variety,* August 3, 1977, 24.

29. Quoted in Rinzler, *The Making of* Star Wars, 284.

30. Myers, "The Studio as Distributor," in Squire, *The Movie Business Book* (1983), 279.

31. Cook, *Lost Illusions,* 50.

32. Myers, "The Studio as Distributor," in Squire, *The Movie Business Book,* 278.

33. *Variety,* August 10, 1977, 3.

34. Cook, *Lost Illusions,* 50.

35. Rinzler, *The Making of* Star Wars, 303–4.

36. Pye and Myles, *The Movie Brats,* 51.

37. Cook, *Lost Illusions,* 31.

38. Both in ibid., 51.

39. McBride, *Steven Spielberg: A Biography,* 271.

40. Ibid., 270, 272.

41. "Watch the Skies" (2001); *Variety,* December 8, 1976, 5.

42. Cook, *Lost Illusions,* 46.

43. Morton, *Close Encounters of the Third Kind,* 298.

44. Quoted in Shone, *Blockbuster: How Hollywood Learned to Stop Worrying and Love the Summer,* 94.

45. The logic of self-reflexiveness in *Close Encounters* is discussed in more general terms in Morris, *The Cinema of Steven Spielberg,* 8–19.

46. McBride, *Steven Spielberg: A Biography,* 266–67.

47. Cook, *Lost Illusions,* 239–45.

48. According to *Variety,* January 16, 1985, 62 and 58 respectively, *Blade Runner* cost $27 million and earned $14.8 million in rentals, and *The Thing,* $15 million and $10 million. *Alien*

cost $11 million and eventually earned $40.3 million. According to *Variety*, May 30, 1979, 5, it received an initial "mini-multiple" release on only ninety screens, partly because it was first released exclusively in 70 mm with a six-track Dolby magnetic soundtrack. Discussions of these and other dystopian science-fiction films are legion. For summary overviews, see Cook, *Lost Illusions*, 249–51; Prince, *A New Pot of Gold*, 336–40; and Ryan and Kellner, *Camera Politica*, 254–58.

49. *Variety*, May 29, 1977, 20.

50. Ibid., January 14, 1976, 4.

51. Rickitt, *Special Effects*, 86.

52. According to Rickitt, this look was produced by putting Scotchlite tape on the sets and the actors' costumes.

53. *Variety*, December 20, 1978, 3; December 27, 1978, 3. The latter noted that the figure of "501 situations" cited in the former had now been corrected.

54. Quoted in McBride, *Steven Spielberg: A Biography*, 287.

55. McBride, *Steven Spielberg: A Biography*, 310.

56. Mott and Saunders, *Steven Spielberg*, 88.

57. Ibid.

58. McBride, *Steven Spielberg: A Biography*, 321.

59. *Variety*, June 17, 1981, 3, 35; June 24, 1981, 1.

60. Ibid., August 12, 1981, 3; September 16, 1981, 1, 82.

61. Ibid., January 13, 1982, 15; Sackett, *The Hollywood Reporter Book of Box-Office Hits*, 278; McBride, *Steven Spielberg: A Biography*, 322.

62. McBride, *Steven Spielberg: A Biography*, 287.

63. Simonet, "Conglomerates and Content," in Austin, *Current Research in Film*, 154–62.

64. *Variety*, January 14, 1981, 110.

65. Ibid.

66. Ibid., January 16, 1985, 62.

67. Murphy, "Distribution and Exhibition: An Overview," in Squire, *The Movie Business Book* (1983), 250, 249, 258. According to Murphy in *Variety*, July 16, 1980, 30, ticket sales had risen from 912 million to 1,333 million and grosses from $1,294 million to $2,653 million between 1969 and 1978.

68. Ibid., 259.

69. Ibid., 260.

70. Cook, *Lost Illusions*, 350.

71. *Variety*, February 6, 1980, 38.

72. Ibid., May 19, 1976, 19.

73. Ibid., December 17, 1980, 32.

74. Ibid., March 17, 1976, 3.

75. Ibid., January 4, 1978, 21. *Smokey and the Bandit* went on to earn $59,859,515 in domestic rentals both from its initial run and from what *Variety*, November 23, 1977, 3, called "a series of saturation revival runs in Dixie exchange areas."

76. Ibid., May 28, 1980, 32 and January 17, 1980, 39; Meisel, "Industry," 62.

77. Cook, *Lost Illusions*, 293–94; Prince, *A New Pot of Gold* 295–98.

78. Meisel, "Industry," 62; *Variety*, December 31, 1980, 23; January 5, 1983, 4.

79. Paul, *Laughing Screaming*, 36–173, and "The Impossibility of Romance," in Neale, *Genre and Contemporary Hollywood*, esp. 117–25.

80. The figures for all these films are derived from *Variety*, February 21, 1990, 226, 234, and 242.

81. Thrower, *Nightmare USA*, 19–21.

82. *Variety*, August 8, 1979, 30; January 21, 1981, 3. Simonet, "Industry," 66, describes a four-hundred- to five-hundred-theater release as "conventional," a seven-hundred-theater release as a "broader opening," and a one-thousand-theater release as a form of "saturation."

83. *Variety,* February 9, 1983, 4, 46. See also *Variety,* June 17, 1981, 18; August 5, 1981, 7, 28; November 4, 1981, 6, 30; January 27, 1982, 100; August 25, 1982, 1, 51; October 20, 1982, 38; December 1, 1982, 5, 28; March 30, 1983, 4, 135; August 31, 1983, 7, 30.

84. Ibid., April 14, 1982, 7.

85. Ibid.

86. Ibid., June 13, 1979, 7; January 9, 1980, 28; January 31, 1980, 1; November 5, 1980, 26; January 7, 1981, 1.

87. Biskind, *Down and Dirty Pictures,* 15–18, 43–49; Cook, *Lost Illusions,* 216–17; King, *American Independent Cinema,* 20–21; Pierson, *Spike, Mike, Slackers, and Dykes,* 6–20.

88. *Variety,* February 6, 1980, 3; March 5, 1980, 6; October 21, 1981, 34.

89. For details on all these films, see ibid., June 2, 1976, 16; September 1, 1976, 3; November 24, 1977, 3; January 11, 1978, 35; March 5, 1980, 6; February 25, 1981, 30.

90. There appears to be some confusion about the role of Universal. According to Cimino's commentary on the British edition of the DVD (OPTD0773), EMI provided the production funds. *Variety's* review (November 29, 1978, 24) credits the film as "a Universal release of a Universal-EMI production," while Cook, *Lost Illusions,* 330, states flatly that *The Deer Hunter* was "the only successful film produced and distributed by EMI Films Ltd. before it was acquired by Thorn in 1979." Universal clearly played a major role in the film's distribution, though the nature and scope of its role in the film's production remains obscure.

91. Wood, *Hollywood from Vietnam to Reagan—and Beyond,* 246–48.

92. Schreger, "The Second Coming of Sound," 36 (emphasis in original).

93. *Variety,* December 13, 1978, 5, 8, 41; December 20, 1978, 10; January 24, 1979, 6; February 28, 1979, 13; April 25, 1979, 5.

94. Cowie, *The* Apocalypse Now *Book,* esp. 1–125.

95. Ibid., 13, 118.

96. Ibid., 110, 122–23; *Variety,* March 2, 1977, 3, 32; July 18, 1978, 23.

97. *Variety,* August 22, 1979, 8; September 5, 1979, 8; September 19, 1979, 5. Cowie, *The* Apocalypse Now *Book,* 124–25, notes that total rentals as of May 17, 1980 were $33,967,382, that "advances had been recouped in almost all territories to which *Apocalypse* had been sold," but that the "picture still languished in deficit," largely because of interest payments on loans and participants' shares in revenues.

98. Cook, *Lost Illusions,* 391–92; Cowie, *The* Apocalypse Now *Book,* 99–112.

99. Bach, *Final Cut. Variety's* review (November 26, 1980, 14) noted that "scenes with dialog which should supply plot and background information are either almost incomprehensible or else so abrupt that they do little to 'explain' what's going on."

100. Cook, *Lost Illusions,* 63.

101. *Variety,* November 26, 1980, 3, 29; April 29, 1981, 3, 6, 26, 43.

102. Ibid., April 29, 1981, 43; December 23, 1981, 3, 34; January 16, 1985, 62.

103. Frayling, *Sergio Leone,* 379–459.

104. Quoted in ibid., 450.

105. *Variety,* June 13, 1984, 4.

106. Frayling, *Sergio Leone,* 462.

107. *Variety,* November 18, 1981, 14; December 2, 1981, 3, 34.

108. Ibid., December 2, 1981, 16.

109. Ibid., December 9, 1981, 3; January 6, 1982, 36.

110. Eberts and Ilott, *My Indecision Is Final,* 65–78.

111. Ibid., 96.

112. Ibid., 135.

113. Ibid., 135–36.

114. *Variety,* January 26, 1983, 3; April 27, 1983, 4.

115. *The Mission* cost $24.5 million and earned $8.3 million in North American rentals; *Revolution* cost $22 million and earned under $1 million.

116. *A Passage to India* cost $14.5 million and earned $13.4 million in North American rentals; *Out of Africa* cost $30 million and earned $43.1 million.

117. Eberts and Ilott, *My Indecision Is Final,* 231–32.

Notes to Chapter 11

1. *HR,* January 2, 1986, 1; *Variety,* January 15, 1986, 41.

2. Prince, *A New Pot of Gold,* 92; Wasser, *Veni, Vidi, Video,* 153.

3. *Variety,* November 27, 1985, 119; Cook, *Lost Illusions,* 92–93; Lafferty, "Feature Films on Prime-Time Television," in Balio, *Hollywood in the Age of Television,* 252; Segrave, *Movies at Home,* 126; Wasser, *Veni, Vidi, Video,* 153.

4. Prince, *A New Pot of Gold,* 93.

5. Hilmes, *Hollywood and Broadcasting,* 174.

6. Balio, "Introduction to Part II," in Balio, *Hollywood in the Age of Television,* 265.

7. Segrave, *Movies at Home,* 142.

8. Prince, *A New Pot of Gold,* 102.

9. Wasser, *Veni, Vidi, Video,* 101.

10. Prince, *A New Pot of Gold,* 104.

11. Segrave, *Movies at Home,* 190.

12. These rental figures derive from *Variety,* February 21, 1990, 216, and are slightly lower than the $82 million cited in Prince, *A New Pot of Gold,* 448. Unless otherwise specified, figures for the number of screens on which films were released or subsequently shown are all derived either from *Variety,* which now routinely listed these figures on a weekly basis, or from individual title entries in the Internet Movie Database (www.imdb.com) or The-Numbers.dot.com.

13. Prince, *A New Pot of Gold,* 105.

14. Ibid., 106.

15. *Days of Thunder* earned $40 million in domestic rentals, *The Rock,* $74 million.

16. Prince, *A New Pot of Gold,* 107.

17. Wasser, *Veni, Vidi, Video,* 153.

18. Maltby, *Hollywood Cinema,* 192. According to *Variety,* February 21, 1990, 220, *Batman* cost $50 million. It earned an additional $25 million from foreign theatrical markets and an additional $40 million from pay cable, syndication, and network TV. Its distribution and marketing costs in these and in all other formats and markets amounted to $70 million.

19. Maltby, *Hollywood Cinema;* Squire, *The Movie Business Book* (1992 ed.), 322.

20. *Platoon* earned $69,937,092 in domestic rentals; *Dirty Dancing,* $25,009,305; *sex, lies, and videotape,* $11 million; and *Ninja Turtles,* $67,650,000.

21. Wyatt, "Independents, Packaging, and Inflationary Pressure in 1980s Hollywood" in Prince, *A New Pot of Gold,* 144.

22. Ibid., 145.

23. Ibid., 148–49. For a detailed account of *Cut Throat Island,* see Parish, *Fiasco: A History of Hollywood's Iconic Flops,* 211–29.

24. Wyatt, "Independents, Packaging, and Inflationary Pressure in 1980s Hollywood," in Prince, *A New Pot of Gold,* 145–46; Wasser, *Veni, Vidi, Video,* 179. *Twins* cost $17 million and earned $57,165,127 in domestic rentals, *Kindergarten Cop,* $26 million and $47,365,485.

25. Wasser, *Veni, Vidi, Video,* 177.

26. *Variety,* February 22, 1989, 22; Wasser, *Veni, Vidi, Video,* 155.

27. Balio, "Introduction to Part II," in Balio, *Hollywood in the Age of Television,* 280.

28. *Variety,* February 5, 1986, 3.

29. Ibid., October 22, 1986, 506.

30. Ibid., October 29, 1990, 76.

31. Ibid.

32. Ibid.

33. Ibid.

34. Ibid., February 24, 1988, 295.

35. Wasser, *Veni, Vidi, Video,* 156.

36. Childs, "Home Video," in Squire, *The Movie Business Book* (1992), 333.

37. Bart, *Boffo!,* 74.

38. King, *American Independent Cinema,* 33.

39. For accounts of the *Lord of the Rings* films, see Bart, *Boffo!,* 51–66; Margolis, Cubitt, King, and Jutel, *Studying the Event Film;* Thompson, *The Frodo Franchise.* By the late 1990s, grosses rather than rentals seem to have become the preferred measure of a film's box-office performance, possibly because box-office figures had become a publicly discussed and advertised feature of Hollywood discourse and grosses were always higher and therefore much more impressive than rentals. See Acland, *Screen Traffic,* 4, and Wyatt and Vlesmas, "The Drama of Recoupment," in Sandler and Studlar, *Anatomy of a Blockbuster,* 40–43.

40. Tzioumakis, *American Independent Cinema,* 260–66.

41. Spaulding, "Life Upside Down," 40.

42. *Variety,* January 16–22, 1995, 1.

43. Ibid., January 9, 1980, 9.

44. Coca-Cola Co., Form 10-K, 1982, 5, quoted in Prince, *A New Pot of Gold,* 40.

45. *Variety,* October 29, 1990, 76.

46. Ibid., January, 14, 1991, 12.

47. Prince, *A New Pot of Gold,* 79, 84. As Prince goes on to point out, the Supreme Court's ruling in the Paramount case in 1948 had "refused to find that theater ownership by the majors was illegal in itself. Assessments about legality would depend on the trade practices that accompanied, or were intended to be accomplished by, such ownership." As a result, Gulf + Western, MCA, and Columbia Tri-Star were all "able to purchase theater chains outright" in the 1980s.

48. Maltby, *Hollywood Cinema,* 190.

49. Acland, *Screen Traffic,* 74, 75; *Variety,* January 28, 1991, 6; August 22–28, 1994, 1, 65. The number of theaters and screens in the United States tended to fluctuate thereafter, but they never fell below 7,070 and 27,805, respectively.

50. Acland, *Screen Traffic,* 73–75.

51. Reardon, "The Studio Distributor," in Squire, *The Movie Business Book* (1992), 312.

52. *Variety,* December 19, 1994–January 1, 1995, 10.

53. Fellman, "Theatrical Distribution," in Squire, *The Movie Business Book* (2006), 365.

54. *Variety,* January 4–10, 1999, 28; March 11–17, 2002, 21.

55. Reardon, "The Studio Distributor," in Squire, *The Movie Business Book* (1992), 312–13.

56. Ibid., 313.

57. Ibid.

58. These films were among the biggest box-office hits of the period. Their domestic rentals were as follows: *The Little Mermaid,* $40,227,000; *Home Alone,* $140,099,000; *Beauty and the Beast,* $69,415,000; *Hook,* $69 million; *Aladdin,* $117,740,683; *Mrs. Doubtfire,* $109,761,240; *The Santa Clause,* $72,348,689.

59. Russell, *The Historical Epic and Contemporary Hollywood,* 66. The film's use of the full width of the wide-screen frame was unusual; most directors and cinematographers composed

shots with the ratio of TV screens and screenings in mind. See Neale, "Widescreen Composition in the Age of Television," in Neale and Smith, *Contemporary Hollywood Cinema*, 130–41.

60. *Variety,* June 20, 1990, 1, 27; May 18, 1992, 3, 15. One hundred sixty-three 70 mm prints and approximately 1,300 35 mm prints were struck for the initial release of *Far and Away.* Both *Dances with Wolves* and *Wyatt Earp* were subsequently made available in even longer "Director's Cuts," running 237 and 215 minutes respectively.

61. As Burgoyne, *The Hollywood Historical Film,* 102, has pointed out, *Schindler's List* is not usually categorized as a biopic, but it is based on Thomas Keneally's biography of Oskar Schindler, and it draws "on the forms and patterns of the biographical film."

62. Domestic rentals for these films were as follows: *Rain Man,* $86,813,000; *Parenthood,* $50,004,367; *Ghost,* $98.2 million; *Pretty Woman,* $81,905,530; *Fried Green Tomatoes,* $37,402,827; *Unforgiven,* $44.4 million; *Forrest Gump,* $156 million; *Apollo 13,* $84,309,770. The importance of the over-twenty-fives, the over-forties, and women in particular is noted in *Variety,* February 10, 1992, 5, 10; November 29, 1993, 74; April 18–24, 1994, 11, 14. According to *Variety,* April 10–16, 1995, 11, between 30 percent and 36 percent of moviegoers in the mid-1990s were over forty.

63. Ibid., January 16–22, 1995, 11.

64. Ibid., January 11–17, 1999, 7.

65. Ibid., March 15–21, 1989, 1; January 3, 1990, 5. By the end of the decade, *Variety,* March 8–14, 1999, 23, noted: "Of the 104 films released during the 1990s that have earned at least $100 million, 24 opened in June." It also noted that "summer is the most productive period overall, with 57 blockbusters opening from May through August."

66. Maltby, *Hollywood Cinema,* 198. For blow-by-blow accounts of one or more summers between 1990 and 2003, see Bart, *The Gross;* Hayes and Bing, *Open Wide;* Shone, *Blockbuster: How Hollywood Learned to Stop Worrying and Love the Summer,* 257–381. It should be noted here that, precisely because they provided an alternative, the "counterprogramming" of niche productions and art-house imports has increased during the summer season too. See *Variety,* May 3–9, 1999, 11, 14. As *Variety* points out, the traditional season for films like these had once been the fall.

67. For some or all of these trends, and in addition to those cited already, see Arroyo *Action/Spectacle Cinema;* Keane, *Disaster Movies,* 73–121; King, *Spectacular Narratives;* King and Krzywinska, *Science Fiction Cinema,* 58–113; and Tasker, *Action and Adventure Cinema.*

68. Higgins, "Suspenseful Situations," 79. The others include Neale, *Genre and Hollywood,* 196–202. Both derive their focus on situations from Brewster and Jacobs, *Theatre to Cinema,* 19–29, and in turn from Meisel, *Realizations: Narrative, Pictorial, and Theatrical Arts in Nineteenth-Century England,* 39–51.

69. Higgins, "Suspenseful Situations," 77.

70. Ibid., 78.

71. One of the first proponents of a new Cinema of Attractions was Arroyo, *Action/Spectacle Cinema,* vii, 2, 22.

72. *Variety,* June 13, 1990, 7, 10; June 28, 1993, 11; November 22, 1993, 1, 83.

73. Ibid., February 13–19, 1995, 1, 28.

74. Balio, "A Major Presence in All of the World's Important Markets," in Neale and Smith, *Contemporary Hollywood Cinema,* 58. According to *Variety,* October 21, 1991, 1, 95, the new investors included Fujisankei, a Japanese TV and publishing house; Canal Plus, a French pay-cable company; and the Dutch record company, Polygram. According to Maltby, *Hollywood Cinema,* 216, in the year 2000, "nearly 20 per cent of the $15 billion spent on Hollywood production was German investment money."

75. Acland, *Screen Traffic,* 140–41; Balio, "A Major Presence in All of the World's Important

Markets," in Neale and Smith, *Contemporary Hollywood Cinema,* 60; *Variety,* February 6–12, 1995, 1, 15; April 8–14, 1996, 9, 15; September 23–29, 1996, 17, 23.

76. Acland, *Screen Traffic,* 142; *Variety,* April 29–May 5, 1996, 11, 14, 15. The definition of a wide release was relative. According to *Variety,* April 15–21, 1996, 27, *Twister,* which had opened on 2,414 screens in the United States and Canada, opened on 219 in Japan. As Acland points out, the uneven patterns in screen growth and an overall decline in the number of screens in Eastern Europe and in parts of Asia and Africa were effectively ignored in the industry's press, thus producing a highly selective impression of uninterrupted global growth.

77. Acland, "Opening Everywhere," in Maltby, Stokes, and Allen, *Going to the Movies,* 366.

78. *Variety,* April 3–9, 1995, 1, 46.

79. Rickitt, *Special Effects,* 41.

80. Cubitt, "Digital Filming and Special Effects," in Harries, *The New Media Book,* 26.

81. Wood, *Digital Encounters,* 56–8, 73–78.

82. Whissel, "Tales of Upward Mobility," 23–34.

83. Rickitt, *Special Effects,* 240.

84. Coate and Kallay, "Presented in 70 mm," 261.

85. Allen, "From *Bwana Devil* to *Batman Forever,*" in Neale and Smith, *Contemporary Hollywood Cinema,* 119.

86. Allen, "*Jurassic Park,*" in Cook, *The Cinema Book,* 144–45.

87. Allen and Kuhn, "Sound," in Cook, *The Cinema Book,* 145.

88. Epstein, *The Big Picture,* 214.

89. McDonald, *Video and DVD Industries,* 93.

90. Wasser, "Ancillary Markets—Video and DVD," in McDonald and Wasko, *The Contemporary Film Industry,* 129.

91. Drake, "Distribution and Marketing," in McDonald and Wasko, *The Contemporary Film Industry,* 77.

92. Epstein, *The Big Picture,* 214.

93. Klinger, *Beyond the Multiplex.*

94. On the development of IMAX, see Carr and Hayes, *Wide Screen Movies,* 183–87; Enticknap, *Moving Image Technology,* 71–72; Wollen, "The Bigger the Better: From CinemaScope to IMAX," in Hayward and Wollen, *Future Visions: New Technologies of the Screen,* 10–30.

95. *In 70 mm: The 70 mm Newsletter* 57 (June): 1999, 16; Davis, "The Fall and Rise of *Fantasia,*" in Stokes and Maltby, *Hollywood Spectatorship,* 74. A restored version of the original *Fantasia* had been used for an experimental digital sound system in Los Angeles in 1985: "The system used digital audio recorded as video content on a video cassette and decoded in the theater" (Sherlock, "*Widescreen Movies* Corrections," 41).

96. McDonald, "IMAX: The Hollywood Experience," in Belton, Hall, and Neale, forthcoming. The aspect ratio of an IMAX frame is 1.44:1. Conversions of 35 mm films to IMAX mask off the top and bottom of the IMAX frame using hard-matte printing, much as in 35 mm nonanamorphic wide-screen projection.

97. Sharon Waxman, "Top Directors See the Future, and They Say It's in 3-D," *NYT,* May 22, 2007, accessed at www.nytimes.com/2007/05/22/movies/22dime.html.

98. Walters, "The Great Leap Forward," 38.

Notes to Conclusion

1. According to the Internet Movie Database, *Gladiator* cost an estimated $103 million and grossed $187,670,866 in North America and $258,264,745 abroad; *Pirates of the Caribbean: The Curse of the Black Pearl* cost $140 million, and grossed $305,388,685 domestically and $346,800,000 abroad.

2. According to the Internet Movie Database, *Treasure Planet* cost an estimated $140 million but grossed only $38,120,554 in North America and $53,700,000 abroad; *The Alamo* (2004) cost an estimated $95 million and grossed only $22,406,362 in North America.

3. According to *Variety*, February 21, 1990, 242, 238, and 222, respectively, *A Bridge Too Far* earned $20.4 million domestically but cost $24 million, *Annie* earned $37.7 million domestically but cost $51.5 million, and *Willow* earned $25 million domestically but cost $35 million.

4. According to the Internet Movie Database, *There's Something about Mary* cost $23 million and grossed $176,483,808 in North America alone; *The Sixth Sense* cost $55 million and grossed $293,501,675 in North America and a further $379,300,000 abroad. According to Drake, "Distribution and Marketing," in McDonald and Wasko, *The Contemporary Film Industry*, 67, production and promotion costs on *My Big Fat Greek Wedding*, which went on to gross $241 million in North America, amounted to a mere $5 million and $35 million respectively.

BIBLIOGRAPHY

References to trade paper, newspaper, and Internet sources are carried in the Notes only. All other published sources are listed hereunder.

Abel, Richard. *Americanizing the Movies and "Movie-Mad" Audiences, 1910–1914.* Berkeley: University of California Press, 2006.

———. "Look There! It's an American Subject!" In Quaresima, Raengo, and Vichi, *La nascita dei generi cinematografici*, 379–90.

———. "Nickelodeons." In Abel, *Encyclopedia of Early Cinema*, 478–80.

———. *The Red Rooster Scare: Making American Cinema, 1900–1910.* Berkeley: University of California Press, 1999.

Abel, Richard, ed. *Encyclopedia of Early Cinema.* London: Routledge, 2005.

Abel, Richard, and Rick Altman, eds. *The Sounds of Early Cinema.* Bloomington: Indiana University Press, 2001.

Aberdeen, J. A. *Hollywood Renegades: The Society of Motion Picture Producers.* Los Angeles: Cobblestone, 2000.

Acland, Charles R. "'Opening Everywhere': Multiplexes and the Speed of Cinema Culture." In Maltby, Stokes, and Allen, *Going to the Movies,* 369–82.

———. *Screen Traffic: Movies, Multiplexes, and Global Culture.* Durham, NC: Duke University Press, 2003.

Allen, Michael. "From *Bwana Devil* to *Batman Forever:* Technology in Contemporary Hollywood Cinema." In Neale and Smith, *Contemporary Hollywood Cinema,* 109–29.

———. "*Jurassic Park.*" In Cook, *The Cinema Book,* 144–45.

Allen, Michael, and Annette Kuhn. "Sound." In Cook, *The Cinema Book,* 144–45.

Allen, Robert C. "Vitascope/Cinématographe: Initial Patterns of American Film Industrial Practice." In Fell, *Film before Griffith,* 144–52.

Allvine, Glendon. *The Greatest Fox of Them All.* New York: Lyle Stuart, 1969.

Altman, Rick. *The American Film Musical.* Bloomington: Indiana University Press/London: BFI, 1989.

———. *Silent Film Sound.* New York: Columbia University Press, 2004.

Alvarez, Max. "The Origins of the Film Exchange." *Film History* 17, no. 4 (2005): 431–65.

Anderson, Michael. "The Motion Picture Patents Company." PhD dissertation, University of Wisconsin–Madison, 1983.

Arroyo, José, ed. *Action/Spectacle Cinema: A Sight and Sound Reader.* London: BFI, 2000.

Austin, Bruce A., ed. *Current Research in Film: Audiences, Economics, and Law,* vol. 2. Norwood: Ablex, 1986.

Babington, Bruce, and Peter William Evans. *Biblical Epics: Sacred Narrative in the Hollywood Cinema.* Manchester: Manchester University Press, 1993.

Bach, Steven. *Final Cut: Dreams and Disaster in the Making of* Heaven's Gate. New York: William Morrow, 1985.

Balio, Tino. *Grand Design: Hollywood as a Modern Business Enterprise, 1930–1939.* New York: Scribner's, 1993.

———. "Introduction to Part II." In Balio, *Hollywood in the Age of Television,* 259–96.

———. "'A Major Presence in All of the World's Important Markets': The Globalization of Hollywood in the 1990s." In Neale and Smith, *Contemporary Hollywood Cinema,* 58–73.

———. "Part I: A Novelty Spawns Small Businesses, 1894–1908." In Balio, *Hollywood in the Age of Television,* 3–25.

———. "Part IV: Retrenchment and Reorganization, 1948–." In Balio, *The American Film Industry* (1985), 401–47.

———. *United Artists: The Company Built by the Stars.* Madison: University of Wisconsin Press, 1976.

———. *United Artists: The Company That Changed the Film Industry.* Madison: University of Wisconsin Press, 1987.

Balio, Tino, ed. *The American Film Industry.* Madison: University of Wisconsin Press, 1976 and 1985.

———. *Hollywood in the Age of Television.* Boston: Unwin Hyman, 1990.

Barr, Charles. "CinemaScope: Before and After." *Film Quarterly* (Spring 1963): 4–24.

Barrios, Richard. *A Song in the Dark: The Birth of the Musical Film.* New York: Oxford University Press, 1995.

Bart, Peter. *Boffo! [How I Learned to Love the Blockbuster and Fear the Bomb].* New York: Hyperion/Miramax, 2006.

———. *The Gross: The Hits, The Flops—The Summer That Ate Hollywood.* New York: St. Martin's Griffin, 1999.

Basinger, Jeanine. *Silent Stars.* Hanover, NH: Wesleyan University Press, 1999.

———. *The World War II Combat Film: Anatomy of a Genre.* Middleton, CT: Wesleyan University Press, 2003 [1986].

Baxter, John. *Stanley Kubrick: A Biography.* London: HarperCollins, 1997.

Beaupré, Lee. "How to Distribute a Film." In Kerr, *The Hollywood Film Industry,* 185–203.

Behlmer, Rudy. *Behind the Scenes: The Making of . . .* Hollywood: Samuel French, 1990.

Behlmer, Rudy, ed. *Memo from Darryl F. Zanuck: The Golden Years at Twentieth Century-Fox.* New York: Grove Press, 1993.

———. *Memo from David O. Selznick.* Los Angeles: Samuel French, 1989 [1972].

Belton, John. "CinemaScope: The Economics of Technology." *The Velvet Light Trap* 21 (Summer 1985): 35–43.

———. "The Rivoli." . . . *in 70 mm: The 70 mm Newsletter* 12, no. 59 (1999): 4–9, accessible at www.in70mm.com/newsletter/1999/59/rivoli/theatre.htm.

———. *Widescreen Cinema.* Cambridge, MA: Harvard University Press, 1992.

Belton, John, Sheldon Hall, and Steve Neale, eds. *Widescreen Worldwide.* Bloomington, IN: Libbey, forthcoming.

Berg, A. Scott. *Goldwyn: A Biography.* London: Hamish Hamilton, 1989.

Bernstein, Matthew. *Walter Wanger: Hollywood Independent.* Minneapolis: University of Minnesota Press, 1994.

Bertellini, Giorgio. "Shipwrecked Spectators: Italy's Immigrants at the Movies in New York, 1906–1916." *The Velvet Light Trap* 44 (1999): 39–53.

Birchard, Robert S. *Cecil B. DeMille's Hollywood.* Lexington: University Press of Kentucky, 2004.

Biskind, Peter. *Down and Dirty Pictures: Miramax, Sundance, and the Rise of the Independent Film.* London: Bloomsbury, 2004.

———. *Easy Riders, Raging Bulls: How the Sex 'n' Drugs 'n' Rock 'n' Roll Generation Saved Hollywood.* London: Bloomsbury, 1998.

Bizony, Piers. 2001: *Filming the Future.* London: Aurum Press, 1994.

Bogdanovich, Peter. "Letter from Hollywood." *Movie* 17 (Winter 1969/70): 38.

Bordwell, David. "CinemaScope: The Modern Miracle You See without Glasses." In his *Poetics of Cinema.* New York: Routledge, 2008, 281–325.

———. *Figures Traced in Light: On Cinematic Staging.* Berkeley: University of California Press, 2005.

———. *On the History of Film Style.* Cambridge, MA: Harvard University Press, 1997.

Borneman, Ernest. "United States versus Hollywood: The Case Study of an Antitrust Suit." *Sight and Sound* 19, nos. 10 and 11 (1951). Reprinted in Balio, *The American Film Industry,* 449–62.

Bowser, Eileen. "*The Birth of a Nation:* Production." In Usai, *The Griffith Project.* Vol. 8, *Films Produced in 1914–15,* 55–62.

———. *The Transformation of Cinema, 1907–1915.* New York: Scribner's, 1990.

Boyle, John W., ASC. "And Now . . . Cinerama." *American Cinematographer* (November 1952), accessible at http://widescreenmuseum.com/widescreen/ac-cinerama.htm.

Bradby, David, Louis James, and Bernard Sharratt, eds. *Performance and Politics in Popular Drama: Aspects of Popular Entertainment in Theatre, Film, and Television, 1800–1976.* Cambridge: Cambridge University Press, 1980.

Brewster, Ben. "Deep Staging in French Films, 1900–1914." In Elsaesser, *Early Cinema: Space, Frame, Narrative,* 45–55.

———. "Multiple-Reel/Feature Films: USA." In Abel, *Encyclopedia of Early Cinema,* 656–57.

———. "Periodization of Early Cinema." In Keil and Stamp, *American Cinema's Transitional Era: Audiences, Institutions, Practices,* 66–75.

———. "Staging in Depth." In Abel, *Encyclopedia of Early Cinema,* 605–8.

Brewster, Ben, and Lea Jacobs. *Theatre to Cinema: Stage Pictorialism and the Early Feature Film.* Oxford: Oxford University Press, 1997.

Bridges, Herb, and Terryl C. Boodman. Gone with the Wind: *The Definitive Illustrated History of the Book, the Movie, and the Legend.* Englewood Cliffs, NJ: Prentice-Hall, 1989.

Britton, Andrew. "American Cinema in the '70s: *Jaws.*" *Movie* 23 (Winter 1976/77): 27–32.

Brown, Gene. *Movie Time: A Chronology of Hollywood and the Movie Industry from Its Beginnings to the Present.* New York: Macmillan, 1995.

Brownlow, Kevin. *David Lean.* London: Richard Cohen, 1996.

Bruck, Connie. *When Hollywood Had a King: The Reign of Lew Wasserman, Who Leveraged Talent into Power and Influence.* New York: Random House, 2003.

Buckland, Warren. *Directed by Steven Spielberg: Poetics of the Contemporary Hollywood Blockbuster.* New York: Continuum, 2006.

Burgoyne, Robert. *The Hollywood Historical Film.* Oxford: Blackwell, 2008.

Cameron, Ian, and Douglas Pye, eds. *The Movie Book of the Western.* London: Studio Vista, 1996.

Canjels, Rudmer. "Beyond the Cliffhanger: Distributing Silent Serials—Local Practices, Changing Forms, Cultural Transformations." PhD dissertation, University of Utrecht, 2005.

Carli, Philip H. "*The Birth of a Nation:* Music." In Usai, *The Griffith Project.* Vol. 8, *Films Produced in 1914–15,* 87–91.

Carr, Robert E., and R. M. Hayes. *Wide Screen Movies: A History and Filmography of Wide Gauge Filmmaking.* Jefferson, NC: McFarland, 1988.

Chapman, James. *License to Thrill: A Cultural History of the James Bond Films.* London: I. B. Tauris, 1999.

Childs, Richard "Reg" B. "Home Video." In Squire, *The Movie Business Book* (1992), 328–37.

Clark, Donald, and Christopher Anderson. *John Wayne's* The Alamo: *The Making of the Epic Film.* Hillside, IL: Midwest Publishing, 1994.

Clark, Frances Mullin. "Rome: New Directions." *Sight and Sound* 19, no. 1 (1950): 12.

Coate, Michael. "Roadshow: The Sound of Money," accessible at www.fromscripttodvd.com/sound_of_music_40th_tribute.htm, 2006.

Coate, Michael, and William Kallay. "Presented in 70 mm." *Widescreen Review Presents: The Ultimate Widescreen DVD Movie Guide* 1, no. 1 (2001): 257–96.

Cohan, Steven. *Masked Men: Masculinity and the Movies in the 50s.* Bloomington: Indiana University Press, 1997.

Cohen, Paula Marantz. *Silent Film and the Triumph of the American Myth.* Oxford: Oxford University Press, 2001.

Coles, David. "Magnified Grandeur: The Big Screen, 1926–31." *70 mm: The 70 mm Newsletter* 14, no. 64 (2001): 4–8.

Collins, Jim, Hilary Radner, and Ava Preacher Collins, eds. *Film Theory Goes to the Movies.* New York: Routledge, 1993.

Conant, Michael. *Anti-Trust in the Motion Picture Industry.* Berkeley: University of California Press, 1960.

———. "The Impact of the Paramount Decrees." In Balio, *The American Film Industry* (1976), 346–70.

———. "The Paramount Decrees Reconsidered." In Balio, *The American Film Industry* (1985), 537–73.

Cook, David A. *Lost Illusions: American Cinema in the Shadow of Watergate and Vietnam, 1970–1979.* New York: Scribner's, 2000.

Cook, Pam, ed. *The Cinema Book.* London: BFI, 2007 [1985].

Cosandey, Roland, André Gaudreault, and Tom Gunning, eds. *Une invention du diable? Cinéma des premiers temps et religion.* Sainte Foy: Les Presses du L'Université Laval/Lausanne: Editions Payout Lausanne, 1992.

Cossar, Harper. *Screen Space: Widescreen, Aspect Ratios, and Style.* Lexington: University Press of Kentucky, forthcoming.

Cowie, Peter. *The Apocalypse Now Book.* London: Faber and Faber, 2000.

———. *The Godfather Book.* London: Faber and Faber, 1997.

Coyne, Michael. *The Crowded Prairie: American National Identity in the Hollywood Western.* London: I. B. Tauris, 1997.

Crafton, Donald. *The Talkies: American Cinema's Transition to Sound, 1926–1931.* New York: Scribner's, 1997.

Cripps, Thomas. "The Reaction of the Negro to *The Birth of a Nation*" (1963). Reprinted in Silva, *Focus on* The Birth of a Nation, 111–24.

Cubitt, Sean. "Digital Filming and Special Effects." In Harries, *The New Media Book,* 7–29.

Custen, George F. *Bio/Pics: How Hollywood Constructed Public History.* New Brunswick, NJ: Rutgers University Press, 1992.

Cutts, John. "Long Shot." *Films and Filming* 16, no. 8 (1970): 20–21.

D'Antonio, Joanne. *Andrew Marton.* Metuchen, NJ: Directors Guild of America and Scarecrow Press, 1991.

Davis, Amy M. "The Fall and Rise of *Fantasia.*" In Stokes and Maltby, *Hollywood Spectatorship: Changing Perceptions of Cinema Audiences,* 63–78.

DeBauche, Leslie Midkiff. *Reel Patriotism: The Movies and World War I.* Madison: University of Wisconsin Press, 1997.

deCordova, Richard. *Picture Personalties: The Emergence of the Star System in America.* Urbana: University of Illinois Press, 1990.

DeMille, Cecil B. *The Autobiography of Cecil B. DeMille,* edited by Donald Hayne. London: W. H. Allen, 1960.

Dennett, Andrea Stulman, and Nina Warnke. "Disaster Spectacles at the Turn of the Century." *Film History* 4, no. 2 (1990): 101–11.

Deutchman, Ira. "Independent Distribution and Marketing." In Squire, *The Movie Business Book* (1992), 320–27.

Drake, Philip. "Distribution and Marketing." In McDonald and Wasko, *The Contemporary Film Industry,* 63–82.

Duckett, Victoria. "Theater, Legitimate." In Abel, *Encyclopedia of Early Cinema,* 626–28.

Dyer, Richard. "American Cinema of the '70s: *The Towering Inferno.*" *Movie* 21 (Autumn 1975): 30–33.

Eames, John Douglas. *The MGM Story.* London: Pyramid, 1990 [1975].

Eberts, Jake, and Terry Ilott. *My Indecision Is Final: The Rise and Fall of Goldcrest Films.* London: Faber and Faber, 1990.

Eisenschitz, Bernard. *Nicholas Ray: An American Journey.* London: Faber and Faber, 1993.

Eldridge, David. *Hollywood's History Films.* London: I. B. Tauris, 2006.

Eliot, Marc. *Walt Disney: Hollywood's Dark Prince.* London: André Deutsch, 1994.

Elley, Derek. *The Epic Film: Myth and History.* London: Routledge & Kegan Paul, 1984.

Elsaesser, Thomas, ed. *Early Cinema: Space, Frame, Narrative.* London: BFI, 1990.

Elsaesser, Thomas, and Adam Barker. "Introduction" to "The Continuity System: Griffith and Beyond." In Elsaesser, *Early Cinema: Space, Frame, Narrative,* 293–317.

Elsaesser, Thomas, Alexander Horwath, and Noel King, eds. *The Last Great American Picture Show: New Hollywood Cinema in the 1970s.* Amsterdam: Amsterdam University Press, 2004.

Enticknap, Leo. *Moving Image Technology: From Zoetrope to Digital.* London: Wallflower Press, 2005.

Epstein, Edward Jay. *The Big Picture: The New Logic of Money and Power in Hollywood.* New York: Random House, 2005.

Erb, Cynthia. *Tracking King Kong: A Hollywood Icon in World Culture.* Detroit: Wayne State University Press, 1998.

Erffmeyer, Thomas Edward. "The History of Cinerama: A Study of Technological Innovation and Industrial Management." PhD dissertation, Northwestern University, 1985.

Eyles, Allen. "CinemaScope and the Fox Circuit." *Picture House* 2 (Autumn 1982): 9–12.

———. "When Exhibitors Saw Scarlett: The War over *Gone with the Wind.*" *Picture House* 27 (2002): 23–32.

Eyman, Scott. *Lion of Hollywood: The Life and Legend of Louis B. Mayer.* New York: Simon and Schuster, 2005.

Fadiman, William. "Runaways." *Films and Filming* 8, no. 10 (1962): 40–41.

Fell, John L., ed. *Film before Griffith.* Berkeley: University of California Press, 1983.

Fellman, Daniel R. "Theatrical Distribution." In Squire, *The Movie Business Book* (2006), 362–74.

Finler, Joel W. *The Hollywood Story.* London: Octopus, 1988.

Flamini, Roland. *Scarlett, Rhett, and a Cast of Thousands: The Filming of Gone with the Wind.* London: André Deutsch, 1976.

Fordin, Hugh. *MGM's Greatest Musicals: The Arthur Freed Unit.* New York: Da Capo Press, 1996 [1975].

Frayling, Christopher. *Sergio Leone: Something to Do with Death.* London: Faber and Faber, 2000.

Friedman, Lester D., ed. *American Cinema of the 1970s: Themes and Variations.* New Brunswick, NJ: Rutgers University Press, 2007.

Fuller, Kathryn H. *At the Picture Show: Small-Town Audiences and the Creation of Movie Fan Culture.* Washington, DC: Smithsonian Institution Press, 1996.

Fulton, A. R. *Motion Pictures: The Development of an Art from Silent Films to the Age of Television.* Norman: University of Oklahoma Press, 1960.

Gabler, Neil. *Walt Disney: The Triumph of the American Imagination.* New York: Knopf, 2007.

Gaines, Jane. *Fire and Desire: Mixed-Race Movies in the Silent Era.* Chicago: University of Chicago Press, 2001.

Gaines, Jane, and Neil Lerner. "The Orchestration of Affect: The Motif of Barbarism in Breil's *The Birth of a Nation* Score." In Abel and Altman, *The Sounds of Early Cinema,* 252–68.

Galbraith, Stuart, IV. "A History and Analysis of the Roadshow Mode of Motion Picture Exhibition." Master's dissertation, University of Southern California, 1997.

Garity, William E., and Watson Jones. "Experiences in Road-Showing Disney's *Fantasia,*" *Journal of the Society of Motion Picture Engineers,* July 1942, accessible at www.widescreenmuseum .com/sound/Fantasound3.htm.

Gateward, Frances. "Movies and the Legacies of War and Corruption." In Friedman, *American Cinema of the 1970s: Themes and Variations,* 95–115.

Gibson, Emily, with Barbara Firth. *The Original Million Dollar Mermaid: The Annette Kellerman Story.* Crows Nest, New South Wales: Allen and Unwin, 2005.

Glancy, H. Mark. "MGM Film Grosses, 1924–1948: The Eddie Mannix Ledger." *Historical Journal of Film, Radio, and Television* 12, no. 2 (1992): 127–44.

———. "Warner Bros. Film Grosses, 1921–51: The William Schaefer Ledger." *Historical Journal of Film, Radio, and Television* 15, no. 1 (1995): 55–73.

———. *When Hollywood Loved Britain: The Hollywood "British" Film, 1939–45.* Manchester: Manchester University Press, 1999.

Golden, Eve. *Vamp: The Rise and Fall of Theda Bara.* New York: Enterprise, 1996.

Gomery, Douglas. *The Coming of Sound.* New York: Routledge, 2005.

———. "The Coming of Sound to the American Cinema: A History of the Transformation of an Industry." PhD dissertation, University of Wisconsin–Madison, 1974 [John Douglas Gomery].

———. "The Hollywood Blockbuster: Industrial Analysis and Practice." In Stringer, *Movie Blockbusters,* 72–83.

———. *Shared Pleasures: A History of Movie Presentation in the United States.* London: BFI, 1992.

———. "Writing the History of the American Film Industry: Warner Bros. and Sound." *Screen* 17, no. 1 (1976): 40–53.

Gordon, Bernard. *Hollywood Exile, or How I Learned to Love the Blacklist.* Austin: University of Texas Press, 1999.

Gottlieb, Carl. *The* Jaws *Log.* New York: Newmarket Press, 2001 [1975].

Grant, Barry Keith, ed. *Film Genre Reader III.* Austin: University of Texas Press, 2003.

Greene, Eric. Planet of the Apes *as American Myth: Race, Politics, and Popular Culture.* Hanover, NH: Wesleyan University Press, 1998 [1996].

Grieveson, Lee. *Policing Cinema: Movies and Censorship in Early Twentieth-Century America.* Berkeley: University of California Press, 2004.

Griffith, Richard. "Where Are the Dollars?" *Sight and Sound* (December 1949, 33–34; January 1950, 39–40; and March 1950, 44–45).

Guback, Thomas. "Hollywood's International Market." In Balio, *The American Film Industry* (1985), 463–86.

———. *The International Film Industry: Western Europe and America since 1945.* Bloomington: Indiana University Press, 1969.

Gunning, Tom. "The Cinema of Attractions: Early Film, Its Spectator and the Avant Garde." *Wide Angle* 8, no. 3/4 (1986): 31–45.

———. "Colorful Metaphors: The Attraction of Color in Early Silent Cinema." *Fotogenia* 1 (1994), available at www.muspe.unibo.it/period/fotogen/num01/engo1.htm.

———. "*Intolerance:* Narrative Structure." In Usai, *The Griffith Project.* Vol. 9, *Films Produced in 1916–18,* 46–52.

Gussow, Mel. *Darryl F. Zanuck: "Don't Say Yes until I Finish Talking."* London: W. H. Allen, 1971.

Hall, Ben M. *The Best Remaining Seats: The Golden Age of the Movie Palace.* New York: Da Capo, 1988 [1975].

Hall, Sheldon. "Hard Ticket Giants: Hollywood Blockbusters in the Widescreen Era." PhD dissertation, University of East Anglia, 1999.

———. "*How the West Was Won:* History, Spectacle and the American Mountains." In Cameron and Pye, *The Movie Book of the Western,* 255–61.

Hampton, Benjamin B. *History of the American Film Industry: From Its Beginnings to 1931.* New York: Dover, 1970 [1931].

Hanson, Patricia, and Alan Gevinson, eds. *The American Film Institute Catalog of Motion Pictures Produced in the United States: Feature Films, 1911–1920.* Berkeley: University of California Press, 1988.

Hanssen, F. Andrew. "Revenue Sharing and the Coming of Sound." In Sedgwick and Pokorny, *An Economic History of Film,* 86–120.

Harmetz, Aljean. *On the Road to Tara: The Making of* Gone with the Wind. New York: Harry N. Abrams, 1996.

Harries, Dan, ed. *The New Media Book.* London: BFI, 2002.

Harris, Mark. *Scenes from a Revolution: The Birth of the New Hollywood.* Edinburgh: Canongate, 2008.

Haskell, Molly. *Frankly, My Dear*: Gone with the Wind *Revisited.* New Haven: Yale University Press, 2009.

Haver, Ronald. *David O. Selznick's Hollywood.* London: Secker and Warburg, 1980.

———. A Star Is Born: *The Making of the 1954 Movie and Its 1983 Restoration.* London: André Deutsch, 1988.

Hay, Peter. *MGM: When the Lion Roars.* Atlanta: Turner, 1991.

Hayes, Dade, and Jonathan Bing. *Open Wide: How Hollywood Box Office Became a National Obsession.* New York: Hyperion/Miramax, 2004.

Hayes, R. M. *3-D Movies: A History and Filmography of Stereoscopic Cinema.* Jefferson, NC: McFarland, 1999 [1990].

Hayward, Philip, and Tana Wollen, eds. *Future Visions: New Technologies of the Screen.* London: BFI, 1993.

Heffernan, Kevin. *Ghouls, Gimmicks, and Gold: Horror Films and the American Movie Business, 1953–1968.* Durham, NC: Duke University Press, 2004.

Hendricks, Gordon. "The History of the Kinetoscope." In Balio, *The American Film Industry* (1985), 43–56.

Herzog, Charlotte Kopac. "Motion Picture Theater and Film Exhibition, 1896–1932." PhD dissertation, Northwestern University, 1980.

Heston, Charlton. *In the Arena: The Autobiography.* London: HarperCollins, 1995.

Higashi, Sumiko. *Cecil B. De Mille and American Film Culture: The Silent Era.* Berkeley: University of California Press, 1994.

Higgins, Scott. "Suspenseful Situations: Melodramatic Narrative and the Contemporary Action Film." *Cinema Journal* 47, no. 2 (2008): 74–96.

Hilmes, Michelle. *Hollywood and Broadcasting.* Urbana: University of Illinois Press, 1990.

Hincha, Richard. "Selling CinemaScope: 1953–1956." *The Velvet Light Trap* 21 (Summer 1985): 44–53.

———. "Twentieth Century-Fox's CinemaScope: An Industrial Organization Analysis of Its Development, Marketing, and Adoption." PhD dissertation, University of Wisconsin–Madison, 1989.

Hirschhorn, Clive. *The Hollywood Musical.* London: Octopus, 1981.

Hoberman, J. "*Nashville* Contra *Jaws;* Or 'The Imagination of Disaster' Revisited." In Elsaesser, Horwath, and King, *The Last Great American Picture Show: New Hollywood Cinema in the 1970s,* 195–222.

Holden, Anthony. *The Oscars: The Secret History of Hollywood's Academy Awards.* London: Little, Brown, 1993.

Holliss, Richard, and Brian Sibley. *The Disney Studio Story.* London: Octopus, 1988.

———. Snow White and the Seven Dwarfs *and the Making of the Classic Film.* New York: Hyperion, 1987.

Hollyman, Burns St. Patrick. "The First Picture Shows in Austin, Texas (1894–1911)." *Journal of the University Film Association* 29, no. 3 (1977): 3–8.

Holt, Jennifer. "In Deregulation We Trust: The Synergy of Politics and Industry in Reagan-Era Hollywood." *Film Quarterly* 55, no. 2 (2001): 22–29.

Horwitz, Rita. "George Kleine and the Early Motion Picture Industry." In Horwitz and Harrison with White, *The George Kleine Collection of Early Motion Pictures in the Library of Congress: A Catalog,* xiii–xxv.

Horwitz, Rita, and Harriet Harrison, with Wendy White. *The George Kleine Collection of Early Motion Pictures in the Library of Congress: A Catalog.* Washington, DC: Library of Congress, 1980.

Hovet, Ted. "Realism and Spectacle in *Ben-Hur* (1888–1959)." PhD dissertation, Duke University, 1995.

Howe, A. L. "A Banker Looks at the Picture Business." *Journal of the Screen Producers Guild* (March 1969), quoted in Pye and Myles, *The Movie Brats,* 39.

Hugo, Chris. "American Cinema in the '70s: The Economic Background." *Movie* 27/28 (Winter 1980/Spring 1981): 43–49.

———. "U.S. Film Industry: Economic Background Part Two." *Movie* 31/32 (Winter 1986): 84–87.

Irwin, Will. *The House That Shadows Built.* New York: Doubleday, 1928.

Jacobs, Diane. *Hollywood Renaissance.* South Brunswick, NY: Barnes/Tantivy, 1977.

Jacobs, Lewis. *The Rise of the American Film: A Critical History.* New York: Harcourt Brace, 1939.

Jewell, Richard B. "RKO Film Grosses, 1929–1951: The C. J. Tevlin Ledger." *Historical Journal of Film, Radio, and Television* 14, no. 1 (1994): 37–49.

Kaplan, Fred. "Riches from Ruins." *Jump Cut* 6 (1975): 3–4.

Kaufman, J. B. "*The Birth of a Nation:* Distribution and Reception." In Usai, *The Griffith Project.* Vol. 8, *Films Produced in 1914–15,* 91–98.

Keane, Stephen. *Disaster Movies: The Cinema of Catastrophe.* London: Wallflower, 2001.

Keil, Charlie. "*The Birth of a Nation:* Style and Technique." In Usai, *The Griffith Project.* Vol. 8, *Films Produced in 1914–15,* 62–69.

———. "*Intolerance:* Style and Technique." In Usai, *The Griffith Project.* Vol. 9. *Films Produced in 1916–18,* 57–62.

Keil, Charlie, and Shelley Stamp, eds. *American Cinema's Transitional Era: Audiences, Institutions, Practices.* Berkeley: University of California Press, 2004.

Kelley, William van Doren. "Natural Color Cinematography." *Transactions of the Society of Motion Picture Engineers* 10 (May 1920), quoted in Koszarski, *An Evening's Entertainment,* 128.

Kenaga, Heidi. "The West before the Cinema Invaded It": Famous Players–Lasky's "Epic" Westerns, 1923–25. PhD dissertation, University of Wisconsin–Madison, 1999.

Kermode, Mark. *The Exorcist.* London: BFI, 1997; rev. 2nd ed., 2003.

Kerr Paul, ed. *The Hollywood Film Industry.* London: Routledge & Kegan Paul/BFI, 1986.

Kezich, Tullio, and Alessandra Levantesi. *Dino: The Life and Times of Dino De Laurentiis.* New York: Miramax, 2004.

Kim, Erwin. *Franklin J. Schaffner.* Metuchen, NJ: Scarecrow Press, 1985.

Kimble, Greg. "*How the West Was Won*—in Cinerama." *American Cinematographer* (October 1983): 46–50, 89–90.

King, Geoff. *American Independent Cinema.* London: I. B. Tauris, 2005.

———. *New Hollywood Cinema: An Introduction.* London: I. B. Tauris, 2002.

———. *Spectacular Narratives: Hollywood in the Age of the Blockbuster.* London: I. B. Tauris, 2000.

King, Geoff, and Tanya Krzywinska. *Science Fiction Cinema: From Outerspace to Cyperspace.* London: Wallflower, 2000.

King, Neil. *Heroes in Hard Times: Cop Action Movies in the U.S.* Philadelphia: Temple University Press, 1999.

King, Rob. "'Made for the Masses with an Appeal to the Classes': The Triangle Film Corporation and the Failure of Highbrow Film Culture." *Cinema Journal* 44, no. 2 (2005).

Klinger, Barbara. *Beyond the Multiplex: Cinema, New Technologies, and the Home.* Berkeley: University of California Press, 2006.

Knight, Arthur. "The Reluctant Audience." *Sight and Sound* 22, no. 4 (1953): 191–92.

Kohler, Richard, and Walter Lassally. "The Big Screens." *Sight and Sound* 24, no. 3 (1955): 120–26.

Kolker, Robert Phillip. *A Cinema of Loneliness.* New York: Oxford University Press, 1980; rev. 2nd ed., 1988.

Koszarski, Richard. *An Evening's Entertainment: The Age of the Silent Feature Picture, 1915–1928.* New York: Scribner's, 1990.

———. *Von: The Life and Films of Erich von Stroheim.* New York: Limelight Editions, 2001.

Krämer, Peter. *The New Hollywood: From* Bonnie and Clyde *to* Star Wars. London: Wallflower Press, 2005.

Krause, Martin, and Linda Witkowski. *Walt Disney's* Snow White and the Seven Dwarfs*: An Art in Its Making.* New York: Hyperion, 1994.

Lafferty, William. "Feature Films on Prime-Time Television." In Balio, *Hollywood in the Age of Television,* 235–56.

Lahue, Kalton C. *Dreams for Sale: The Rise and Fall of the Triangle Film Corporation.* South Brunswick: A. S. Barnes, 1971.

Lambert, Gavin. *GWTW: The Making of* Gone with the Wind. Boston: Little, Brown, 1973.

Lang, Robert. "*The Birth of a Nation:* History, Ideology and Narrative Form." In Lang, *The Birth of a Nation,* 3–24.

Lang, Robert, ed. *The Birth of a Nation.* New Brunswick, NJ: Rutgers University Press, 1994.

Larsen, Ernest. "Lemmings and Escapism." *Jump Cut* 8 (1975): 20.

Leider, Emily W. *Dark Lover: The Life and Death of Rudolph Valentino.* London: Faber and Faber, 2003.

Lenning, Arthur. "Myth and Fact: The Reception of *The Birth of a Nation.*" *Film History* 16, no. 2 (2004): 117–41.

Lev, Peter. *American Films of the 70s: Conflicting Visions.* Austin: University of Texas Press, 2000.

Lewis, Howard Thompson. "Goldstein, Incorporated, Advertising, Maintenance of Broadway Exploitation Theater." *Harvard Business Reports.* Vol. 8, *Cases on the Motion Picture Industry.* New York: McGraw-Hill, 1930, reproduced and edited by David Pierce (1999), accessible at www.cinemaweb.com/silentfilm/bookshelf/31_rs_10.htm.

Lewis, Howard T. *The Motion Picture Industry.* New York: Van Nostrand, 1933.

Lewis, Jon, ed. *The New American Cinema.* Durham, NC: Duke University Press, 1998.

Lichtenfeld, Eric. *Action Speaks Louder: Violence, Spectacle, and the American Action Movie.* Westport, CT: Praeger, 2004.

Limbacher, James L. *Four Aspects of the Film.* New York: Brussel & Brussel, 1968.

Lobban, Grant. "Coming in 70 mm: Is There a Future for 70 mm Theatrical Prints?" *Cinema Technology* (April 1995).

———. "In the Splendor of 70 mm." *. . . in 70 mm: The 70 mm Newsletter* 15, no. 67 (2002): 14–22, accessible at www.in70mm.com/newsletter/2002/67.

LoBrutto, Vincent. *Stanley Kubrick.* London: Faber and Faber, 1997.

Londoner, David J. "The Changing Economics of Entertainment." In Balio, *The American Film Industry* (1985), 603–30.

Lowry, Edward. "Edwin J. Hadley: Traveling Film Exhibitor." In Fell, *Film before Griffith,* 131–43.

Luckett, Moya. "*Fantasia:* Cultural Constructions of Disney's 'Masterpiece.'" In Smoodin, *Disney Discourse: Producing the Magic Kingdom,* 214–36.

Madsen, Axel. "The Changing of the Guard." *Sight and Sound* 39, no. 2 (1970): 63–64, 111.

———. "Fission-Fusion-Fission." *Sight and Sound* 37, no. 3 (1968): 124–26.

———. *The New Hollywood: American Movies in the '70s.* New York: Crowell, 1975.

Malamud, Margaret. "The Greatest Show on Earth: Roman Entertainments in Turn-of-the-Century New York." *Journal of Popular Culture* 35, no. 3 (2001): 43–58.

Maltby, Richard. *Harmless Entertainment: Hollywood and the Ideology of Consensus.* Metuchen, N.J.: Scarecrow Press, 1983.

———. *Hollywood Cinema.* Oxford: Blackwell, 2003 [1995].

———. "'Nobody Knows Everything': Post-Classical Historiographies and Consolidated Entertainment." In Neale and Smith, *Contemporary Hollywood Cinema,* 21–44.

Maltby, Richard, Melvyn Stokes, and Robert C. Allen, eds. *Going to the Movies: Hollywood and the Social Experience of Cinema.* Exeter: Exeter University Press, 2008.

Man, Glenn. "Movies and Conflicting Ideologies." In Friedman, *American Cinema of the 1970s: Themes and Variations,* 135–56

Manso, Peter. *Brando.* London: Weidenfeld and Nicholson, 1994.

Margolis, Harriet, Sean Cubitt, Barry King, and Thierry Jutel, eds. *Studying the Event Film:* The Lord of the Rings. Manchester: Manchester University Press, 2008.

Marks, Martin Miller. *Music and the Silent Film: Contexts and Case Studies.* New York: Oxford University Press, 1997.

Martin, Mel. *The Magnificent Showman: The Epic Films of Samuel Bronston.* Albany, GA: BearManor Media, 2007.

Mayer, David. "*The Birth of a Nation:* Theatrical Sources." In Usai, *The Griffith Project.* Vol. 8, *Films Produced in 1914–15,* 81–87.

———. *Playing Out the Empire:* Ben-Hur *and Other Toga Plays and Films, A Critical Anthology.* Oxford: Clarendon Press, 1994.

McArthur, Benjamin. *Actors and American Culture, 1880–1920.* Iowa City: University of Iowa Press, 2000.

McBride, Joseph. *Searching for John Ford.* New York: St. Martin's Press, 2001.

———. *Steven Spielberg: A Biography.* London: Faber and Faber, 1997.

McCarthy, Todd. *Howard Hawks: The Grey Fox of Hollywood.* New York: Grove Press, 1997.

McDonald, Paul. "IMAX: The Hollywood Experience." In Belton, Hall, and Neale (forthcoming).

———. *Video and DVD Industries.* London: BFI, 2007.

McDonald, Paul, and Janet Wasko, eds. *The Contemporary Hollywood Film Industry.* Oxford: Blackwell, 2008.

McKenna, Anthony T. "Joseph E. Levine: Showmanship, Reputation and Industrial Practice, 1945–1977." PhD dissertation, University of Nottingham, 2008.

McLaughlin, Robert. *Broadway and Hollywood: A History of Economic Interaction.* New York: Arno Press, 1974.

McNamara, Brooks. *The Shuberts of Broadway: A History Drawn from the Collections of the Shubert Archive.* New York: Oxford University Press, 1990.

Meisel, Martin. *Realizations: Narrative, Pictorial, and Theatrical Arts in Nineteenth-Century England.* Princeton, NJ: Princeton University Press, 1983.

Meisel, Myron. "Industry." *Film Comment* 18, no. 2 (1982): 60–66.

Merritt, Russell. "D. W. Griffith's *Intolerance:* Reconstructing an Unattainable Text." *Film History* 4, no. 4 (1990): 37–75.

———. "*Intolerance:* Production and Distribution." In Usai, *The Griffith Project.* Vol. 9, *Films Produced in 1916–18,* 39–46.

———. "On First Looking into Griffith's Babylon: A Reading of a Publicity Still." *Wide Angle* 3, no. 1 (1979): 12–21.

Monaco, James. *American Film Now: The People, The Power, The Money, The Movies.* New York: Oxford University Press, 1979.

Monaco, Paul. *The Sixties, 1960–1969.* New York: Scribner's, 2001.

Morgan, Hal, and Dan Symmes. *Amazing 3-D.* London: Vermilion/Little, Brown, 1982.

Morris, Nigel. *The Cinema of Steven Spielberg: Empire of Light.* London: Wallflower Press, 2007.

Morton, Ray. Close Encounters of the Third Kind: *The Making of Steven Spielberg's Classic Film.* New York: Applause Theatre and Film, 2007.

Mott, Donald R., and Cheryl McAllister Saunders. *Steven Spielberg.* London: G. K. Hall, 1986.

Murphy, A. D. "Distribution and Exhibition: An Overview." In Squire, *The Movie Business Book* (1983), 343–62.

Murphy, Robert. *Sixties British Cinema.* London: BFI, 1992.

Musser, Charles. *The Emergence of Cinema: The American Screen to 1907.* New York: Scribner, 1990.

———. "Itinerant Exhibitors." In Abel, *Encyclopedia of Early Cinema,* 340–42.

———. "On 'Extras,' Mary Pickford, and Red-Light Filmmaking in the United States, 1913." *Griffithiana* 17, no. 50 (1994): 149–75.

Musser, Charles, with Carol Nelson. *High-Class Moving Pictures: Lyman H. Howe and the Forgotten Era of Traveling Exhibition, 1880–1920.* Princeton, NJ: Princeton University Press, 1991.

Myers, Peter S. "The Studio as Distributor." In Squire, *The Movie Business Book* (1983), 275–84.

Neale, Steve. *Genre and Hollywood.* London: Routledge, 2001.

———. "Widescreen Composition in the Age of Television." In Neale and Smith, *Contemporary Hollywood Cinema,* 130–41.

Neale, Steve, ed. *Genre and Contemporary Hollywood.* London: BFI, 2002.

Neale, Steve, and Murray Smith, eds. *Contemporary Hollywood Cinema.* London: Routledge, 1998.

Nelson, Al P., and Mel R. Jones. *A Silent Siren Song: The Aitken Brothers' Hollywood Odyssey, 1905–1926.* New York: Cooper Square Press, 2000.

Niver, Kemp. *Klaw and Erlanger Present Famous Plays in Pictures,* edited by Bebe Bersten. Los Angeles: Locare Research Group, 1976.

Nowell-Smith, Geoffrey, ed. *The Oxford History of World Cinema.* Oxford: Oxford University Press, 1996.

Nowell-Smith, Geoffrey, and Steven Ricci, eds. *Hollywood and Europe: Economics, Culture, National Identity, 1946–95.* London: BFI, 1998.

Nowotny, Robert A. *The Way of All Flesh Tones: A History of Color Motion Picture Processes, 1895–1929.* New York: Garland, 1983.

Ohmer, Susan. "The Science of Pleasure: George Gallup and Audience Research in Hollywood." In Stokes and Maltby, *Identifying Hollywood's Audiences,* 61–80.

Parish, James Robert. *Fiasco: A History of Hollywood's Iconic Flops.* New York: John Wiley, 2006.

Paul, William. "The Impossibility of Romance: Hollywood Comedy, 1978–1999." In Neale, *Genre and Contemporary Hollywood,* 117–29.

———. *Laughing Screaming: Modern Hollywood Horror and Comedy.* New York: Columbia University Press, 1994.

———. "Screens." In Abel, *Encyclopedia of Early Cinema,* 573–76.

Pearson, Roberta. "The Menace of the Movies: Cinema's Challenge to the Theater in the Transitional Period." In Keil and Stamp, *American Cinema's Transitional Era: Audiences, Institutions, Practices,* 315–31.

Pfiel, Fred. *White Guys: Studies in Postmodernism and Difference.* London: Verso, 1995.

Pierson, John. *Spike, Mike, Slackers, and Dykes.* London: Faber and Faber, 1995.

Pratley, Gerald. *The Cinema of David Lean.* South Brunswick, NJ: Barnes/Tantivy, 1974.

Prince, Stephen. *A New Pot of Gold: Hollywood under the Electronic Rainbow, 1980–1989.* New York: Scribner's, 2000.

Pryluck, Calvyn. "Industrialization of Entertainment in the United States." In Austin, *Current Research in Film: Audiences, Economics, and Law,* vol. 2, 117–35.

———. "The Itinerant Movie Show and the Development of the Film Industry." *Journal of the University Film and Video Association* 25, no. 4 (1983): 11–22.

Pye, Michael, and Lynda Myles. *The Movie Brats: How the Film Generation Took Over Hollywood.* London: Faber and Faber, 1979.

Quaresima, Leonardo, Alessandra Raengo, and Laura Vichi, eds. *La nascita dei generi cinematografici.* Udine: Forum, 1998.

Quinn, Michael. "Distribution, the Transient Audience, and the Transition to the Feature Film." *Cinema Journal* 40, no. 2 (2001): 35–56.

———. "Early Feature Distribution and the Development of the Motion Picture Industry: Famous Players and Paramount: 1912–1921." PhD dissertation, University of Wisconsin–Madison, 1998 [Michael Joseph Quinn].

———. "Paramount and Early Feature Distribution: 1914–1921." *Film History* 11, no. 1 (1999).

———. "USA: Distribution." In Abel, *Encyclopedia of Early Cinema,* 659–61.

Ramsaye, Terry, ed. *The International Motion Picture Almanac, 1936–37.* New York: Quigley, 1936.

———. *The Motion Picture Almanac, 1934–35.* New York: Quigley, 1934.

Reardon, D. Barry. "The Studio Distributor." In Squire, *The Movie Business Book* (1992), 310–19.

Reeves, Hazard E. "The Development of Stereo Magnetic Recording for Film." *Journal of the Society of Motion Picture and Television Engineers* (October and November 1982): 947–53; 1087–90.

———. "This Is Cinerama." *Film History* 11, no. 1 (1999): 85–97.

Rhodes, John David. "'Our Beautiful and Glorious Art Lives': The Rhetoric of Nationalism in Early Italian Film Periodicals." *Film History* 12, no. 3 (2000): 308–21.

Richards, Jeffrey. *Hollywood's Ancient Worlds.* London: Continuum, 2008.

———. *Visions of Yesterday.* London: Routledge & Kegan Paul, 1973.

Rickitt, Richard. *Special Effects: The History and Technique.* New York: Billboard, 2007.

Rinzler, J. W. *The Making of* Star Wars. London: Ebury Press, 2007.

Robinson, David. *From Peep Show to Palace: The Birth of American Film.* New York: Columbia University Press, 1996.

Roddick, Nick. *A New Deal in Entertainment: Warner Brothers in the 1930s*. London: BFI, 1983.

———. "Only the Stars Survive: Disaster Movies in the Seventies." In Bradby, James, and Sharratt, *Performance and Politics in Popular Drama: Aspects of Popular Entertainment in Theatre, Film, and Television, 1800–1976*, 243–69.

Rosen, David N. "Drugged Popcorn." *Jump Cut* 8 (1975): 19–20.

Rosendorf, Neal Moses. "'Hollywood in Madrid': American Film Producers and the Franco Regime, 1950–1970." *Historical Journal of Film, Radio, and Television* 27, no. 1 (2007): 77–109.

———. "The Life and Times of Samuel Bronston, Builder of 'Hollywood in Madrid': A Study in the International Scope and Influence of American Popular Culture." PhD dissertation, Harvard University, 2000.

Rubin, Martin. *Showstoppers: Busby Berkeley and the Tradition of Spectacle*. New York: Columbia University Press, 1993.

Rubin, Stephen Jay. *The James Bond Films*. London: Talisman, 1981.

Russell, James. *The Historical Epic and Contemporary Hollywood: From* Dances with Wolves *to* Gladiator. New York: Continuum, 2007.

Ryan, Michael, and Douglas Kellner. *Camera Politica: The Politics and Ideology of Contemporary Hollywood Film*. Bloomington: Indiana University Press, 1988.

Sackett, Susan. *The Hollywood Reporter Book of Box-Office Hits*. New York: Billboard, 1996.

Salt, Barry. *Film Style and Technology: History and Analysis*. London: Starword, 1992 [1983].

Sandler, Kevin S., and Gaylyn Studlar, eds. Titanic: *Anatomy of a Blockbuster*. New Brunswick, NJ: Rutgers University Press, 1997.

Sanjek, Russell, updated by David Sanjek. *Pennies from Heaven: The American Popular Music Business in the Twentieth Century*. New York: Da Capo Press, 1996.

Schaefer, Eric. *"Bold! Daring! Shocking! True!" A History of the Exploitation Film, 1919–1959*. Durham, NC: Duke University Press, 1999.

Schatz, Thomas. *Boom and Bust: American Cinema in the 1940s*. New York: Scribner's, 1997.

———. *The Genius of the System: Hollywood Filmmaking in the Studio Era*. London: Simon and Schuster, 1988.

———. "The New Hollywood." In Collins, Radner, and Collins, *Film Theory Goes to the Movies*, 8–36.

Schickel, Richard. *D. W. Griffith: A Biography*. London: Pavilion, 1984.

Schreger, Charles. "The Second Coming of Sound." *Film Comment* 14, no. 5 (1978): 34–37.

Sedgwick, John, and Michael Pokorny, eds. *An Economic History of Film*. London: Routledge, 2005.

Segrave, Kerry. *American Films Abroad: Hollywood's Domination of the World's Movie Screens*. Jefferson, NC: McFarland, 1997.

———. *Movies at Home: How Hollywood Came to Television*. Jefferson, NC: McFarland, 1999.

Sergi, Gianluca. *The Dolby Era: Film Sound in Contemporary Hollywood*. Manchester: Manchester University Press, 2004.

Sherlock, Daniel J. "*Widescreen Movies* Corrections" (1994–2004), accessible at www.film-tech.com/tips/nsmc.html.

Shipman, David. "The All-Conquering Governess." *Films and Filming* 12, no. 11 (1966): 16–20.

Shivas, Mark. "*How the West Was Won*." *Movie* 6 (January 1963): 28–29.

Shone, Tom. *Blockbuster: How Hollywood Learned to Stop Worrying and Love the Summer*. London: Simon and Schuster, 2004.

Silva, Fred, ed. *Focus on* The Birth of a Nation. Englewood Cliffs, NJ: Prentice-Hall, 1971.

Silverman, Stephen. *The Fox That Got Away: The Last Days of the Zanuck Dynasty at Twentieth Century-Fox*. Secaucus, NJ: Lyle Stuart, 1988.

Siminoski, Ted. "The *Billy Jack* Phenomenon: Filmmaking with Independence & Control." *The Velvet Light Trap* 13 (Fall 1974): 36–39.

Simmon, Scott. *The Films of D. W. Griffith.* Cambridge: Cambridge University Press, 1993.

Simonet, Thomas. "Conglomerates and Content: Remakes, Sequels, and Series in the New Hollywood." In Austin, *Current Research in Film: Audiences, Economics, and Law,* vol. 2, 154–62.

———. "Industry." *Film Comment* 16, no. 1 (1980): 66–69.

Singer, Ben. "Feature Films, Variety Programs." In Keil and Stamp, *American Cinema's Transitional Era,* 76–100.

Singer, Ben, and Charlie Keil. "USA: Production." In Abel, *Encyclopedia of Early Cinema,* 655–58.

Sklar, Robert. "Hub of the System: New York's Strand Theater and the Paramount Case." *Film History* 6, no. 2 (1984): 187–205.

———. "'The Lost Audience': 1950s Spectatorship and Historical Reception Studies." In Stokes and Maltby, *Identifying Hollywood's Audiences,* 81–92.

———. *Movie-Made America: A Cultural History of American Movies.* London: Chappell/Elm Tree, 1978.

Slide, Anthony. *The American Film Industry: A Historical Dictionary.* New York: Greenwood Press, 1986.

———. *Silent Topics: Essays on Undocumented Areas of Silent Film.* Lanham, MD: Scarecrow Press, 2005.

Smith, Andrew Brodie. *Shooting Cowboys and Indians: Silent Western Films, American Culture, and the Birth of Hollywood.* Boulder: University Press of Colorado, 2003.

Smith, Bradford. "A Religious Spectacle in Theatre and Film: Max Reinhardt's *The Miracle* (1911–1912)." In Cosandey, Gaudreault, and Gunning, *Une invention du diable? Cinéma des premiers temps et religion,* 311–18.

Smith, Jeff. *The Sounds of Commerce: Marketing Popular Film Music.* New York: Columbia University Press, 1998.

Smoodin, Eric, ed. *Disney Discourse: Producing the Magic Kingdom.* New York: Routledge, 1994.

Smyth, J. E. *Reconstructing American Historical Cinema: From* Cimarron *to* Citizen Kane. Lexington: University Press of Kentucky, 2006.

Soares, André. *Beyond Paradise: The Life of Ramon Novarro.* New York: St. Martin's Press, 2002.

Sobchack, Vivian. "'Surge and Splendor': A Phenomenology of the Hollywood Epic." *Representations* 29 (Winter 1990): 24–49.

Solomon, Aubrey. *Twentieth Century-Fox: A Corporate and Financial History.* Lanham, MD: Scarecrow Press, 1988.

Solomon, Jon. *The Ancient World in the Cinema.* New Haven, CT: Yale University Press, 2001 [1978].

Spaulding, Jeffrey. "Life Upside Down: The 25th Annual 'Grosses Gloss,'" *Film Comment* 36, no. 2 (2000): 40–42.

Spears, Jack. *The Civil War on Screen and Other Essays.* New York: A. S. Barnes, 1977.

Spellerberg, James. "The Ideology of CinemaScope." *The Velvet Light Trap* 21 (Summer 1985): 26–34.

———. "Technology and the Film Industry: The Adoption of CinemaScope." PhD dissertation, University of Iowa, 1980.

Squire, Jason E., ed. *The Movie Business Book.* New York: Simon and Schuster, 1983.

———. *The Movie Business Book.* Englewood Cliffs, NJ: Prentice-Hall, 1992.

———. *The Movie Business Book.* Maidenhead: McGraw-Hill, 2006.

Staiger, Janet. "Announcing Wares, Winning Patrons, Voicing Ideals: Thinking about the History and Theory of Film Advertising." *Cinema Journal* 29, no. 3 (1990): 3–31.

Stanfield, Peter. "Country Music and the 1939 Western." In Cameron and Pye, *The Movie Book of the Western*, 22–33.

Stokes, Melvyn, and Richard Maltby, eds. *Hollywood Spectatorship: Changing Perceptions of Cinema Audiences*. London: BFI, 2001.

———. *Identifying Hollywood's Audiences*. London: BFI, 1999.

Stones, Barbara. *America Goes to the Movies: 100 Years of Motion Picture Exhibition*. North Hollywood: National Association of Theatre Owners, 1993.

Street, Sarah. *Transatlantic Crossings: British Feature Films in the USA*. New York: Continuum, 2002.

Streible, Dan. "Boxing Films." In Abel, *Encyclopedia of Early Cinema*, 80–82.

Stringer, Julian, ed. *Movie Blockbusters*. London: Routledge, 2003.

Stubbs, Jonathan. "Inventing England: Representations of English History in Hollywood Cinema, 1950–1964." PhD dissertation, University of East Anglia, 2007.

Studlar, Gaylyn. *This Mad Masquerade: Stardom and Masculinity in the Jazz Age*. New York: Columbia University Press, 1996.

Suid, Lawrence H. *Guts and Glory: The Making of the American Military Image in Film*. Lexington: University Press of Kentucky, 2002.

Suras, Constantine. *The Epic in Film: From Myth to Blockbuster*. Lanham, MD: Rowman and Littlefield, 2008.

Swadkins, Keith H. "Whatever Happened to Cinerama?" *The Perfect Vision* 4, no. 16 (1993): 31–37.

Swatrz, Mark E. "Motion Pictures on the Move." *Journal of American Culture* 9, no. 3 (1986): 1–7.

Tasker, Yvonne. *Spectacular Bodies: Gender, Genre, and the Action Cinema*. London: Routledge, 1993.

Tasker, Yvonne, ed. *Action and Adventure Cinema*. London: Routledge, 2004.

Telotte, J. P. "The New Hollywood Musical." In Neale, *Genre and Contemporary Hollywood*, 48–61.

Thomas, David O. "From Page to Screen in Smalltown America: Early Motion Picture Exhibition in Winona, Minnesota." *Journal of the University Film Association* 33, no. 3 (1981): 3–13.

Thompson, Kristin. *The Frodo Franchise:* The Lord of the Rings *and Modern Hollywood*. Berkeley: University of California Press, 2007.

Thompson, Kristin, and David Bordwell. *Film History: An Introduction*. New York: McGraw-Hill, 2003 [1994].

Thomson, David. *Showman: The Life of David O. Selznick*. London: André Deutsch, 1993.

Thrower, Stephen. *Nightmare USA: The Untold Story of the Exploitation Independents*. Godalming: FAB Press, 2007.

Tibbetts, John C. *The American Theatrical Film: Stages in Development*. Bowling Green, OH: Bowling Green State University Press, 1985.

Toeplitz, Jerzy. *Hollywood and After: The Changing Face of Hollywood Cinema*. London: George Allen and Unwin, 1974.

Tomadjoglu, Kimberley. "Rome's Premiere Film Studio: Società Italiana Cines." *Film History* 12, no. 3 (2000): 262–75.

Travers, Peter, and Stephanie Reiff. *The Story behind* The Exorcist. New York: Crown, 1974.

Turner, Adrian. *A Celebration of* Gone with the Wind. London: Gallery Books, 1991.

———. "Quaking in the Stalls." *Films Illustrated* 4, no. 38 (1975): 292–95.

Tzioumakis, Yannis. *American Independent Cinema: An Introduction*. Edinburgh: Edinburgh University Press, 2006.

Uricchio, William, and Roberta E. Pearson. *Reframing Culture: The Case of Vitagraph's Quality Films*. Princeton, NJ: Princeton University Press, 1993.

Usai, Paolo Cherchi. "*Cabiria*, an Incomplete Masterpiece: The Quest for the Original 1914 Version." *Film History* 2, no. 2 (1988): 155–65.

———. "Color." In Abel, *Encyclopedia of Early Cinema*, 138–41.

———. "Italy: Spectacle and Melodrama." In Nowell-Smith, *The Oxford History of World Cinema*, 123–29.

Usai, Paolo Cherchi, ed. *The Griffith Project*. Vol. 8, *Films Produced in 1914–15*. London: BFI, 2004.

———. *The Griffith Project*. Vol. 9, *Films Produced in 1916–18*. London: BFI, 2005.

Vardac, Nicholas. *Stage to Screen: Theatrical Origins of Early Films: David Garrick to D. W. Griffith*. Cambridge, MA: Harvard University Press, 1949.

Vertrees, Alan David. *Selznick's Vision:* Gone with the Wind *and Hollywood Filmmaking*. Austin: University of Texas Press, 1997.

Vidor, King. *A Tree Is a Tree*. London: Longman, Green, 1954.

Vincent, Tom. "Standing Tall and Wide: A History of VistaVision." Master's dissertation, University of East Anglia, 1993.

Wagstaff, Christopher. "Italian Genre Films in the World Market." In Nowell-Smith and Ricci, *Hollywood and Europe: Economics, Culture, National Identity, 1946–95,* 74–85.

Walker, Alexander. *Hollywood, England: The British Film Industry in the Sixties*. London: Harrap, 1986 [1974].

———. *National Heroes: British Cinema in the Seventies and Eighties*. London: Harrap, 1985.

———. *Stardom: The Hollywood Phenomenon*. Harmondsworth: Penguin, 1974 [1970].

Waller, Gregory A. "Robert Southard and the History of Traveling Film Exhibition." *Film Quarterly* 57, no. 2 (2003/4): 2–14.

Walters, Ben. "The Great Leap Forward." *Sight and Sound* 19, no. 3, n.s. (2009): 38–43.

Wasko, Janet. *Movies and Money: Financing the American Film Industry*. Norwood, NJ: Ablex, 1982.

Wasser, Frederick. "Ancillary Markets—Video and DVD." In McDonald and Wasko, *The Contemporary Film Industry,* 120–31.

———. *Veni, Vidi, Video: The Hollywood Empire and the VCR*. Austin: University of Texas Press, 2001.

Whissel, Kristen. "Tales of Upward Mobility: The New Verticality and Digital Special Effects." *Film Quarterly* 59, no. 4 (2006): 23–34.

Whitfield, Eileen. *Pickford: The Woman Who Made Hollywood*. Toronto: Macfarlane, Walter and Ross, 1997.

Whittington, William. *Sound Design and Science Fiction*. Austin: University of Texas Press, 2007.

Williams, Linda. "*The Birth of a Nation*: Politics." In Usai, *The Griffith Project*. Vol. 8, *Films Produced in 1914–15,* 98–107.

———. *Playing the Race Card: Melodramas of Black and White from Uncle Tom to O. J. Simpson*. Princeton, NJ: Princeton University Press, 2001.

Wilmeth, Don B. *The Language of American Popular Entertainment: A Glossary of Argot, Slang, and Terminology*. Westport, CT: Greenwood, 1981.

Wollen, Tana. "The Bigger the Better: From CinemaScope to IMAX." In Hayward and Wollen, *Future Visions: New Technologies of the Screen,* 10–30.

Wood, Aylish. *Digital Encounters*. London: Routledge, 2007.

———. "Timespaces in Spectacular Cinema: Crossing the Great Divide of Spectacle Versus Narrative." *Screen* 43, no. 4 (2002): 370–86.

Wood, Robin. *Hollywood from Vietnam to Reagan—and Beyond.* New York: Columbia University Press, 2003 [1986].

Wyatt, Justin. "From Roadshowing to Saturation Release: Majors, Independents, and Marketing/Distribution Innovations." In Lewis, *The New American Cinema,* 64–86.

———. *High Concept: Movies and Marketing in Hollywood.* Austin: University of Texas Press, 1994.

———. "Independents, Packaging, and Inflationary Pressure in 1980s Hollywood." In Prince, *A New Pot of Gold: Hollywood under the Electronic Rainbow, 1980–1989,* 142–59.

Wyatt, Justin, and Katherine Vlesmas. "The Drama of Recoupment: On the Mass Media Negotiation of *Titanic.*" In Sandler and Studlar, Titanic: *Anatomy of a Blockbuster,* 29–45.

Wyke, Maria. *Projecting the Past: Ancient Rome, Cinema, and History.* New York: Routledge, 1997.

Yacowar, Maurice. "The Bug in the Rug: Notes on the Disaster Genre" (1977). In Grant, *Film Genre Reader III,* 277–95.

Name Index

Page numbers in italics refer to illustrations or picture captions.

COMPANIES, INSTITUTIONS, AND ORGANIZATIONS

Theaters and Exhibition Venues

TECHNICAL DEVICES, FORMATS, AND PROCESSES

TITLE INDEX

Indexed below are all the films cited in this book (including the Notes), as well as the titles of books, newspapers, periodicals, plays, songs, and TV series mentioned in the main text. Foreign-language productions are normally listed under their English-language title. British films are listed under their American release title where this is different from the original (for example, *A Matter of Life and Death* is listed under *Stairway to Heaven*). Original and alternative titles are cross-referenced to the main entry. Dates represent the year of first U.S. exhibition, and are not necessarily the same as the date of first release in other countries. Page numbers in italics refer to illustrations or picture captions.

Subject Index

3-D. *See* Name Index: Technical Devices, Formats, and Processes

70mm. *See* wide gauge; Name Index: Technical Devices, Formats, and Processes

Adaptation, 47, 53, 84, 100–103, 121–22, 197–98; comic books, 222, 240, 255; literary, 21, 44, 45, 285n37, 296n113, 298n239; musical theater, 106, 183–84, 195, 215; Shakespeare, 101–3, 169, 176; television, 236; theater, 47, 54, 84, 106, 183–84

Animation, 106–11, 251, 253–55, 282n78, 283n101

Antitrust legislation, 112, 124, 128, 140, 236

Art house films, 169–70

Audience demographics, 43, 45, 56, 57, 167–68, 170, 188, 189–90, 206–7, 212, 246–47; adult, 229, 233–34, 297n9; polling, 113–14; youth, 189–92, 293n54, 297nn8, 17, 18

Biblicals, 54, 136–37, 162, 178–79

Biopics, 103, 106, 118, 121, 122, 165, 196, 203, 204, 249, 307n16

Blockbusters, 177–86, 212, 250; definition of, 1; origin of term, 139

Boxing films, 3, 11, 24

Box office. *See* revenue

Censorship, 17, 40, 101, 121–22, 131–32, 189, 196; overseas, 104, 229

CGI. *See* special effects; Name Index: Technical Devices, Formats, and Processes

Cinema of Spectacular Situations, 5, 251. *See also* spectacle

Cold War, 163

Color processes, 6, 54, 60, 62–68, 73, 140. *See also* Name Index: Technical Devices, Formats, and Processes

Colossal (term), 137

Comedy, 225–27, 241, 251

Costume film, 51, 52, 88, 136, 181

Country films, 226–27

Disaster (genre), 100, 205–7, 255, 299n68, 300nn74, 77

Distribution, 13–14, 41, 46, 47, 83, 89–90, 125–26, 128, 171, 176, 198–99, 223, 214–42; auction selling, 128–29, 137, 139; backlogs, 119–22, 124; block booking, 18, 47, 49, 95, 125, 285n60; day-and-date releasing, 97–98, 130; exchanges, 14, 46; open booking, 46, 47; overseas, 48, 103–5, 123, 135–36, 139, 153, 160, 250; platform releasing, 247–49; run-zone-clearance, 17, 83, 120, 156; saturation releasing, 45, 130, 132, 134, 172, 174, 196, 211, 213, 226, 260–61; showcase releasing, 174–75, 192, 226, 294n72; states rights, 3, 9–10, 11, 12, 17, 24–25, 27–26, 29, 35, 42, 44, 46, 271n3, 273n66;